The Age of Information has revealed an enlightened perspective of the planet Earth. A new consciousness has surfaced, recognizing that our survival and the survival of other species depends on the understanding and preservation of the complex interrelationships that exist between the human and physical environments.

The Concise EARTHBOOK is designed to place the world at your fingertips. Space travel and satellite photography have inspired a new style of environmental mapping that offers unique insight into the land use and life conditions of humans, animals and plants throughout the world. This new age atlas brings the world home in a way that will nurture and strengthen our geographic literacy and environmental awareness.

The Concise Edition of the EARTHBOOK delivers the people and places of the world in a compact size and format—places you want to locate, travel to or dream about.

EARTHBOOKS INCORPORATED

THE CONCISE WORLD

STATISTICS

The World	6- 7	**Africa**	28-38
Europe	8-15	**North-America**	38-42
Asia	16-25	**South-America**	42-47
Australia	24-27		

READER INFORMATION

Reader information	48	**Legend**	49

EUROPE

Europe, environment, flags 50-51

British Isles and Central Europe 52-53
Belgium, Czechoslovakia, Federal Republic of Germany, German Democratic Republic, Luxembourg, Netherlands, Poland

Northern Europe 54-55
Denmark, Finland, Iceland, Norway, Sweden

Spain, Italy, France 56-57

The Balkans 58-59
Bulgaria, Cyprus, Greece, Hungary, Romania, Turkey

The Middle East 60-61
Bahrain, Iran, Iraq, Israel, Jordan, Kuwait, Lebanon, Qatar, Syria, United Arab Emirates

Western Soviet Union 62-63
European USSR, Western Siberia

ASIA

Asia, environment, flags 64-65

South West Asia 66-67
Afghanistan, Iran, Pakistan

Eastern Soviet Union 68-69
Eastern Siberia, Mongolia

China and Japan 70-71
incl. Mongolia, North Korea, South Korea, Taiwan

India and South East Asia 72-73
incl. Bangladesh, Bhutan, Burma, Cambodia, Laos, Nepal, Sri Lanka, Thailand, Vietnam

The East Indies 74-75
Brunei, Indonesia, Malaysia, Philippines

AUSTRALIA

Australasia, environment, flags 76-77

Australia 78-79

New Guinea and New Zealand 80-81

Oceania 82-83
Melanesia, Micronesia, Polynesia

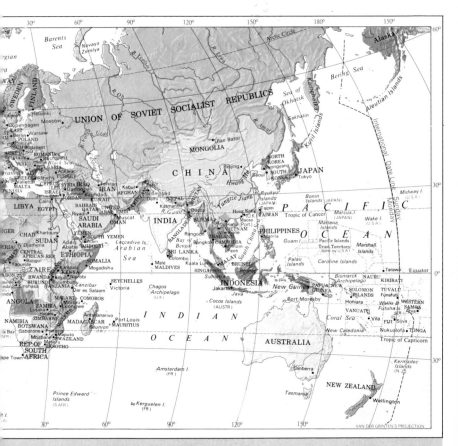

Country	Page	Country	Page	Country	Page	Country	Page
...lawi	95	Oman	89	Sierra Leone	90	Tunisia	87
...alaysia	74	Pakistan	67	Singapore	74	Turkey	59
...ldives	72	Panama	105	Solomon Islands	81	Tuvalu	82
...li	86	Papua New Guinea	80	Somalia	93	Uganda	92
...lta	57	Paraguay	112	South Korea	74	Union of Soviet	62, 68
...uritania	86	Peru	108, 109	South Yemen	89	Socialist Republics	
...uritius	94	Philippines	75	Spain	56	(U.S.S.R)	
...xico	104	Poland	53	Sri Lanka	72	United Arab Emirates	60
...naco	57	Portugal	56	Sudan	88, 92	United Kingdom and	
...ngolia	68, 70	Qatar	60	Surinam	109	Northen Ireland	52
...rocco	86	Republic of Ireland	52	Swaziland	95	United States	98, 102-103
...zambique	95	Republic of South Africa	94	Sweden	54	Uruguay	112
...mibia	94	Romania	58	Switzerland	57	Vanuatu	82
...uru	82	Rwanda	92	Syria	60	Vatican State	57
...pal	72	Saint Kitts-Nevis	105	Taiwan	71	Venezuela	108
...therlands	52	Saint Lucia	105	Tanzania	92	Vietnam	73
...w Zealand	81	Saint Vincent	105	Thailand	73	Western Samoa	82
...aragua	104	San Marino	57	The Bahamas	105	Yemen	89
...er	87	São Tome and Principe	57	The Gambia	86	Yugoslavia	58
...eria	91	Saudi Arabia	60, 89	Togo	90	Zaire	92
...rth Korea	71	Senegal	86	Tonga	82	Zambia	94
...rway	54	Seychelles	93	Trinidad and Tobago	105	Zimbabwe	94

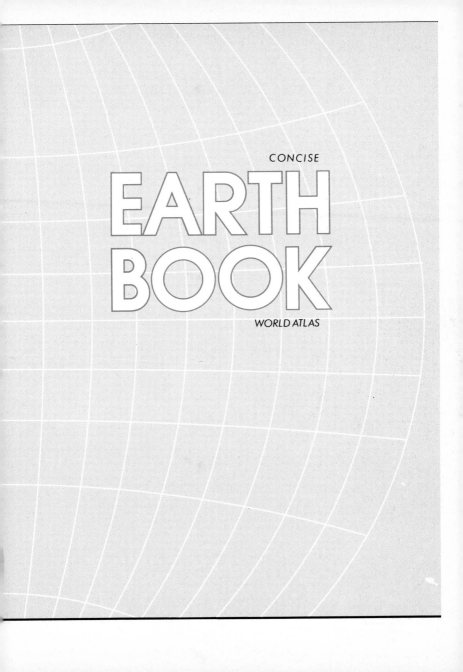

CONCISE

EARTH BOOK

WORLD ATLAS

Published in the United States of America by
EARTHBOOKS INCORPORATED, Denver, Colorado.

The Concise EARTHBOOK©
EARTHBOOKS INCORPORATED

Designed, edited drawn and reproduced by the
cartographers, geographers, artists and technicians
at ESSELTE MAP SERVICE.

Cover Design: Turnbull & Company

Esselte Map Service AB (Sweden)
    (Title) Concise EARTHBOOK
    Includes Glossary and Index
    1. Atlases   1. Title
    ISBN No. 1-877731-02-1 (previously ISBN 0-87746-101-5)

Printed in Yugoslavia

AFRICA

Africa, environment, flags   **84-85**

North-West Africa   **86-87**
Algeria, Libya, Morocco, Mauretania, Niger, Tunisia

The Nile Valley and Arabia   **88-89**
Bahrain, Egypt, Iraq, Israel, Jordan, Kuwait, Lebanon, Oman, Qatar, Saudi-Arabia, Southern Yemen, Sudan, Syria, United Arab Emirates, Yemen

West Africa   **90-91**
Benin, Burkina, Cameroon, Chad, Congo, Equatorial Guinea, Gabon, Ghana, Guinea, Guinea-Bissau, Ivory Coast, Liberia, Mali, Niger, Nigeria, São Tomé and Príncipe, Senegal, Sierra Leone, The Gambia, Togo

East Africa   **92-93**
Central Africa, Ethiopia, Kenya, Sudan, Tanzania, Uganda, Zaire

Southern Africa   **94-95**
Angola, Botswana, Comores, Madagascar, Malawi, Mauritius, Mozambique, Namibia, Lesotho, South Africa, Swaziland, Zambia, Zimbabwe

NORTH AMERICA

North America, environment, flags   **96-97**

Alaska and Western Canada   **98-99**
incl. the Aleutian islands

Eastern Canada   **100-101**

The United States   **102-103**
incl. Mexico

Central America and the West Indies   **104-105**
Belize, The Caribbean Archipelago, Costa Rica, Cuba, El Salvador, Guatemala, Honduras, Mexico, Nicaragua

SOUTH AMERICA

South America, environment, flags   **106-107**

South America, northern part   **108-109**
Brazil, Colombia, Ecuador, Guyana, Panama, Peru, Surinam, Venezuela

South America, central part   **110-111**
Bolivia, Brazil, Chile, Peru

South America, southern part   **112-113**
Argentina, Bolivia, Brazil, Chile, Paraguay, Uruguay

POLAR REGIONS

The Arctic, environment   **114**

The Antarctica, environment   **115**

THE WORLD

The World, environment   **116-117**

The World, political   **118-119**

The World, Time Zones   **120-121**

Animals on the Edge of Extinction   **122-123**

INDEX

Index   **125-184**

THE WORLD'S longest, greatest, highest, largest

Area: 150.243.000 km²
(Land: 26%, Water: 71%, Ice: 3%)
Population: 4,025,281,000

Greenland

Mount McKinley

NORTH AMERICA

Great Br

Missouri   Lake Superior

Mississippi

Milwaukee Depth

Amazon

SOUTH AMERICA

Lago Titicaca

Cerro Aconcagua

Grande de Tierra
del Fuego

World's Longest Rivers

1.	Nile (Africa)	6.690 km
2.	Amazon (South America)	6.570 km
3.	Mississippi-Missouri (North America)	6.020 km
4.	Yangtze (Asia)	5.980 km
5.	Yenisey (Asia)	5.870 km

Greatest Depth in each ocean

Arctic: North Polar Basin	5.500 m
Atlantic: Milwaukee Depth (Puerto Rico Trench)	9.219 m
Indian: Java Trench	7.450 m
Pacific: Challenger Deep (Mariana Trench)	11.034 m

Highest Mountain in each continent

Africa: Kilimanjaro	5.895 m
(Antarctica Vinson Massif)	5.140 m
Asia: Mt. Everest	8.848 m
Europe: Mont Blanc	4.810 m
North America: Mount McKinley	6.194 m
Oceania: Puncak Jaya	5.030 m
South America: Cerro Aconcagua	6.959 m

Largest Island in each continent

Africa: Madagascar	587.000 km²
(Antarctica: Alexander 1)	43.200 km²
Asia: Borneo	737.000 km²
Europe: Great Britain	219.000 km²
North America: Greenland	2.131.000 km²
Oceania: New Guinea	790.000 km²
South America: Grande de Tierra del Fuego	48.000 km²

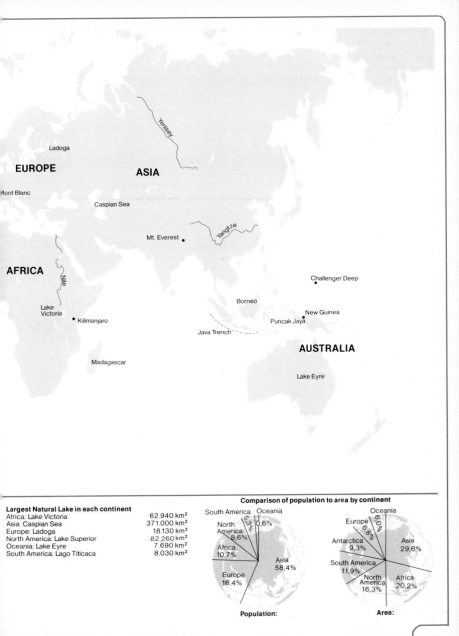

Largest Natural Lake in each continent

Africa: Lake Victoria	62.940 km²
Asia: Caspian Sea	371.000 km²
Europe: Ladoga	18.130 km²
North America: Lake Superior	82.260 km²
Oceania: Lake Eyre	7.690 km²
South America: Lago Titicaca	8.030 km²

Comparison of population to area by continent

Population:

South America 5,3%
Oceania 0,6%
North America 8,6%
Africa 10,7%
Asia 58,4%
Europe 16,4%

Area:

Oceania 6,0%
Europe 6,8%
Antarctica 9,3%
Asia 29,6%
South America 11,9%
North America 16,3%
Africa 20,2%

EUROPE

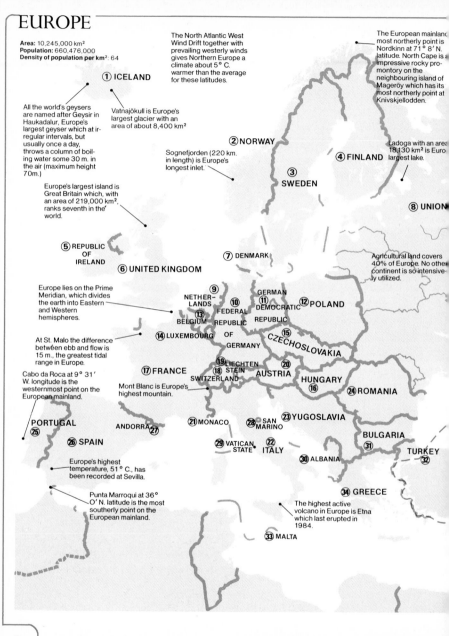

Area: 10,245,000 km²
Population: 660,476,000
Density of population per km²: 64

The North Atlantic West Wind Drift together with prevailing westerly winds gives Northern Europe a climate about 5° C. warmer than the average for these latitudes.

The European mainland most northerly point is Nordkinn at 71° 8′ N. latitude. North Cape is an impressive rocky promontory on the neighbouring island of Mageröy which has its most northerly point at Knivskjellodden.

① ICELAND

All the world's geysers are named after Geysir in Haukadalur. Europe's largest geyser which at irregular intervals, but usually once a day, throws a column of boiling water some 30 m. in the air (maximum height 70m.)

Vatnajökull is Europe's largest glacier with an area of about 8,400 km²

② NORWAY

Sognefjorden (220 km. in length) is Europe's longest inlet.

③ SWEDEN

④ FINLAND

Ladoga with an area 18,130 km² is Europe's largest lake.

Europe's largest island is Great Britain which, with an area of 219,000 km², ranks seventh in the world.

⑧ UNION

⑤ REPUBLIC OF IRELAND

⑥ UNITED KINGDOM

⑦ DENMARK

Agricultural land covers 40% of Europe. No other continent is so intensively utilized.

Europe lies on the Prime Meridian, which divides the earth into Eastern and Western hemispheres.

⑨ NETHER-LANDS

⑩ FEDERAL REPUBLIC OF GERMANY

⑪ GERMAN DEMOCRATIC REPUBLIC

⑫ POLAND

⑬ BELGIUM

At St. Malo the difference between ebb and flow is 15 m., the greatest tidal range in Europe.

⑭ LUXEMBOURG

⑮ CZECHOSLOVAKIA

Cabo da Roca at 9° 31′ W. longitude is the westernmost point on the European mainland.

⑰ FRANCE

⑲ LIECHTEN STEIN

⑱ SWITZERLAND

⑳ AUSTRIA

⑯ HUNGARY

㉔ ROMANIA

Mont Blanc is Europe's highest mountain.

㉑ MONACO

㉘ SAN MARINO

㉓ YUGOSLAVIA

PORTUGAL ㉕

ANDORRA ㉗

㉙ VATICAN STATE

㉒ ITALY

BULGARIA
㉛

TURKEY
㉜

㉖ SPAIN

Europe's highest temperature, 51° C., has been recorded at Sevilla.

㉚ ALBANIA

Punta Marroqui at 36° 0′ N. latitude is the most southerly point on the European mainland.

㉞ GREECE

The highest active volcano in Europe is Etna which last erupted in 1984.

㉝ MALTA

...IET SOCIALIST REPUBLICS

...Volga is 3,690 km.
...g, Europe's longest
...r. It also has the
...atest rate of flow.

...traditional boundary
...ween Europe and
...a divides both Turkey
...the U.S.S.R. into a
...opean and an Asian
...

...g this line Europe
...ends to about 60° E.
...gitude in the Ural
...untains.

...RUS

㉚	ALBANIA
㉗	ANDORRA
⑳	AUSTRIA
⑬	BELGIUM
㉛	BULGARIA
㉟	CYPRUS
⑮	CZECHOSLOVAKIA
⑦	DENMARK
⑩	FEDERAL REPUBLIC OF GERMANY
④	FINLAND
⑰	FRANCE
⑪	GERMAN DEMOCRATIC REPUBLIC
㉞	GREECE
⑯	HUNGARY
①	ICELAND
㉒	ITALY
⑲	LIECHTENSTEIN
⑭	LUXEMBOURG
㉝	MALTA
㉑	MONACO
⑨	NETHERLANDS
②	NORWAY
⑫	POLAND
㉕	PORTUGAL
⑤	REPUBLIC OF IRELAND
㉔	ROMANIA
㉘	SAN MARINO
㉖	SPAIN
③	SWEDEN
⑱	SWITZERLAND
㉜	TURKEY
⑧	UNION OF SOVIET SOCIALIST REPUBLICS
⑥	UNITED KINGDOM AND NORTHERN IRELAND
㉙	VATICAN STATE
㉓	YUGOSLAVIA

① ICELAND

Lýðveldið Ísland
(Republic of Iceland)

Area: 102,819 km²
Population: 240,000
Population growth per annum: 1.1%
Life expectancy at birth: males 73 years, females 79 years
Literacy: 99,9%
Capital with population: Reykjavik 87,000
Other important cities with population: Akureyri 14,000
Language: Icelandic
Religion: Protestant
Currency: Króna = 100 aurar

The Island of the Norse sagas, Iceland's "althingi" claims to be the world's oldest parliament, enacting laws since 930. The Icelanders kept the old Norse myths and sagas alive by oral tradition until Snorri Sturluson collected them in his epic Edda. A sight to be seen is the world famous Geysir. Independent 930, JUN 17, 1944.

② NORWAY

Kongeriket Norge
(Kingdom of Norway)

Area: 386,974 km² (including Svalbard and Jan Mayen)
Population: 4,130,000
Population growth per annum: 0.4%
Life expectancy at birth: males 72 years, females 78 years
Literacy: 99%
Capital with population: Oslo 447,000
Other important cities with population: Bergen 207,000, Trondheim 134,000
Language: Norwegian
Religion: Protestant
Currency: Norwegian krone = 100 öre

Norway, proclaimed 'The land of the Midnight Sun" might rather be called the Land of Fiords. These spectacular inlets between vertical mountain walls dissect Norway, and have made the Norwegians a people who sail and fish. The Sogne Fiord is 220 km. long — the Europe's longest bay. Independent 1905.

③ SWEDEN

Konungariket Sverige
(Kingdom of Sweden)

Area: 449,964 km²
Population: 8,350,000
Population growth per annum: 0.2%
Life expectancy at birth: males 72 years, females 79 years
Literacy: 99%
Capital with population: Stockholm 651,000 (metropolitan area 1,409, 000)
Other important cities with population: Göteborg 424,000 Malmö 230,000
Language: Swedish
Religion: Protestant
Currency: Swedish krona = 100 öre

The metallurgical industry that gave the world "Swedish steel" has traditions that reach beyond the Viking Age. The world's oldest company, Stora, chartered in 1280, is still working the mine of Falun, that produced the copper that once made Sweden a great power.

④ FINLAND

Suomen Tasavatta — Republiken Finland
(Republic of Finland)

Area: 337,032 km²
Population: 4,870 000
Population growth per annum: 0.6%
Life expectancy at birth: males 69 years, females 77 years
Literacy: 99%
Capital with population: Helsinki (Helsingfors) 484,000
Other important cities with population: Tampere (Tammerfors) 170.000, Turku (Åbo) 165,000
Language: Finnish, Swedish
Religion: Protestant
Currency: Markka (mark) = 100 penniä (penni)

The "land of a thousand lakes" (actually almost a hundred thousand) has also become known as "the land that pays its debts" — by repaying not only U.S. loans but also a huge war indemnity to the Soviet Union after World War II. Exporting high quality manufactured goods to East and West has brought prosperity to the Finns. Independent DEC 6, 1917

⑤ REPUBLIC OF IRELAND

Poblacht na L'Éireann
(Eire)

Area: 70,283 km²
Population: 3,440,000
Population growth per annum: 1.1%
Life expectancy at birth: males 70 years, females 75 years
Literacy: 99%
Capital with population: Dublin 526,000
Other important cities with population: Cork 150,000, Limerick 76,000
Language: Irish, English
Religion: Roman Catholic
Currency: Irish pound (punt Eirenmach) = 100 pighne

"The Emerald Isle" is perhaps most famous for its people — for boisterous bards, for poets and playwrights and Irish Eyes — but also for Irish coffee, whiskey and Guinness beer. Ireland justly prides itself also on the Book of Kells — and maybe more reluctantly for the Blarney Stone, kissed by many. Independent 1916, 1922.

⑥ THE UNITED KINGDOM OF GREAT BRITAIN AND NORTHERN IRELAND

Area: 244,104 km²
Population: 56,780,000
Population growth per annum: — 0.1%
Life expectancy at birth: males 70 years, females 76 years
Literacy: 99%
Capital with population: London 6,755,000
Other important cities with population: Birmingham 1,013,000, Leeds 714,000, Sheffield 543,000
Language: English
Religion: Protestant, Roman Catholic, Moslem
Currency: British pound = 100 pence

Britannia ruled the waves for over three hundred years, and finally gracefully resigned from the role of "peacekeeper" after the Pax Britannica had been broken by two world wars. The sun may have set over the Empire, but it still shines on the Union Jack in many places all over the world.

⑦ DENMARK

Kongeriget Danmark
(Kingdom of Denmark)

Area: 43,069 km²
Population: 5,112,000
Population growth per annum: 0.2%
Life expectancy at birth: males 71 years, females 77 years
Literacy: 99%
Capital with population: Köbenhavn
(Copenhagen) 483,000, (Greater Copenhagen 1,400,000)
Other important cities with population: Aarhus 250,000,
Odense 170,000
Language: Danish
Religion: Protestant (Lutherans)
Currency: Danish krone = 100 øre

*Danish kings have ruled not only all of Scandinavia but also
England. Today no other country has larger overseas territories.
They include the world's largest island, Greenland. Friendly
Denmark now serves as an important link between the Nordic
countries and the rest of Europe, especially the E.E.C.*

⑧ UNION OF SOVIET SOCIALIST REPUBLICS

Soyuz Sovyetskikh
Sotsialisticheskikh Respublik

Area: 22,402,200 km²
Population: 276,300,000
Population growth per annum: 0.9 %
Life expectancy at birth: males 65 years, females 74 years
Literacy: 99%
Capital with population: Moskva (Moscow) 8,537,000
Other important cities with population:
Leningrad 4,800,000, Baku 1,660,000,
Kuybyshev 1,250,000
Language: Slavic (Russian, Ukrainian, Byelorussian, Polish),
Altaic (Turkish, etc.) Other Indo-European, Uralian,
Caucasian.
Religion: Orthodox, Moslem
Currency: Rubel = 100 kopek

*The U.S.S.R. is a country that is almost a continent not only in
size, but also in diversity. It covers 1/6 of the Earth's land area,
and is larger than South America. 75% is traditionally considered to be part of Asia, but 75% of its people live in the European part. In comprises 120 different peoples, dominated by
the Russians.*

⑨ NETHERLANDS

Koninkrijk der Nederlanden
(Kingdom of the Netherlands)

Area: 41,548 km²
Population: 14,395,000
Population growth per annum: 0.6%
Life expectancy at birth: males 72 years, females 78 years
Literacy: 99%
Capital with population: Amsterdam 994,000
Other important cities with population:
Rotterdam 1,025,500, S-Gravenhage (The Hague)
(672,000)
Language: Dutch
Religion: Roman Catholic (40%), Protestant (35%)
Currency: Guilder = 100 cents

*More than one third of the country lies below sealevel. Some
Dutch say that 'God created the world, except the Netherlands,
which we had to create ourselves'. This task was begun in the
15th century, when they learned to reclaim their slowly sinking
land from the encroaching sea. Independent APR 19, 1839.*

⑩ FEDERAL REPUBLIC OF GERMANY

Bundesrepublik Deutschland

Area: 248,687 km²
Population: 61,420,000
Population growth per annum: − 0.3 %
Life expectancy at birth: males 69 years, females 75 years
Literacy: 99%
Capital with population: Bonn 293,000
Other important cities with population: Berlin 1,860,000,
Hamburg 1,620,000, Munich 1,285,000
Language: German
Religion: Protestant (49%), Roman Catholic (45%)
Currency: D-mark = 100 pfennig

*Like the mythical Phoenix, West Germany has miraculously
sprung from the pyre of total defeat and destruction since
1945. In economic and industrial importance the western half
of divided Germany now ranks fourth in the world. The Grand
Tour must include the Rhine valley with its castles and
vineyards. Independent SEP 6, 1949.*

⑪ GERMAN DEMOCRATIC REPUBLIC

Deutsche Demokratische Republik

Area: 108,333 km²
Population: 16,700,000
Population growth per annum: 0%
Life expectancy at birth: males 69 years, females 75 years
Literacy: 99%
Capital with population: Berlin 1,185,000
Other important cities with population: Leipzig 560,000.
Dresden 525,000, Karl-Marx-Stadt 320,000
Language: German
Religion: Protestant (80%)
Currency: Mark (of the GDR) = 100 pfennig

*The republic is divided nation with a divided capital. The fears
and the rivalries of the victorious powers after World War II
prevented the reestablishment of a German "Reich". Thus part
of the old capital, Berlin, is now a West German enclave, by road
and railway over 150 km. (100 miles) inside East Germany.
Independent OCT 7, 1949.*

⑫ POLAND

Polska Rzeczpospolita Ludowa
(Polish Peoples Republic)

Area: 312,683 km²
Population: 36,400,000
Population growth per annum: 1.0 %
Life expectancy at birth: males 67 years, females 75 years
Literacy: 98%
Capital with population: Warszawa (Warsaw) 1,630,000
Other important cities with population: Lódź 850,000
Kraków 725,000
Language: Polish
Religion: Roman Catholic
Currency: Zloty = 100 groszy

*The Polish people do not give up. Time and again conquering ar-
mies have swept over Poland and divided the spoils. After World
War II the Soviet Union pushed the land westwards over former
German land, annexing 1/3 of pre-war Poland in the east.
Independent 966, NOV 10, 1918.*

11

⑬ BELGIUM

Royaume de Belgique —
Koninkrijk België
(Kingdom of Belgium)

Area: 30,519 km²
Population: 9,850 000
Population growth per annum: 0.1%
Life expectancy at birth: males 69 years, females 75 years
Literacy: 98%
Capital with population: Bruxelles 980,000 (Brussels)
Other important cities with population:
Antwerpen 490,000, Gent 240,000
Language: Flemish (Dutch), French, German
Religion: Roman Catholic
Currency: Belgian franc = 100 centimes

*The country at "the crossroads of Western Europe" is
dominated by the capital Brussels. Brussels is also the capital of
the E.E.C. The difficulties in uniting Europe are mirrored in the
Belgian nation. The Dutch-speaking Flemings and French-
speaking Walloons stick together against others, but often
quarrel amongst themselves. Independent OCT 4, 1830.*

⑭ LUXEMBOURG

Grand-Duché Luxembourg)
(Grand Duchy of Luxembourg)

Area: 2,586 km²
Population: 366,000
Population growth per annum: —0.04%
Life expectancy at birth: males 68 years, females 75 years
Literacy: 100%
Capital with population: Luxembourg 79,000
Other important cities with population: none
Language: Luxemburgish, French, German
Religion: Roman Catholic (94%)
Currency: Luxembourg franc = 100 centimes

*Historically Luxembourg has always had strong ties with one or
another of its neighbours while maintaining independence in
form if not in fact. It also formed some sort of a nucleus for the
Coal and Steel Union that evolved into the E.E.C. Indep. 1866.*

⑮ CZECHOSLOVAKIA

Československá Socialistická
Republika
(Czechoslovak Socialist Republic)

Area: 127,869 km²
Population: 15,400 000
Population growth per annum: 0.7%
Life expectancy at birth: males 67 years, females 74 years
Literacy: 99%
Capital with population: Praha (Prague) 1,185,000
Other important cities with population: Bratislava 395,000,
Brno 380,000
Language: Czech, Slovak
Religion: Roman Catholic (55%), Protestant (10%)
Currency: Koruna = 100 haléřu

*Haseks fictionary "Good soldier Schweik" in many ways
epitomizes the survival instincts of his fellow citizens. Both
Czechs and Slovaks have always striven for freedom, but
throughout the centuries have been forced to bow to foreign
rule. Mining and manufacturing have a long history in
Czechoslovakia. Independent OCT 28, 1918.*

⑯ HUNGARY

Magyar Népköztársaság
(Hungarian People's Republic)

Area: 93,032 km²
Population: 10,680,000
Population growth per annum: 0.4%
Life expectancy at birth: males 67 years, females 73 years
Literacy: 98%
Capital with population: Budapest 2,064,000
Other important cities with population:
Debrecen 205,000, Miskolc 212,000
Language: Hungarian (Magyar)
Religion: Roman Catholic (65%), Protestant (25%)
Currency: Forint = 100 fillér

*Hungary is in many ways an enclave in Eastern Europe — a
Finno-Ugric nation surrounded by Slav neighbors, a land of
plains, the famous puszta, and rolling hills, encircled by higher
mountain lands — and, within limits, more prosperous and
"capitalistic" than the other Soviet satellites. Independent 1001.*

⑰ FRANCE

République Française
(French Republic)

Area: 547,026 km²
Population: 54,539,000
Population growth per annum: 0.3%
Life expectancy at birth: males 70 years, females 78 years
Literacy: 99%
Capital with population: Paris 2,320,000
(Greater Paris 8,550,000)
Other important cities with population: Marseille 915,000,
Lyon 465,000
Language: French
Religion: Roman Catholic (90%) Islam (4%)
Currency: French franc = 100 centimes

*France is one of the great powers of the world. The French
language is still the language of diplomacy. France is culturally
the world's leading nation, and most former French colonies remain members of the French Commonwealth. France is also the
leading European nation on the space frontier. National day:
JULY 14, (1789)*

⑱ SWITZERLAND

Schweiz - Suisse - Svizzera
(Swiss Confederation)

Area: 41,293 km²
Population: 6,400,000
Population growth per annum: 0.2 %
Life expectancy at birth: males 72 years, females 78 years
Literacy: 99%
Capital with population: Bern 144,000
Other important cities with population: Zürich 363,000,
Basel 180,000
Language: German, French, Italian, Romansch
Religion: Roman Catholic (49%), Protestant (48%)
Currency: Swiss franc = 100 centimes (rappen)

*The Financial Pole of the world is claimed to be in situated in
some undefined spot in Zürich. Through centuries of neutrality
and economic stability, Switzerland has grown into a global
center of banking. Besides quality watches, tourism somehow
seems to have been invented in this land of few natural
resources. Independent AUG 1, 1291.*

⑲ LIECHTENSTEIN
Fürstentum Liechtenstein
(Principality of Liechtenstein)

Area: 160 km²
Population: 27,000
Population growth per annum: 7.0%
Life expectancy at birth: not available
Literacy: 100 %
Capital with population: Vaduz 5,000
Other important cities with population: none
Language: German
Religion: Roman Catholic
Currency: Swiss franc = 100 centimes

Liechtenstein epitomizes the notion "postage stamp state" — because of its size and its fame among collectors of stamps. It is also an anomaly surviving principality from the times when Europe was divided among many princes and kings, before their
realms were united into nations. Independent MAY 3, 1342.

⑳ AUSTRIA
Republik Österreich
(Republic of Austria)

Area: 83,853 km²)
Population: 7,550,000
Population growth per annum: —0.1%
Life expectancy at birth: males 68 years, females 75 years
Literacy: 98%
Capital with population: Wien (Vienna) 1,530,000
Other important cities with population: Graz 243,000,
Linz 200,000
Language: German
Religion: Roman Catholic (89%), Protestant (6%)
Currency: Schilling = 100 groschen

Austria is the only state pledged both by law and treaties to neutrality. Vienna, for centuries the capital of the "Holy Roman Empire", the seat of the Habsburg Emperors, still bears the imprint of bygone greatness, and remains the cultural capital of Central Europe. Indep. 1276, 1804, 1918, APR 27, 1945.

㉑ MONACO
Principauté de Monaco
(Principality of Monaco)

Area: 1,95 km²
Population: 27,000
Population growth per annum: —3.0%
Life expectancy at birth: males 70 years, females 78 years
Literacy: 99%
Capital with population: Monaco-Ville 1,700
Other important cities with population: none
Languages: French, Monegasque
Religion: Roman Catholic
Currency: French-or Monegasque franc = 100 centimes

Monaco proves that gambling can pay provided you run the bank! The Monte Carlo Casino has been the Mecca of gamblers since 1858 and also made Monaco a fashionable tourist resort. The citizens of microscopic Monaco do not pay income tax. Independent 1297.

㉒ ITALY
Repubblica Italiana
(Italian Republic)

Area: 301,268 km²
Population: 56,930,000
Population growth per annum: 0.4%
Life expectancy at birth: males 70 years, females 76 years
Literacy: 98%
Capital with population: Roma (Rome) 2,830,000
Other important cities with population: Milano 1,500,000,
Napoli 1,200,000
Language: Italian
Religion: Roman Catholic
Currency: Lira = 100 centesimi

All roads lead to Rome, still the Eternal City — the city of the Pope, of the Sistine Chapel, of the Colosseum and innumerable monuments of Imperial Rome. But Italy is also the land of Saint Francis and Leonardo, of Pisa, Venice and Florence — and to-day of Milan, Torino and Cortina d'Ampezzo. Independent FEB 18, 1861.

㉓ YUGOSLAVIA
Socijalistička Federativna Republika
Jugoslavija
(Socialist Federal Republ. of Yogoslavia)

Area: 255,804 km²
Population: 22,850,000
Population growth per annum: 0.9%
Life expectancy at birth: males 67 years, females 72 years
Literacy: 85%
Capital with population: Beograd (Belgrade) 1,407,000
Other important cities with population: Zagreb 1,175,000,
Skopje 507,000, Ljubljana 305,000
Language: Serbo-Croatian, Macedonian, Slovenian,
Albanian
Religion: Orthodox (41%), Roman Catholic (32%),
Moslem (12%)
Currency: Yugoslavian dinar = 100 para

Few would in 1918 have placed any money on the survival of any country in the Balkan Peninsula and least of them all Yugoslavia with its mosaic of quarrelling religions — three — and combative peoples — five — speaking four different languages. Independent DEC 1, 1918.

㉔ ROMANIA
Republica Socialistă România
(Socialist Republic of Romania)

Area: 237,500 km²
Population: 22,600,000
Population growth per annum: 0.9%
Life expectancy at birth: males 68 years, females 73 years
Literacy: 98%
Capital with population: Bucuresti (Bucharest) 1,835,000
Other important cities with population:
Constanţa 285,000, Cluj-Napoca 271,000
Language: Romanian
Religion: Orthodox (70%), Roman Catholic (14%)
Currency: Leu = 100 bani

A land that is still Roman after almost two thousand years! Rome sett-led the fertile Dacia and made an everlasting imprint. In spite of that, the frontier province was lost less than two centuries after conquest. The people today speak a language based on Latin. Transylvania is known for fictitious Count Dracula. Independent 1877.

13

㉕ PORTUGAL
República Portuguesa
(Republic of Portugal)

Area: 92,082 km²
Population: 9,930,000
Population growth per annum: 0.9%
Life expectancy at birth: males 66 years, females 74 years
Literacy: 80%
Capital with population: Lisboa (Lisbon) 818,000
Other important cities with population: Porto 330,000
Language: Portuguese
Religion: Roman Catholic
Currency: Escudo = 100 centavos

In spite of its small size, Portugal managed to become one of the world's great powers, and to acquire and retain a global empire for half a millennium. Portugal produces famous wines, such as madeira and port (from Oporto), and every second wine bottle in the world is sealed with Portuguese cork.

㉖ SPAIN
Reino de España
(Kingdom of Spain)

Area: 504,782 km²
Population: 38,220,000
Population growth per annum: 1.0 %
Life expectancy at birth: males 70 years, females 76 years
Literacy: 97%
Capital with population: Madrid 3,188,000
Other important cities with population:
Barcelona 1,755,000, Sevilla 654,000,
Zaragoza 600,000
Language: Spanish, Catalan, Basque
Religion: Roman Catholic
Currency: Spanish peseta = 100 céntimos

Proud Spain, once one of the world's great powers that sent the Great Armada to England in a bid to become master of the oceans, is today still the cultural leader in the Iberic World. It gave the world people such as Cervantes, Loyola, Goya, and Picasso.

㉗ ANDORRA
Principat d'Andorra
(Principality of Andorra)

Area: 453 km²
Population: 41,600
Population growth per annum: not available
Life expectancy at birth: males 70 years, females 76 years
Literacy: 100%
Capital with population: Andorra la Vella 10,500
Other important cities with population: none
Language: Catalan
Religion: Roman Catholic
Currency: French franc, Spanish peseta

Conducting trade between Spain and France is and has been the main business of this Pyrenean principality, jointly ruled by the Spanish Bishop of Urgel and the Head of State of France. Outside Andorra some call it smuggling. Tourism also benefits from the absence of customs duties. Independent 1278.

㉘ SAN MARINO
Repubblica di San Marino
(Republic of San Marino)

Area: 61 km²
Population: 22,000
Population growth per annum: not available
Life expectancy at birth: not available
Literacy: not available
Capital with population: San Marino 5,000
Other important cities with population: none
Language: Italian
Religion: Roman Catholic
Currency: Italian lira = 100 centesimi

The only surviving city state of medieval Italy, San Marino is still governed by two Capitani Reggenti, democratically elected for a period of only six months. Sale of postage stamps was an important industry, but is now dwarfed by the tourist trade. Over 3.5 million visit San Marino each year. Independent 1263.

㉙ VATICAN CITY STATE
Stato della Citta del Vaticano

Area: 0.44 km²
Population: 1,000
Population growth per annum: —
Life expectancy at birth: —
Literacy: —
Capital with population: —
Other important cities with population: —
Language: Italian
Religion: Roman Catholic
Currency: Vatican City lira, Italian lira = 100 centesimi

The spiritual importance of the Pope is inversely proportionate to the size of his worldly domains, the world's smallest state. Relative to its size it certainly contains greater treasures of art than any other state in the world, such as the Sistine Chapel and the Pietà. Independent FEB 11, 1929.

㉚ ALBANIA
Rebublika Popullore
Socialiste e Shqipërisë

Area: 28,748 km²
Population: 2,850 000
Population growth per annum: 2.4%
Life expectancy at birth: males 68 years, females 71 years
Literacy: 75%
Capital with population: Tirana 198,000
Other important cities with population: Shkodra 63,000
Language: Albanian
Religion: Religions are not allowed since 1967
Currency: Lek = 100 qindarka

A desire for self-sufficiency has turned Albania into a virtually unknown "white spot" on the map. This nation is Europe's only Moslem country, but has declared itself "the world's first atheist state". It is so dogmatically communist, that it has broken all ties with other communist countries. Independent NOV 11,1912.

㉛ BULGARIA
Narodna Republika Bålgarija
(Peoples Republic of Bulgaria)

Area: 110,912 km²
Population: 8,930,000
Population growth per annum: 0.6%
Life expectancy at birth: males 69 years, females 75 years
Literacy: 95%
Capital with population: Sofiya 1,080,000
Other important cities with population: Plovid 310,000,
  Varna 260,000
Language: Bulgarian
Religion: Orthodox (85%), Moslem (13%)
Currency: Lev = 100 stótinki

*The Bulgarians do not forget that Russia helped to liberate their
country from Turkish rule that lasted for over five centuries. Today it is counted among the most loyal allies of the Soviet Union.
Europe's "vegetable and fruit garden" is also the tourist "Riviera"
of Eastern Europe. Independent SEPT 22, 1908.*

㉜ TURKEY
Türkiye Cumhuriyeti
(Republic of Turkey)

Area: 779,452 km²
Population: 48,000,000
Population growth per annum: 2.5%
Life expectancy at birth: males 58 years, females 63 years
Literacy: 70%
Capital with population: Ankara 1,877,000
Other important cities with population: Istanbul 2,773,000,
  Izmir 758,000,
Language: Turkish
Religion: Moslem
Currency: Turkish lira = 100 kuruş

*The land that for centuries served as a link between Europe and
Asia now also provides the two continents with a physical link,
the huge bridge over the Bosporus. The world famous cathedral
of Hagia Sofia, built by emperor Justinian 532-537, was turned
into a mosque after the fall of Constantinople in 1453.*

㉝ MALTA
Repubblika ta'Malta
(Republic of Malta)

Area: 316 km²
Population: 330,000
Population growth per annum: 0.9%
Life expectancy at birth: males 69 years, females 73 years
Literacy: 83%
Capital with population: Valletta 14,000
Other important cities with population: none
Language: Maltese, English
Religion: Roman Catholic
Currency: Lira Maltija (Maltese Lira) = 100 cents = 1000 mils

*For unprecedented valour during World War II the people of
Malta were collectively awarded the George Cross, Britain's
highest civilian decoration. Malta still proudly carries the cross
in its national flag. From 1530 to 1798 Malta was ruled by the
Knights Hospitallers — since Known as the Knights of Malta.
Independent SEP 21, 1964.*

㉞ GREECE
Elleniki Dimokratia
(Hellenic Republic)

Area: 131,944 km²
Population: 9,750,000
Population growth per annum: 0.6%
Life expectancy at birth: males 71 years, females 75 years
Literacy: 95%
Capital with population: Athinai (Athens) 900,000
  (Greater Athens 3,000,000)
Other important cities with population:
  Thessaloníki 400,000, Pátrai 140,000
Language: Greek
Religion: Greek Orthodox (97%)
Currency: Drachma = 100 lepta

*The cradle of European civilization is now a member of the
E.E.C. and thus takes an active part in shaping the Europe of the
future. Greece may well have the world's largest merchant fleet
— even if few sail under Greek flag. Venerable Parthenon, temple of Pallas Athena, still crowns Athen's Acropolis.
Independent FEB 3, 1830.*

㉟ CYPRUS
Kypriaki Dimokratia —
Kibris Cumhuriyeti
(Republic of Cyprus)

Area: 9,251 km²
Population: 655,000
Population growth per annum: 0.4%
Life expectancy at birth: males 70 years, females 74 years
Literacy: 89%
Capital with population: Nicosia 161,000
Other important cities with population: Limassol 107,000,
  Famagusta 40,000
Language: Greek, Turkish
Religion: Orthodox (77%)
Currency: Cyprus pound = 100 cents

*The very name of the metal copper is derived from the island's
original name, Kypros, as it in ancient times was the world's
leading producer of copper. The Greek goddess of love,
Aphrodite, was said to have been born here out of the surf. Actually Cyprus itself is a child of the sea, a part of former deep
ocean crust lifted high above sealevel. Indep. AUG 16,1960.*

ASIA

Area: 44,493,000 km²
Population: 2,349,048,000
Density of population per km²: 53

The Asian mainland's northernmost point is Cape Chelyuskin at 77° 44′ N. latitude.

Lowest surface temperature in the northern hemisphere, – C., was recorded at Oymyakon.

Northeastern Siberia has the most extreme continental climate in the world. The variation between the warmest month of Summer (average temperature of up to 17°C.) and the coldest month of Winter (below −50°C.) is greater than anywhere else. Winter here is colder than in any other populated spot.

The coniferous forests of Siberia, the Taiga, are the most extensive in the world. The wide-stretched lowlands rank second after those of the Amazon Basin.

There is no clear, natural boundary between Asia and Europe which together form the Eurasian mainland. The boundary is usually drawn along the crest of the Ural Mountains then follows the Ural River to the Caspian Sea to the Black Sea via the Manych Depression and the Sea of Azov.

① UNION OF SOVIET SOCIALIST REPUBLICS

The Ob drainage system of 3 million km² is the largest in Asia

The deepest lake in the world is Lake Baykal, 1940 m.

Baba Burun at 26° 3′ E. longitude is the Asian mainland's westernmost cape.

TURKEY ⑤

The Caspian Sea (371,000 km²) is the largest lake in the world.

The deserts and steppes of Central Asia are the most extensive area of inland drainage in the world. They cover about a third of the continent.

② MONGOLIA

⑥ LEBANON ⑦
⑬ ISRAEL SYRIA
⑭ JORDAN
Asia's highest surface temperature, 50°C., has been recorded at Baghdad.

The Fedchenko Glacier is Asia's largest, 1,350 km² in size.

The earth's largest variety of grass – bamboo can reach up to 40 m length and up tom 30 in thickness in China

Asia's and the world's deepest depression is the Dead Sea in the Jordan Valley, −402 m.
⑰
SAUDI ARABIA

⑧ IRAQ
⑮ KUWAIT
⑨ IRAN
AFGHANISTAN ⑩

Tibet is the Roof of the World, 2 million km² above 4.000 m. high.

Mount Everest (Qomolangma Feng) is the world's highest mountain, 8,848 m.

CHINA ⑪

⑱ BAHRAIN
⑲ QATAR ⑳ UNITED ARAB EMIRATES
PAKISTAN ⑯

The Arabian Peninsula is the world's largest and extends over 2,5 million km² (larger than Greenland).

NEPAL
⑤ BHUTAN ㉖

The world's heaviest fall, 26,461 mm., was recorded at Cherrapunji in 1860-61.

㉑ YEMEN
SOUTH YEMEN ㉒
㉓ OMAN

Himalaya is the world's highest mountain range with nine of the world's ten highest peaks and altogether fourteen reaching above 8,000 m.

BANGLA-DESH ㉗
INDIA ㉔
㉘
BURMA
㉚ LAOS
VIETN ㉛
THAILAND ㉙
CAMBODIA ㉟

In Summer the east-bound Southwest Monsoon Current replaces the westerly North Equatorial Current in the Indian Ocean, just as the South West Monsoon replaces the Northeast Trade Winds.

㉞ SRI LANKA

㉝ MALDIVES

Cape Buru at 1° 25′N. latitude is the southernmost point of the Asian mainland.

MALAYSIA ㊲
SINGAPORE ㊳

B

16

Cape Dezhneva at 169°
45′ E. longitude is the
most easterly point on
the Asian mainland.

The world's lowest
temperature, —88.3° C.,
was recorded in Antarc-
tica in 1960.

Klyuchevskaya Sopka,
4750 m., is Asia's
highest active volcano.
The most recent eruption
was in 1962.

The northern part of the
Sea of Okhotsk is frozen
over in February and
March

The Sikhote-Alin Range
was bombarded in 1947
by the greatest swarm of
meteorites known to
humankind, over 10,000
meteorites weighing
together some 100,000
kg.

JAPAN
⑫
On the average Tokyo is
shaken by an earthquake
every week.

NORTH
KOREA

SOUTH
KOREA
④

longest river in Asia
fourth longest in the
d, is the Yangtze,
0 km.

②
WAN

The East Asian seas are
hit by more than twenty
typhoons (tropical
storms) during the period
September-November
every year, the earth's
most severely hit region.

㊱ PHILIPPINES

Borneo, 737,000 km², is
Asia's largest island and
ranks third in the world.

ONESIA

⑩	AFGHANISTAN
⑱	BAHRAIN
㉗	BANGLADESH
㉖	BHUTAN
㊴	BRUNEI
㉘	BURMA
⑪	CHINA
㉟	CAMBODIA
㉔	INDIA
㊵	INDONESIA
⑨	IRAN
⑧	IRAQ
⑬	ISRAEL
⑫	JAPAN
⑭	JORDAN
⑮	KUWAIT
㉚	LAOS
⑥	LEBANON
㊲	MALAYSIA
㉝	MALDIVES
②	MONGOLIA
㉕	NEPAL
③	NORTH KOREA
㉓	OMAN
⑯	PAKISTAN
㊱	PHILIPPINES
⑲	QATAR
⑰	SAUDI ARABIA
㊳	SINGAPORE
④	SOUTH KOREA
㉒	SOUTH YEMEN
㉞	SRI LANKA
⑦	SYRIA
㉙	THAILAND
㉜	TAIWAN
⑤	TURKEY
①	UNION OF SOVIET SOCIALIST REPUBLICS
⑳	UNITED ARAB EMIRATES
㉛	VIETNAM
㉑	YEMEN

① UNION OF SOVIET SOCIALIST REPUBLICS
Soyuz Sovyetskikh Sotsialisticheskikh Respublik

Area: 22,402,200 km²
Population: 276,300,000
Population growth per annum: 0.9%
Life expectancy at birth: males 65 years, females 74 years
Literacy: 99%
Capital with population: Moskva (Moscow) 8,537,000
Other important cities with population:
Leningrad 4,800,000, Baku 1,660,000,
Kuybyshev 1,250,000
Language: Altaic (Turkish etc.), other Indo-European,
Uralian Caucasian
Religion: Orthodox, Moslem
Currency: Rubel = 100 kopek

The U.S.S.R. is a country that is almost a continent not only in size, but also in diversity. It covers 1/6 of the Earth's land area, and is larger than South America. 75% is traditionally considered to be part of Asia, but 75% of its people live in the European part. In comprises 120 different peoples, dominated by the Russians.

② MONGOLIA
Bügd Nayramdakh Mongol Ard Uls
(Mongolian People's Republic)

Area: 1,565,000 km²
Population: 1,820,000
Population growth per annum: 2.9%
Life expectancy at birth: males 61 years, females 65 years
Literacy: 80%
Capital with population: Ulaanbaatar (Ulan Bator) 400,000
Other important cities with population: Darkhan 52,000
Language: Mongol, Russian, Chinese
Religions: Buddhist
Currency: Tugrik = 100 möngö

The home of Genghis Khan is now as then a land of unbroken horizons where trees are as rare as people on the windswept grasslands. The Mongols have now exchanged their horses for motor bikes and so only disappear faster out of view. One third of Mongolia is part of the mighty Gobi Desert. Independent JAN 5, 1946.

③ NORTH KOREA
Chosun Minchu-chui Inmin
Konghwa-guk
(Democratic People's
Republic of Korea)

Area: 122,098 km²
Population: 18,490,000
Population growth per annum: 3.2%
Life expectancy at birth: males 70 years, females 78 years
Literacy: 85%
Capital with population: P'yŏngyang 1,280,000
Other important cities with population: Hamhŭng 420,000,
Ch'ŏngjin 265,000
Languages: Korean
Religion: Buddhist (activities discouraged)
Currency: Won = 100 chon

Korea is a victim of the 20th century. During the scramble for colonies it was annexed by Japan, and after the Japanese capitulation in 1945 it was divided into two zones of occupation by the U.S.A. and the U.S.S.R. along 38° N lat. The cold war began here and grew into a real war 1950-53. Korea remains divided. Independent NOV 9, 1948.

④ SOUTH KOREA
Han Kook
(Republic of Korea)

Area: 98,992 km²
Population: 39,950,000
Population growth per annum: 1.6%
Life expectancy at birth: 68 years
Literacy: 92%
Capital with population: Sŏul (Seoul) 8,367,000
Other important cities with population: Pusan 3,160,000,
Taegu 1,607,000
Language: Korean
Religion: Buddhist, Confucianist, Christian
Currency: Won = 100 chon

In the shadow of China, the Korean people have managed to maintain a national identity — and true independence during most of their history — and also to achieve great cultural feats of their own. Here books were being printed as early as a thousand years ago. Independent AUG 15, 1948.

⑤ TURKEY
Türkiye Cumhuriyeti
(Republic of Turkey)

Area: 779,452 km²
Population: 48,000,000
Population growth per annum: 2.5%
Life expectancy at birth: males 58 years, females 63 years
Literacy: 70%
Capital with population: Ankara 1,877,000
Other important cities with population: Istanbul 2,773,000,
Izmir 758,000
Language: Turkish
Religion: Moslem
Currency: Turkish lira = 100 kurş

The land that for centuries served as a link between Europe and Asia now also provides the two continents with a physical link, the huge bridge over the Bosporus. The world famous cathedral of Hagia Sofia, built by emperor Justinian 532-537, was turned into a mosque after the fall of Constantinople in 1453.

⑥ LEBANON
Al-Jumhouriya al-Lubnaniya
(Republic of Lebanon)

Area: 10,452 km²
Population: 3,500,000
Population growth per annum: 0.8%
Life expectancy at birth: males 63 years, females 67 years
Literacy: 75%
Capital with population: Bayrút (Beirut) 702,000
Other important cities with population:
Tarábulus (Tripoli) 175,000
Language: Arabaic
Religion: Moslem (50%), Christian (50%)
Currency: Lebanese pound = 100 piastres

Since Phoenician times international trade has been the blood of life here at the crossroads of the Levant, populated by fiercely proud clans from all over the Middle East. The lone cedar tree of the flag is almost the last remnant of the mighty forests that once covered Mt. Lebanon. Independent JUN 1, 1944.

⑦ SYRIA
Al-Jamhouriya al Arabia as-Souriya
(Syrian Arab republic)

Area: 185,180 km²
Population: 9,840,000
Population growth per annum: 3.8%
Life expectancy at birth: males 63 years, females 66 years
Literacy: 65%
Capital with population: Dimashq (Damascus) 1,251,000
Other important cities with population:
Halab (Aleppo) 1,525,000 Hims (Homs) 630,000
Language: Arabic
Religion: Moslem (88%), Christian
Currency: Syrian pound = 100 piaster

Long before Rome was founded all caravan trails and trade routes "of the world" converged on the capital of Syria, Damascus. Herod, St. Paul and Ibn Battuta as well as Alexander the Great, Julius Caesar and Genghis Khan have all passed through Damascus. Independent JAN 1, 1944.

⑧ IRAQ
Al Jumhouriya al 'Iraqia
(Republic of Iraq)

Area: 434,924 km²
Population: 14,000,000
Population growth per annum: 3.4%
Life expectancy at birth: males 54 years, females 57 years
Literacy: 70%
Capital with population: Baghdad 3,200,000
Other important cities with population: Al Basrah 400,000,
Al Mawsil (Mosul) 350,000
Language: Arabic, Kurdish
Religion: Moslem (95%)
Currency: Iraqi dinar = 20 dirham = 1000 fils

The ancient "Land Between the Rivers", Mesopotamia, is today known as Iraq. The name is said to be derived from a word meaning "origin", a very apt name. Here the wheel and the plow were invented. Here the oldest maps and written records have been found as well as the oldest Codes of Law. Independent 1932.

⑨ IRAN
Jomhori-e-Islami-e-Irân
(Islamic Republic of Iran)

Area: 1,648,100 km²
Population: 43,830,000
Population growth per annum: 3.0%
Life expectancy at birth: males 53 years, females 54 years
Literacy: 48%
Capital with population: Tehrān 4,500,000
Other important cities with population: Esfahān 700,000,
Mashhad 700,000
Language: Farsi (persian), Turkic languages, Kurdish
Religion: Shiá Moslems (93%)
Currency: Rial = 100 dinars

Through milennia Iran previously called Persia — has influenced the history and culture of all people. Iran has nurtured Cyrus, Darius and Xerxes, Zoroaster, Firdawsi and Omar Khayyam — and ayatollah Khomeini. Iranians invented polo and developed chess.

⑩ AFGHANISTAN
De Afghanistan Democrateek
Jamhuriat
(Democratic Republic of Afganistan)

Area: 647,497 km²
Population: 17,500,000 (of which 23% are
refugees outside the country)
Population growth per annum: 2.5%
Life expectancy at birth: males 40 years, females 41 years
Literacy: 10%
Capital with population: Kabul 900,000
Other important cities with population: Kandahar 180,000
Herat 140,000
Language: Pushtu, Dari (Persian)
Religion: Islam (90% Sunni Moslems)
Currency: Afghani = 100 puls

The crossroads of Asia — and once more, a theater of war. Throughout history, conquering armies have marched through the green valleys beneath Afghanistan's forbidding mountains, but no one has ever been able to subjugate its warlike tribes, so fiercely independent, that they were not even united into an emirate before 1747. Independent 1747.

⑪ CHINA
(Peoples Republic of China)

Area: 9,561,000 km²
Population: 1,008,175,000
Population growth per annum: 1.4%
Life expectancy at birth: males 62 years, females 69 years
Literacy: 75%
Capital with population: Beijing (Peking) 5,550,000
Other important cities with population: Shanghai
6,300,000, Tianjin 5,200,000, Shenuang 4,000,000
Language: Mandarin Chinese, Shanghai-, Canton-, Fukien-,
Hakka- dialects, Tibetan, Vigus (Turkic)
Religion: Officially atheist, Confucanist, Buddhist, Taoist.
Currency: Yuan = 10 jiap = 100 fen

The length of the historical records of China are paralleled only by the Great Wall one of the greatest human-made structures 4,000 kms, 2,500 miles). China is the world's most populous nation, human-made, and will without doubt be one of the superpowers of the future. Independent OCT 1, 1949.

⑫ JAPAN
Nippon (or Nihon)

Area: 377,765 km²
Population: 119,500,000
Population growth per annum: 0.9%
Life expectancy at birth: males 73 years, females 78 years
Literacy: 99%
Capital with population: Tōkyō 8,150,000
Other important cities with population:
Yokohama 2,870,000 Nagoya 2,060,000,
Kyōto 1,460,000
Language: Japanese
Religion: Buddhist, Shinto, Roman Catholic
Currency: Yen = 100 sen

Japan has learned to live with earthquakes. Minor tremors are registered more than twice a day, and on average the earth here trembles perceptibly once a week. Only a few cause damage to buildings, as houses here are either very light structures or built to resist even severe shocks.

19

⑬ ISRAEL
Medinat Israel — State of Israel

Area: 20,770 km²
Population: 4,150,000
Population growth per annum: 2.6%
Life expectancy at birth: males 71 years, females 73 years
Literacy: 88%
Capital with population: Yerushalayim (Jerusalem) 430,000
Other important cities with population:
Tel Aviv-Yafo 330,000, Hefa (Haifa) 226,000
Language: Hebrew, Arabic
Religion: Judaism (85%), Moslem (11%)
Currency: Shekel = 100 agorot

The unprecedented rebirth of a land and a language after almost two thousand years must be considered a miracle. This fulfillment of an cient prophecies is due to the tenacity and spirit of the Jewish people. A majority of human kind considers Jerusalem Holy. Independent MAY 14, 1948.

⑭ JORDAN
Al Mamlaka al Urduniya al Hashemiyah
(The Hashemite Kingdom of Jordan)

Area: 97,740 km²
(incl. 5,880 km² on the West Bank)
Population: 3,500,000
Population growth per annum: 3.7%
Life expectancy at birth: males 58 years, females 62 years
Literacy: 58%
Capital with population: 'Ammān 1,230,000
Other important cities with population: Az Zarqā' 270,000, Irbid 140,000
Language: Arabic
Religion: Moslem (80% Sunni Moslems)
Currency: Jordan dinar = 1000 fils

Once the rulers of the arid lands east of River Jordan controlled the trade routes across the desert, and accumulated wealth from the incense trade, as can be seen from the glory of the rose-red ruins of Petra. Independent MAR 22, 1946.

⑮ KUWAIT
Dowlat al Kuwait
(State of Kuwait)

Area: 17,818 km²
Population: 1,910,,000
Population growth per annum: 6.0%
Life expectancy at birth: males 67 years, females 72 years
Literacy: 71%
Capital with population: Al Kuwayt (Kuwait) 280,000
Other important cities with population: none
Language: Arabic
Religion: Moslem (70% Sunni Moslems)
Currency: Kuwait dinar = 1000 fils

The name Kuwait today associates with oil and wealth. Once sturdy dhows sailing to far away African and East Indian ports brought renown to Kuwait. The real Sindbad the Sailor may have lived here. Independent JUN 19, 1961.

⑯ PAKISTAN
(Islamic Republic of Pakistan)

Area: 887,747 km²
Population: 89,000,000
Population growth per annum: 2.8%
Life expectancy at birth: males 52 years, females 50 years
Literacy: 23%
Capital with population: Islamabad 201,000
Other important cities with population: Karachi 5,103,000, Lahore 2,920,000, Faisalabad 1,092,000
Language: Urdu, Punjabi
Religion: Moslem (sunni Moslems)
Currency: Pakistani rupie = 100 paisa

By peaceful agreement, but through tumultuous upheaval the Islamic nation of Pakistan was created out of parts of former British India. Until 1971 it also comprised Bangladesh 2,000 km. away, then known as East Pakistan. Independent AUG 14, 1947.

⑰ SAUDI ARABIA
Al-Mamlaka-al-'Arabiya as-Sa'udiya
(Kingdom of Saudi Arabia)

Area: 2,149,690 km²
Population: 10,970,000
Population growth per annum: 4.2%
Life expectancy at birth: males 53 years, females 56 years
Literacy: 25%
Capital with population: Ar Riyād (Riyadh) 1,250,000
Other important cities with population: Jiddah 1,300,000, Makkah (Mecca) 550,000
Language: Arabic
Religion: Moslem
Currency: Rial = 100 halalas

Like the genie released from Aladdin's oil lamp, the wealth of oil released from the rocks of the desert have brought fabulous palaces and gardens to its owners. Modern cities, industries, universities and motorways have been created overnight. Independent SEP 20, 1932.

⑱ BAHRAIN
Mashyaka al Bahrayn
(State of Bahrain)

Area: 622 km²
Population: 380,000
Population growth per annum: 2.8%
Life expectancy at birth: males 64 years, females 68 years
Literacy: 40%
Capital with population: Al Manāmah 122,000
Other important cities with population: Al Muharraq 62,000
Language: Arabic
Religion: Islam (Sunni Moslems)
Currency: Bahrain dinar = 100 fils

The popular joke, that Bahrain gas stations should give free fuel to every buyer of water for coolant, is of course not true. It reflects the lack of water that troubles oil-rich Bahrain. It will be solved by a pipeline following the giant causeway to the mainland. Independent AUG 15, 1971.

⑲ QATAR
Dawlat Qatar
(State of Qatar)

Area: 11,437 km²
Population: 260 000
Population growth per annum: 6.5%
Life expectancy at birth: males 55 years, females 58 years
Literacy: 40%
Capital with population: Ad Dawhah 190,000
Other important cities with population: none
Language: Arabic
Religion: Moslem
Currency: Riyal = 100 dirham

A black underground sea of oil has become the source of wealth to Qatar, instead of the Gulf's warm blue waters and its pearl oysters. Independent SEP 1, 1971.

⑳ UNITED ARAB EMIRATES
Al Imarat al Arabiya al Muttahida

Area: 92,100 km²
Population: 1,175,000
Population growth per annum: 7.3%
Life expectancy at birth: males 60 years, females 74 years
Literacy: 53%
Capital with population: Alu Zaly (Abu Dhabi) 240,000
Other important cities with population: Dubayy 278,000
Language: Arabic
Religion: Islam
Currency: UAE dirham = 100 fils

Pearl-fishing and clandestine trade (by some called smuggling) sustained the people on the Trucial Coast after the more lucrative slave trade was abolished by the Perpetual Maritime Truce Treaty, signed by Great Britain and the seven sheiks 1853. Oil has now brought prosperity. Independent DEC 2, 1971.

㉑ YEMEN
Al Jamhuriyah al Arabiya al Yamaniya
(Yemen Arab Republic)

Area: 195,000 km²
Population: 7,160,000
Population growth per annum: 2.3%
Life expectancy at birth: males 37 years, females 39 years
Literacy: 12%
Capital with population: San'a 278,000
Other important cities with population: Hodeida 130,000, Taż 120,000
Language: Arabic
Religion: Moslem
Currency: Yemen paper riyal = 100 rial

The Roman name for Yemen "Arabia Felix" or Lucky Arabia was more apt then than today. The old great dams filled up with silt and were destroyed by floods, and incense no longer fetches its weight in silver or gold.

㉒ SOUTH YEMEN
Jumhurijah al-Yemen al Dimuqratiya al Sha'abijah
(Peoples Democratic)

Area: 287,682 km²
Population: 2,030,000
Population growth per annum: 1.8%
Life expectancy at birth: males 40 years, females 42 years
Literacy: 25%
Capital with population: Baladıyat 'Adan (Aden) 295,000
Other important cities with population: Al Mukallā 100,000
Language: Arabic
Religion: Moslem
Currency: South Yemen dinar = 1000 fils

This is the land of ancient skyscrapers. The high-rise buildings that form the skyline of Hadramaut are mainly built of mud bricks. They are 6-7 stories high, but seem higher as every story has 2 rows of windows.

㉓ OMAN
(Sultanate of Oman)

Area: 212,457 km²
Population: 1,500 000
Population growth per annum: 3.0%
Life expectancy at birth: males 46 years, females 48 years
Literacy: 20%
Capital with population: Masqat 50,000
Language: Arabic
Religion: Moslem
Currency: Rial = 1000 biazas

Like his rival, the King of Portugal, the Sultan of Oman once ruled over a far-flung transocean empire. The red flag of the Sultan flew over forts and trading posts on Asian and African coasts, such as Mombasa and Zanzibar.

㉔ INDIA
Bharat
(Republic of India)

Area: 3,184,290 km²
Population: 683,810,000
Population growth per annum: 2.0%
Life expectancy at birth: males 50 years, females 49 years
Literacy: 36%
Capital with population: Delhi 5,720,000
Other important cities with population:
Bombay 8,230,000, Calcutta 9,170,000,
Madras 4,280,000
Language: Hindi, English
Religion: Hindu (83%), Moslem (11%)
Currency: Rupee = 100 Paise

Like the images of Hindu gods that have several eyes, heads and arms (symbolizing their paradoxical nature), the subcontinent and nation of India has many diverse and contradictory features. India is the serene Taj Mahal in cool white marble, and Calcutta with its teeming millions, holy cows and also nuclear power. Independent JAN 26, 1950.

㉕ NEPAL
Sri Nepala Sarkar
(Kingdom of Nepal)

Area: 145,391 km²
Population: 16,100,000
Population growth per annum: 2.3%
Life expectancy at birth: males 43 years, females 44 years
Literacy: 20%
Capital with population: Katmandu 195,000
Other important cities with population: Patan 50,000
Language: Nepali, Indian Languages
Religion: Hindu (90%), Buddist (7%)
Currency: Nepalese Rupee = 2 mohur = 100 paisa

*By avoiding involvement in the affairs of the outside world the
mountain kingdom of Nepal has like Switzerland managed to
remain independent. Nepal shares with China the world's
highest peak, Chomolungma, the "Goddess Mother of the
World" to the Tibetans, since 1865 also known as Mt. Everest.*

㉖ BHUTAN
Druk Gaykhab
(Kingdom of Bhutan)

Area: 46,600 km²
Population: 1,250,000
Population growth per annum: 2.2%
Life expectancy at birth: males 44 years, females 43 years
Literacy: 5%
Capital with population: Thimphu 21,000
Other important cities with population: none
Language: Dzongka, Nepali
Religion: Buddhist (70%), Hindu
Currency: Ngultrum = 100 chetrums (Indian rupee also used)

*Bhutan's official name Druk Yul translates Land of the Dragon.
This is an apt name, as the mountainous former hermit kingdom
has many fairy-tale qualities . The only real dragons to be found
are those on the national flags.*

㉗ BANGLADESH
(Peoples Republic of Bangladesh)

Area: 143,998 km²
Population: 96,000,000
Population growth per annum: 2.8%
Life expectancy at birth: males 46 years, females 46 years
Literacy: 25%
Capital with population: Dakha 3,500,000
Other important cities with population:
Ghittagong 1,390,000, Khulna 650,000
Language: Bengali, English
Religion: Islam (80%), Hindu
Currency: Taka = 100 poisha

*The fertile delta lands of Ganges and Brahmaputra, created by
floods, have long been more than overpopulated. Troubled by
alternating droughts and torrential rains, poor Bangladesh is fre-
quently plagued by hurricanes and devastating tidal floods.
Independent DEC 20, 1971.*

㉘ BURMA
Pyidaungsu Socialist Thammada
Myanma Naingngandaw
(Socialist Republic of the Union of
Burma)

Area: 676,552 km²
Population: 35,310,000
Population growth per annum: 2.4%
Life expectancy at birth: males 51 years, females 54 years
Literacy: 78%
Capital with population: Rangoon 2,460,000
Other important cities with population: Mandalay 420,000,
Bassein 360,000
Language: Burmese
Religions: Buddhist (85%)
Currency: Kyat = 100 pyas

*Burma is still the land of the gilded pagodas, where time flows as
slowly as the mighty Irrawaddy. In this land of yesterday veteran
cars are in everyday use, and elephants haul teak logs to the
rivers. Burma's socialists have governed the country since
1948. Independent JAN 4, 1948.*

㉙ THAILAND
Prathes Thai
(Kingdom of Thailand)

Area: 514,000 km²
Population: 50,000,000
Population growth per annum: 2.3%
Life expectancy at birth: males 58 years, females 63 years
Literacy: 84%
Capital with population: Krung Thep (Bangkok) 5,470,000
Other important cities with population: Chiang Mai
105,000
Language: Thai
Religion: Buddhist (93%), Moslem (4%)
Currency: Baht = 100 Satang

*Thailand has throughout history managed to survive and main-
tain independence by deft diplomacy and careful observation
of prevailing wind directions. Internally the king retains power
in much the same way.*

㉚ LAOS
(The Lao People's Democratic
Republic)

Area: 236,800 km²
Population: 3,500,000
Population growth per annum: 2.4%
Life expectancy at birth: males 42 years, females 45 years
Literacy: 28%
Capital with population: Vientiane 120,000
Other important cities with population:
Luang Prabang 45,000
Language: Lao
Religion: Buddhist
Currency: Kip = 100 at

*Reverence for royalty has always transcended life in Laos. A
royal prince led the communists to victory in 1975 and abolished monarchy. Several hundred huge carved burial urns,
presumably containing royal remains from prehistoric times,
still dot the Plain of Jars. Independent JUN 20, 1954.*

㉛ VIETNAM
Cộng Hòa Xã Hội Chu Nghĩa Việt Nam
(Socialist Republic of Vietnam)

Area: 329,566 km²
Population: 60,000,000
Population growth per annum: 2.3%
Life expectancy at birth: males 51 years, females 54 years
Literacy: 73%
Capital with population: Hanoi 2,570,000
Other important cities with population:
Ho Chi Minh 3,500,000, Hai Phong 1,300,000
Language: Vietnamese, French, English
Religion: Buddhist
Currency: Dong = 10 hao = 10 xu

The proud and martial Vietnamese of the Red River basin have been called the Prussians of Indo-China. With military aid from the U.S.S.R and captured U.S. arms they have now become the strongest military power of South East Asia. Independent JUL 20, 1954.

㉜ TAIWAN
(Republic of China)

Area: 36,174 km²
Population: 18,800,000
Population growth per annum: 1.8%
Life expectancy at birth: males 70 years, females 75 years
Literacy: 89%
Capital with population: Taipei 2,400,000
Other important cities with population:
Kaohsiung 1,260,000
Language: Chinese
Religion: Confucianist, Buddist, Taoist
Currency: New Taiwan dollar = 100 cents

The Chinese governments in Peking and Taipei do agree in one important respect: There is only one China, and Taiwan is no more than a Chinese province. The main difference is that the authority of the rulers in Taipei does not extend to any part of ancient, mainland China proper.

㉝ MALDIVES
Divehi Jumhuriya
(Republic of Maldives)

Area: 298 km²
Population: 168,000
Population growth per annum: 2.9%
Life expectancy at birth: not available
Literacy: 36%
Capital with population: Malé 40,000
Other important cities with population: none
Languages: Divehi
Religion: Moslem (Sunni Moslems)
Currency: Rufiyaa = 100 laaris

In the days when the dhows carried carpets, ivory and slaves over the Indian Ocean, the thousand coral islands of the Maldives lay at the crossroads of the ocean. Now even the names of the atolls, Tiladummati, Fadiffolu, Miladummadulu sound of long lost fame and tales of far away lands. Independent NOV 11, 1968.

㉞ SRI LANKA
(Democratic Socialist
Republic of Sri Lanka)

Area: 65,610 km²
Population: 14,850,000
Population growth per annum: 1.7%
Life expectancy at birth: males 64 years, females 67 years
Literacy: 84%
Capital with population: Colombo 586,000
Other important cities with population:
Dehiwela-Mt. Lavinia 175,000, Moratuwa 136,000
Language: Sinhala, Tamil
Religion: Buddhist (70%), Hindu (17%), Christian, Moslem
Currency: Sri Lanka rupee = 100 cents

Ceylon is even today a land of legends. On the top of Adam's Peak there is a 1.5 m. (5 ft.) long foot print, claimed to be left in the rock by Adam (or by Buddha, or Sheva, or St. Thomas according to preference). Independent 1947.

㉟ CAMBODIA
(Cambodian People's Republic)

Area: 181,035 km²
Population: 6,680,000
Population growth per annum: 2.9%
Life expectancy at birth: males 44 years, females 47 years
Literacy: 48%
Capital with population: Phnom Penh 500,000
Other important cities with population:
Battambang 50,000
Language: Khmer
Religion: Buddhist
Currency: Riel = 100 sen

Clashing radical ideologies have once more made life only worse for everyone. Pleasant Kampuchea now lies in ruins like mighty remains from its glorious past. Famous Angkor, for over 500 years the capital of all Indochina, has so far been spared further destruction. Independent OCT 9, 1970.

㊱ PHILIPPINES
República de Filipinas ·
Republika ng Pilipinas
(Republic of the Philippines)

Area: 300,000 km²
Population: 53,350,000
Population growth per annum: 2.7%
Life expectancy at birth: males 59 years, females 62 years
Literacy: 88%
Capital with population: Manila 1,600,000
Other important cities with population:
Quezon City 1,200,000, Davao 620,000, Cebu 500,000
Language: Pilipino, English, Spanish
Religion: Roman Catholic (80%), Islam (7%)
Currency: Philippine pesó = 100 centavos

East and west meet in this island nation, east of the Asian mainland, yet west of the Pacific. The people of this fomer colony of Spain (1521-1899) and the United States (1899-1942) are of Malayo-Polynesian stock but speak Spanish, English and Pilipino. Most are Roman Catholics but some are Moslems. Independent JUL 4, 1946.

㊲ MALAYSIA

Area: 329,749 km²
Population: 15,070,000
Population growth per annum: 2.5%
Life expectancy at birth: males 62 years, females 65 years
Literacy: 75%
Capital with population: Kuala Lumpur 450,000
Other important cities with population:
George Town 300,000, Ipoh 250,000
Language: Bahasa Malaysia, Chinese
Religion: Moslem 50%, Buddhist (26%), Hindu (9%)
Currency: Ringgit = 100 sen

In this land reigning rajahs (and sultans) each in turn serve five years as 'Supreme Head of State'. This unusual system of royal rotation has brought unity and stability to the geographically divided nation. In Sarawak the world's largest cave (700×300 m.) has been found. Independent SEP 16, 1963.

㊳ SINGAPORE
(Republic of Singapore)

Area: 618 km²
Population: 2,530,000
Population growth per annum: 1.2%
Life expectancy at birth: males 69 years, females 73 years
Literacy: 84%
Capital with population: Singapore 2,350,000
Other important cities with population: none
Language: Chinese, Malay, Tamil, English
Religion: Buddhist, Taoist, Moslem, Hindu, Christian
Currency: Singapore-dollar = 100 cents

A modern City state, living off free entrepot trade and local manufacturing industries requiring skilled labour, Singapore survives without hinterland. Independent AUG 9, 1965.

AUSTRALIA

Area: 8,945,000 km²
Population: 23,446,000
Density of population per km²: 2,6

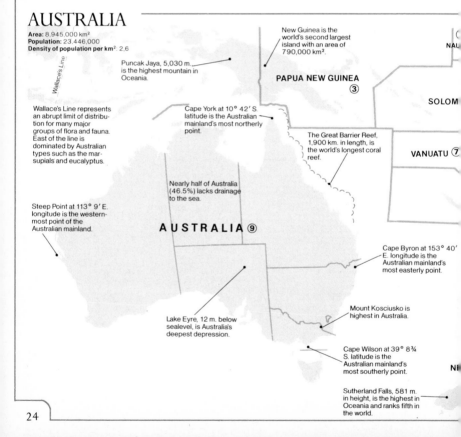

Wallace's Line

New Guinea is the world's second largest island with an area of 790,000 km².

NAU

Puncak Jaya, 5,030 m, is the highest mountain in Oceania.

PAPUA NEW GUINEA ③

SOLOM

Wallace's Line represents an abrupt limit of distribution for many major groups of flora and fauna. East of the line is dominated by Australian types such as the marsupials and eucalyptus.

Cape York at 10° 42′ S. latitude is the Australian mainland's most northerly point.

The Great Barrier Reef, 1,900 km. in length, is the world's longest coral reef.

VANUATU ⑦

Nearly half of Australia (46.5%) lacks drainage to the sea.

Steep Point at 113° 9′ E. longitude is the westernmost point of the Australian mainland.

AUSTRALIA ⑨

Cape Byron at 153° 40′ E. longitude is the Australian mainland's most easterly point.

Mount Kosciusko is highest in Australia.

Lake Eyre, 12 m. below sealevel, is Australia's deepest depression.

Cape Wilson at 39° 8¾ S. latitude is the Australian mainland's most southerly point.

NI

Sutherland Falls, 581 m. in height, is the highest in Oceania and ranks fifth in the world.

㊴ BRUNEI

Area: 5,765 km²
Population: 213,000
Population growth per annum: not available
Life expectancy at birth: not available
Literacy: not available
Capital with population: Bandar Seri Begawan 51,000
Other important cities with population: none
Language: Malay, English
Religion: Moslem (64%), Buddhist, Christian
Currency: Brunei dollar = 100 cents

A land flowing with oil — where the citizens can use their own money to buy "milk and honey" — as they do not have to pay any income taxes! No wonder the Sultan of Brunei can continue to rule — with broad popular support. Independent DEC 31, 1983.

㊵ INDONESIA
Republik Indonesia
(Republic of Indonesia)

Area: 1,919,400 km²
Population: 158,000,000
Population growth per annum: 1.7%
Life expectancy at birth: males 46 years, females 49 years
Literacy: 64%
Capital with population: Jakarta 6,500,000
Other important cities with population:
  Surabaya 2,000,000   Bandung 1,500,000,
  Medan 1,400,000
Language: Bahasa Indonesia
Religion: Moslem (92%)
Currency: Rupiah = 100 sen

Panta rei (all flows) ought to be the motto of this nation of over 13,000 islands. No other state has so many active volcanoes. On Java alone there are 27. Here the island volcano of Krakatoa, 1,800 m. (6,000 ft.) high, disintegrated in 1883 in the most catastrophic eruption in history. Independent AUG 17, 1945.

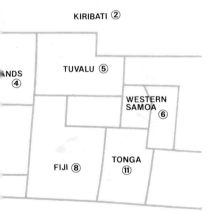

KIRIBATI ②

TUVALU ⑤

⑨ AUSTRALIA

⑧ FIJI

② KIRIBATI

① NAURU

⑩ NEW ZEALAND

③ PAPUA NEW GUINEA

④ SOLOMON ISLANDS

⑪ TONGA

⑤ TUVALU

⑦ VANUATU

⑥ WESTERN SAMOA

The area around Lake Taupo is a unique landscape of volcanic features such as bubbling mud cauldrons, hot springs, solfataras and fumaroles. The geyser Waimangu used to be the world's greatest, the column of water could reach as high as 450 m.

① NAURU
(Republic of Nauru)

Area: 21,3 km²
Population: 8,400
Population growth per annum: 1.5%
Life expectancy at birth: not available
Literacy: 99%
Capital with population: Yaren
Other important cities with population: none
Language: Nauruan, English
Religion: Protestant (60%), Roman Catholic (30%)
Currency: Australian dollar = 100 cents

It is easy to drive around all of Nauru in a car in less time that it takes for an astronaut to circle the Earth, as the total circumference is only 34 km. (21 miles). Independent JUN 31, 1970.

② KIRIBATI
(Republic of Kiribati)

Area: 886 km²
Population: 60,000
Population growth per annum: not available
Life expectancy at birth: not available
Literacy: not available
Capital with population: Bairiki 20,000
Other important cities with population: none
Language: Kiribati, English
Religion: Protestant (50%), Roman Catholic (50%)
Currency: Australian dollar = 100 cents

No other nation is spread so thinly as Kiribati, with land size — smaller than New York City scattered over an area wider than the contiguous United States! Kiribati always has two days, as it is divided by the dateline. Independent JUL 12, 1979.

③ PAPUA NEW GUINEA

Area: 461,691 km²
Population: 3,260,000
Population growth per annum: 2.7%
Life expectancy at birth: males 51 years, females 50 years
Literacy: 32%
Capital with population: Port Moresby 124,000
Other important cities with population: Lae 62,000
Language: English, numerous, local languages
Religions: Animist, Protestant, Roman Catholic
Currency: Kina = 100 toe

The official "Pidgin English" developed here during the last hundred years is quite a new language, using mainly English words. E.g. "Ars bilong diwai" means "roots" (Diwai is a melanesian word for tree, belong equals of — and ars is just the very bottom of anything. Independent SEP 16, 1975.

④ SOLOMON ISLANDS

Area: 29,785 km²
Population: 258,000
Population growth per annum: 3.0%
Life expectancy at birth: not available
Literacy: not available
Capital with population: Honiara 24,000
Other important cities with population: none
Language: English, numerous local languages
Religion: Protestant (75%), Roman Catholic (19%)
Currency: Solomon Island dollar = 100 cents

The Solomon Islands suffered heavily during World War II during the battles of Guadalcanal and the Coral Sea. Yet some islands still profit from the spoils of war by exporting scrap iron. Independent JUL 7, 1978.

⑤ TUVALU

Area: 24,6 km²
Population: 7,300
Population growth per annum: 1.6%
Life expectancy at birth: males 57 years, females 59 years
Literacy: not available
Capital with population: Funafuti 2,100
Other important cities with population: none
Language: Samoan, English
Religion: Protestant
Currency: Australian dollar = 100 cents

Tuvalu comprises nine low coral atolls (formerly also called Lagoon or Ellice islands) in the very centre of the island world of the South Pacific. In spite of the fact that an atoll can measure 10-20 km. across its land area is almost negligible. Independent OCT 1, 1978.

⑥ WESTERN SAMOA
Samoa i Sisifo
(Independent State of
Western Samoa)

Area: 2,831 km²
Population: 156,000
Population growth per annum: 1.3%
Life expectancy at birtn: 63%
Literacy: 90%
Capital with population: Apia 33,200
Other important cities with population: none
Language: Samoan, English
Religion: Protestant (75%), Roman Catholic (22%)
Currency: Tala = 100 sene

Truly Polynesian Samoa is in many ways an incarnation of the South Sea Islands — complete with beaches and palms and friendly people, but it is at the same time a modern society with TV, colleges, and all the rest. Independent JAN 1, 1962.

⑦ VANUATU
(Republic of Vanuatu)

Area: 14,763 km²
Population: 117,000
Population growth per annum: 2.7%
Life expectancy at birth: not available
Literacy: not available
Capital with population: Vila 14,000
Other important cities with population: none
Language: Bislama, English, French
Religion: Protestant (68%), Roman Catholic (16%)
Currency: Vatu

Two colonial powers, France and Great Britain ruled the former Condominium of the New Hebrides in quaint harmony with strict and sometimes silly division of authority 1906-80. Independent JUL 30, 1980.

⑧ FIJI
(Dominion of Fiji)

Area: 18,376 km²
Population: 670,000
Population growth per annum: 1.8%
Life expectancy at birth: males 70 years, females 73 years
Literacy: 75%
Capital with population: Suva 71,000
Other important cities with population: Lautoka 26,000
Language: English, Fijian, Hindustani
Religion: Christian (49%), Hindu (40%)
Currency: Fijian dollar = 100 cents

Volcanic soil, tropical sunshine and gentle trade winds bringing regular rainfall favour sugar cane cultivation. Sugar has become the major product of Fiji. Independent OCT 10, 1970.

⑨ AUSTRALIA
(Commonwealth of Australia)

Area: 7,686,848 km²
Population: 15,450,000
Population growth per annum: 1.2%
Life expectancy at birth: males 70 years, females 76 years
Literacy: 99%
Capital with population: Canberra 256,000
Other important cities with population: Sydney 3,281,000, Melbourne 2,804,000, Brisbane 1,090,000
Language: English, aboriginal languages
Religion: Christian Protestant (61%), Catholic (27%)
Currency: Australian dollar = 100 cents

The only land that is quite different, Australia comprises an entire continent with a quite different fauna and flora — eucalyptus trees and kangaroos, egg-laying mammals and koalas, the living teddy bears. The 1,900 km. long Great Barrier Reef is the world's longest coral reef. Independent JAN 1, 1901.

⑩ NEW ZEALAND

Area: 268,704 km²
Population: 3,200,000
Population growth per annum: 1.1%
Life expectancy at birth: males 70 years, females 76 years
Literacy: 99%
Capital with population: Wellington 342,000
Other important cities with population: Auckland 864,000, Christchurch 322,000
Language: English, Maori
Religion: Protestant
Currency: New Zealand dollar = 100 cents

Far from being the opposite of England, green and civilized New Zealand is at the Antipodes seen from Britain — that is exactly at the other side of the Earth. New Zealand England is rich in beautiful scenery. Independent 1931.

⑪ TONGA
(Kingdom of Tonga)

Area: 748 km²
Population: 99,000
Population growth per annum: not available
Life expectancy at birth: not available
Literacy: not available
Capital with population: Niku'alofa 20,000
Other important cities with population: none
Language: English
Religion: Protestant (85%), Roman Catholic (15%)
Currency: Pa'anga = 100 seniti

The "Friendly Islands", Captain Cook's name for Tonga, are not easy to reach due to lack of good harbours. The island of Niuafo'ou has become known among philatelists as "Tin Can Island" because of the method used to collect and deliver mail. Independent JUN 4, 1970.

AFRICA

Area: 30,293,000 km²
Population: 431,209,000
Density of population per km²: 14

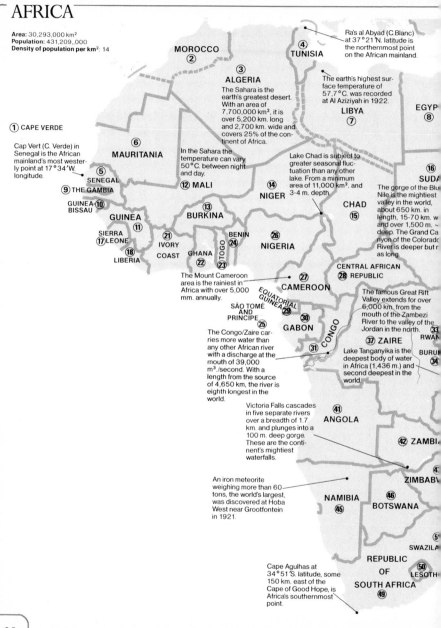

Ra's al Abyad (C.Blanc) at 37°21'N. latitude is the northernmost point on the African mainland.

The earth's highest surface temperature of 57,7°C. was recorded at Al Aziziyah in 1922.

① CAPE VERDE

Cap Vert (C. Verde) in Senegal is the African mainland's most westerly point at 17°34'W. longitude.

The Sahara is the earth's greatest desert. With an area of 7,700,000 km², it is over 5,200 km. long and 2,700 km. wide and covers 25% of the continent of Africa.

In the Sahara the temperature can vary 50°C. between night and day.

Lake Chad is subject to greater seasonal fluctuation than any other lake. From a minimum area of 11,000 km². and 3-4 m. depth.

The gorge of the Blu Nile is the mightiest valley in the world, about 650 km. in length, 15-70 km. w and over 1,500 m. ~ deep. The Grand Ca nyon of the Colorado River is deeper but n as long.

The Mount Cameroon area is the rainiest in Africa with over 5,000 mm. annually.

The famous Great Rift Valley extends for over 6,000 km. from the mouth of the Zambezi River to the valley of the Jordan in the north.

Lake Tanganyika is the deepest body of water in Africa (1,436 m.) and second deepest in the world.

The Congo/Zaire carries more water than any other African river with a discharge at the mouth of 39,000 m³./second. With a length from the source of 4,650 km, the river is eighth longest in the world.

Victoria Falls cascades in five separate rivers over a breadth of 1.7 km. and plunges into a 100 m. deep gorge. These are the continent's mightiest waterfalls.

An iron meteorite weighing more than 60 tons, the world's largest, was discovered at Hoba West near Grootfontein in 1921.

Cape Agulhas at 34°51'S. latitude, some 150 km. east of the Cape of Good Hope, is Africa's southernmost point.

Country labels

- ② MOROCCO
- ④ TUNISIA
- ③ ALGERIA
- ⑦ LIBYA
- ⑧ EGYP
- ⑥ MAURITANIA
- ⑤ SENEGAL
- ⑨ THE GAMBIA
- ⑩ GUINEA-BISSAU
- ⑪ GUINEA
- ⑫ MALI
- ⑬ BURKINA
- ⑭ NIGER
- ⑮ CHAD
- ⑯ SUDA
- ⑰ SIERRA LEONE
- ⑱ LIBERIA
- ㉑ IVORY COAST
- ㉒ GHANA
- ㉓ TOGO
- ㉔ BENIN
- ㉖ NIGERIA
- ㉗ CAMEROON
- ㉘ CENTRAL AFRICAN REPUBLIC
- ㉙ EQUATORIAL GUINEA
- ㉕ SÃO TOMÉ AND PRINCIPE
- ㉚ GABON
- ㉛ CONGO
- ㊲ ZAIRE
- ㉝ RWAN
- ㉞ BURU
- ㊶ ANGOLA
- ㊷ ZAMBI
- ZIMBABV
- ㊻ BOTSWANA
- ㊺ NAMIBIA
- SWAZILA
- ㊾ REPUBLIC OF SOUTH AFRICA
- ㊿ LESOTH

The Nile (with Kagera) is the world's longest river (6,690 km.) Some two-thirds of the water in the lower river comes from the Abbysinian Highlands since most of the water from Lake Victoria evaporates in the marshlands of the Sudd.

Lake Assale in the Danakil Desert is Africa's deepest depression, 174 m. below sealevel.

②⓪ DJIBOUTI

⑲ ETHIOPIA
Ranked the world's hottest place Massawa has an average year round temperature of 30.2°C.

Ra's Hafun at 51°25'E. longitude is the most easterly point on the African mainland.

SOMALIA

㊱ SOMALIA

NDA

KENYA
㉟

Kilimanjaro is the highest mountain in Africa and one of the world's highest volcanoes. The mountain rises nearly 5,000 m. above the surrounding savanna.

㊵ SEYCHELLES

e Victoria (62,940 ².) is Africa's largest e and the third gest in the world.
ANZANIA
㊳

㊴ COMOROS

③
ALAWI

AMBIQUE ㊹

㊽ MADAGASCAR

㊼ MAURITIUS

Madagascar (587,000 km².) is Africa's largest island and ranks fourth in the world.

rica's highest waterfall
th a drop of 948 . lies
the Tugela in the
akensberg. It is also
e world's second
ghest falls.

③ ALGERIA
㊶ ANGOLA
㉔ BENIN
㊻ BOTSWANA
⑬ BURKINA
㉞ BURUNDI
㉗ CAMEROON
① CAPE VERDE
㉘ CENTRAL AFRICAN REP.
⑮ CHAD
㊴ COMOROS
㉛ CONGO
⑳ DJIBOUTI
⑧ EGYPT
㉙ EQUATORIAL GUINEA
⑲ ETHIOPIA
㉚ GABON
㉒ GHANA
⑪ GUINEA
⑩ GUINEA-BISSAU
㉑ IVORY COAST
㉟ KENYA
㊿ LESOTHO
⑱ LIBERIA
⑦ LIBYA
㊽ MADAGASCAR
㊸ MALAWI
⑫ MALI
⑥ MAURITANIA
㊼ MAURITIUS
② MOROCCO
㊹ MOZAMBIQUE
㊺ NAMIBIA
⑭ NIGER
㉖ NIGERIA
㊾ REPUBLIC OF SOUTH AFRICA
㉝ RWANDA
㉕ SÃO TOMÉ AND PRINCIPE

⑤ SENEGAL
㊵ SEYCHELLES
⑰ SIERRA LEONE
㊱ SOMALIA
⑯ SUDAN
㊿ SWAZILAND
㊳ TANZANIA
⑨ THE GAMBIA
㉓ TOGO
④ TUNISIA
㉜ UGANDA
㊲ ZAIRE
㊷ ZAMBIA
㊼ ZIMBABWE

29

① CAPE VERDE
República de Cabo Verde
(Republic of Cape Verde)

Area: 4,033 km²
Population: 296,000
Population growth per annum: 1.7%
Life expectancy at birth: males 58 years, females 62 years
Literacy: 37%
Capital with population: Praia 38,000
Other important cities with population: Mindelo 40,000
Language: Portuguese, Crioulo
Religion: Roman Catholic
Currency: Escudo = 100 centavos

Heat and drought are two words that characterize the volcanic islands, named after a cape on the mainland, 580 km. to the east. Salt is produced by evaporation an industry with good natural prospects. Independent JUL 5, 1975.

② MOROCCO
Al-Mamlaka al-Maghrebia
(Kingdom of Morocco)

Area: 458,730 km²
Population: 21,160,000
Population growth per annum: 3.2%
Life expectancy at birth: males 54 years, females 57 years
Literacy: 24%
Capital with population: Rabat 440,000
Other important cities with population: Dar el Beida (Casablanca) 1,400,000, Marrakech 330,000
Language: Arabic, Berber
Religion: Moslem, (Sunni Moslems)
Currency: Dirham = 100 centimes

East and West meet in Morocco. For the "western" world it is a land of the Near East — and for the "eastern", Islamic world it is a land of the Maghreb, The West. The mosques and palaces of cities such as Marrakech and Fez are famous in the west as well as in the east. Independent MAR 28, 1956.

③ ALGERIA
al-Jumhuriya al-Jazairia
ad-Dimuqratiya ash-Shabiya
(Democratic and Popular Republ. of Algeria)

Area: 2,381,740 km²
Population: 21,460,000
Population growth per annum: 3.3%
Life expectancy at birth: males 54 years, females 56 years
Literacy: 46%
Capital with population: Al Jazair (Algiers) 2,500,000
Other important cities with population: Oran 630,000, Constantine 385,000
Language: Arabic
Religion: Islam (Sunni Moslems)
Currency: Algerian dinar = 100 centimes

Four-fifths of the land is desert. The prosperous and fertile coastal area is just a thin gilt edge along the northern rim of the majestic Sahara. Covering 7.7 million km². (5,200 by 2,700 km.), the Sahara is the world's greatest desert, so that the barren wastes of Algeria comprise only 25% of the Sahara! Independent JUL 3, 1962.

④ TUNISIA
Al-Djoumhouria Attunisia
(Republic of Tunisia)

Area: 164,150 km²
Population: 6,970,000
Population growth per annum: 2.5%
Life expectancy at birth: males 57 years, females 58 years
Literacy: 62%
Capital with population: Tunis 557,000
Other important cities with population: Sfax 232,000, Sousse 85,000
Language: Arabic
Religion: Moslem
Currency: Tunisian dinar = 100 millimes

A nation with many ties. Ties of history and culture link it forever to all its Mediterranean neighbours, and very strongly to France. Ties of language and blood bind it to the Arabic West, Maghreb. This is also the land of Carthage, that fought Rome for the hegemony of "the world". Independent MAR 20, 1956.

⑤ SENEGAL
République du Sénégal
(Republic of Senegal)

Area: 196,192 km²
Population: 6,270,000
Population growth per annum: 2.6%
Life expectancy at birth: males 41 years, females 44 years
Literacy: 10%
Capital with population: Dakar 800,000
Other important cities with population: Thies 130,000 Kaolack 116,000
Language: French, Tribal languages
Religion: Moslem (80%), Christian (10%), Animist
Currency: CFA-franc = 100 centimes

The Gateway to West Africa. The leading metropolis of the area, Dakar, is favoured by a magnificent natural harbour. The location near Cap Vert, the most westerly point of the mainland made Dakar the natural staging post for transatlantic flights to South America until the 1960's. Independent AUG 20, 1960.

⑥ MAURITANIA
Republique Islamique de Mauritanie
(Islamic Republic of Mauritania)

Area: 1,030,700 km²
Population: 1,830,000
Population growth per annum: 2.8%
Life expectancy at birth: males 41 years, females 44 years
Literacy: 17%
Capital with population: Nouakchott 135,000
Other important cities with population: none
Language: French, Arabic
Religion: Moslem
Currency: Ouguiya = 5 khoum

For the Arabs and the Islamic World, Mauretania is the Far West, the Land of the Sunset. Only a fraction of the vast country is habitable, and the lack of water is a severe handicap to any development. Independent NOV 28, 1960.

⑦ LIBYA

Al-Jamahiriya Al-Arabiya-Al Libya
Al-Shabiya Al-Ishtrakiya
(Socialist People's Libyan Arab jamahiriya)

Area: 1,759,540 km²
Population: 3,500,000
Population growth per annum: 4.1%
Life expectancy at birth: males 54 years, females 57 years
Literacy: 40 %
Capital with population: Tripoli (Tarabulus) 860,000
Other important cities with population: Beghasi 300,000
Language: Arabic
Religion: Moslem
Currency: Libyan dinar = 1000 dirham

*Elusive Libya retains in our times some of the enigmatic
features of Africa. The central volcanic area, the Black Hills
that are clearly visible on space images of Africa, were recently mapped with the aid of satellite photos.*

⑧ EGYPT

Jumhuriyat Misr al-Arabiya
(Arab Republic of Egypt)

Area: 1,001,449 km²
Population: 46,000,000
Population growth per annum: 2.6%
Life expectancy at birth: males 54 years, females 56 years
Literacy: 40%
Capital with population: Al Qahirah (Cairo)9,000,000
Other important cities with population: Al Iskandariyah
(Alexandria) 3,000,000, Al Jizah (Giza) 2,000,000
Language: Arabic
Religion: Islam (Sunni Moslems 90%)
Currency: Egyptian pound = 100 piastres

*The whole of inhabitable Egypt is nothing but an oasis — total-
ly dependent on the water of the Nile. In general the width of
the cultivated and settled land is only 3-15 km. Of the seven
wonders of the ancient world, Egypt had two, and even if the
Pharos has been destroyed, the Pyramids still stand. Independent FEB 28. 1922.*

⑨ THE GAMBIA

(Republic of The Gambia)

Area: 11,295 km²
Population: 700,000
Population growth per annum: 2.8%
Life expectancy at birth: males 39 years, females 43 years
Literacy: 12 %
Capital with population: Banjul 45,000
Other important cities with population: none
Language: English, Mandinka, Wolof
Religion: Moslem (85%), Christian, Animist
Currency: Dalasi = 100 bututs

*The land that is a river. This former British colonial enclave in-
side Senegal is now joined with Senegal in the Confederation
of Senegambia. Here Alex Haley found his roots, as described
in his bestseller. Independent FEB 18, 1965.*

⑩ GUINEA-BISSAU

(Republic of Guinea-Bissau)

Area: 36,125 km²
Population: 830,000
Population growth per annum: 1.7%
Life expectancy at birth: males 39 years, females 43 years
Literacy: 9%
Capital with population: Bissau 110,000
Other important cities with population: none
Language: Portuguese, Criolo
Religion: Tribal (50%), Moslem (38%), Christian (5%)
Currency: Guinea-Bissau peso = 100 centavos

*A new name heralds a new era. For more than 500 years this
land was known as Portuguese Guinea. No other land has
been a colony for so many years. Guinea Bissau has an excep-
tional un-African archipelago coast. Independent SEP 24,
1973.*

⑪ GUINEA

République populaire
et révolutionnaire de Guinée
(Republic of Guinea)

Area: 245,857 km²
Population: 5,410,000
Population growth per annum: 2.5%
Life expectancy at birth: males 42 years, females 45 years
Literacy: 48 %
Capital with population: Conakry
Other important cities with population: Kankan 100,000
Language: French, tribal languages
Religion: Moslems (75%), Tribal
Currency: Syli = 100 cauris

*The name Guinea rings with a chink of gold — since 1663,
when coins were struck in England out of pure 22 carat gold
from Guinea. In Britain prices can still be quoted in guineas.
Guinea still has natural resources that could bring prosperity to
this very poor country. Independent OCT 2, 1958.*

⑫ MALI

République du Mali
(Republic of Mali)

Area: 1,240,142 km²
Population: 7,720,000
Population growth per annum: 2.7%
Life expectancy at birth: males 44 years, females 44 years
Literacy: 10%
Capital with population: Bamako 405,000
Other important cities with population: Ségou 65,000
Language: French, Bambara
Religion: Moslem (65%), Animist (30%), Christian (5%)
Currency: Mali franc = 100 centimes

*Half Sahara and half Sahel, half desert and half savanna land,
Mali has been hard hit by years of drought. Once the kings of
Mali controlled the trade routes of the Sahara and the minarets
of fabled Timbuktu attracted both traders and adventurers to
cross the sand seas. Independent SEP 22, 1960.*

⑬ BURKINA

République de Burkina Faso
(People's Democratic Republic
of Burkina)

Area: 274,122 km²
Population: 6,700,000
Population growth per annum: 2.6%
Life expectancy at birth: males 42 years, females 45 years
Literacy: 7%
Capital with population: Ouagadougou 286,000
Other important cities with population:
Bobu Dioulasso 165,000
Language: French, Sudanic tribal languages
Religion: Animist (50%), Moslem (20%)
Currency: CFA-franc = 100 centimes

*A land at the mercy of the winds. The dreaded dry Harmattan
blowing from Sahara is a harbinger of death — the blessed
Guinea Monsoon from the south an angel of life with its
seasonal rain. The savanna lands here depend on a precarious
balance between precipitation and evaporation. Independent
AUG 5, 1960.*

⑭ NIGER

République du Niger
(Republic of Niger)

Area: 1,267,000 km²
Population: 6,270,000
Population growth per annum: 2.9%
Life expectancy at birth: males 41 years, females 44 years
Literacy: 5%
Capital with population: Niamey 225,000
Other important cities with population: Zinder 60,000,
Language: French, Hausa, Djerma
Religion: Moslem (85%), Animist
Currency: CFA-franc = 100 centimes

*A name that is more of an incantation than a description. This is
a land-locked, dry and infertile part of Sahara, and the mighty
Niger crosses only a narrow corner. The Tuaregs still cross the
desert with salt caravans. Independent AUG 3, 1960.*

⑮ CHAD

République du Tchad
(Republic of Chad)

Area: 1,284,000 km²
Population: 5,120,000
Population growth per annum: 2.0%
Life expectancy at birth: males 39 years, females 41 years
Literacy: 15%
Capital with population: N'djamena 303,000
Other important cities with population: Moundou 66,000
Language: French, Arabic, Sudanese languages
Religion: Animist, Moslem (45%), Christian (5%)
Currency: CFA-franc = 100 centimes

*Land-locked Chad can be called a coastal land, as it is part of
the Sahel, "the coast" of the sand sea of Sahara. It is drained
to the shallow central basin of Lake Chad, the ever changing
lake that varies from 10,000-50,000 km². and from 1 to 4 m.
in average depth. Independent AUG 11, 1960.*

⑯ SUDAN

Jamhuryat es-Sudan Al Democratia'
(The Democratic Republic of Sudan)

Area: 2,505,813 km²
Population: 21,440,000
Population growth per annum: 2.8%
Life expectancy at birth: males 46 years, females 48 years
Literacy: 20%
Capital with population: Al Khartum (Khartoum) 476,000,
(Metropolitanarea 1,350,000)
Other important cities with population: Bur Sudan 207,000
Language: Arabic, various tribal languages
Religion: Moslem (70%) Christian, Animist
Currency: Sudanese pound = 100 piaster

*In Sudan there are two countries in one. There are the Islamic,
Arabic-speaking northern desert lands, and there are the
Christian, Nilotic southern savanna lands. In spite of the name,
most of the world's gum arabic comes from the acacia forests
of Sudan. Independent JAN 1, 1956.*

⑰ SIERRA LEONE

(Republic of Sierra Leone)

Area: 73,326 km²
Population: 3,350,000
Population growth per annum: 2.6%
Life expectancy at birth: males 44 years, females 48 years
Literacy: 15%
Capital with population: Freetown 300,000
Other important cities with population: Makeni 1,000,000,
Kenema 775,000
Language: English, Tribal languages
Religion: Animist, Moslem (30%)
Currency: Leone = 100 cents

*A new homeland for freed slaves. Under British protection
repatriated slaves from Great Britain founded Freetown at one
of the few good natural harbours of West Africa back in 1787.
Later it was used as a settlement for Africans rescued from
slaveships. Sierra Leone became independent in APR 27,
1961.*

⑱ LIBERIA

(Republic of Liberia)

Area: 111,369 km²
Population: 1,900,000
Population growth per annum: 3.5%
Life expectancy at birth: males 52 years, females 54 years
Literacy: 24%
Capital with population: Monrovia 425,000
Other important cities with population: none
Language: English
Religion: Moslem (21%), Christian (35%), Traditional (43%)
Currency: Liberian dollar = 100 cents

*As the name implies, Liberia is a free nation, and has been
since it was established in 1822 for freed slaves from the USA.
In 1847 it became the continent's first independent republic
and remained so during the days of the "Scramble for Africa"
when this was divided into colonies.*

⑲ ETHIOPIA
Hebretesbawit Ityopia
(Socialist Ethiopia)

Area: 1,221,900 km²
Population: 42,020,000
Population growth per annum: 1.8%
Life expectancy at birth: males 38 years, females 41 years
Literacy: 8%
Capital with population: Addis Ababa 1,400,000
Other important cities with population: Asmara 45,000,
Gondar 80,000
Language: Amharic, other Semitic and Hamitic languages,
Arabic, English
Religion: Orthodox Christian (40%), Moslem (40%)
Currency: Ethiopian birr = 100 cents

*The nation that is an archipelago on dry land. For centuries
Ethiopia was a Christian island in a Moslem sea. It is still an
archipelago of densely populated islands of high plateaus,
separated by deep river gorges and hot lowlands — and a
linguistic archipelago of over 70 ethnic groups.*

⑳ DJIBOUTI
Jumhouriyya Djibouti
(Republic of Djibouti)

Area: 23,000 km²
Population: 340,000
Population growth per annum: 2.2%
Life expectancy at birth: 50 years
Literacy: 20%
Capital with population: Djibouti 150,000
Other important cities with population: Tadjourah
Language: French, Arabic
Religion: Islam
Currency: Djibouti franc = 100 centimes

*The nation is a railway terminal — and vice versa. The entrepôt
port would not and could not exist as an independent unity
without the railway to Addis-Ababa. This railway was built in
1915 and has since served as the major link between central
Ethiopia and the world. Independent JUN 27, 1977.*

㉑ IVORY COAST
République de la Côte d'Ivoire
(Republic of Ivory Coast)

Area: 322,464 km²
Population: 8,500,000
Population growth per annum: 3.5%
Life expectancy at birth: males 44 years, females 48 years
Literacy: 24%
Capital with population: Abidjan 1,850,000
Other important cities with population: Bouaké 640,000,
Man-Danané 450,000
Language: French, tribal languages
Religion: Moslem (15%), Christian (12%), Indigenous (63%)
Currency: CFA-franc = 100 centimes

*The Cocoa Coast would be more apt but less poetic name for
this land. Cocoa and coffee long ago replaced ivory and slaves
as the staples of the Ivory Coast. No nation produces more
cocoa. Other agricultural products are pineapples, bananas
and palm oil. Independent AUG 7, 1960.*

㉒ GHANA
(Republic of Ghana)

Area: 238,305 km²
Population: 12,210,000
Population growth per annum: 3.1%
Life expectancy at birth: males 47 years, females 50 years
Literacy: 30%
Capital with population: Accra 750,000
Other important cities with population:
Sekondi-Takoradi 300,000,
Language: English, 50 tribal languages
Religion: Christian (42%), Traditional beliefs, Moslem (12%)
Currency: Cedi = 100 pesewas

*The former Gold Coast is at the same time a historic truth and a
fitting description. One man and his dreams brought first independence and then financial ruin to his once — prosperous
country. Many foreign flags have flown over Gold Coast — Portuguese, Swedish, Danish, Dutch and British. Independent
MAR 6, 1957.*

㉓ TOGO
République Togolaise
(Republic of Togo)

Area: 56,785 km²
Population: 2,890,000
Population growth per annum: 2.7%
Life expectancy at birth: males 44 years, females 48 years
Literacy: 10%
Capital with population: Lomé 283,000
Other important cities with population: none
Language: French, Tribal languages
Religion: Animist, Christian (25%), Moslem (10%)
Currency: CFA-franc = 100 centimes

*An artificial nation. During the scramble for Africa, the Ger-
mans, like all other colonial powers just grabbed as much land
as they could regardless of tribal, linguistic and other natural
boundaries. Part of their colonial patchwork finally emerged as
free Togo. Independent APR 27, 1960.*

㉔ BENIN
République Populaire du Benin
(Peoples Republic of Benin)

Area: 112,622 km²
Population: 3,830 000
Population growth per annum: 3.0%
Life expectancy at birth: males 44 years, females 48 years
Literacy: 20%
Capital with population: Porto Novo 105,000
Other important cities with population: Cotonou 490,000
Language: French, local dialects
Religion: Roman Catholic, Islam, Animist
Currency: CFA-franc = 100 centimes

*Coastal Benin is a country apart island — studded lagoons that
are neither sea nor land. Here the fishing villages were built on
stilts to escape occasional floods and to give some protection
against slavers. Independent AUG 1, 1960.*

㉕ SÃO TOMÉ AND PRINCIPE

São Tomé e Principe
(Democratic Republic of Sao Tome and Principe)

Area: 964 km²
Population: 102,000
Population growth per annum: 3.4%
Life expectancy at birth: not available
Literacy: 50 %
Capital with population: São Tomé 20,000
Other important cities with population: none
Language: Portuguese
Religion: Roman Catholic
Currency: Dobra = 100 centimos

These tropical islands in the cool Benguela current are favoured by fertile volcanic soil. At the turn of the century they were the world's leading producers of cocoa — but now others produce more. Coconuts and coffee are also grown. Independent JUL 12, 1975.

㉖ NIGERIA

(Federal Republic of Nigeria)

Area: 923,768 km²
Population: 82,390,000
Population growth per annum: 3.2%
Life expectancy at birth: males 46 years, females 49 years
Literacy: 25%
Capital with population: Lagos 1,061,000
Other important cities with population: Ibadan 850,000, Ogbomosho 435,000, Kano 400,000
Language: English, Hausa, Yoruba, Ibo
Religion: Moslem (55%), Christian (25%)
Currency: Naira = 100 kobo

Nigeria is Africa's most populous country in more than one sense. No other can match its over 80 millions and its over 250 linguistic groups (and tribes). It is hard to believe that this prosperous nation once was justly called "The White Man's Grave" (due to the coastal malaria swamps). Independent OCT 1, 1960.

㉗ CAMEROON

Rèpublique du Cameroun
(United Republic of Cameroon)

Area: 475,442 km²
Population: 9,060,000
Population growth per annum: 2.3%
Life expectancy at birth: males 44 years, females 48 years
Literacy: 34%
Capital with population: Yaoundé 314,000
Other important cities with population: Douala 460,000
Language: English, French, Bantu, Sudanic
Religion: Moslem (25%), Roman Catholic (20%), Protestant (15%), Animist
Currency: CFA-franc = 100 centimes

An ethnic kaleidoscope, the country was a German colony, then two separate League of Nations mandates (French and British) before becoming a unitary republic. There are some two hundred different African ethnic groups. The famous Mt. Cameroon, that rises 4,070 m. up from the sea, serves at times as a natural lighthouse. The volcano erupted as recently as 1959. Indep.JAN 1, 1960.

㉘ CENTRAL AFRICAN REPUBLIC

République Centrafricaine

Area: 622,984 km²
Population: 2,520,000
Population growth per annum: 2.7%
Life expectancy at birth: 44 years
Literacy: 20%
Capital with population: Bangui 390,000
Other important cities with population: Berbérati 95,000
Language: French, local dialects
Religion: Animist (57%), Roman Catholic (20%), Protestant (15%)
Currency: CFA-franc = 100 centimes

At this crossroads of Africa the savannas meet the rain forests and the Bantu peoples mingle with the nilo-saharan groups and others. Even the rivers are running in opposite directions: the Ubangi towards Congo, the Shari to Lake Chad. Indep. AUG 13, 1960.

㉙ EQUATORIAL GUINEA

Repùblica de Guinea Ecuatorial
(Republic of Equatorial)

Area: 28,051 km²
Population: 398,000
Population growth per annum: 2.3%
Life expectancy at birth: males 44 years, females 48 years
Literacy: 20%
Capital with population: Malabo 27,000
Other important cities with population: none
Language: Spanish, Fang, English
Religion: Roman Catholic (60%)
Currency: Ekuele = 100 céntimos

As an antithesis, a part of the mainland of Africa belongs to the main island of Equatorial Guinea. On Bioko the lingua franca has become pidgin English and on Pagalu Portuguese patois in spite of the fact that Spanish was the official language! Indep. OCT 12, 1968.

㉚ GABON

Rèpublique Gabonaise
(Gabonese Republic)

Area: 267,667 km²
Population: 1,370,000
Population growth per annum: 1.0%
Life expectancy at birth: males 42 years, females 45 years
Literacy: 65%
Capital with population: Libreville 350,000
Other important cities with population: Port Gentil 78,000
Language: French, Bantu dialects
Religion: Roman Catholic (42%), Animist, Protestant
Currency: CFA-franc = 100 centimes

Like some brand names Gabon has become almost a household word, because of the widespread use of mahogany plywood for furniture and doors. In addition to timber, Gabon produces oil, manganese and uranium. Independent AUG 17, 1960.

㉛ CONGO
République Populaire du Congo
(Peoples Republic of the Congo)

Area: 342,000 km²
Population: 1,740 000
Population growth per annum: 2.6%
Life expectancy at birth: males 44 years, females 48 years
Literacy: 80%
Capital with population: Brazzaville 422,000
Other important cities with population:
Pointe Noire 185,000
Language: French, bantu dialects
Religion: Animist (47%), Roman Catholic (40%),
Protestant (12%)
Currency: CFA-franc = 100 centimes

*Without the Congo River there wouldn't be any Congo. The
sole reason for establishing the French colony north of the
great river was to explore and exploit as much as possible of
the basin (in competition with the Belgians). The name of the
capital still honours the founding explorer de Brazza.
Independent AUG 15, 1960.*

㉜ UGANDA
(Republic of Uganda)

Area: 236,860 km²
Population: 14,000,000
Population growth per annum: 3.0%
Life expectancy at birth: males 51 years, females 54 years
Literacy: 25%
Capital with population: Kampala 340,000
Other important cities with population: none
Language: English, Swahili, Tribal languages
Religion: Roman Catholic (35%), Protestant (25%),
Moslem (10%), Animist
Currency: Uganda shilling = 100 cents

*Once and future Pearl of Africa? Here people has
demonstrated once more that they are their own worst enemy
in their lust for power. The setting of the gem remains: fertile
lands wity an abundance of water, and magnificent scenery:
The fabled Mountains of the Moon, the Ruwenzori, and the
source lakes of the Nile. Independent SEP 9, 1962.*

㉝ RWANDA
Republika y'u Rwanda
(Republic of Rwanda)

Area: 26,338 km²
Population: 5,650,000
Population growth per annum: 3.0%
Life expectancy at birth: males 44 years, females 48 years
Literacy: 37%
Capital with population: Kigali 157,000
Other important cities with population: none
Language: French, Kinyarwandu, Swahili
Religion: Animist, Roman Catholic (40%)
Currency: Rwanda franc = 100 centimes

*This tiny nation contains some spectacular features: some of
the true sources of the Nile, some of the last mountain gorillas
and some active volcanoes in the Virunga Mountains. Independent JUL 7, 1962.*

㉞ BURUNDI
(Republic of Burundi)

Area: 27,834 km²
Population: 4,560 000
Population growth per annum: 2.2%
Life expectancy at birth: males 39 years, females 43 years
Literacy: 25%
Capital with population: Bujumbura 160,000
Other important cities with population: none
Language: French, Kirundi
Religion: Roman Catholic 78%
Currency: Burundi franc = 100 centimes

*A free colony. The hamitic Tutsi established colonial rule over
the Hutu — the Bantu majority of the people as early as the
17th century. The Europeans came over two hundred years
later and left after seventy years. The Tutsi still rule Burundi.
Independent JUL 1, 1962.*

㉟ KENYA
Jamhuri ya Kenya
(Republic of Kenya)

Area: 582,646 km²
Population: 19,500,000
Population growth per annum: 4.0%
Life expectancy at birth: males 51 years, females 56 years
Literacy: 40 %
Capital with population: Nairobi 1,200,000
Other important cities with population: Mombasa 340,000,
Kisumu 155,000
Language: Swahili, English
Religion: Protestant (37%), Roman Catholic (22%),
Moslem (5%), Others
Currency: Kenya Shilling = 100 cents

*If there is a Safari Land in the world, it must be Kenya. The word
safari (from the Arabic word for travel) rings with adventure.
Here the adventurer's dreams may still be realized. In parks
such as famous Amboseli close-ups of lions can be taken
against the background of snow-capped Kilimanjaro.
Independent DEC 12, 1963.*

㊱ SOMALIA
Jamhuryadda Dimugradiga Somaliya
(Somali Democratic Republic)

Area: 637,657 km²
Population: 3,860,000
Population growth per annum: 7.9%
Life expectancy at birth: males 41 years, females 45 years
Literacy: 5%
Capital with population: Muqdisho 600,000
Other important cities with population: Hargeysa 150,000
Language: Somali
Religion: Moslem
Currency: Somali shilling = 100 centesimi

*The land of frankincense and myrrh — today as in the days of
ancient Egypt. Incense resins and carvings of aromatic
resinous wood are still an important product of this droughtrid-
den land of semideserts and dry savannas. Some of its proud
camel herders now farm irrigated lands. Independent JUL 1,
1960.*

㊲ ZAIRE
République du Zaïre
(Republic of Zaire)

Area: 2,344,885 km²
Population: 31,940,000
Population growth per annum: 2.8%
Life expectancy at birth: males 44 years, females 48 years
Literacy: males 40%, females 15%
Capital with population: Kinshasa 2,450,000
Other important cities with population: Kananga 705,000,
Lubumbashi 455,000
Language: French, Bantu-an Sudan dialects
Religion: Roman Catholic 48%, Animist, Protestant (12%)
Currency: Zaire = 100 makuta

*The heart of Africa. Within Zaire (former Belgian Congo) can
be found sophisticated Kinshasa and rain forests with pygmy
tribes, uranium and diamond mines as well as leaking river
steamers, steaming rain forests but also prosperous farmland
— and some 200 different ethnic groups.
Independent JUN 30, 1960.*

㊳ TANZANIA
(United Republic of Tanzania)

Area: 945,050 km²
Population: 19,730,000
Population growth per annum: 2.9%
Life expectancy at birth: 52 years
Literacy: 66%
Capital with population: Dar es Salaam 757,000
Other important cities with population:
Zanzibar (Town) 111,000, Mwanza 111,000
Language: Swahili, English, local dialects
Religion: Animist, Christian (30%), Moslem (30%)
Currency: Tanzanian shilling = 100 cents

*Arid Tanzania is full of natural wonders: The snow-capped,
perfect volcanic cone on Mt Kilimanjaro, highest in Africa; Lake
Victoria, third largest in the World; Lake Tanganyika, second
deepest; the Serengeti Plains with the last prim of eval herds
wild animals; the serene Ngorongoro Crater.*

㊴ COMOROS
Republique fédérale islamique
des Comores
(Federal Islamic Republic of the Comoros)

Area: 1,862 km²
Population: 370,000
Population growth per annum: 2.2%
Life expectancy at birth: males 47 years, females 45 years
Literacy: 15%
Capital with population: Moroni 25,000
Other important cities with population: none
Language: French, Arabic
Religion: Islam
Currency: CFA-franc = 100 centimes

*Essence is the very essence of the economy of the Comoro
Islands that produce exotic ilang-ilang, citronella and jasmine
essences as well as vanilla extract and cloves. Independent
JUL 6, 1975.*

㊵ SEYCHELLES
(Republic of Seychelles)

Area: 443 km²
Population: 65,000
Population growth per annum: 3.1%
Life expectancy at birth: 66 years
Literacy: 60%
Capital with population: Victoria 14,000
Other important cities with population: none
Language: English, French, Creole
Religion: Roman Catholic (91%), Protestant (8%)
Currency: Seychelles rupee = 100 cents

*The islands of the love fruit — the world's largest, the sea (or
double) coconut. This gigantic fruit, that may weigh 20-25 kg.
(50 pounds), contains 3-4 smooth bilobed nuts with
unavoidable associations to the human body. They grow only
on the Seychelles, and their origin was long a mystery.
Independent JUN 29, 1976.*

㊶ ANGOLA
República Popular de Angola
(People's Republic of Angola)

Area: 1,246,700 km²
Population: 7,770,000
Population growth per annum: 2.5%
Life expectancy at birth: males 40 years, females 43 years
Literacy: 20 %
Capital with population: Luanda 475,000
Other important cities with population: Huambo 62,000
Language: Portuguese, various Bantu languages
Religion: Roman Catholic, Animist
Currency: Kwanza = 100 lwei

*Accessibility shaped the destiny of Angola. In contrast to other
parts of Africa there are good harbours here and neither forbidding deserts nor feverish swamps bar the routes to the in-
terior. Thus Angola became one of the first European colonies
on the African mainland. Independent NOV 11, 1975.*

㊷ ZAMBIA
(Republic of Zambia)

Area: 752,620 km²
Population: 6,240,000
Population growth per annum: 3.2%
Life expectancy at birth: males 47 years, females 50 years
Literacy: 54%
Capital with population: Lusaka 538,000
Other important cities with population: Kitwe 315,000,
Ndola 285,000
Language: English, Bantu dialects
Religion: Christian (60%), Animist
Currency: Kwacha = 100 ngwee

*A colony for less than 40 years! Here colonial rule was not
established until 1924 (as the result of Cecil Rhode's dream of
extending British rule from the Cape to Cairo) but by 1964 the
winds of change brought freedom to Zambia. The Victoria Falls
are Zambia's most famous sight. Independent OCT 24, 1964.*

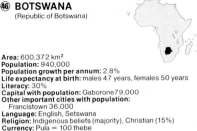

㊸ MALAWI
(Republic of Malawi)

Area: 118,484 km²
Population: 6,100 000
Population growth per annum: 3.2%
Life expectancy at birth: males 44 years, females 48 years
Literacy: 25%
Capital with population: Lilongwe 103,000
Other important cities with population: Blantyre 220,000
Language: English, Chichewa
Religion: Animist, Christian (30%), Moslem (15%)
Currency: Kwacha = 100 tambala

A self-sufficient land of farmers, striving to build a better future. This is expressed also in their names for the units of currency. One kwacha (dawn) is divided into 100 tambalas (cockerels).

㊶ BOTSWANA
(Republic of Botswana)

Area: 600,372 km²
Population: 940,000
Population growth per annum: 2.8%
Life expectancy at birth: males 47 years, females 50 years
Literacy: 30%
Capital with population: Gaborone 79,000
Other important cities with population:
Francistown 36,000
Language: English, Setswana
Religion: Indigenous beliefs (majority), Christian (15%)
Currency: Pula = 100 thebe

Land-locked Botswana lies in the center of the mountainbowl of southern Africa. Here lies the Kalahari desert and here the Cubango River loses itself in a maze of salt swamps and shallow lakes without outlet, such as famed Lake Ngami. Independent SEP 30, 1966.

㊹ MOZAMBIQUE
República Popular de Moçambique
(People's Republic of Mozambique)

Area: 799,380 km²
Population: 13,140,000
Population growth per annum: 2.6%
Life expectancy at birth: males 44 years, females 48 years
Literacy: 14%
Capital with population: Maputo 755,000
Other important cities with population: Nampula 156,000
Beira 230,000
Language: Portuguese, Bantu languages
Religion: Roman Catholic (18%), Moslem (10%), Animist
Currency: Metical = 100 centavos

Geographical facts force "all-black" Mozambique to live in an uneasy partnership with "all-white" South Africa. Mozambique has water-power (Cabora Bassa, 1.4 GW.) and people-power but few minerals. South Africa needs contract workers and electricity in its mines. Independent JUN 15, 1975.

㊼ ZIMBABWE

Area: 390,308 km²
Population: 7,530,000
Population growth per annum: 3.4%
Life expectancy at birth: males 52 years, females 55 years
Literacy: 45 %
Capital with population: Harare 656,000
Other important cities with population: Bulawayo 414,000,
Chitungwiza 175,000
Language: English, Bantu dialects
Religion: Christian, Animist
Currency: Zimbabwe dollar = 100 cents

A nation with well-deserved pride. Zimbabwe is named after the impressive ruin-city that also is the firm foundation of the national spirit. These massive stone walls and towers were built more than a thousand years ago by Bantu kings — ancestors to the people of today's Zimbabwe. Independent APR 18, 1980.

㊺ NAMIBIA
(SOUTH-WEST AFRICA)
Namibia (Suidwes-Afrika)
(U.N. trusteeship, ruled by South Africa)

Area: 823,168 km²
Population: 1,040,000
Population growth per annum: not available
Life expectancy at birth: not available
Literacy: not available
Capital with population: Windhoek 89,000
Other important cities with population: none
Language: Afrikaans, English, German
Religion: Protestant (40%)
Currency: South African rand = 100 cents

Poor but potentially rich, a nation but yet kept in colonial bondage, Namibia awaits full freedom. This former German colony was given as a mandate under the auspices of the League of Nations in 1919. South Africa refuses to set Namibia free.

㊽ MADAGASCAR
Repoblika Demokratika n'i
Madagascar
(Democratic Republic of Madagascar)

Area: 587,041 km²
Population: 9,740,000
Population growth per annum: 2.6%
Life expectancy at birth: males 44 years, females 48 years
Literacy: 53%
Capital with population: Antananarivo 500,000
Other important cities with population: Toamasina 60,000
Language: Merina, French
Religion: Animist, Christian (40%), Moslem (10%)
Currency: Malagasy franc = 100 centimes

The fourth largest island of all — and in most aspects an Asian island. Geologically it is a segment of the same block as India, and the population is of Indo-Melanesian stock. The endemic wildlife comprises rare species, such as the bug-eyed aye-aye and the hedgehog-like tenrec.

㊾ REPUBLIC OF SOUTH AFRICA

Area: 1,225,824 km²
Population: 31,850,000
Population growth per annum: 2.8%
Life expectancy at birth: males 59 years, females 62 years
Literacy: Whites 98%, Asians 85%, Coloureds 75%
Capital with population: Cape Town 1,108,000
Pretoria 528,000
Other important cities with population:
Johannesburg 1,540,000 Durban 506,000
Language: Afrikaans, English
Religion: Protestant, Roman Catholic
Currency: Rand = 100 cents

Humans are their own enemies in rich South Africa. The original natives, the bushmen, fled into the Kalahari desert at the arrival of the Bantu tribes and the original Dutch Boers. The peoples of South Africa are now torn apart by worsening racial conflicts, aggravated by the in famous Apartheid ideology. Independent MAY 31, 1910, 1931.

㊿ LESOTHO

(Kingdom of Lesotho)

Area: 30,355 km²
Population: 1,470,000
Population growth per annum: 2.4%
Life expectancy at birth: males 49 years, females 51 years
Literacy: 55%
Capital with population: Maseru 45,000
Other important cities with population: none
Language: Sesotho, English
Religion: Roman Catholic (40%), Protestant (40%)
Currency: Lote = 100 lisente

An encircled nation, but not a subjugated land. This free black enclave in "white" South Africa is a reminder to its neighbours that all people are created equal. Independent OCT 4, 1966.

NORTH AMERICA

Area: 24,454,000 km²
Population: 346,418,000
Density of population per km²: 14

Cape Prince of Wales at 168° 4′ W. longitude is the North American mainland's most westerly point.

Mount McKinley is North America's highest peak, 6,194 m.

The Malaspina Glacier, covering an area of 3,8 km², is the largest on th North American mainla

The United States bou Alaska from Russia in 1867 for $ 7,200,000

Snake River Canyon (Hell's Canyon) on the boundary between Ida and Oregon is the worl deepest ravine, 2,400 in depth.

The world's loftiest trees — up to 111 m. tall — grow in the redwood forests of California.

Death Valley is the co nent's deepest depre sion, 86 m. below sealevel, and also its h test place (highest rec ed temperature of 56 C.).

⑩ BELIZE
① CANADA
⑭ COSTA RICA
⑤ CUBA
⑧ DOMINICAN REPUBLIC
⑪ EL SALVADOR
⑨ GUATEMALA
⑦ HAITI
⑫ HONDURAS
⑥ JAMAICA
③ MEXICO
⑬ NICARAGUA
⑮ PANAMA
④ THE BAHAMAS
② UNITED STATES

(51) SWAZILAND

(Kingdom of Swaziland)

Area: 17,365 km²
Population: 630,000
Population growth per annum: 2.8%
Life expectancy at birth: males 44 years, females 48 years
Literacy: 65%
Capital with population: Mbabane 23,000
Other important cities with population: none
Language: Swazi, English
Religion: Protestant (60%), Roman Catholic, Animist
Currency: Lilangeni = 100 cents

The proud Swazi people claim a history of five hundred years, but in their country their 'rights' are not older than those of their white neighbours on the other side of the Drakensberg Mountains. British protection kept Swaziland out of the Boer's hands. Independent SEP 6, 1968.

(52) MAURITIUS

Area: 2,045 km²
Population: 990,000
Population growth per annum: 1.6%
Life expectancy at birth: males 61 years, females 67 years
Literacy: 61%
Capital with population: Port-Louis 150,000
Other important cities with population: Beau-Bassin (Rose Hill) 90,000
Language: English, French, Creole
Religion: Hindu (53%), Roman Catholic (25%), Moslem (16%)
Currency: Mauritius rupee = 100 cents

In relation to size no land on Earth has as many different languages — spoken by so many diverse ethnic groups: English (official), Hindi, Creole, Urdu, Tamil, French, Chinese, Arabic and a few African languages. Indep. MAR 12, 1968.

Cape Murchison on the Boothia Peninsula at 71° 59' N. latitude is the northernmost point on the continent's mainland.

Greenland, with an area of 2,131,000 km², is the world's largest island. Only 341,700 km² is ice-free land. Measurement of the icecap has revealed that Greenland is in fact a number of separate islands covered by ice that in places is up to 4,000 m. thick.

North America's lowest temperature, −78°C., was recorded in the valley of the MacKenzie River.

Four of the world's ten largest lakes are found in North America.

Chubb Crater on the Ungava Peninsula is the world's largest meteorite crater, 3.5 km. in diameter and more than 400 m. deep.

Cape Charles at 55° 39' W. longitude is the North American mainland's easternmost point.

C A N A D A
①

Lake Superior, with an area of 82,260 km², is the world's largest fresh water lake and ranks as the world's second largest lake after the Caspian Sea.

Yellowstone is the world's oldest national park, founded 1872. The park is well known for its teeming animal life and for more than a hundred splendid geysers including The Giant, the biggest in the world.

The tidal range in the Bay of Fundy is the largest in the world, 19.6 m. between ebb and flow.

The strongest wind ever to be recorded at the earth's surface, 103 m./sek., was measured in New Hampshire in 1934.

North America's highest waterfall and third highest in the world is Yosemite Falls, 739 m.

② UNITED STATES

The Mississippi-Missouri is North America's longest river and with a length of 6,020 km. is third longest in the world.

Mammoth Cave in Kentucky is the world's longest with 240 km. of passages on five levels, two lakes, three rivers and eight waterfalls below ground.

The world's mightiest flow of water is the Gulf Stream, 30-40 km. wide with a flow of 55 million m³ per second at a rate of 3-5 knots.

the gorge of the Blue s bigger than the d Canyon on the Col- o River which is 350 ong, up to 21 km. and reaches a depth 300 m.

④ THE BAHAMAS

Between June and November the Gulf of Mexico and Caribbean Sea are hit by destructive tropical storms, hurricanes, with torrential rainfall and wind forces up to 100 m./second.

CUBA
⑤

HAITI
⑦

⑧ DOMINICAN REPUBLIC

⑥ JAMAICA

③ MEXICO

BELIZE ⑩

⑨ GUATEMALA

HONDURAS

⑫ ⑬ NICARAGUA

⑪ EL SALVADOR

The Isthmus of Panama is generally considered to be the boundary between North and South America. The southernmost point on the North American mainland is Punta Naranjas at 8° 13' N. latitude.

⑭ COSTA RICA

⑮ PANAMA

39

① CANADA

Area: 9,976,139 km²
Population: 25,130,000
Population growth per annum: 1.5%
Life expectancy at birth: males 70 years, females 77 years
Literacy: 99%
Capital with population: Ottawa 295,000
Other important cities with population:
  Montréal 1,000,000, Toronto 600,000, Calgary 595,000
Language: English, French
Religion: Roman Catholic (46%), Protestant (36%)
Currency: Canadian dollar = 100 cents

A nation that spans a continent, Canada is the world's second largest country. Halifax on the Atlantic is closer to Great Britain than to Vancouver on the Pacific. When the sun rises over Newfoundland it is still midnight in Yukon. The 19.6 m (55 ft) tides in the Bay of Fundy are the world's greatest. Independent JUL 1, 1867.

② UNITED STATES OF AMERICA

Area: 9,363,123 km²
Population: 234,250,000
Population growth per annum: 0.9%
Life expectancy at birth: males 69 years, females 77 years
Literacy: 99%
Capital with population: Washington 638,000
Other important cities with population:
  New York 7,100,000, Chicago 3,000,000,
  Los Angeles 3,000,000
Language: English
Religion: Protestant (33%),Roman Catholic (23%), Judaism (3%)
Currency: US dollar = 100 cents

U.S.A. is a powerful nation. The economic strength and military might of the nation can hardly be overestimated. It is the world's leading producer of most important commodities: oil, gas, coal, steel, paper. It is also found at the top of most lists of world records and extremes — and especially those of engineering feats. Independent JUL 4, 1776.

③ MEXICO
Estados Unidos Mexicanos
(United Mexican States)

Area: 1,972,547 km²
Population: 76,790,000
Population growth per annum: 3.0%
Life expectancy at birth: males 62 years, females 67 years
Literacy: 74 %
Capital with population: Mexico City 13,000,000
Other important cities with population:
  Guadalajara 2,300,000, Monterrey 2,000,000
Language: Spanish
Religion: Roman Catholic
Currency: Mexican peso = 100 centavos

The centre of power in Central America lies as before in Mexico. In the early 19th century, the Spanish viceroy ruled half of Northern America from here, and today the nation is ranked high among the powers of the Third World. The famous pyramids of Teotihuacán manifest the greatness of Mexico. Independent SEP 16, 1810.

④ THE BAHAMAS
(Commonwealth of the Bahamas)

Area: 13,935 km²
Population: 230,000
Population growth per annum: 3.7%
Life expectancy at birth: males 64 years, females 69 years
Literacy: 89 %
Capital with population: Nassau 139,000
Other important cities with population: Freeport 16,000
Language: English
Religion: mainly Protestant
Currency: Bahamian dollar = 100 cents

A thousand coral reefs and not one but 700 coral islands in the sun. For the industrial eastern USA the beaches of the Bahamas are conveniently close — as Mediterranean shores are to northwestern Europe. Blue underwater caves attract scuba divers. Independent JUL 10, 1973.

⑤ CUBA
República de Cuba
(Republic of Cuba)

Area: 121,046 km²
Population: 10,000 000
Population growth per annum: 0.8%
Life expectancy at birth: males 71 years, females 74 years
Literacy: 96%
Capital with population: La Habana (Havana) 1,950,000
Other important cities with population:
  Santiago de Cuba 565,000, Camagüey 480,000
Language: Spanish
Religion: Roman Catholic
Currency: Cuban peso = 100 centavos

The Sugar Island. Sugar and Cuba are now almost synonymous words, but it is a fact that the sugar cane was imported to Cuba from the Old World by the Spaniards. The Cubans themselves are also descendants of immigrants from the Old World: the Spaniards and their negro slaves. Independent DEC 10, 1898.

⑥ JAMAICA

Area: 10,991 km²
Population: 2,310,000
Population growth per annum: 1.4%
Life expectancy at birth: males 68 years, females 73 years
Literacy: 82%
Capital with population: Kingston 650,000
Other important cities with population:
  St. Catherine 220,000, Clarendon 195,000
Language: English
Religion: Protestant (75%), Roman Catholic
Currency: Jamaica dollar = 100 cents

Pirate Island has become Island in the Sun and Land of the Rasta — as Fifteen men on a dead man's chest has been replaced by the inspired music of the Rastafarians. The bottle of rum is still available. Only scuba divers can today visit infamous Port Royal on the bottom of Kingston Bay. Independent AUG 6, 1962.

⑦ HAITI
Rêpublique d'Haiti
(Republic of Haiti)

Area: 27,750 km²
Population: 5,200,000
Population growth per annum: 2.4%
Life expectancy at birth: males 49 years, females 52 years
Literacy: 23%
Capital with population: Port-au-Prince 460,000
Other important cities with population: Cap Haïtien 55,000
Language: French, Creole
Religion: Roman Catholic (66%), Protestant (11%)
Currency: Guorde = 100 centimes

Historically the land of voodo, of mystery and magic. Officially all are Roman catholics, but the undercurrent of ancient African religions is still strong here. Slaves who won their freedom against Spanish, British and French armies created here the world's first Negro republic. Independent JAN 1, 1804.

⑧ DOMINICAN REPUBLIC
Repblica Dominicana

Area: 48,442 km²
Population: 5,980,000
Population growth per annum: 2.6%
Life expectancy at birth: males 58 years, females 62 years
Literacy: 62%
Capital with population: Santo Domingo 1,300,000
Other important cities with population: Santiago (de los Caballeros) 280,000, La Romana 90,000
Language: Spanish
Religion: Roman Catholic
Currency: RD peso = 100 centavos

This is in all but name Columbu's country. Here lie his mortal remains in a lead casket in the cathedral of Santo Domingo. The city that he founded is the oldest European city in the New World, and the island itself carries the name he gave it, Hispaniola — "the Spanish (Island)". Independent FEB 27, 1844.

⑨ GUATEMALA
República de Guatemala
(Republic of Guatemala)

Area: 108,889 km²
Population: 6,580,000
Population growth per annum: 3.0%
Life expectancy at birth: males 57 years, females 59 years
Literacy: 47%
Capital with population: Guatemala 1,300,000
Other important cities with population: Quezaltenango 66,000
Language: Spanish, Indian dialects
Religion: Roman Catholic
Currency: Quetzal = 100 centavos

A land of awe inspiring ruins and memories of its brilliant past during the reign of the Mayas — of once glorious cities like Tikal and Uaxactún. It is also a land of melodious place names like Chichicastenango (a famous market town) and Sololà. Independent 1821, 1839.

⑩ BELIZE

Area: 22,965 km²
Population: 158 000
Population growth per annum: not available
Life expectancy at birth: 60 years
Literacy: 80%
Capital with population: Belmopan 2,900
Other important cities with population: Belize City 40,000
Language: English, Spanish
Religion: Roman Catholic (60%), Protestant
Currency: Belize dollar = 100 cents

Belize is an anomaly — the only British enclave in Latin America. The forests yield valuable timber — mahogany and rosewood — and chicle latex, the original "gum" used for making chewing gum before the development of synthetic gum. Independent SEP 21, 1981.

⑪ EL SALVADOR
República de El Salvador
(Republic of El Salvador)

Area: 21,393 km²
Population: 5,300,000
Population growth per annum: 2.9%
Life expectancy at birth: males 60 years, females 65 years
Literacy: 40%
Capital with population: San Salvador 884,000
Other important cities with population: Santa Ana 210,000, San Miguel 160,000
Language: Spanish
Religion: Roman Catholic
Currency: Colón = 100 centavos

This is truly the land of volcanoes. The average distance between active volcanoes here is less than 30 km. (19 miles)! Politically the nation is disrupted by even more serious eruptions of violence, aggravated by outside interference. Independent 1839, 1841.

⑫ HONDURAS
República de Honduras
(Republic of Honduras)

Area: 112,088 km²
Population: 4,090,000
Population growth per annum: 3.8%
Life expectancy at birth: males 55 years, females 59 years
Literacy: 47%
Capital with population: Tegucigalpa 534,000
Other important cities with population: San Pedro Sula 398,000, El Progreso 105,000
Language: Spanish
Religion: Roman Catholic
Currency: Lempira = 100 centavos

The word banana republic must have been coined with Honduras in mind. Bananas thrive in the fertile volcanic soil and the warm, humid climate of the tropical coastlands. The forest covers impressive Maya ruins, such as Copán. Independent 1821, NOV 5, 1838.

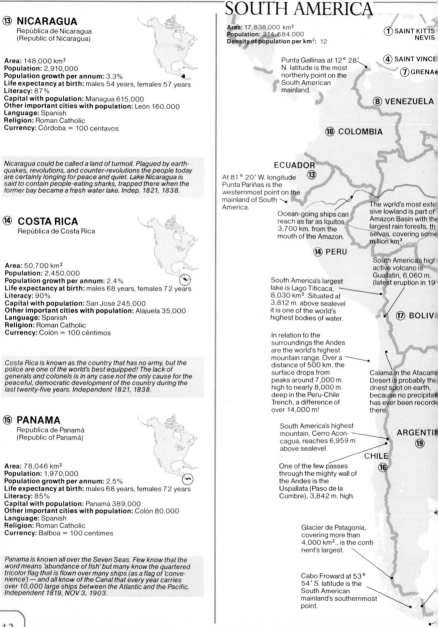

⑬ NICARAGUA
República de Nicaragua
(Republic of Nicaragua)

Area: 148,000 km²
Population: 2,910,000
Population growth per annum: 3.3%
Life expectancy at birth: males 54 years, females 57 years
Literacy: 87%
Capital with population: Managua 615,000
Other important cities with population: León 160,000
Language: Spanish
Religion: Roman Catholic
Currency: Córdoba = 100 centavos

*Nicaragua could be called a land of turmoil. Plagued by earth-
quakes, revolutions, and counter-revolutions the people today
are certainly longing for peace and quiet. Lake Nicaragua is
said to contain people-eating sharks, trapped there when the
former bay became a fresh water lake. Indep. 1821, 1838.*

⑭ COSTA RICA
República de Costa Rica

Area: 50,700 km²
Population: 2,450,000
Population growth per annum: 2.4%
Life expectancy at birth: males 68 years, females 72 years
Literacy: 90%
Capital with population: San José 245,000
Other important cities with population: Alajuela 35,000
Language: Spanish
Religion: Roman Catholic
Currency: Colón = 100 céntimos

*Costa Rica is known as the country that has no army, but the
police are one of the world's best equipped! The lack of
generals and colonels is in any case not the only cause for the
peaceful, democratic development of the country during the
last twenty-five years. Independent 1821, 1838.*

⑮ PANAMA
República de Panamá
(Republic of Panamá)

Area: 78,046 km²
Population: 1,970,000
Population growth per annum: 2.5%
Life expectancy at birth: males 68 years, females 72 years
Literacy: 85%
Capital with population: Panamá 389,000
Other important cities with population: Colón 80,000
Language: Spanish
Religion: Roman Catholic
Currency: Balboa = 100 centimes

*Panama is known all over the Seven Seas. Few know that the
word means 'abundance of fish' but many know the quartered
tricolor flag that is flown over many ships (as a flag of 'conve-
nience') — and all know of the Canal that every year carries
over 10,000 large ships between the Atlantic and the Pacific.
Independent 1819, NOV 3, 1903.*

SOUTH AMERICA

Area: 17,838,000 km²
Population: 214,684,000
Density of population per km²: 12

① SAINT KITTS NEVIS

④ SAINT VINCE

⑦ GRENA

Punta Gallinas at 12° 28′
N. latitude is the most
northerly point on the
South American
mainland.

⑧ VENEZUELA

⑩ COLOMBIA

ECUADOR

At 81° 20′ W. longitude
Punta Pariñas is the
westernmost point on the
mainland of South
America.

⑬

Ocean-going ships can
reach as far as Iquitos,
3,700 km. from the
mouth of the Amazon.

⑭ PERU

The world's most exte
sive lowland is part of
Amazon Basin with the
largest rain forests, th
selvas, covering some
million km³.

South America's high
active volcano is
Guallatiri, 6,060 m.
(latest eruption in 19

South America's largest
lake is Lago Titicaca,
8,030 km². Situated at
3,812 m. above sealevel
it is one of the world's
highest bodies of water.

⑰ BOLIV

In relation to the
surroundings the Andes
are the world's highest
mountain range. Over a
distance of 500 km. the
surface drops from
peaks around 7,000 m.
high to nearly 8,000 m.
deep in the Peru-Chile
Trench, a difference of
over 14,000 m!

Calama in the Atacam
Desert is probably the
driest spot on earth,
because no precipitat
has ever been record
there.

South America's highest
mountain, Cerro Acon-
cagua, reaches 6,959 m.
above sealevel.

ARGENTI
⑲

CHILE
⑯

One of the few passes
through the mighty wall of
the Andes is the
Uspallata (Paso de la
Cumbre), 3,842 m. high.

Glacier de Patagonia,
covering more than
4,000 km²., is the conti-
nent's largest.

Cabo Froward at 53°
54′ S. latitude is the
South American
mainland's southernmost
point.

42

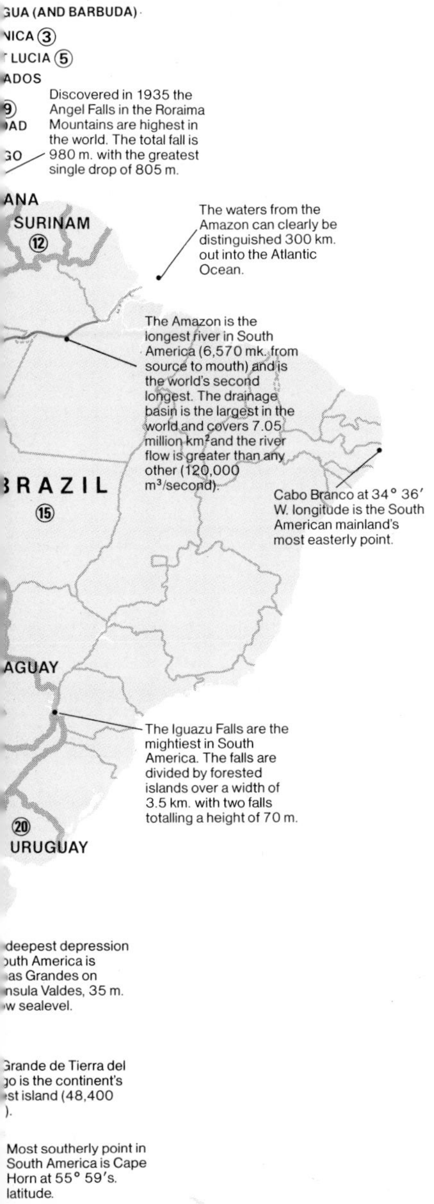

GUA (AND BARBUDA)

NICA ③

LUCIA ⑤

ADOS

⑨
AD

GO

Discovered in 1935 the Angel Falls in the Roraima Mountains are highest in the world. The total fall is 980 m. with the greatest single drop of 805 m.

ANA

SURINAM ⑫

The waters from the Amazon can clearly be distinguished 300 km. out into the Atlantic Ocean.

The Amazon is the longest river in South America (6,570 mk. from source to mouth) and is the world's second longest. The drainage basin is the largest in the world and covers 7.05 million km² and the river flow is greater than any other (120,000 m³/second).

BRAZIL ⑮

Cabo Branco at 34° 36' W. longitude is the South American mainland's most easterly point.

AGUAY

The Iguazu Falls are the mightiest in South America. The falls are divided by forested islands over a width of 3.5 km. with two falls totalling a height of 70 m.

⑳
URUGUAY

deepest depression
uth America is
as Grandes on
nsula Valdes, 35 m.
w sealevel.

Grande de Tierra del
go is the continent's
st island (48,400
).

Most southerly point in South America is Cape Horn at 55° 59's. latitude.

②	ANTIGUA (AND BARBUDA)
⑲	ARGENTINA
⑥	BARBADOS
⑰	BOLIVIA
⑮	BRAZIL
⑯	CHILE
⑩	COLOMBIA
③	DOMINICA
⑬	ECUADOR
⑦	GRENADA
⑪	GUYANA
⑱	PARAGUAY
⑭	PERU
①	SAINT KITTS -NEVIS
⑤	SAINT LUCIA
④	SAINT VINCENT
⑫	SURINAM
⑨	TRINIDAD AND TOBAGO
⑳	URUGUAY
⑧	VENEZUELA

① SAINT KITTS-NEVIS
Federation of Saint Christopher and Nevis

Area: 261 km²
Population: 45,000
Population growth per annum: not available
Life expectancy at birth: not available
Literacy: not available
Capital with population: Basseterre 15,000
Other important cities with population: none
Language: English
Religion: Protestant (76%), Roman Catholic (8%)
Currency: EC-dollar = 100 cents

St. Kitts cultivates tourists and sugar. The pleasant climate in the trade wind tropics favours both of the main industries. Palms and beaches correspond to the common "image" of the Caribbean. Independent SEP 19, 1983.

② ANTIGUA (AND BARBUDA)

Area: 442 km²
Population: 79,000
Population growth per annum: not available
Life expectancy at birth: not available
Literacy: not available
Capital with population: Saint Johns 25,000
Other important cities with population: none
Language: English
Religion: Christian (predominantly Church of England)
Currency: East Caribbean dollar = 100 cents

Antigua and Barbuda are names known to collectors of stamps, to naval strategy planners, some students of colonial history and a few in the sugar trade, and of course, to the proud and in-dependent islanders of the Lesser Antilles. Ind. NOV 1, 1981.

③ DOMINICA
(Commonwealth of Dominica)

Area: 751 km²
Population: 82,000
Population growth per annum: 2.7%
Life expectancy at birth: males 57 years, females 59 years
Literacy: not available
Capital with population: Roseau 20,000
Other important cities with population: none
Language: English, French patois
Religion: Roman Catholic
Currency: French franc = 100 centimes

Dominica can be called the only Caribbean country among all the Caribbean lands. Only here still lives a sizeable remnant of the once dreaded Carib Indians — whose name is perpetuated in the equally dreadful word cannibal. Indep. NOV 3, 1978.

④ SAINT VINCENT (AND THE GRENADINES)

Area: 389 km²
Population: 123,000
Population growth per annum: 5.9%
Life expectancy at birth: males 59 years, females 60 years
Literacy: 95 %
Capital with population: Kingstown 33,000
Other important cities with population: none
Language: English
Religion: Protestant (75%), Roman Catholic (13%)
Currency: EC-dollar = 100 cents

Many different kinds of fruit are grown on the islands — coconuts, mangoes, avocados, guavas just to mention a few, but not the pomegranates used for making grenadine syrup (an ingredient of many cocktails). Most of the 600 volcanic Grenadine Islands belong to St. Vincent. Ind. OCT 27, 1979.

⑤ SAINT LUCIA

Area: 616 km²
Population: 127,000
Population growth per annum: 1.8%
Life expectancy at birth: males 65 years, females 70 years
Literacy: 78%
Capital with population: Castries 45,000
Other important cities with population: none
Language: English, French patois
Religion: Roman Catholic
Currency: EC-dollar = 100 cents

Bananas, cocoa and coconuts are the chief products of St. Lucia instead of sugar as on most other Antillean Islands. A growing number of tourists are discovering the pleasant beaches of St. Lucia. Independent FEB 22, 1979.

⑥ BARBADOS

Area: 431 km²
Population: 250,000
Population growth per annum: 1.4%
Life expectancy at birth: males 68 years, females 73 years
Literacy: 97%
Capital with population: Bridgetown 7,500
Other important cities with population: none
Language: English
Religion: Protestant
Currency: Barbados dollar = 100 cents

Tourists and sugar cane thrive here on the most easterly of the Windward Islands. The gentle trade winds blow with a constant 5-6 m./s. to keep the surf rolling in and the sky clear of clouds. Independent NOV 30, 1966.

⑦ GRENADA
(State of Grenada)

Area: 344 km²
Population: 115,000
Population growth per annum: 1.0%
Life expectancy at birth: 69 years
Literacy: 85%
Capital with population: Saint George's 7,500
Other important cities with population: none
Language: English
Religion: Roman Catholic
Currency: E C dollar = 100 cents

Grenada is one of the "spice islands" of the world. It produces more than one third of the nutmeg on the world market. In the world of the super powers Grenada has also had an importance without relation to its tiny size. Independent FEB 7, 1974.

⑩ COLOMBIA
República de Colombia
(Republic of Colombia)

Area: 1,141,748 km²
Population: 27,410,000
Population growth per annum: 2.1%
Life expectancy at birth: males 60 years, females 65 years
Literacy: 82%
Capital with population: Bogotá 4,900,000
Other important cities with population:
  Medellín 1,800,000, Cali 1,200,000, Barranquilla 900,000
Language: Spanish
Religion: Roman Catholic
Currency: Colombian peso = 100 centavos

Colombia may have been the legendary land of El Dorado — the gold-covered king. Today it could be called the land of green gold — as 90% of all emeralds in the world come from mines in Colombia. However high quality coffee is the country's main export product. Independent DEC 17, 1819.

⑧ VENEZUELA
República de Venezuela
(Republic of Venezuela)

Area: 912,050 km²
Population: 15,260,000
Population growth per annum: 3.5%
Life expectancy at birth: males 64 years, females 69 years
Literacy: 86%
Capital with population: Caracas 2,700,000
Other important cities with population:
  Maracaibo 845,000, Barquismeto 459,000
Language: Spanish
Religion: Roman Catholic
Currency: Bolivar = 100 céntimos

Venice has been called a floating city, and Venezuela — "little Venice" — a land floating on oil. Over 4,000 oil drilling derricks stand now in the shallow waters of the Maracaibo lagoon like the houses on stilts that gave the country its name. In the southeast the Angel Falls, highest in the world, plunge 980 m. down (805 m. uninterrupted). Independent 1821, 1830.

⑪ GUYANA
(Cooperative Republic of Guyana)

Area: 215,000 km²
Population: 830,000
Population growth per annum: 2.2%
Life expectancy at birth: males 67 years, females 72 years
Literacy: 85%
Capital with population: Georgetown 187,000
Other important cities with population: none
Language: English, Hindi, Creole
Religion: Hindu (37%), Protestant (32%),
  Roman Catholic (13%), Islam (9%)
Currency: Guyana dollar = 100 cents

Guyana is an East Indian country in the West Indies, as the major part of the inhabitants are descendants of immigrants from India. Of all the world's waterfalls only nine are higher than the near 500 m. high uninterrupted cascades of the King George VI Falls, north of the Roraima Plateau. Indep. MAY 26, 1966.

⑨ TRINIDAD AND TOBAGO

Area: 5,128 km²
Population: 1,160,000
Population growth per annum: 1.5%
Life expectancy at birth: males 66 years, females 72 years
Literacy: 92%
Capital with population: Port of Spain 56,000
Other important cities with population:
  San Fernando 40,000
Language: English, Spanish
Religion: Roman Catholic (31%), Protestant (26%),
  Hindu (23%), Moslem (6%)
Currency: Trinidad and Tobago dollar = 100 cents

A melting pot where everything is transformed. Cultures traditions, and people from five continents have been mixed and combined under the sun of Trinidad. A different melting pot an "inexhaustible" lake of asphalt, Pitch Lake, is unique in the world. Independent AUG 31, 1962.

⑫ SURINAM

Area: 163,820 km²
Population: 370,000
Population growth per annum: 1.3%
Life expectancy at birth: males 65 years, females 70 years
Literacy: 80%
Capital with population: Paramaribo 68,000
Other important cities with population: none
Language: Dutch
Religion: Hindu (29%), Protestant (20%), Moslem (19%),
  Roman Catholic (18%)
Currency: Suriname guilder or florin = 100 cents

A country for $ 24? In a deal with Britain in the 15th century the Dutch acquired this British colony in exchange for New Amsterdam — later better known as the city of New York — in turn bought for $24. 90% of today's Surinam is covered with dense rainforest. Independent NOV 25, 1975.

⑬ ECUADOR
República del Ecuador
(Republic of Ecuador)

Area: 283,561 km²,
  (disputed area 190,807 km² not included)
Population: 8,810,000
Population growth per annum: 3.0%
Life expectancy at birth: males 58 years, females 62 years
Literacy: 84%
Capital with population: Quito 920,000
Other important cities with population:
  Guaqaquil 1,300,000, Cuenca 270,000
Language: Spanish, Quechuan, Jivaroan
Religion: Predominantly Roman Catholic
Currency: Sucre = 100 centavos

A "heavy" item in Ecuador's export statistics is featherweight balsa timber. The Spanish word balsa denotes both raft and the timber, lighter than cork. The Indians used it for building sailing rafts as early as prehistoric times. The logs for Heyerdahl's famous Kon-Tiki were cut in Ecuador in 1947. Independent MAY 13, 1830.

⑭ PERU
República del Perú
(Republic of Peru)

Area: 1,285,216 km²
Population: 18,300,000
Population growth per annum: 2.7%
Life expectancy at birth: males 56 years, females 59 years
Literacy: 72%
Capital with population: Lima 3,100,000
Other important cities with population: Callao 300,000
Language: Spanish, Quechua, Aymará
Religion: Roman Catholic
Currency: Sol = 100 centavos

The Inca's land of gold and silver was turned into a land of guano and fishmeal. The conquistadores stripped the land of its im-mense treasures of golden artwork. The stone buildings of Machu Picchu's breath-taking eagle's nest-city still remain — hidden and forgotten for five centuries until discovered by Hiram Bingham in 1911. Independent JUL 28, 1821.

⑮ BRAZIL
República Federativa do Brasil
(Federative Republic of Brazil)

Area: 8,511,965 km²
Population: 120,000,000
Population growth per annum: 2.4%
Life expectancy at birth: males 60 years, females 64 years
Literacy: 68%
Capital with population: Brasília 410,000,
  (Federal district 1,200,000)
Other important cities with population:
  São Paulo 7,000,000, Rio de Janeiro 5,100,000
Language: Portuguese
Religion: Roman Catholic (89%), Protestant (7%)
Currency: Cruzeiro = 100 centavos

Only four countries in the world are larger than Brazil, The mighty Amazon carries more water than any other river (120 000 m²/s at the mouth) and is navigable for ocean-going ships up to Iquitos, 3 700 km from the sea. Brasilia, created by presi-dent Kubitscheck and architects Oscar Niemeyer and Lúcio Costa, became capital in 1960. Independent SEP 7, 1822.

⑯ CHILE
República de Chile
(Republic of Chile)

Area: 756,945 km²
Population: 11,490,000
Population growth per annum: 1.7%
Life expectancy at birth: males 62 years, females 69 years
Literacy: 90%
Capital with population: Santiago 3,450,000
Other important cities with population:
  Viña del Mar 300,000, Varpariso 270,000
Language: Spanish
Religion: Predominantly Roman Catholic
Currency: Chilean peso = 100 centavos

The "narrowest" country in the world, Chile, is nearly twenty-five times longer than it is wide (175 by 4 300 km) and stretches from the tropics down to the stormy Cape Horn in the "Furious Fifties". At Calama in the Atacama Desert no rainfall has ever been recorded. Independent SEP 18, 1810.

⑰ BOLIVIA
República de Bolivia
(Republic of Bolivia)

Area: 1,098,580 km²
Population: 5,900,000
Population growth per annum: 2.6%
Life expectancy at birth: males 47 years, females 51 years
Literacy: 75%
Capital with population: La Paz 650,000 and Sucre 65,000
Other important cities with population:
  Santa Cruz 260,000, Cochabamba 200,000
Language: Spanish, Quechua (34%), Aymará (25%)
Religion: Roman Catholic
Currency: Bolivian peso = 100 centavos

Tin mining is the main source of wealth in land-locked Bolivia. Most of the population live on the dry, cold tablelands, higher than many peaks in the European Alps. Lake Titicaca, shared with Peru, is the, worlds highest (3 812 m) navigable body of water. Independent AUG 6, 1825.

⑱ PARAGUAY
República del Paraguay
(Republic of Paraguay)

Area: 406,752 km²
Population: 3,000,000
Population growth per annum: 3.3%
Life expectancy at birth: males 62 years, females 66 years
Literacy: 82%
Capital with population: Asunción 460,000
Other important cities with population: Caaguazu 73,000
Language: Spanish, Guaraní (90%)
Religion: Roman Catholic
Currency: Guaraní = 100 céntimos

Here one man's will is, and has been, law — by unbroken tradi-tion from Jesuit times. The pope was replaced by the King of Spain, he in turn by the founding dictator "El Supremo" and so on. General Alfredo Stroessner seized power in 1954. The Ig-uaçu falls of the Parana cascade 82 m. over a width of four km. between hundreds of forest islands. Independent MAY 14, 1811.

⑲ ARGENTINA
República Argentina
(Argentine Republic)

Area: 2,777,815 km²
Population: 27,950,000
Population growth per annum: 1.3%
Life expectancy at birth: males 66 years, females 73 years
Literacy: 94 %
Capital with population: Buenos Aires 2,900,000,
(Greater Buenos Aires 9,900,000)
Other important cities with population: Còrdoba 970,000,
Rosario 880,000, Mendoza 600,000
Language: Spanish
Religion: Roman Catholic
Currency: Arg. peso = 100 centavos

*The home of the tango and the gaucho, Argentina is a Europe in
miniature. It is situated on southern latitudes, and it, was
populated by settlers from all over Europe. It has the continents
highest peak, Aconcagua, and its lowest spot, Salinas Grandes
on the Peninsula Valdés, 35 m. below sea level. Independent
MAR 25, 1810.*

⑳ URUGUAY
República Oriental del Uruguay
(Oriental Republic of Uruguay)

Area: 186,926 km²
Population: 2,990,000
Population growth per annum: 0.6%
Life expectancy at birth: males 66 years, females 73 years
Literacy: 94%
Capital with population: Montevideo 1,362,000
Other important cities with population: Salto 80,000,
Paysandá 80,000
Language: Spanish
Religion: Roman Catholic
Currency: Nuevo peso (new peso) = 100 centésimos

*A country of rolling grasslands with grazing cattle and cultivated
fields. As in other agricultural lands, more people live in the
capital than in all the other towns put together. Independent
AUG. 25, 1825.*

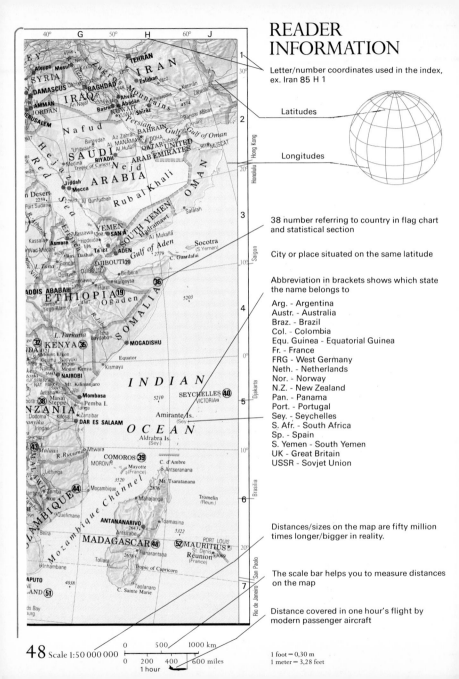

READER INFORMATION

Letter/number coordinates used in the index, ex. Iran 85 H 1

Latitudes

Longitudes

38 number referring to country in flag chart and statistical section

City or place situated on the same latitude

Abbreviation in brackets shows which state the name belongs to

Arg. - Argentina
Austr. - Australia
Braz. - Brazil
Col. - Colombia
Equ. Guinea - Equatorial Guinea
Fr. - France
FRG - West Germany
Neth. - Netherlands
Nor. - Norway
N.Z. - New Zealand
Pan. - Panama
Port. - Portugal
Sey. - Seychelles
S. Afr. - South Africa
Sp. - Spain
S. Yemen - South Yemen
UK - Great Britain
USSR - Sovjet Union

Distances/sizes on the map are fifty million times longer/bigger in reality.

The scale bar helps you to measure distances on the map

Distance covered in one hour's flight by modern passenger aircraft

48 Scale 1:50 000 000

0   500   1000 km

0   200   400   600 miles
1 hour

1 foot = 0,30 m
1 meter = 3,28 feet

Symbols   Scale 1:10 000 000, 1:20 000 000

🚩Bombay More than 5 000 000 inhabitants

🛶Milano 1 000 000-5 000 000 inhabitants

■Zürich 250 000-1 000 000 inhabitants

●Dijon 100 000-250 000 inhabitants

● Dover   25 000-100 000 inhabitants

○ Torquay   Less than 25 000 inhabitants

° Tachiumet   Small sites

WIEN   National capital

Atlanta   State capital

—— Major road

—— Other road

– – – – Road under construction

—— Railway

– – – – Railway under construction

······· Train ferry

▬▬▬▬ National boundary

▬ ▬ ▬ ▬ Disputed national boundary

—— State boundary

- - - - - Disputed state boundary

▬▬▬▬ Undefined boundary in the sea

ᐧ 4807   Height above sea-level in metres

ᐧ3068   Depth in metres

National park

∴ Niniveh   Ruin

=   Pass

KAINJI DAM   Dam

- - - - - -   Wadi

·······   Canal

—⊢—   Waterfalls

Reef

Symbols   Scale 1:30 000 000 1:50 000 000 1:54 000 000 1:60 000 000 1:75 000 000

🛶Shanghai More than 5 000 000 inhabitants

■Barcelona 1 000 000-5 000 000 inhabitants

●Venice 250 000-1 000 000 inhabitants

● Aberdeen   50 000-250 000 inhabitants

○ Beida   Less than 50 000 inhabitants

○ Mawson   Scientific station

CAIRO   National capital

—— Major road

—— Railway

– – – – Railway under construction

▬▬▬▬ National boundary

▬ ▬ ▬ ▬ Disputed national boundary

—— State boundary

- - - - - Disputed state boundary

▬▬▬▬ Undefined boundary in the sea

ᐧ 8848   Height above sea-level in metres

ᐧ11034   Depth in metres

2645   Thickness of ice cap

∴ Thebes   Ruin

Dam

- - - - -   Wadi

·······   Canal

—⊢—   Waterfalls

Reef

Colour Key

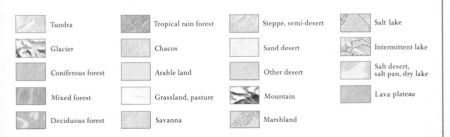

Tundra

Glacier

Coniferous forest

Mixed forest

Deciduous forest

Tropical rain forest

Chacos

Arable land

Grassland, pasture

Savanna

Steppe, semi-desert

Sand desert

Other desert

Mountain

Marshland

Salt lake

Intermittent lake

Salt desert, salt pan, dry lake

Lava plateau

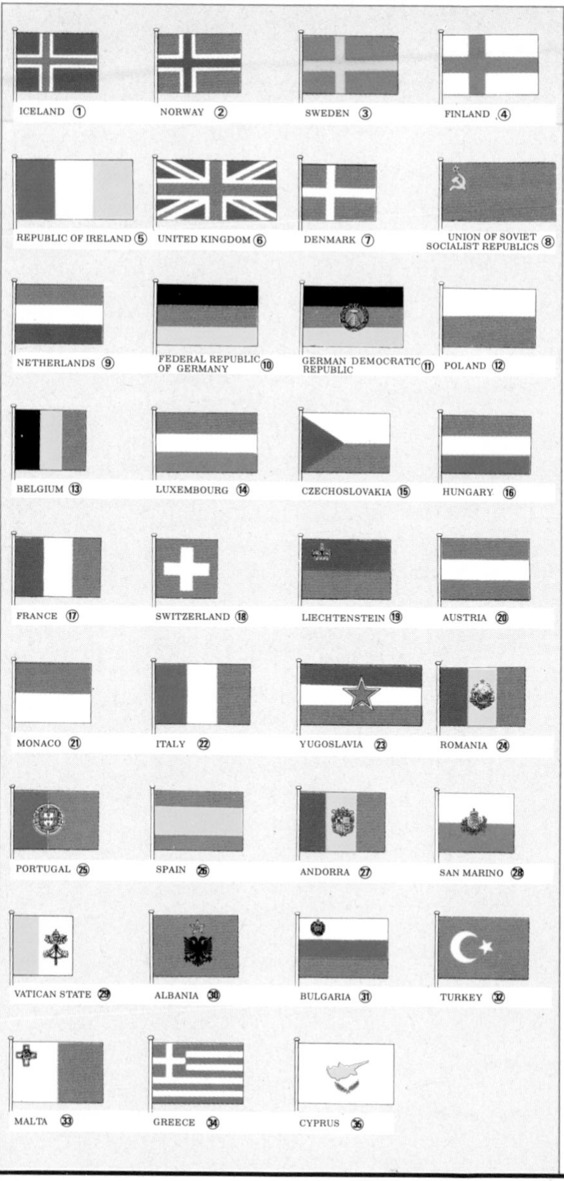
ICELAND ①
NORWAY ②
SWEDEN ③
FINLAND ④
REPUBLIC OF IRELAND ⑤
UNITED KINGDOM ⑥
DENMARK ⑦
UNION OF SOVIET SOCIALIST REPUBLICS ⑧
NETHERLANDS ⑨
FEDERAL REPUBLIC OF GERMANY ⑩
GERMAN DEMOCRATIC REPUBLIC ⑪
POLAND ⑫
BELGIUM ⑬
LUXEMBOURG ⑭
CZECHOSLOVAKIA ⑮
HUNGARY ⑯
FRANCE ⑰
SWITZERLAND ⑱
LIECHTENSTEIN ⑲
AUSTRIA ⑳
MONACO ㉑
ITALY ㉒
YUGOSLAVIA ㉓
ROMANIA ㉔
PORTUGAL ㉕
SPAIN ㉖
ANDORRA ㉗
SAN MARINO ㉘
VATICAN STATE ㉙
ALBANIA ㉚
BULGARIA ㉛
TURKEY ㉜
MALTA ㉝
GREECE ㉞
CYPRUS ㉟

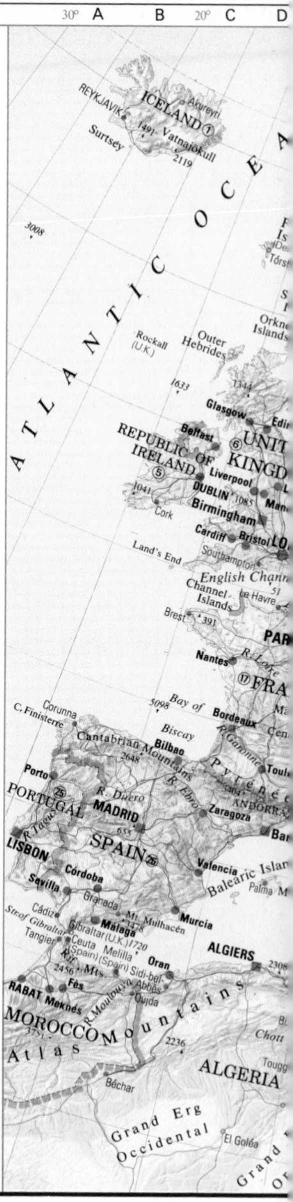
30° A B 20° C D
REYKJAVIK
ICELAND ①
Akureyri
1491 Vatnajökull
2119
Surtsey
ATLANTIC OCEA
3008
Rockall (U.K.)
Outer Hebrides
1633
1344
Glasgow
Belfast
REPUBLIC OF IRELAND ⑤
⑥ UNIT KINGD
Liverpool
DUBLIN
1085
1041
Cork
Birmingham
Cardiff
Bristol
Land's End
Southampton
English Chann
Channel Islands
Le Havre
Brest
391
Nantes
R. Loire
⑰ FRA
5098
Bay of Biscay
Bordeaux
Corunna
C. Finisterre
Cantabrian Mountains
2648
Bilbao
Porto
㉕
PORTUGAL
R. Duero
R. Ebro
Pyrénées
ANDORRA
MADRID
Zaragoza
R. Tagus
655
LISBON
SPAIN ㉖
Córdoba
Valencia
Balearic Islan
Palma
Sevilla
Granada
Mt. Mulhacén
3478
Murcia
Cádiz
Str. of Gibraltar
Gibraltar (U.K.) 1720
Málaga
Tangier
Ceuta (Spain)
Melilla (Spain)
Oran
ALGIERS
Sidi-bel-Abbès
Rif Mts
2456
Fès
Oujda
RABAT
Meknès
R. Moulouya
MOROCCO
3751
Atlas Mountains
2236
ALGERIA
Béchar
Grand Erg Occidental
El Goléa

Scale 1:30 000 000

51

foot = 0,30 m
meter = 3,28 feet

Scale 1:10 000 000

| 0 | 100 | 200 | 300 | 400 | 500 km |

| 0 | 100 | 200 | 300 miles |

1/2 hour

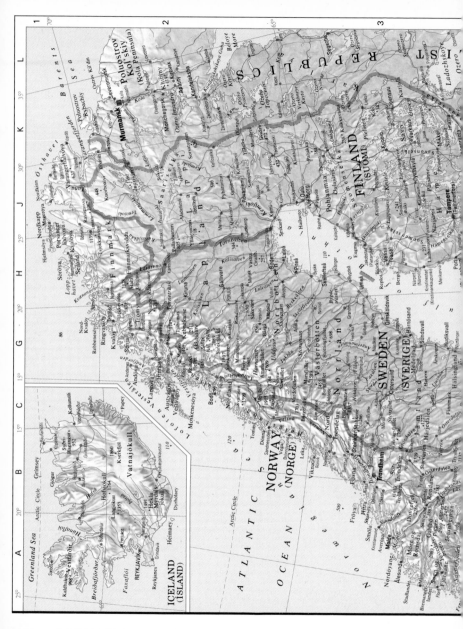

Scale 1:10 000 000

ot = 0,30 m
eter = 3,28 feet

| 0 | 100 | 200 | 300 | 400 | 500 km |

| 0 | 100 | 200 | 300 miles |

1/2 hour

1 foot = 0,30 m
1 meter = 3,28 feet

A 20° B 25° C 30°

Bratislava
Slovakia
Miskolc
BUDAPEST
Debrecen
HUNGARY
(MAGYARORSZÁG)
Szeged
Arad
Zagreb
Hrvatska
(Croatia)
Osijek
Novi Sad
Timişoara
Banat
BEOGRAD
(BELGRADE)
YUGOSLAVIA
Sarajevo
Niš
SOFIYA
(SOFIA)
Plovdiv
Makedonija
Skopje
TIRANA
ALBANIA
(SHQIPËRIA)
Makedhonía
THESSALONÍKI
(Salonica)

Uzhgorod
Ivano-Frankovsk
Chernovtsy
Carpathians
Oradea
Cluj Napoca
Transilvania
Tîrgu Mureş
Sibiu
ROMANIA
Braşov
Craiova
Valachia
BUCUREŞTI
(BUCHAREST)
Ploieşti
Ruse
Stara Planina
Stara Zagora
Burgas
BULGARIA

Belt'sy
Moldaviya
Iaşi
Kishinev
Bendery
Tiraspol'
Nikola
Ode

Galaţi
Brăila
Delta Dunării
(Mouths of the Danube)
Insulă Sacalin
Medgidia
Constanţa
Varna
Dobrudža

Adriatic Sea
Dubrovnik

GREECE
(HELLAS)
Thessalía
Ípiros
Kérkira (Corfu)
ATHINAI
(ATHENS)
Piraiévs
Peloponnisos
(Peloponnese)
Iónioi Nísoi
(Ionian Islands)
Iónion Pélagos
(Ionian Sea)

Istanbul
İzmit
Adapaza
Bursa
Balıkesir
İzmir
Denizli
Antalya
Anad
Kikládhes
(Cyclades)
Ródhos
(Rhodes)
Kárpathos
Kásos

MEDITERRANEAN SEA
Kritikón Pélagos
(Sea of Crete)
Kríti (Crete)
Iráklion

45°
40°
35°
1
2
3
4

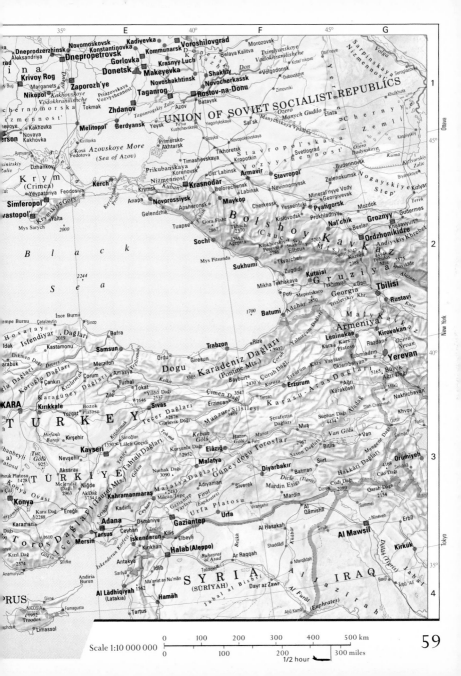

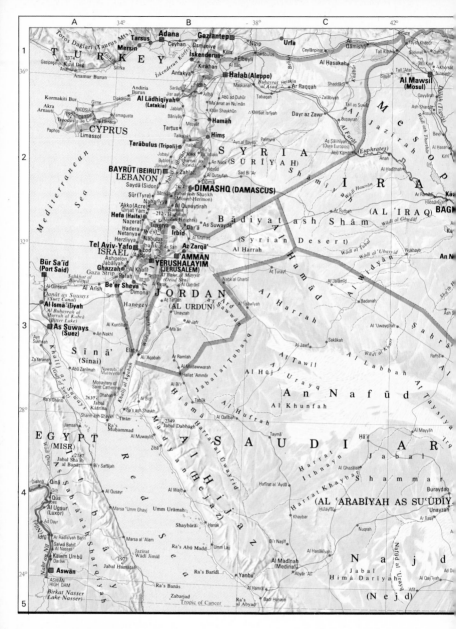

THE MIDDLE EAST

1 foot = 0,30 m
1 meter = 3,28 feet

Scale 1:10 000

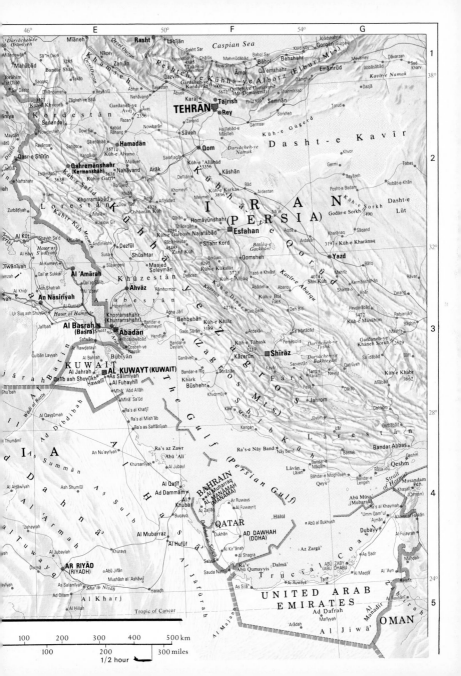

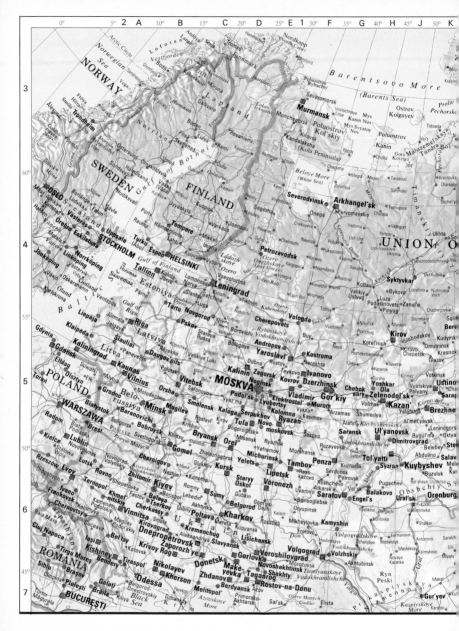

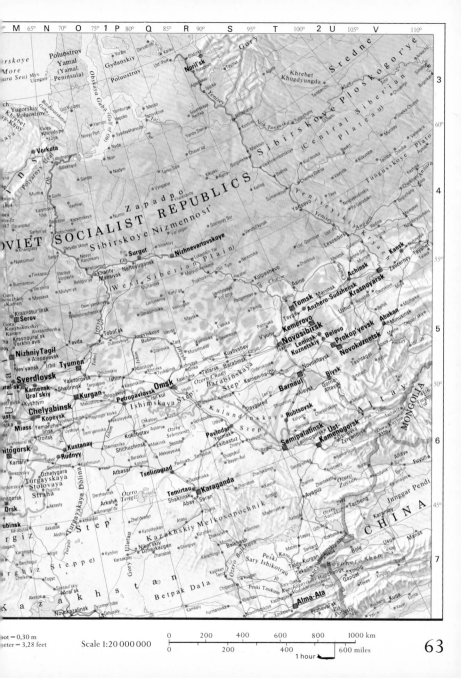

Scale 1:20 000 000

63

UNION OF SOVIET SOCIALIST REPUBLICS ① MONGOLIA ② NORTH KOREA ③ SOUTH KOREA ④

TURKEY ⑤ LEBANON ⑥ SYRIA ⑦ IRAQ ⑧

IRAN ⑨ AFGHANISTAN ⑩ CHINA ⑪ JAPAN ⑫

ISRAEL ⑬ JORDAN ⑭ KUWAIT ⑮ PAKISTAN ⑯

SAUDI ARABIA ⑰ BAHRAIN ⑱ QATAR ⑲ UNITED ARAB EMIRATES ⑳

YEMEN ㉑ SOUTH YEMEN ㉒ OMAN ㉓ INDIA ㉔

NEPAL ㉕ BHUTAN ㉖ BANGLADESH ㉗ BURMA ㉘

THAILAND ㉙ LAOS ㉚ VIETNAM ㉛ TAIWAN ㉜

MALDIVES ㉝ SRI LANKA ㉞ CAMBODIA ㉟ PHILIPPINES ㊱

MALAYSIA ㊲ SINGAPORE ㊳ BRUNEI ㊴ INDONESIA ㊵

64   ASIA

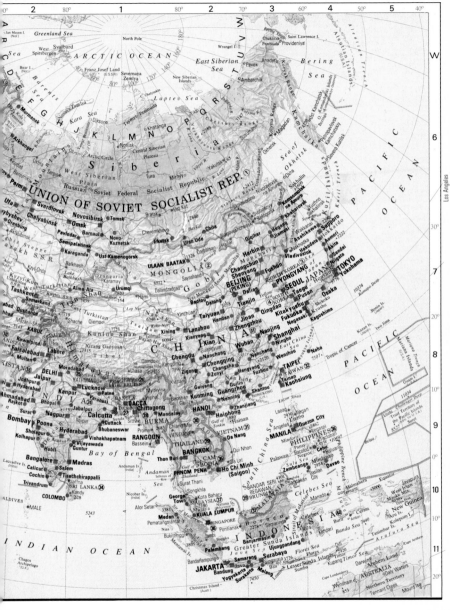

Greenland Sea
Jan Mayen I. (Nor.)
West Spitsbergen *Svalbard*
North Pole
Wrangel I.
Chukotski Peninsula *Providenya*
Saint Lawrence I.

ARCTIC OCEAN

Bear I.
Franz Josef Land (USSR)
Severnaya Zemlya
New Siberian Islands
East Siberian Sea
Pevek
Anadyr
Aleutian Islands (USA)
Aleutian Trench

W

Barents Sea
Novaya Zemlya
Kara Sea
Dikson
Laptev Sea
Ambarchik
Kolyma Range
Bering Sea

Murmansk
Arctic Circle
Taymyr Peninsula
Central Siberian Plateau
Norilsk
Verkhoyansk Range
Kamchatka
Petropavlovsk Kamchatskiy

P A C I F I C

Arkhangel
West Siberian Plain
S i b e r i a
Yakutsk
Sea of Okhotsk

Perm
Russian Soviet Federal Socialist Republic

UNION OF SOVIET SOCIALIST REP.

O C E A N

Sverdlovsk
Chelyabinsk
Novosibirsk
Tomsk
Bratsk
Ust Kut
Komsomolsk
Khabarovsk
Sakhalin

Kuybyshev
Orenburg
Omsk
Barnaul
Novo-Kuznetsk
Irkutsk
Ulan Ude
Chita

Pavlodar
Semipalatinsk
Cheremkhovo
L. Baykal

MONGOLIA ②
Blagoveshchensk
Vladivostok
Sapporo
Hokkaido

Karaganda
Ust-Kamenogorsk
ULAAN BAATAR
Asahikawa
Hakodate
Aomori

Kyzyl-Kum
Balkhash
Dzungaria
Sayshand
Gobi
NORTH KOREA ③
PYONGYANG
Akita
Sendai

Tashkent
Alma-Ata
Ürümqi
Harbin
Changchun
SEOUL
JAPAN
TOKYO

Samarkand
Tian Shan
Hami
BEIJING (PEKING)
Shenyang
Fushun
SOUTH KOREA ④
Taegu
Yokohama

Dushanbe
Kunlun Shan
Baotou
Datong
Tianjin
Dalian
Pusan
Osaka

KABUL
Kashgar
Xizang (Tibet)
Yinchuan
Taiyuan
Jinan
Kitakyushu
Fukuoka
Nagasaki
Kagoshima

Rawalpindi
Lahore
Lanzhou
Handan
Zhengzhou
CHINA
Xian
Nanjing
Shanghai
Ningbo

Faisalabad
Multan
Chengdu
Chongqing
Wuhan
Nanchang
Wenzhou
TAIPEI

DELHI
Moradabad
KATHMANDU
Guiyang
Changsha
Hengyang
Fuzhou
TAIWAN
Tainan
Kaohsiung

Jaipur
Lucknow
Patna
BANGLA
Kunming
Guangzhou
Guilin
Shantou
HONGKONG

Kanpur
DACCA
Mandalay
HANOI
Nanning
Zhanjiang
MANILA
PHILIPPINES
Quezon City

INDIA
Calcutta
Chittagong
Haiphong
Hainan

Bombay
Poona
Hyderabad
Vishakhapatnam
Cuttack
BURMA
VIETNAM
Da Nang

Bangalore
Madras
RANGOON
THAILAND
Qui Nhon

Bay of Bengal
BANGKOK
CAMBODIA
Ho Chi Minh (Saigon)

COLOMBO
SRI LANKA
PHNOM PENH
MALAYSIA

KUALA LUMPUR
Singapore
Borneo

INDIAN   OCEAN
INDONESIA

Palembang
JAKARTA
Bandung
Surabaya

P A C I F I C

O C E A N

Mariana Islands
Guam (USA)
Tropic of Cancer
Iwo Jima

Philippine Trench
New Guinea
Celebes Sea
Banda Sea
Arafura Sea
AUSTRALIA
Arnhem Land
Northern Territory

Scale 1:75 000 000

0	1000	2000 km
0	400 800	1200 miles
1 hour		

foot = 0,30 m
meter = 3,28 feet

65

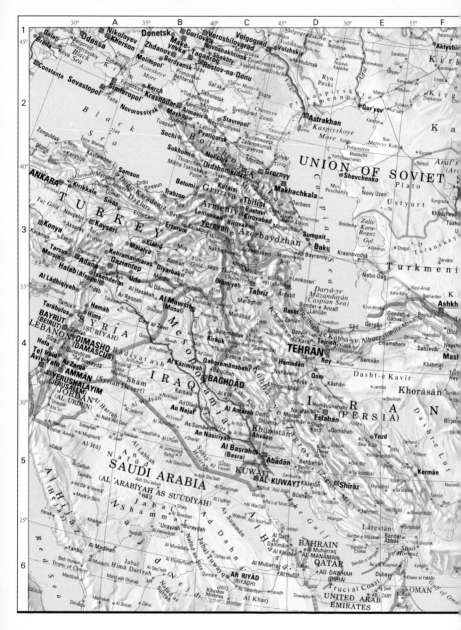

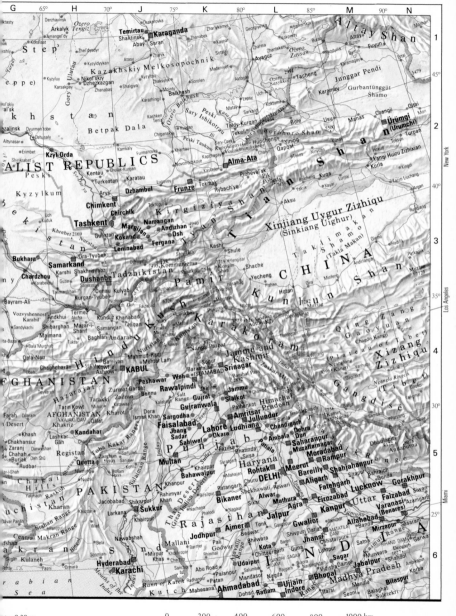

Scale 1:20 000 000

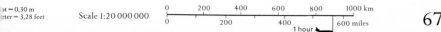

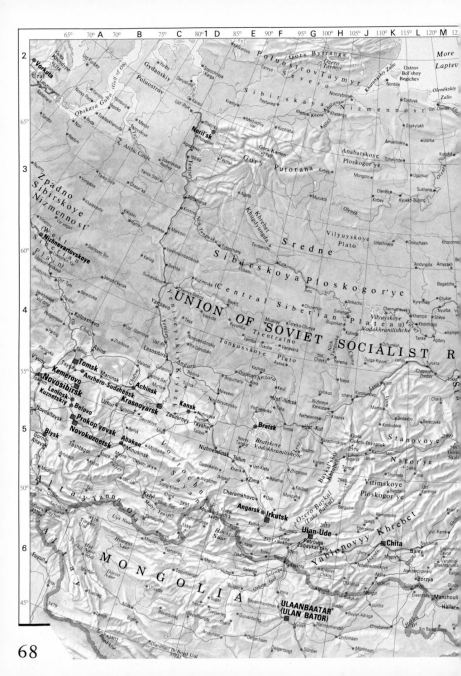

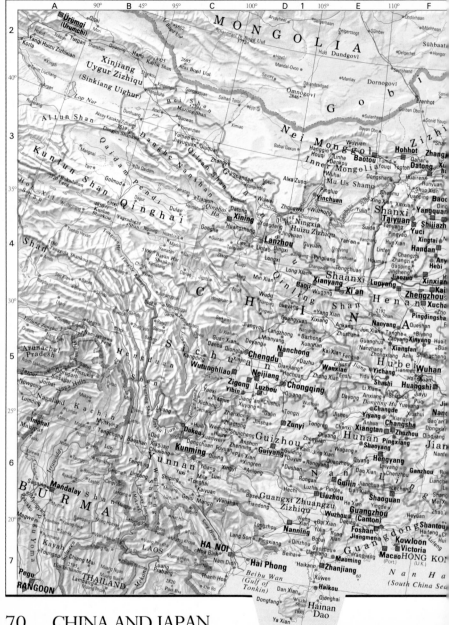

CHINA AND JAPAN

Grid coordinates

65°   A   70°   B   75°   C   80°   D   85°   E

1 — 2 — 3 — 4 — 5 — 6

30° — 25° — Tropic of Cancer — 20° — 15° — 10°

Countries and regions

AFGHANISTAN, PAKISTAN, Jammu and Kashmir, Himachal Pradesh, Punjab, Haryana, Rajasthan, Uttar Pradesh, NEPAL, Sikkim, Bihar, Bengal, Orissa, Madhya Pradesh, Gujarat, Maharashtra, Andhra Pradesh, Karnataka, Tamil Nadu, Chotanagpur, Kathiawar, Kutch, Sind, Registan, Thar Desert (Great Indian Desert), Vindhya Range, Satpura Range, Western Ghats, Eastern Ghats, Coromandel Coast, Malabar Coast

Qing Zang Gaoyuan (Plateau of Tibet), Xizang Zizhi (Tibet), Shan

SRI LANKA (CEYLON), MALDIVES, Lakshadweep (Laccadive Islands), Amindivi Islands

Seas and water bodies

Arabian Sea, INDIAN OCEAN, Bay of Bengal, Gulf of Kutch, Gulf of Khambhat, Gulf of Mannar, Rann of Kutch, Mouths of the Indus, Adams Bridge, Cape Comorin, Dondra Head, Palmyras Point

Cities and towns

Tarin Kowt, Tarakki, Zurmat, Gardez, Zadran, Khakriz, Peshawar, Weh, Rawalpindi, ISLAMABAD, Sopur, Baramula, Srinagar, Banihal Pass, Jammu, Sialkot, Gujrat, Gujranwala, Bannu, Kohat, Salt Range, Jhelum, Kalabagh, Pathankot, Simla, Faisalabad, Sargodha, Jhang Sadar, Sahiwal, Lahore, Okara, Ludhiana, Jullundur, Amritsar, Chandigarh, Dehra Dun, Ambala, Multan, Bahawalpur, Khanpur, Khairpur, Rahimyar Khan, Bhatinda, Sirsa, Saharanpur, Muzaffarnagar, Meerut, DELHI, Rohtak, Moradabad, Rampur, Bareilly, Shahjahanpur, Aligarh, Bikaner, Shekhawati, Churu, Rewari, Mathura, Agra, Firozabad, Fatehgarh, Lucknow, Jacobabad, Sukkur, Shikarpur, Larkana, Khairpur, Nawabshah, Hyderabad, Karachi, Bela, Quetta, Kalat, Jaipur, Ajmer, Jodhpur, Pali, Tonk, Kota, Gwalior, Jhansi, Kanpur, Allahabad, Varanasi (Benares), Faizabad, Gorakhpur, Muzaffarpur, Darbhanga, Patna, Monghyr, Bhagalpur, KATMANDU, Udaipur, Chittaurgarh, Bhilwara, Guna, Bhopal, Sagar, Jabalpur, Satna, Mirzapur, Sasaram, Gaya, Ranchi, Jamshedpur, Durgapur, Burdwan, Asansol, Howrah, Calcutta, Cuttack, Bhubaneshwar, Berhampur, Ahmadabad, Nadiad, Dohad, Ratlam, Ujjain, Indore, Khandwa, Itarsi, Betul, Amravati, Nagpur, Bhandara, Durg, Raipur, Bilaspur, Raurkela, Sambalpur, Jamnagar, Rajkot, Junagadh, Veraval, Bhavnagar, Vadodara, Bharuch, Surat, Dhule, Jalgaon, Bhusawal, Akola, Burhanpur, Nasik, Malegaon, Manmad, Aurangabad, Nander, Adilabad, Ulhasnagar, Thana, Bombay, Pune, Ahmadnagar, Sholapur, Bidar, Nizamabad, Warangal, Hyderabad, Vishakhapatnam, Srikakulam, Vizianagaram, Kolhapur, Sangli, Bijapur, Gulbarga, Raichur, Mahbubnagar, Kurnool, Eluru, Rajahmundry, Kakinada, Vijayawada, Machilipatnam, Guntur, Tenali, Ongole, Belgaum, Bagalkot, Yadgir, Nandyal, Hubli, Dharwar, Gadag, Bellary, Anantapur, Cuddapah, Nellore, Gudur, Karwar, Honavar, Davangere, Shimoga, Udipi, Chik Ballapur, Mangalore, Bhadravati, Bangalore, Hassan, Kolar, Gold Fields, Chittoor, Tirupati, Vellore, Kanchipuram, Madras, Mysore, Kozhikode, Ambur, Pondicherry, Calicut, Salem, Erode, Cuddalore, Trichur, Coimbatore, Dindigul, Thanjavur, Karikal, Tiruchchirappalli, Cochin, Alleppey, Madurai, Kumbakonam, Quilon, Trivandrum, Tirunelveli, Tuticorin, Nagercoil, Jaffna, Mullaittivu, Trincomalee, Anuradhapura, Kurunegala, Negombo, COLOMBO, Kandy, Pidurutalagala, Badulla, Ratnapura, Moratuwa, Galle, Matara, Yala

Physical features / mountains

Suleiman Range, Toba Kakar Range, Bolan Pass, Kirthar Range, Aravalli Range, Satpura, Himalaya, Mt Everest 8848, Dhaulagiri, Annapurna, Nanda Devi, Kamet, Gangdise Shan, Nyainqentanglha, Godavari, Krishna, Narmada, Tapti, Mahanadi, Ganges, Indus, Sutlej, Jhelum, Chenab, Ravi, Beas, Yamuna, Chambal

MATATILA DAM, RIHAND DAM

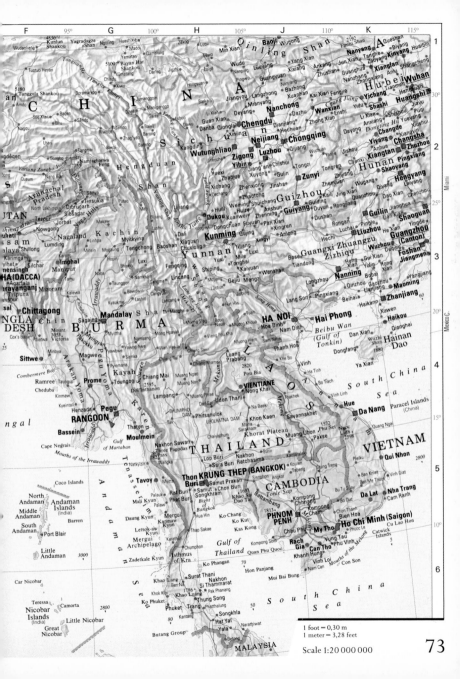

73

1 foot = 0,30 m
1 meter = 3,28 feet

Scale 1:20 000 000

Scale 1:20 000 000

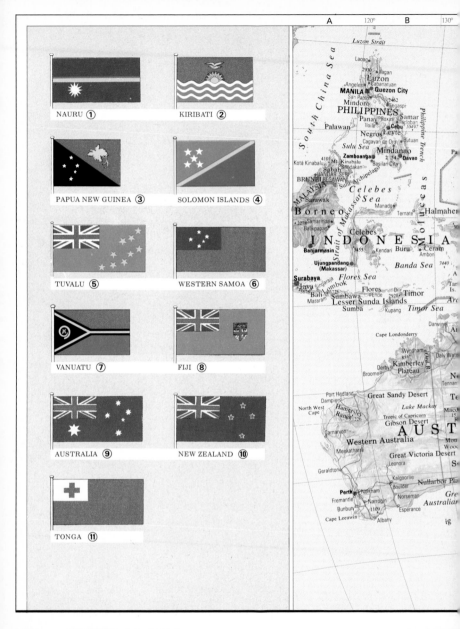

NAURU ①

KIRIBATI ②

PAPUA NEW GUINEA ③

SOLOMON ISLANDS ④

TUVALU ⑤

WESTERN SAMOA ⑥

VANUATU ⑦

FIJI ⑧

AUSTRALIA ⑨

NEW ZEALAND ⑩

TONGA ⑪

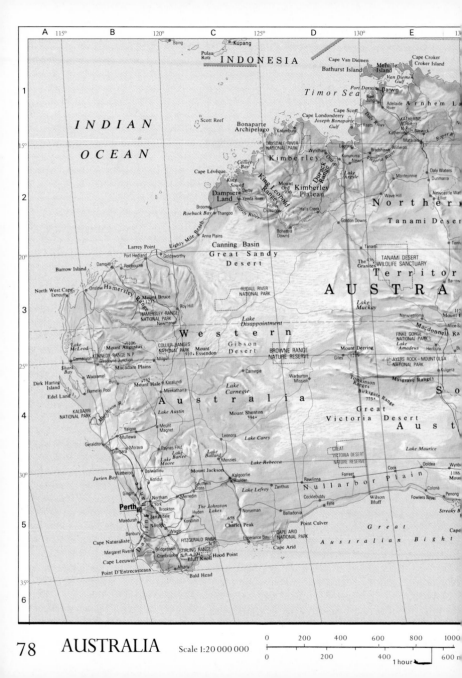

AUSTRALIA Scale 1:20 000 000

1 foot = 0,30 m
1 meter = 3,28 feet

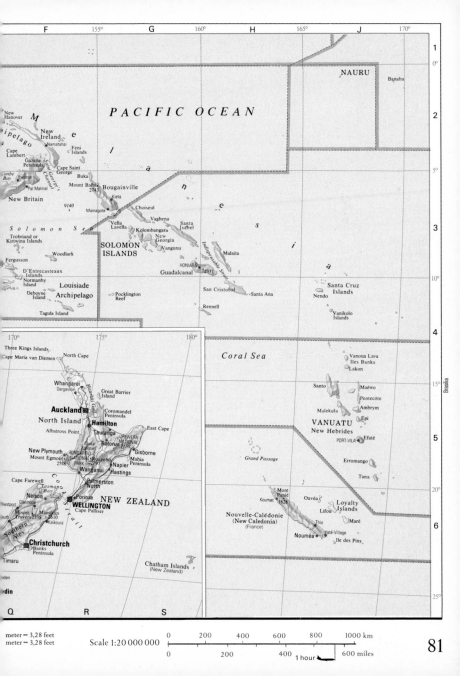

F   155°   G   160°   H   165°   J   170°

1

0°

NAURU

Banaba

M
New
Hanover

New
Ireland

e

Namatahai

Feni
Islands

PACIFIC OCEAN

...ipelago

l

Cape
Lambert

Gazelle
Peninsula

Cape Saint
George

2

5°

...mbe
Bay

Ewasse

Pal Malmal

Buka

Mount Balbi
2743

Bougainville

Kieta

a

New Britain

9140

Mamagota

Choiseul

n

Solomon Sea

Trobriand or
Kiriwina Islands

Woodlark

Fergusson

D'Entrecasteaux
Islands

Normanby
Island

Deboyne
Island

**SOLOMON
ISLANDS**

Vaghena

Vella
Lavella

Kolombangara

New
Georgia

Vangunu

Santa
Isabel

e

Malaita

3

s

i

a

Indispensable Strait

HONIARA

Guadalcanal

2331

Santa Cruz
Islands

10°

**Louisiade
Archipelago**

Pocklington
Reef

San Cristobal

Santa Ana

Rennell

Nendo

Vanikolo
Islands

Tagula Island

4

170°   175°   180°

Three Kings Islands

Cape Maria van Diemen

North Cape

Coral Sea

Vanoua Lava
Iles Banks

Lakon

15°

Whangarei

Dargaville

Great Barrier
Island

Santo

Maéwo

Hauraki Gulf

Auckland

Coromandel
Peninsula

Pentecôte

Ambrym

Malekula

North Island

Hamilton

Tauranga

East Cape

VANUATU
New Hebrides

Epi

Albatross Point

UREWERA
NATIONAL
PARK

Rotorua

Gisborne

PORT-VILA

Efaté

New Plymouth

Mount Egmont
2518

TONGARIRO
NATIONAL
PARK

Lake
Taupo

Ruapehu
2797

Napier

Mahia
Peninsula

Grand Passage

Erromango

Wanganui

Hastings

Tana

Cape Farewell

*Tasman
Bay*

Palmerston
North

Nelson

Blenheim

Porirua

WELLINGTON

NEW ZEALAND

Mont
Panié
1628

Koumac

Ouvéa

Loyalty
Islands

20°

Vestport

...outh

Mount
Travers 2338

Manakau
2610

Cape Palliser

Lifou

Maré

Kaikoura

Nouvelle-Calédonie
(New Caledonia)
(France)

Thio

Yaté-Village

Southern Alps

Cook Strait

Christchurch

Banks
Peninsula

Nouméa

Ile des Pins

Timaru

Chatham Islands
(New Zealand)

6

25°

...den

...din

Q   R   S

Brasilia

meter = 3,28 feet
meter = 3,28 feet

Scale 1:20 000 000

0   200   400   600   800   1000 km

0   200   400   600 miles

1 hour

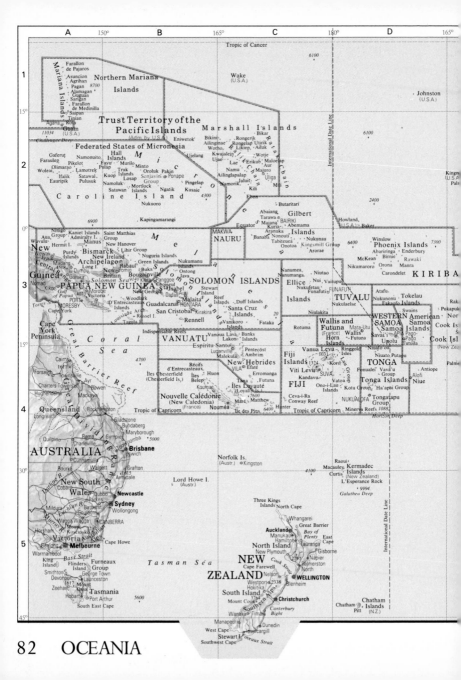

82 OCEANIA

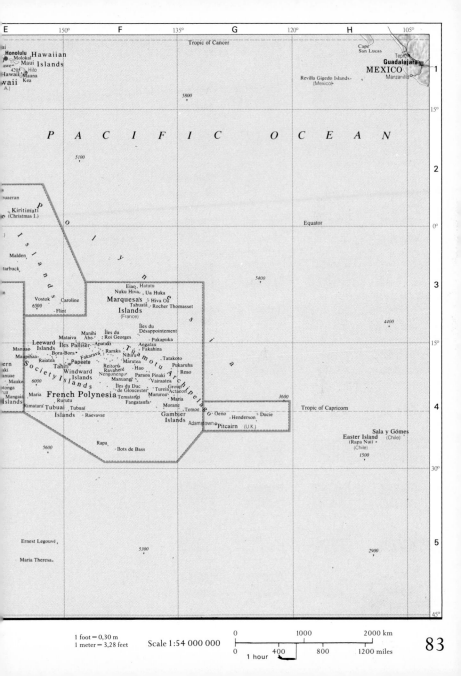

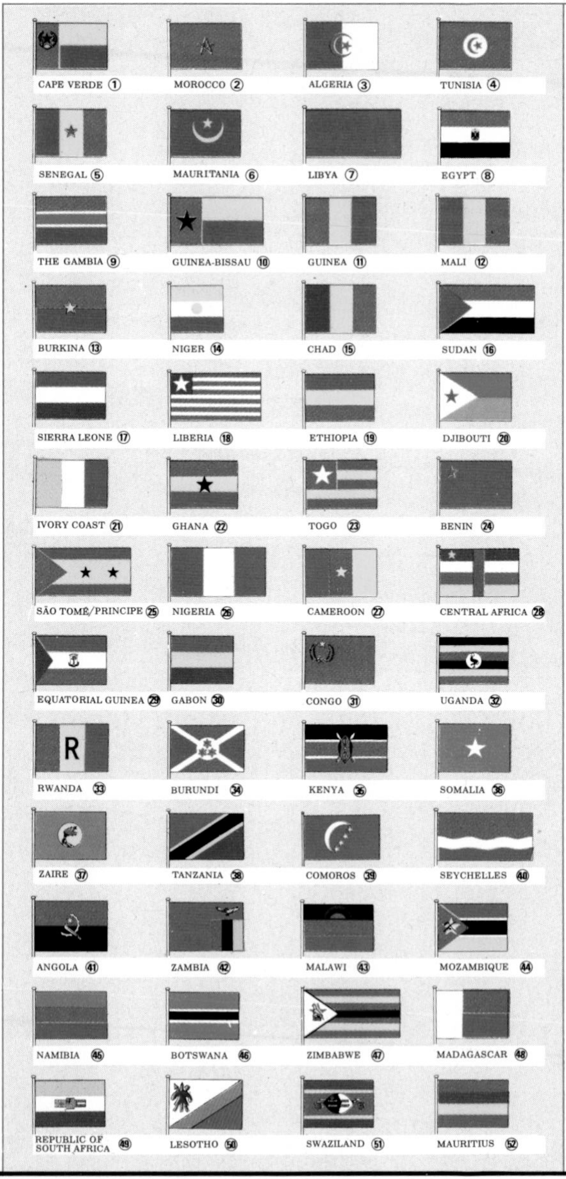
CAPE VERDE ①
MOROCCO ②
ALGERIA ③
TUNISIA ④
SENEGAL ⑤
MAURITANIA ⑥
LIBYA ⑦
EGYPT ⑧
THE GAMBIA ⑨
GUINEA-BISSAU ⑩
GUINEA ⑪
MALI ⑫
BURKINA ⑬
NIGER ⑭
CHAD ⑮
SUDAN ⑯
SIERRA LEONE ⑰
LIBERIA ⑱
ETHIOPIA ⑲
DJIBOUTI ⑳
IVORY COAST ㉑
GHANA ㉒
TOGO ㉓
BENIN ㉔
SÃO TOMÉ/PRINCIPE ㉕
NIGERIA ㉖
CAMEROON ㉗
CENTRAL AFRICA ㉘
EQUATORIAL GUINEA ㉙
GABON ㉚
CONGO ㉛
UGANDA ㉜
RWANDA ㉝
BURUNDI ㉞
KENYA ㉟
SOMALIA ㊱
ZAIRE ㊲
TANZANIA ㊳
COMOROS ㊴
SEYCHELLES ㊵
ANGOLA ㊶
ZAMBIA ㊷
MALAWI ㊸
MOZAMBIQUE ㊹
NAMIBIA ㊺
BOTSWANA ㊻
ZIMBABWE ㊼
MADAGASCAR ㊽
REPUBLIC OF SOUTH AFRICA ㊾
LESOTHO ㊿
SWAZILAND (51)
MAURITIUS (52)

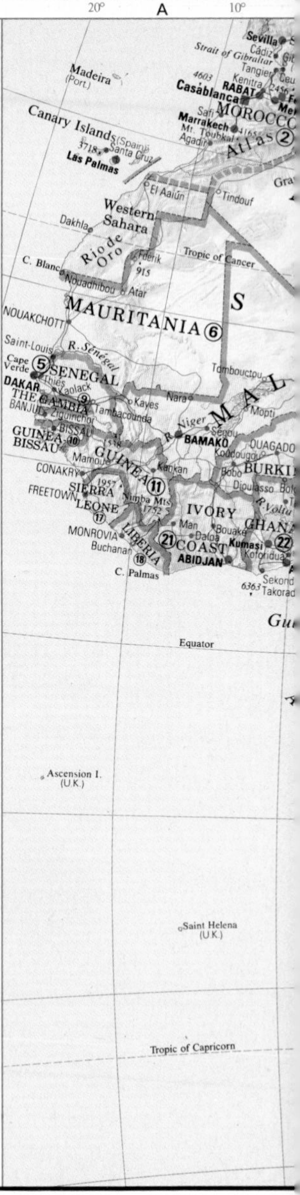
20°
A
10°
Sevilla
Cádiz
Strait of Gibraltar
Tangier
Madeira
(Port.)
4603
Kenitra
RABAT
Casablanca
Safi
MOROCCO
Marrakech
Mt. Toubkal
Agadir
Atlas
②
Canary Islands
(Spain)
3718
Santa Cruz
Las Palmas
El Aaiún
Tindouf
Western
Sahara
Dakhla
Rio de Oro
Fdérik
915
Tropic of Cancer
C. Blanc
Nouadhibou
Atar
S
MAURITANIA ⑥
NOUAKCHOTT
Saint-Louis
R. Sénégal
Cape Verde
⑤
SENEGAL
Tombouctou
DAKAR
Thies
Kaolack
THE GAMBIA
⑨
BANJUL
Ziguinchor
Kayes
Tambacounda
Nara
Mopti
GUINEA-BISSAU
⑩
BISSAU
R. Niger
Ségou
BAMAKO
OUAGADO
Koudougou
Mamou
GUINEA
⑪
Kankan
CONAKRY
Bobo
BURKI
1957
SIERRA LEONE
⑰
FREETOWN
Nimba Mts
1752
Dioulasso
IVORY
R. Volta
Man
Daloa
Bouaké
GHANA
MONROVIA
LIBERIA
⑱
Buchanan
㉑
COAST
Kumasi
㉒
ABIDJAN
Koforidua
C. Palmas
6363
Sekondi
Takoradi
Gu
Equator
Ascension I.
(U.K.)
Saint Helena
(U.K.)
Tropic of Capricorn

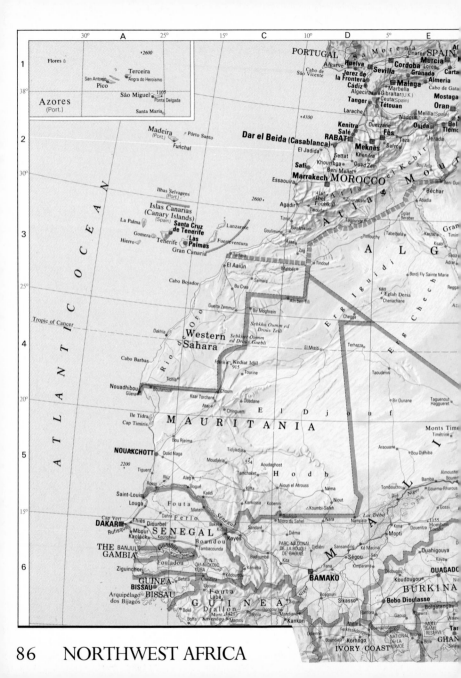

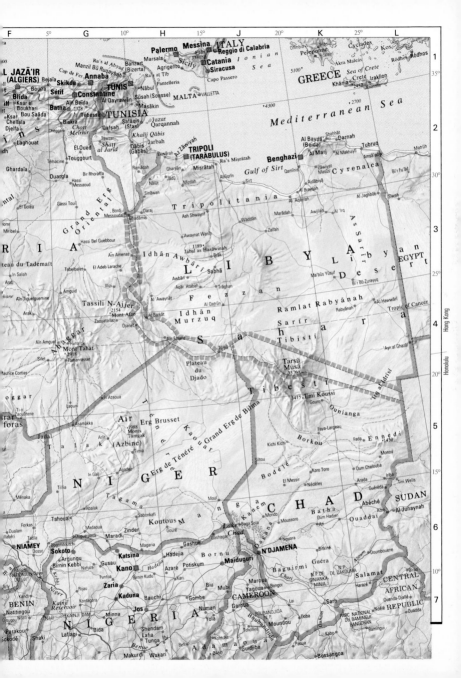

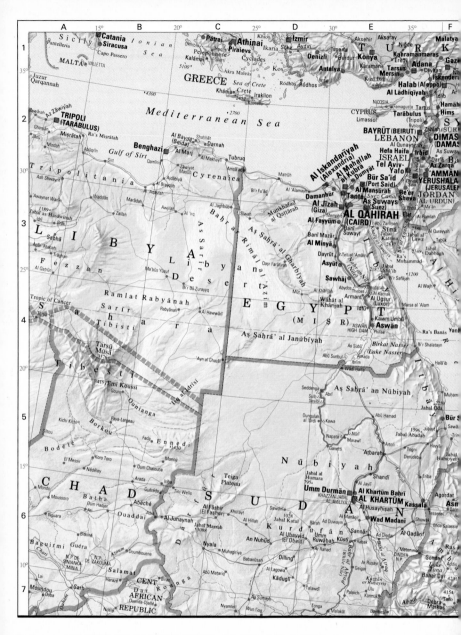

Scale 1:20 000 000

foot = 0,30 m
meter = 3,28 feet

| 0 | 200 | 400 | 600 | 800 | 1000 km |

| 0 | 200 | 400 | 600 miles |

1 hour

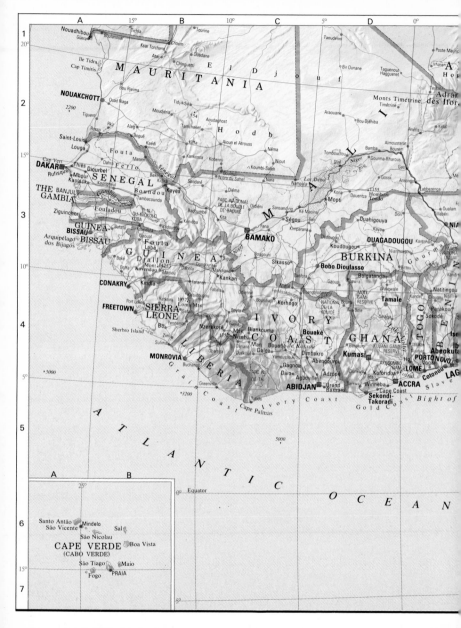

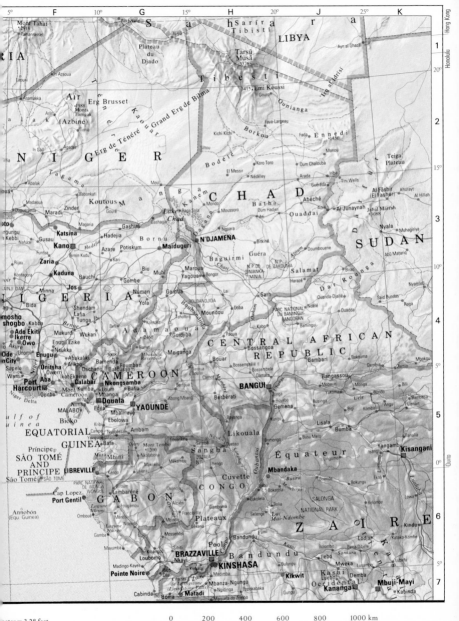

5°   F   10°   G   15°   H   20°   J   25°   K

Mont Tahat
2918
Tamanrasset

Aïn Salah   S   a   h   a   r   a
LIBYA

20°

Plateau
du
Djado

Tarsū Musā
3765
'Ayn al Ghazāl

1

In Azaoua

Aïr
1988
Monts   Erg Brusset
Tamgak
(Azbine)   Kaouar   Grand Erg de Bilma

Tibesti
3415 Emi Koussi
Gouro   Ounianga   'Ira al Idrisi

 RIA

Asamakka

Madaoua

In Gall   Erg de Ténéré

Abalak

Bodélé   Borkou   Faya-Largeau   Enhedi   2459   Teiga
Plateau

Kichi Kichi   Oum Chalouba   Iriba   Tini Wells   Al Fashir
El Fasher   Khurayt

2

15°

Madaoua
Maradi   Zabonkari
Koutous   Gouré
Zinder   Magaria   Gashua
Hadejia

Kanem   N'Guigmi   Lake
Chad   Baga Sola   Mao
Massakori   Moussoro   Mondo   Ati   Abéché   Adré   Al Junaynah
El Geneina   Jabal Marrah
3088   Al Hillah

SUDAN

Kebbi
Nafada

Katsina
Kano
Hadejia
Bornu

Maiduguri   N'DJAMENA   Baguirmi   Guéra   Biltine   Ouaddaï   Doumbouene   Abū Matāriq
Nyala   Muhagiriya

Zaria

Magaria   Gumel   Biu   Mubi

Maiduguri   Batha   Dum Hadjer

Kaduna

Bauchi   Gombe   Marwa
Yagoua   Bongor   Charī   Mongo   N.P. DE
SIANIKA   Salamat   Dar Rounga   Bizo   Nyamēl

Jos

Bida
Minna   Numan   Gamba
Shendam   Yola   Lai   Sarh   PARC NATIONAL
DE BAMINGUI-
BANGORAN   Ndélé   Ouadda   Raga   Said Bundas

NIGERIA

Lafia   Tunga
Ibi
Wukari   Bénoué   Kontcha   BOUBANDJIDA   Moundou   Doba   Koro   Kabo   Bamingui   Ouanda-Djallé   Dar Rounga

mosho   Kabba
shogbo

Ado Ekiti
Ikerre
Owo

Makurdi   Bélel

Adamaoua   2460   Guidjiba

CENTRAL   AFRICAN   REPUBLIC

Mbokou

Ode   Utomi
City   Enugu   Nsukka   Bamenda   Fumban   Meiganga   Bossangoa
Bouar   Bakouma   Zemio

Sapele   Onitsha   Afikpo
Warri   Aba   Abakaliki   Oschang   Batouri   Bossembélé
Bossembélé   Bambari   Bangassou   Monga   Bondo   Bambouti   Lienart

Port   Calabar   Mont Kumba   Loum   Mbanga   Mbia   Carnot   Damara   BANGUI   Mobaye   Yokoma   Uele   Bili   Ango

CAMEROON   Nkongsamba   Bertoua   Bétaré   Gemena   Bangui   Businga   Bogi   Kembé   Banalia

Harcourt   Opobo   Nkambe   Bafia   Abong Mbang   Bétaré Oya   Bétaré

Niger
Delta   Bioko   Douala   YAOUNDÉ   Bertoua   Lisala   Bumba   Yangambi   Kisangani

MALABO   Nimbe
Kribi   Mbalmayo   Bénoya   Likouala   Busu Melo

Bata   Ebolowa

EQUATORIAL
GUINEA   Ambam   Oyem   Minkébé   Ouesso   Bumonga   Ubangui   Ubundu   Bokungu   Lowa

São Tomé   Mont Tembo
1200   Sangha   Yengo   Equateur   Lomami   Lindi

SÃO TOMÉ   Kogo   N'Kolabona   Makokou
AND   Bata   Mbini   PARC   Mékambo   Mbandaka   Buiti   Boende   Velombo

PRINCIPE   LIBREVILLE   Mitzic   Booué   Okondja   CONGO   Cuvette   Bokatola   0°

São Tomé   PARC NATIONAL
DE WONGA-
WONGUÉ   Lambaréné   Koulamoutou   Plateaux   SALONGA   NATIONAL PARK

Cap Lopez
Port Gentil   GABON   Alémbé   Francéville   Mossendjo   Léxana   Selenge   Luc
Mai-Ndombe   Lodja

Annobón
(Equ. Guinea)   Lagune   Gamba
N'Dogo   Mouila   Bambio   ZAIRE

Mayumba   Tchibanga

6

5°

Madingo-Kayés   Kibangou
Loubomo   Sibiti   Pointe Pool   Bandundu   Ilebo   Mweka   Lubumba   Kabinda

BRAZZAVILLE   Bandundu

Pointe Noire   Nkayi   Madimba   Banza-Ngungu   Kikwit   Kananga   Mbuji-Mayi

Cabinda   KINSHASA   Mbanza-Ngungu   Bulungu   Gungu   Kasai   Demba   Kabinda
Chutes de Zaire
(Livingstone Falls)   Ngidinga   Popokabaka   Occidental

Boma   Matadi   Maquela do Zombo

7

5°

Quito

Kindu

E

0

meter = 3,28 feet
meter = 3,28 feet   Scale 1:20 000 000   0   200   400   600   800   1000 km

0   200   400   600 miles
1 hour

91

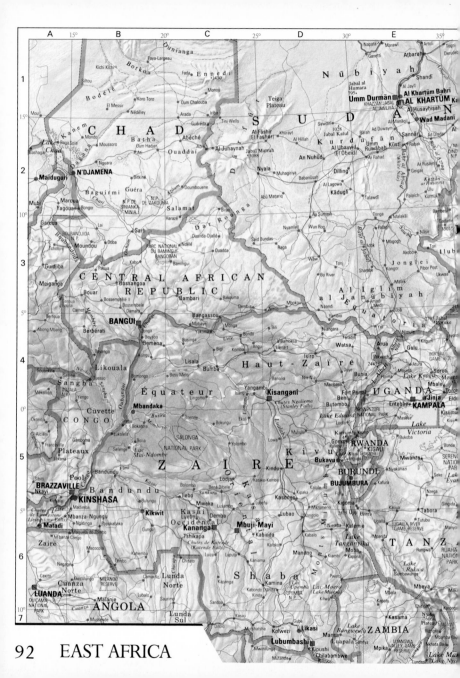

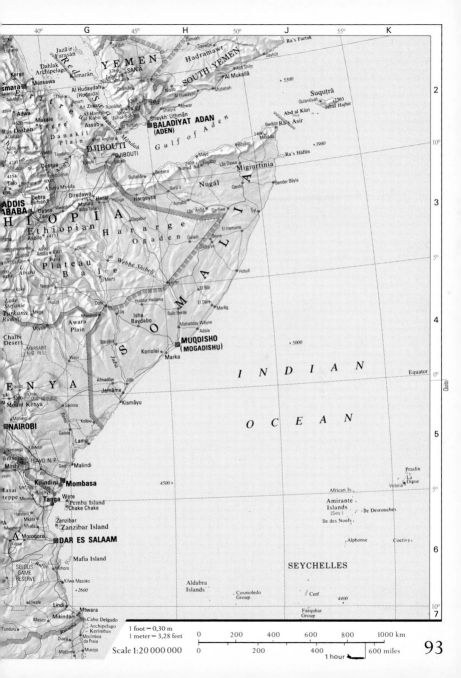

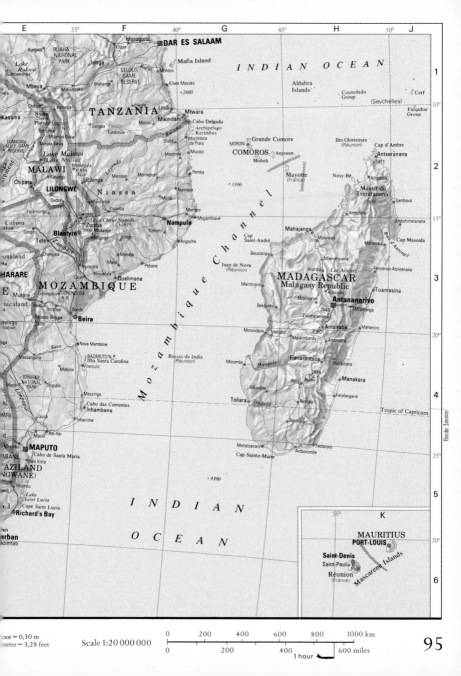

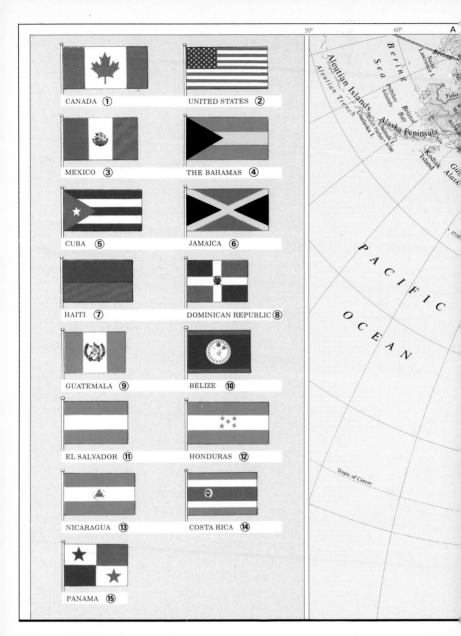

CANADA ①

UNITED STATES ②

MEXICO ③

THE BAHAMAS ④

CUBA ⑤

JAMAICA ⑥

HAITI ⑦

DOMINICAN REPUBLIC ⑧

GUATEMALA ⑨

BELIZE ⑩

EL SALVADOR ⑪

HONDURAS ⑫

NICARAGUA ⑬

COSTA RICA ⑭

PANAMA ⑮

NORTH AMERICA

1 foot = 0,30 m
1 meter = 3,28 feet

Scale 1:50 000 0

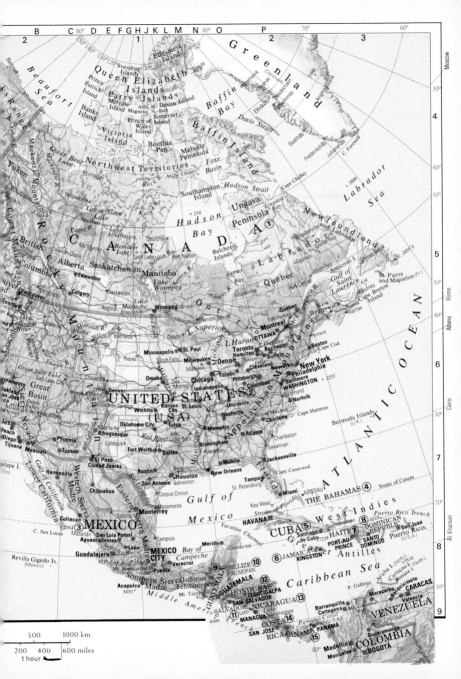

98   ALASKA AND WESTERN CANADA

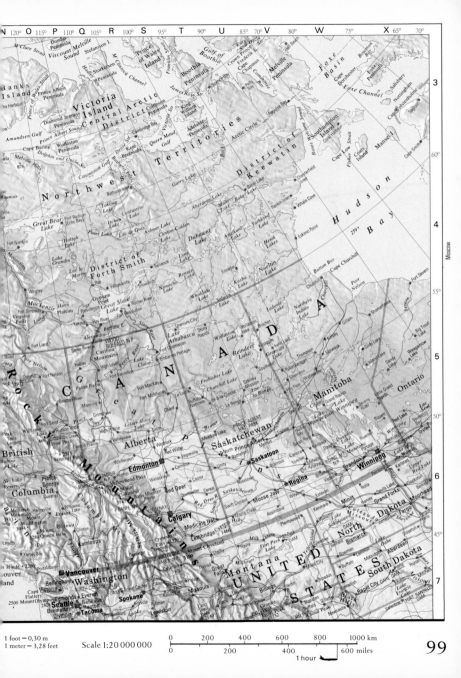

N O 120° 115° P 110° Q 105° R 100° S 95° T 90° U 85° 70° V 80° W 75° X 65° 70°

M'Clure Strait
Viscount Melville Sound
Dundas Peninsula
Stefansson I.
Prince of Wales Island
Gulf of Boothia
Fury and Hecla Str.
Crown Prince Frederik I.
Chapman I.
Foxe Basin
Cape Dorchester
Burton Bay
Mansell I.

Banks Island
Prince Albert Peninsula
M'Clintock Channel
Boothia Peninsula
Melville Peninsula
Foxe Channel
Cape Smith

Diamond Jenness Peninsula
Victoria Island
Central Arctic District
James Ross Str.
Adelaide Peninsula
Arctic Circle
Southampton Island
Coats Island
Nottingham

Amundsen Gulf
Prince Albert Sound
Dolphin and Union Str.
Coronation Gulf
Queen Maud Gulf
Rankin Inlet
Hudson Bay

Northwest Territories
District of Keewatin
Chesterfield
Port Nelson
Fort Severn

Great Bear Lake
District of Forth Smith
Aberdeen Lake
Baker Lake
Rankin Inlet
Eskimo Point
Cape Churchill

Great Slave Lake
Lake Athabasca
Reindeer Lake
Manitoba
Ontario

British Columbia
Rocky Mountains
Alberta
Saskatchewan
Winnipeg

Edmonton
Saskatoon
Regina
Winnipeg

Calgary
Medicine Hat
Moose Jaw
North Dakota
Fargo
Moorhead

Vancouver
Washington
Montana
UNITED STATES
South Dakota

Seattle
Tacoma
Spokane
Billings
Rapid City

1 foot = 0,30 m
1 meter = 3,28 feet

Scale 1:20 000 000

| 0 | 200 | 400 | 600 | 800 | 1000 km |

| 0 | 200 | 400 | 600 miles |

1 hour

99

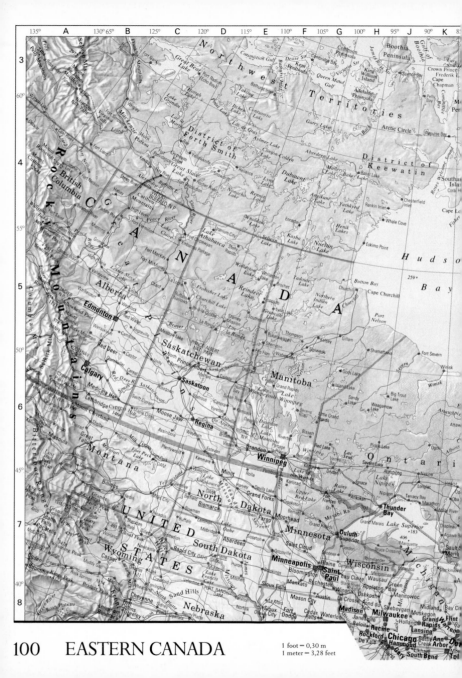

1 foot = 0,30 m
1 meter = 3,28 feet

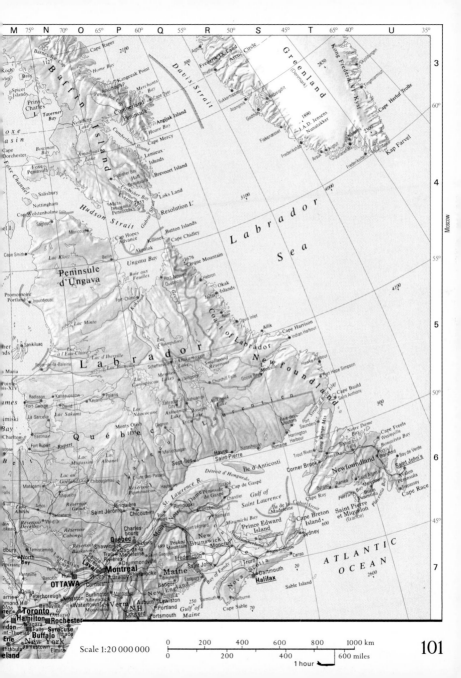

Baffin Island

Cape Raper 2100

Home Bay

Barnes Ice Cap

Cape Hooper

Kangeeak Point

Prins Charles I

Tavener Bay

Penny Highland

Merchants Bay

Cape Dyer

Foxe Basin

Cumberland Peninsula

Nettilling Lake

Angijak Island

Hoare Bay

Cumberland Sound

Spicer Islands

Koch I

Bray I

Davis Strait

Frederick VI Land

Arctic Circle

Greenland (Denmark)

2850

Kap Herluf Trolle

Kong Frederik IX's Land

60°

Ivgtut

Nanortalik

Cape Dorchester

Bowman Bay

Foxe Peninsula

Lake Amadjuak

Foxe Channel

Salisbury

Nottingham

Cap Wolstenholme

Hall Peninsula

Brevoort Island

Loks Land

Gabriel Strait

Resolution I.

3100

Cape Mercy

Meta Incognita Peninsula

Everett Mts

Frobisher Bay

Lemieux Islands

4000

J.A.P. Jensens Nunatakker

1890

Sukkertoppen

Atangmik

Godthåb

Fiskenæsset

Frederikshåb

Kap Farvel

Angmagssalik

Angssaq

Ivgtut

Nanortalik

Cape Smith

Saglouc

Maricourt

Lac Klotz

Bellin

Cap Hopes Advance

Killineq

Button Islands

Akpatok

Cape Chidley

Ungava Bay

1676

Cirque Mountain

Labrador Sea

55°

Peninsule d'Ungava

Baie aux Feuilles

Fort-Chimo

Port Nouveau-Québec

Koksoak

Hebron

Okak

Nutak

Nutak Islands

4100

Kogaluk

Lac Minto

Lac à l'Eau-Claire

Davis Inlet

Aillik

Cape Harrison

Indian Harbour

5

Sanikiluaq

Lac d'Iberville

Labrador

Lac Bienville

Michikamau Lake

Schefferville

Smallwood Réservoir

Menihek Lakes

Melville

Hawke Harbour

Port Hope Simpson

Saint Anthony

Newfoundland

50°

Fort-George

David

Polaris

Radisson

Kaniapiscau

Réservoir Caniapiscau

Keyano

Wabush

Labrador City

Ashuanipi Lake

Churchill Falls

Goose Bay

Ashuanipi Lake

Cape Bauld

300

Lac Naococane

Grand

Eastmain

Fort Rupert

Rupert

Québec

Lac Sakami

Lac Mistassini

Lac Albanel

Lac au Goéland

Chibougamau

Manicouagan

Sept-Îles

Havre-Saint-Pierre

Natashquan

Romaine

Baie-des-Moutons

Harrington Harbour

Trout River

Notre Dame Bay

Cape Freels

Wesleyville

Bonavista Bay

Cape Bonavista

Corner Brook

Newfoundland

Saint John's

Matagami

Amos

Val-d'Or

Réservoir Decelles

Lac Abitibi

Senneterre

Réservoir Gouin

Réservoir Baskatong

Réservoir Cabonga

Baie-Comeau

Forestville

Manicouagan

Fleuve Saint-Laurent

Détroit d'Honguedo

Île d'Anticosti

Gulf of Saint Lawrence

Île de la Madeleine

Avalon Peninsula

Cape Race

6

North Bay

Chicoutimi

Jonquière

Saint-Jérôme

Rivière-du-Loup

St. Lawrence R.

Rimouski

Monts Notre Dame

Péninsule de Gaspé

Cap de Gaspé

Chandler

Miramichi Bay

Cape Breton Island

Sydney

Canso

Charlevoix

Charlesbourg

Québec

Lévis

Trois-Rivières

Cap-de-la-Madeleine

Shawinigan

Drummondville

Peaked Mountain

689

Saint-Léonard

New Brunswick

Fredericton

Prince Edward Island

Northumberland Strait

Moncton

600

ATLANTIC OCEAN

45°

Orillia

Temiscaming

Montreal

Laval

Hull

OTTAWA

Granby

Sherbrooke

Maine

Bangor

Saint John

Bay of Fundy

Eastport

Truro

Dartmouth

Halifax

Sable Island

20

2600

Peterborough

Kingston

Cornwall

St-Jean

Vermont

Burlington

New England

Lewiston

Auburn

Portland

Gulf of Maine

Cape Sable

70

Shelburne

Yarmouth

Belleville

Toronto

Hamilton

Rochester

Syracuse

Buffalo

New York

Jamestown

Elmira

Niagara Falls

Ithaca

Watertown

Adirondack Mountains

NH

Concord

Portsmouth

250

Erie

Cleveland

Lake Erie

Lake Ontario

London

102   THE UNITED STATES

1 foot = 0,30 m
1 meter = 3,28 feet

Scale 1:20 000 000

foot = 0,30 m
meter = 3,28 feets

Scale 1:20 000 000

0   200   400   600   800   1000 km
0   200   400   600 miles
1 hour

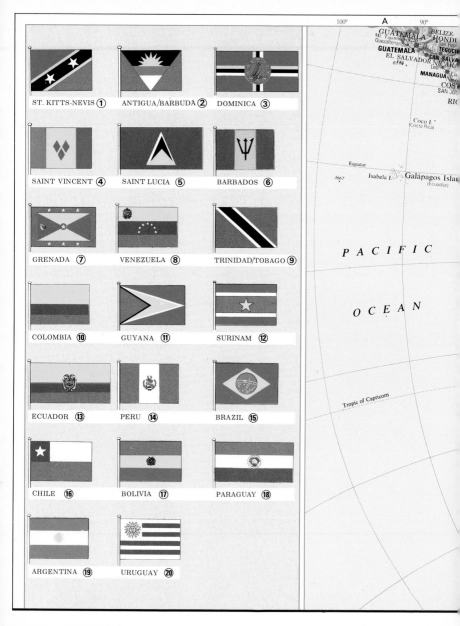

ST. KITTS-NEVIS ①

ANTIGUA/BARBUDA ②

DOMINICA ③

SAINT VINCENT ④

SAINT LUCIA ⑤

BARBADOS ⑥

GRENADA ⑦

VENEZUELA ⑧

TRINIDAD/TOBAGO ⑨

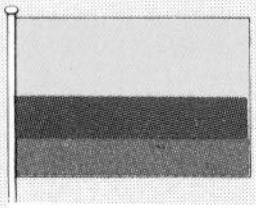
COLOMBIA ⑩

GUYANA ⑪

SURINAM ⑫

ECUADOR ⑬

PERU ⑭

BRAZIL ⑮

CHILE ⑯

BOLIVIA ⑰

PARAGUAY ⑱

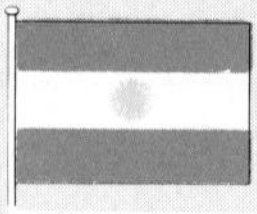
ARGENTINA ⑲

URUGUAY ⑳

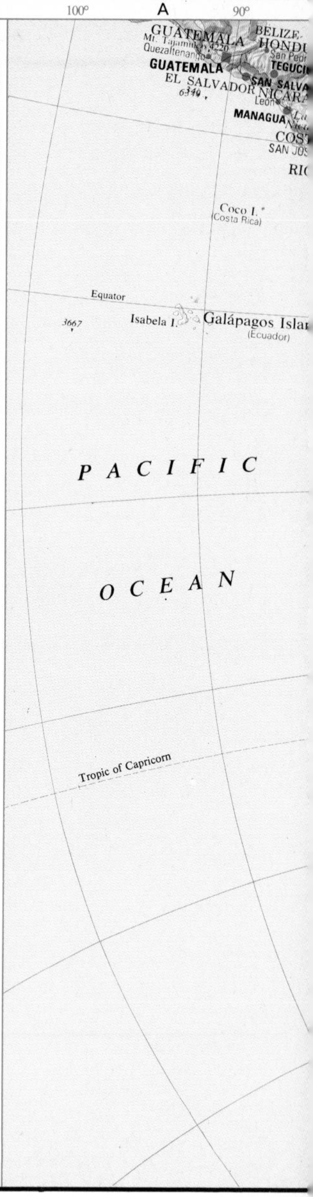
100°
A
90°
GUATEMALA
Quezaltenango
GUATEMALA
EL SALVADOR
MANAGUA
Coco I.
(Costa Rica)
Equator
3667
Isabela I.
(Ecuador)
PACIFIC
OCEAN
Tropic of Capricorn

1 foot = 0,30 m
1 meter = 3,28 feet

Scale 1:50 000 00

South America map

Latitude labels (top): 80° C 70° D 60° E 50° F 40° G 30° H

Right margin labels: Bangkok, Brazzaville, Darwin, Antananarivo, Cape Town, Melbourne

JAMAICA

Caribbean Sea

Puerto Rico (U.S.A.)
ST. KITTS - NEVIS ①
ANTIGUA AND BARBUDA ②
Guadeloupe (France)
DOMINICA ③
Martinique (France) ④
Fort-de-France
ST. LUCIA ⑤
BARBADOS ⑥
ST. VINCENT ⑦
GRENADA ⑦
BRIDGETOWN

Lesser Antilles

P. Gallinas
Santa Marta
Barranquilla
Cartagena
Maracaibo
Barquisimeto
Maracay
VENEZUELA ⑧
CARACAS
Valencia
Barcelona
Ciudad Bolívar
Ciudad Guayana
TRINIDAD AND TOBAGO ⑨
PORT OF SPAIN

PANAMÁ
Colón
MÁ
Medellín
Cúcuta
Bucaramanga
Manizales
BOGOTÁ
Buenaventura
Cali
COLOMBIA ⑩
Ibagué
Pasto

GEORGETOWN
PARAMARIBO
French Guiana
Cayenne
GUYANA ⑪
SURINAM ⑫
Angel Falls
Mt. Roraima
Orinoco R.
Boa Vista
Roraima

ATLANTIC
OCEAN

St. Peter and St. Paul Rocks (Braz.)
Equator 0°

ECUADOR ⑬
Guayaquil
Quito
Cotopaxi
Iquitos

Fernando de Noronha I. (Braz.)

Amazonas
Selva
Manaus
Santarém
Fonte Boa
Letícia
Marajó
Belém
São Luís
Parnaíba
Fortaleza
Maranhão
Teresina
Sobral
C. São Roque
Natal
Mossoró
Ceará
Piauí

PERU ⑭
LIMA
Callao
Huancavelica
Pisco
Cajamarca
Trujillo
Chiclayo
Mt. Huascarán

B R A Z I L

Pôrto Velho
Rondônia
Guajará Mirim
Cobija
Rio Branco
Acre

Caatingas
João Pessoa
Recife ⑮
Campina Grande
Pernambuco
Garanhuns
Maceió

Mato Grosso
Goiás
Barreiras
Bahía
Aracaju
Salvador
Ilhéus

LA PAZ
BOLIVIA ⑰
Lake Titicaca
Cochabamba
Santa Cruz
SUCRE
Oruro
Potosí
Arequipa

Cuiabá
Distrito Federal
Goiânia
BRASÍLIA
Anápolis
Uberlândia
Belo Horizonte
Governador Valadares
Vitória

Brazilian Highlands

PARA-GUAY ⑱
ASUNCIÓN
Mato Grosso do Sul
Campo Grande
São Paulo
Campinas
Rio de Janeiro
Santos
Niterói
Campos

Tropic of Capricorn
Trindade I. (Braz.)
Martin Vaz Is. (Braz.)

CHILE ⑯
Antofagasta
Atacama Desert
Copiapó
La Serena
Valparaíso
SANTIAGO
Talca
Concepción
Temuco
Valdivia
Osorno
Puerto Montt
Chiloé I.

Tucumán
Salta
Córdoba
Mendoza
Rosario
BUENOS AIRES ⑲
ARGENTINA
MONTEVIDEO ⑳
URUGUAY
River Plate
Mar del Plata
Bahía Blanca
Neuquén
Viedma
Gulf of San Matías
Rawson

Pampa

ATLANTIC
OCEAN

Falkland Islands (U.K.)
Stanley

Puerto Aisén
Gulf of San Jorge
Puerto Deseado
Río Gallegos
Strait of Magellan
Punta Arenas
Tierra del Fuego
Cape Horn

South Georgia (U.K.)

MILLER'S BIPOLAR PROJECTION

500   1000 km
200 400   600 miles
1 hour

107

F   60°   G   55°   H   50°   J   45°   K

Bangkok

SAINT LUCIA
CASTRIES
SAINT
VINCENT
KINGSTOWN   BRIDGETOWN
BARBADOS
GRENADA
SAINT GEORGE'S

Lesser Antilles

Porlamar
PORT OF
SPAIN
Tobago
TRINIDAD
AND TOBAGO
Trinidad
San Fernando

A T L A N T I C

1

umaná
la Cruz
lona
Maturín
gre
Ciudad
uayana
Santo Tomé
de Guayana

*Mouths of
the Orinoco*

Morawhanna
Mabaruma
Upata

O C E A N

10°

Guasipati
Tumeremo
El Dorado

Arakaka
Charity
Towakaima
Suddie

*Represa
Raúl Leoni*

New Wellington
New Amsterdam
Nieuw Nickerie
Totness

GEORGETOWN
Parika Wellington
Rosignol
Bartica
New Amsterdam

PARAMARIBO
Nieuw Amsterdam

2

LA

La Gran
Sabana
Roraima
2810
Chiniduik
Depósito

Issano
Mehla
Kamaria Falls
*Churún Merú
(Angel Falls)*

Albina
Paramacca
Kwakoegron
Avanavero Brokopondo
Gurupa

Iracoubo
Sinnamary
Kourou
Saint-Élie
Ile du Diable (Devil's Island)
Cayenne
Guisanbourg
Cabo Orange

5°

GUYANA
SURINAM
Lethem
Dadanawa
Isherton

Julianatop
1280

Maripasoula

**French
Guiana**

Oiapoque
Vila Velha
Cunani

Boa Vista

Guiana

Highlands

Ilha de
Maracá

Roraima
Caracaraí
Vista-Alegre

co Rondón
1789

Catrimani

Serra Acaraí
Northern Perimeter
Highway

Jarapi
Serra do Navio
Amapá

Regina
Amapá
Cabo Norte

*Mouths of
the Amazon*

3

0°

Vila Conceição
Boiaçu

Uatumã
Oriximiná
Óbidos
Almeirim
Gurupá

Ferreira Gomes
Pôrto Grande
Macapá
Pôrto Santana
Chaves
Soure
Curuçá
Salinópolis

Ilha
de Marajó
Capanema
Bragança

ga
Río Negro
Barcelos
Carvoeiro
Moura
Airão

Jatapu
Faro

Serra do
Parintins
Santarém
Pôrto
de Moz
Breves
Cametá

Belém
Vigia
Abaetetuba
Irituia
Camiranga
Santa
Helena
Alcântara

Ururupu
4

Manaus
Manacapuru
Maués
Itacoatiara

Trans-Amazon
Highway
Altamira
Belo Monte
Tucuruí
Baião
Cajuapara
Pinheiro
Turi
Coroatá

São Luís
Rosário

Brazzaville

bufari
ndes
a s

Borba

Itaituba
Jacareacanga
Pimental

Tapajós
Iriri
Xingu

Remanso
Jatobal
Cajuapara
Bacabal

Pindaré Mirim

Presidente
Dutra
Graiaú

5°

B
R
A
Z
I
L
P
a
r
á

Belo Horizonte
Entre Rios

Marabá
Araguatins
Imperatriz
Barra do
Corda

Maranhão
Pastos Bons
Loreto

Flor[ano

Santa Maria
dos Marmelos
Humaitá

Serra do Cachimbo
Prainha

São Félix do Xingu
Xambioá
Araguaína
Carolina
Balsas

Bertolínia
Uruçuí

Canto
do Burití
Bom Jesus

5

ôrto Velho
Jamari
aná
Cariitianas
Nova Vida

Aripuanã
Barracão
do Barreto
Cachimbo

Conceição
do Araguaia
Araguacema
Pau d'Arco

Serra dos Gradaús

Pedro Afonso
Lizarda

Gilbués
Canela
Santa
Filomena

Redenção
da Gurguéia
Parnaguá

Prisão Arcado
Barra
do Ibiapaba

6

ndônia
Rondônia
Pimenta Bueno
Vilhena

Serra do Tombador
Nhamunpará

Cachimbo

Serra Formosa
Piara Açu

Serra do Roncador

Porto Nacional
Natividade
Taguatinga

Peixe
Alvorado
São Miguel
do Araguaia

Goiás

Natal
Corrente

Angical
Barreiras
Corrente

Cariparé
Ibotirama
Bom Jesus
da Lapa

Bahia

Serra dos Parecis

Jaurú
Ubiratí
Lucas
Pôrto Artur

São Félix
Gurupí

Aruanã
Aragarças
Arraias

Correntina

Mato Grosso

oot = 0,30 m
eter = 3,28 feet

Scale 1:20 000 000

0   200   400   600   800   1000 km

0   200   400   600 miles

1 hour

109

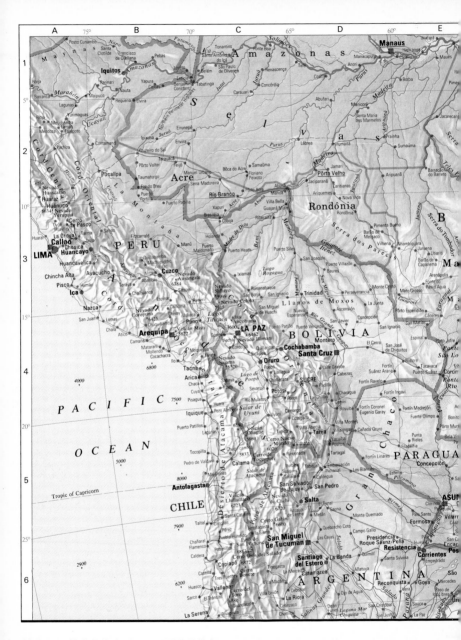

Brazzaville

Santarém
Vitória
Altamira   Belo Monte
Baião
Pinheiro
São Luís
Rosário
Barreirinhas
Primeira Cruz
Granja
Camocim
Acaraú
♦ 4000

Altamira
hway
Iriri
Tucuruí
Pindaré Mirim
Mirim
Coroatá
Urbano
Santos
Brejo
Tianguá
Ipu
Sobral
Pacujá
Fortaleza
Pacatuba

Belo Horizonte
Marabá
Jatobal
Açailândia
Bacabal
Campo Maior
Pirapirau
Piripiri
Coité
Crateús
Senador
Pompeu
Quixadá
Baturité
Aracati
Areia Branca
Macau
Cabo de
São Roque

MARANHÃO
Imperatriz
Barra do
Corda
Grajaú
Presidente
Dutra
Parnarama
TERESINA
PIAUÍ
Elesbão
Veloso
Valença
do Piauí
Picos
Simplício
Mendes
Paulistana
Aroeiras
Frecheirinha
Ouricuri
RIO GRANDE
DO NORTE
NATAL
Nova Cruz

Serra dos Carajás
São Félix do Xingu
Araguacema
Pastos Bons
Floriano
Campo Maior
Oeiras
São João
do Piauí
Petrolina
PERNAMBUCO
Arcoverde
Serra Talhada
Limoeiro
Garanhuns
Palmeira dos
Índios
CARUARU
Caruaru
Serpina
OLINDA
RECIFE

A Z I L
Conceição
do Araguaia
Pedro Afonso
Canela
Barreiras
Remanso
São Raimundo
Rajada
Paulo Afonso
ALAGOAS
Arapiraca
Propriá
Penedo
MACEIÓ

CAMPOS
GOIÁS
Serra dos Gradaús
Serra do Estrondo
Serra do Roncador
Porto Nacional
Natividade
Gurupi
Peixe
Paranã
São Domingos
Correntina
Bahía
BAHIA
Bom Jesus
da Lapa
Paramirim
Feira de
Santana
Alagoinhas
Candeias
SALVADOR
SERGIPE
ARACAJU

osso
Ministro
João Alberto
Pindaba
Rio das Mortes
São Miguel
do Araguaia
Aruanã
Taguatinga
Arraias
Correntina
Caetité
Brumado
Jequié
Vitória da
Conquista
Itabuna
ILHÉUS
3600

rosso
Araguaiana
Goiás
Inhumas
BRASÍLIA
Distrito Federal
Planalto
Central
São Roman
Montes
Claros
Planalto
do Brasil
Canavieiras
Belmonte

Guiratinga
Iporá
GOIÂNIA
Anápolis
Hidrolândia
Jandaia
Rio Verde
Itumbiara
Patos de
Minas
Diamantina
Teófilo Otoni
MINAS GERAIS
Nanuque
Prado
Ponta da Baleia
30

ondonópolis
Alto Garças
Mineiros
Catalão
Araguari
UBERLÂNDIA
Araxá
Sete
Lagoas
Coronel
Fabriciano
GOVERNADOR
VALADARES
Espírito Santo
Linhares

Cuiabá
Verde
Mato Grosso
Cachoeira Alta
UBERABA
Divinópolis
BELO HORIZONTE
Caratinga
VITÓRIA
Vila Velha

CAMPO
GRANDE
Fernandópolis
Três Lagoas
SÃO JOSÉ DO
RIO PRÊTO
Catanduva
Franca
RIBEIRÃO PRÊTO
Passos
Consolação
Nova
Ubá
Moriaé
Cachoeiro de Itapemirim
Itaperuna

ourados
Presidente
Prudente
Araçatuba
Lins
Tupã
Marília
Jaú
Poços de
Caldas
Varginha
NOVA
IGUAÇU
Juiz de
Fora
Petrópolis
Campos

uarama
Maringá
Cruzeiro
do Oeste
Londrina
Bauru
PIRACICABA
CAMPINAS
Jundiaí
VOLTA
REDONDA
Niterói
Rio de Janeiro
Cabo Frio

Paraná
Cascavel
SÃO PAULO
SANTO ANDRÉ
São Vicente
Santos
SÃO JOSÉ DOS
Campos
São Sebastião
RIO DE JANEIRO

Foz do
Iguaçu
Ponta Grossa
CURITIBA
São Francisco do Sul
Joinville
Itajaí
Brusque
ATLANTIC OCEAN
Tropic of Capricorn

Santa Catarina
Blumenau
FLORIANÓPOLIS
Lajes
2400

Santa Rosa
Carazinho
Passo Fundo
Vacaria
Criciúma
Tubarão

rande do Sul
CAXIAS DO SUL
Novo Hamburgo
São Leopoldo
CANOAS
Cachoeira
do Sul
PÔRTO ALEGRE
4000

Brazzaville
Darwin
Antananarivo
1
5°
2
10°
3
15°
4
20°
5
Tropic of Capricorn
25°
6

= 0,30 m
er = 3,28 feet

Scale 1:20 000 000

0   200   400   600   800   1000 km

0   200   400   600 miles

1 hour

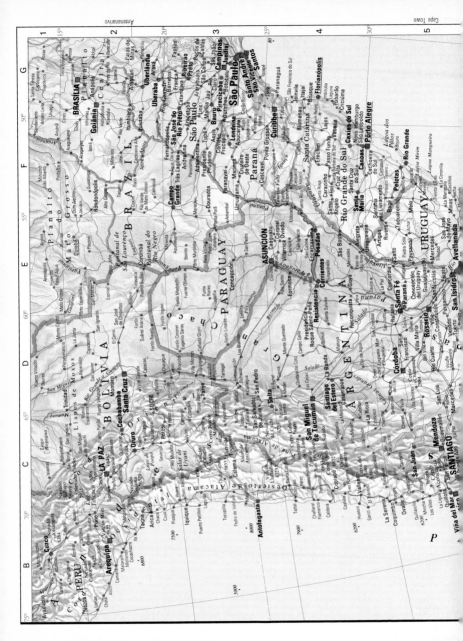

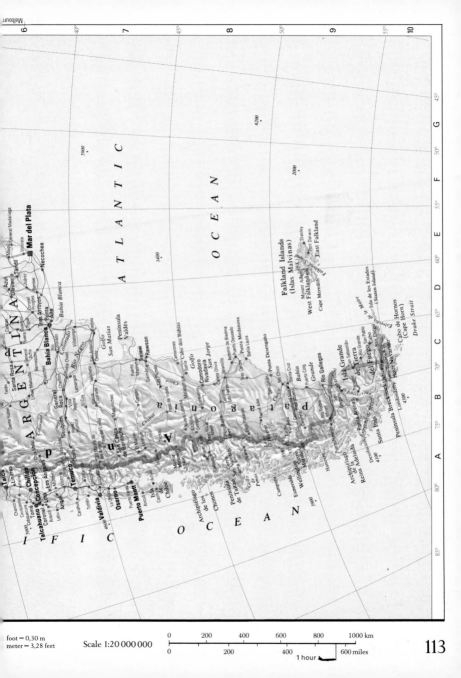

A T L A N T I C

O C E A N

G

F

E

D

C

B

A

45°

50°

55°

60°

65°

70°

75°

80°

85°

Mar del Plata

Necochea

Bahía Blanca

Punta Alta

Tres Arroyos

Azul

Tandil

Olavarría

General Madariaga

ARGENTINA

Santa Rosa

Bahía Blanca

Colorado

Río Negro

Golfo San Matías

Península Valdés

General Roca

Viedma

Telew

Rawson

Golfo San Jorge

Comodoro Rivadavia

Golfo San Jorge

Cabo Tres Puntas

Cabo Blanco

Punta Medanosa

Punta Desengaño

Bahía Grande

Río Gallegos

Puerto Santa Cruz

5900

1400

6200

2000

Falkland Islands
(Islas Malvinas)

Stanley

West Falkland

East Falkland

Mount Adam

Port Darwin

Cape Meredith

Estrecho de Magallanes

Isla Grande
de Tierra
del Fuego

Río Grande

Cabo San Pablo

Cabo San Diego

Isla de los Estados
(Staten Island)

Cabo de Hornos
(Cape Horn)

Drake Strait

Talca

Linares

Chillán

Concepción

Talcahuano

Tomé

Coronel

Los Ángeles

Temuco

Valdivia

Osorno

Puerto Montt

Chiloé

Archipiélago de los Chonos

Península de Taitao

Golfo de Penas

Wellington

Archipiélago de la Reina Adelaida

Punta Arenas

Península Brecknock

Ushuaia

Navarino

4600

5000

4100

4300

3900

P A C I F I C

O C E A N

foot = 0,30 m
meter = 3,28 feet

Scale 1:20 000 000

0   200   400   600   800   1000 km

0   200   400   600 miles

1 hour

113

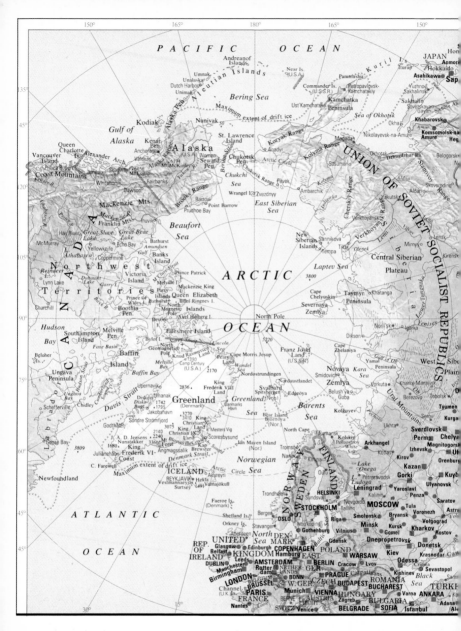

1 foot = 0,30 m
1 meter = 3,28 feet

Scale 1:60 000 000

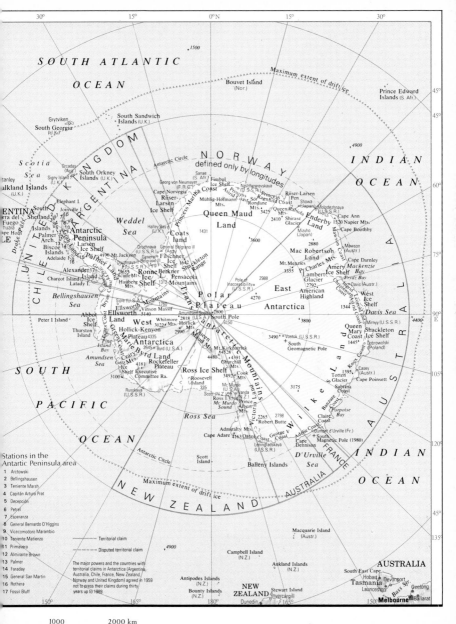

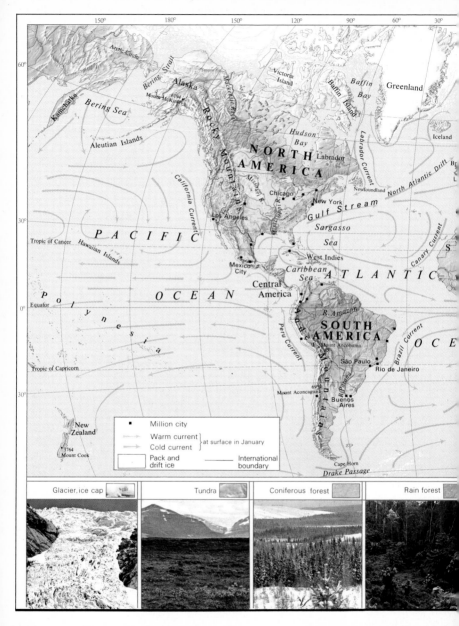

Million city

Warm current ⎤
                 ⎬ at surface in January
Cold current ⎦

Pack and   International
drift ice   boundary

Glacier, ice cap

Tundra

Coniferous forest

Rain forest

116   THE WORLD

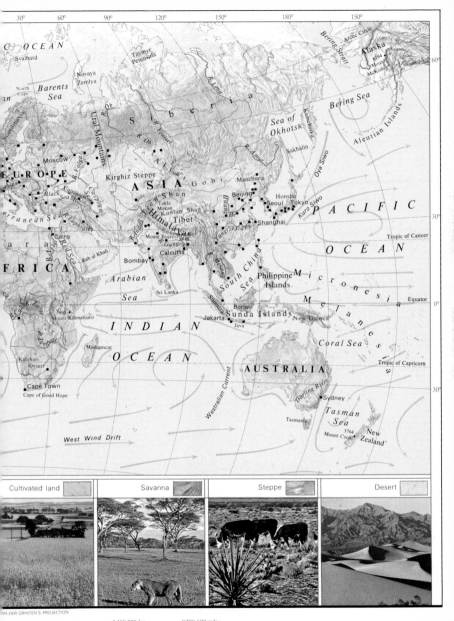

30°   60°   90°   120°   150°   180°   150°

C OCEAN
Svalbard
North Cape

Barents Sea

Taymyr Peninsula

Bering Strait
Arctic Circle
Alaska
6194
Mount McKinley

60°

Novaya Zemlya

R. Lena

EUROPE

Ural Mountains

S i b e r i a

Bering Sea

Moscow

R. Ob

R. Yenisei

Sea of Okhotsk

Aleutian Islands

Kirghiz Steppe

A S I A

Gobi

Manchuria

Sakhalin

Oya Siwo

Black Sea

Caucasus

Caspian Sea

R. Volga

Altai

Shan

Beijing
Seoul
Honshu
Tokyo

Kuro Siwo

PACIFIC

Mediterranean Sea

R. Tigris
R. Euphrates

Takla Makan
Kunlun Shan

Tibet

Yangtze Kiang

Shanghai

30°

Cairo

R. Indus

R. Ganges

Himalayas

Mount Everest

Hwang-ho

OCEAN

Tropic of Cancer

Red Sea

Rub al Khali

Bombay

Calcutta

Arabian

Mekong

South China Sea

M i c r o n e s i a

AFRICA

Sea

Sri Lanka

Philippine Islands

Equator

R. Congo

R. Zaire

Mount Kilimanjaro

Sumatra

Borneo

Jakarta Sunda Islands
Java

New Guinea

M e l a n e s i a

0°

INDIAN

Madagascar

OCEAN

Coral Sea

Tropic of Capricorn

Kalahari Desert

AUSTRALIA

30°

Cape Town
Cape of Good Hope

West Wind Drift

West Australian Current

Darling River

Sydney

Tasman Sea

Tasmania

3764
Mount Cook

New Zealand

Cultivated land	Savanna	Steppe	Desert

AN DER GRINTEN'S PROJECTION

cale 1:180 000 000
: the equator

0 0 400 800 km
30°
60° 200 600 1000 km

0 0 200 600 miles
30°
60° 100 300 500 miles

117

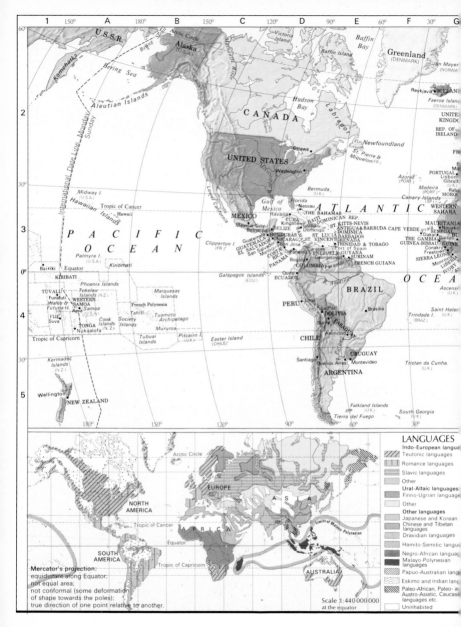

LANGUAGES

Indo-European langua
- Teutonic languages
- Romance languages
- Slavic languages
- Other

Ural-Altaic languages
- Finno-Ugrian language
- Other

Other languages
- Japanese and Korean
- Chinese and Tibetan languages
- Dravidian languages
- Hamito-Semitic langua
- Negro-African langua
- Malayo-Polynesian languages
- Papuo-Australian langua
- Eskimo and Indian lang
- Paleo-African, Paleo- a Austro-Asiatic, Caucas languages etc.
- Uninhabited

Mercator's projection:
equidistant along Equator;
not equal area;
not conformal (some deformation of shape towards the poles);
true direction of one point relative to another.

Scale 1:440 000 000
at the equator

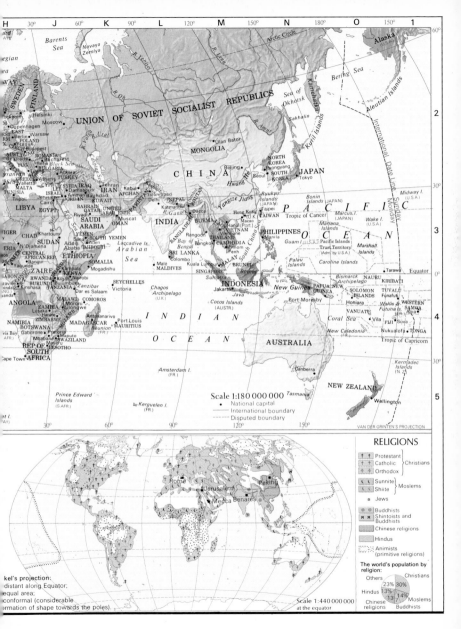

H 30° J 60° K 90° L 120° M 150° N 180° O 150° I

Barents Sea
Novaya Zemlya
Arctic Circle
Alaska
Kamchatka
Bering Sea
Aleutian Islands
International Date Line
Sunday

SWEDEN FINLAND
Helsinki
Moscow
Copenhagen
Warsaw POLAND
Berlin
Prague
Budapest
ROMANIA
Belgrade
Bucharest
YUG.
BULGARIA
Black Sea
Athens
Ankara TURKEY
MALTA
TUNISIA
Tripoli

R. Yenisey
R. Lena
R. Ob
UNION OF SOVIET SOCIALIST REPUBLICS
R. Volga R. Ural
R. Amur
Sea of Okhotsk
Sakhalin
Kuril Islands

Sea of Japan
Ulan Bator
MONGOLIA
CHINA
Beijing
Hwang Ho
NORTH KOREA
Pyongyang
SOUTH Seoul
KOREA
Tokyo JAPAN
Ryukyu Islands (JAPAN)
Bonin Islands (JAPAN)
Midway I. (U.S.A.)

LIBYA EGYPT
Cairo
Alexandria
SYRIA IRAQ
IRAN
Tehran
Kabul
AFGHAN.
Islamabad
Delhi
NEPAL
Katmandu
BHUTAN
Yangtze Jiang
Hong Kong (U.K.)
Macao (Port.)
TAIWAN
Taipei
Tropic of Cancer
Marcus I. (JAPAN)
Wake I. (U.S.A.)

PACIFIC

ISRAEL
Jerusalem
Amman Baghdad
JORDAN
KUWAIT
BAHRAIN
QATAR
Riyadh
SAUDI ARABIA
UNITED ARAB EMIRATES
Muscat
OMAN
R. Ganges
Dacca
BANGLADESH
BURMA
Rangoon
Mandalay (Port.)
Hanoi
VIETNAM
Vientiane
LAOS
Manila
PHILIPPINES
Guam (U.S.A.)
Mariana Islands
Pacific Islands (Trust Territory Adm. by U.S.A.)
Marshall Islands

OCEAN

NIGER CHAD
SUDAN
Khartoum
N'Djamena
CENTRAL AFRICAN REP.
Bangui
Yaoundé
SOUTH YEMEN
YEMEN
Aden
Arabian Sea
INDIA
Bombay
Laccadive Is. (India)
SRI LANKA
Colombo
Malé
MALDIVES
THAILAND
Bangkok
CAMBODIA
Phnom Penh
South China Sea
MALAY
SINGAPORE
BRUNEI
Kuala Lumpur
Borneo
Palau Islands
Caroline Islands

ETHIOPIA
Addis Ababa
SOMALIA
Mogadishu
ZAIRE
Kinshasa
KENYA
Nairobi
UGANDA
RWANDA
Kigali
BURUNDI
Bujumbura
TANZANIA
Dar es Salaam
Zanzibar
SEYCHELLES
Victoria
Chagos Archipelago (U.K.)
INDONESIA
Jakarta
Sumatra
Java
Cocos Islands (AUSTR.)
New Guinea
PAPUA NEW GUINEA
Port Moresby
Bismarck Archipelago
NAURU
SOLOMON ISLANDS
Honiara
KIRIBATI
Tarawa
TUVALU
Equator

ANGOLA
Luanda
ZAMBIA
MALAWI
COMOROS
Moroni
Lusaka
Harare
ZIMBABWE
NAMIBIA
BOTSWANA
Gaborone
MADAGASCAR
Antananarivo
Réunion (FR.)
Port Louis
MAURITIUS
Coral Sea
VANUATU
Vila
New Caledonia (FR.)
FIJI
Suva
WESTERN SAMOA
Wallis & Futuna Is. (FR.)
Nukualofa
TONGA
Tropic of Capricorn

INDIAN

Maputo
SWAZILAND
Mbabane
LESOTHO
Maseru
REP. OF SOUTH AFRICA
Cape Town

OCEAN

AUSTRALIA
Canberra

Amsterdam I. (FR.)
Kerguelen I. (FR.)
Prince Edward Islands (S. AFR.)

Scale 1:180 000 000
• National capital
— International boundary
--- Disputed boundary

Tasmania
Kermadec Islands (N.Z.)
NEW ZEALAND
Wellington

VAN DER GRINTEN'S PROJECTION

30° 60° 90° 120° 150°

Rome
Jerusalem
Mecca Benares
Peking

...kel's projection:
...distant along Equator;
...equal area;
...conformal (considerable
...formation of shape towards the poles).

Scale 1:440 000 000
at the equator

RELIGIONS

† † Protestant
† † Catholic — Christians
† † Orthodox

☾ ☾ Sunnite — Moslems
☾ ☾ Shiite

✡ Jews

☸ ☸ Buddhists

卍 卍 Shintoists and Buddhists

Chinese religions

Hindus

Animists (primitive religions)

The world's population by religion:
Others
23% 30% Christians
Hindus 13%
13% 14% Moslems
Chinese religions
Buddhists

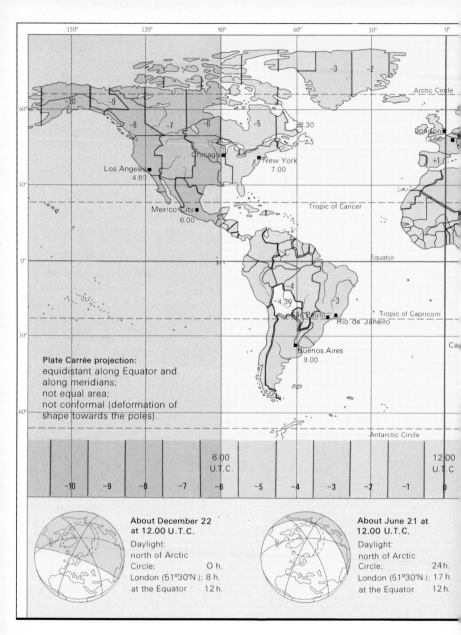

Plate Carrée projection:
equidistant along Equator and
along meridians;
not equal area;
not conformal (deformation of
shape towards the poles).

| -10 | -9 | -8 | -7 | -6 | -5 | -4 | -3 | -2 | -1 | 0 |

6.00 U.T.C.

12.00 U.T.C.

About December 22
at 12.00 U.T.C.

Daylight:
north of Arctic
Circle;   0 h.
London (51°30'N.); 8 h.
at the Equator   12 h.

About June 21 at
12.00 U.T.C.

Daylight:
north of Arctic
Circle;   24 h.
London (51°30'N.); 17 h.
at the Equator   12 h.

120   TIME ZONES

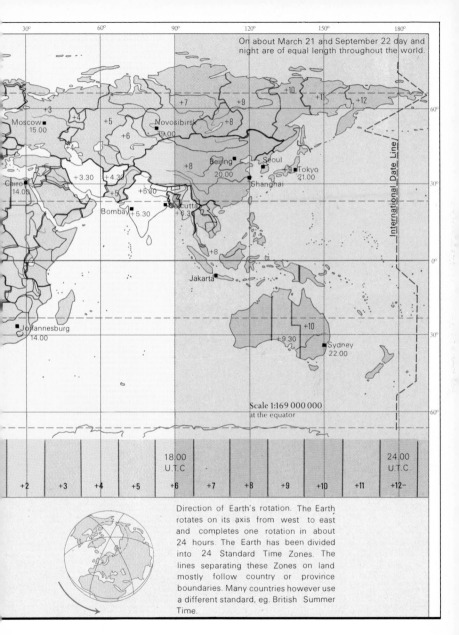

On about March 21 and September 22 day and night are of equal length throughout the world.

30°   60°   90°   120°   150°   180°

+3

Moscow
15.00

+4

+5

+6

Novosibirsk
9.00

+7

+9

+10

+11

+12

+8

+4

+3.30

+4.30

Beijing
20.00

Seoul

Tokyo
21.00

+9

Shanghai

Cairo
14.00

+5

+5.30

Calcutta
+6.30

Bombay
+5.30

+8

Jakarta

Johannesburg
14.00

+10

+9.30

Sydney
22.00

International Date Line

Scale 1:169 000 000
at the equator

60°

30°

0°

30°

60°

18.00
U.T.C.

24.00
U.T.C.

+2   +3   +4   +5   +6   +7   +8   +9   +10   +11   +12−

Direction of Earth's rotation. The Earth rotates on its axis from west to east and completes one rotation in about 24 hours. The Earth has been divided into 24 Standard Time Zones. The lines separating these Zones on land mostly follow country or province boundaries. Many countries however use a different standard, eg. British Summer Time.

121

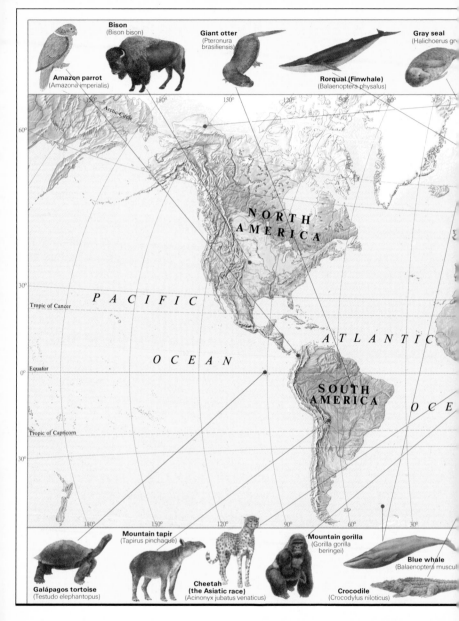

Amazon parrot
(Amazona imperialis)

Bison
(Bison bison)

Giant otter
(Pteronura brasiliensis)

Rorqual (Finwhale)
(Balaenoptera physalus)

Gray seal
(Halichoerus gr

Galápagos tortoise
(Testudo elephantopus)

Mountain tapir
(Tapirus pinchaque)

Cheetah
(the Asiatic race)
(Acinonyx jubatus venaticus)

Mountain gorilla
(Gorilla gorilla beringei)

Blue whale
(Balaenoptera muscul

Crocodile
(Crocodylus niloticus)

ian rhinoceros
(noceros unicornis)

**Ounce
(Snow leopard)**
(Panthera unica)

Walrus
(Odobenus rosmarus)

Giant panda
(Ailuropoda melanoleuca)

Orangutan
(Pongo pygmaeus)

Arctic Circle

ARCTIC OCEAN

EUROPE

ASIA

PACIFIC

Tropic of Cancer

OCEAN

AFRICA

Equator

INDIAN

OCEAN

AUSTRALIA

Tropic of Capricorn

Aye-aye
(Daubentonia
madagascariensis)

Arabian oryx
(Oryx leucoryx)

Tiger
(Leo tigris)

Tasmanian wolf
(Thylacinus cynocephalus)

Kiwi
(Apteryx australis)

VAN DER GRINTEN'S PROJECTION

Scale 1:180 000 000

123

INDEX

A

Aachen 52 E 4
Aalen 53 F 5
Aa Sumayh 92 D 3
Aba 91 F 4
Abaco Island 105 G 2
Abadab, Jabal 88 F 5
Ābādān 61 E 3
Ābādeh 61 F 3
Abadla 86 E 2
Abaetetuba 109 J 4
Abagnar Qi 71 G 2
Abaiang 82 C 2
Abakaliki 91 F 4
Abakan 68 F 5
Abalak 91 F 2
Abancay 110 B 3
Abant Silsilesi 58 D 2
Abariringa 82 D 3
Abarqu 61 F 3
Abarqu, Kavir-e 61 F 3
Abatskoye 63 O 4
Abay 63 O 6
Abaza 68 F 5
Abbai 92 F 2
Abbāsābād 61 G 1
Abbeville 56 D 1
Abbot Ice Shelf 115
'Abd al Kūrī 93 J 2
Abdulino 62 K 5
Abéché 91 J 3
Abemama 82 C 2
Abengourou 90 D 4
Abeokuta 90 E 4
Aberdeen (S.D., U.S.A.)
    102 G 2
Aberdeen (U.K.) 52 C 3
Aberdeen Lake 99 RS 3
Aberystwyth 52 C 4
Abhā' 89 G 5
Abhar 61 E 1
Abidjan 90 CD 4
Abilene 102 FG 5
Abkit 69 T 3
Åbo 55 H 3
Abong Abong, Gunung
    74 A 3
Abong Mbang 91 G 5
Abrantes 56 B 4
'Abri 88 E 4
Abruzzo 57 F 3
Abū ad Duhūr 60 B 2
Abū al Bukhush 61 F 4
Abū 'Alī 61 E 4
Abu Dhabi 61 FG 4
Abufari 109 F 5
Abū Ḩadrīyah 66 D 5
Abū Ḩamad 88 E 5
Abū Jifān 61 E 4
Abū Kamāl 60 C 2

Abū Maṭariq 88 D 6
Abū Mūsa' 61 G 4
Abunā (Brazil) 110 C 3
Abūqrīn 87 J 2
Abū Qumayyis, Ra's 61 F 4
Abu Road 72 B 3
Abū Sunbul 88 E 4
Abuya Myeda 93 FG 2
Abū Ẓaby 89 J 4
Abū Ẓaby (United Arab
    Emirates) 61 FG 4
Abū Zanīmah 60 A 3
Abyad, Ra's al 60 BC 5
Abyār 'Alī 60 C 4
Abydos 88 E 3
Ábyek 61 F 2
Açailândia 109 J 4
Acaponeta 104 AB 3
Acapulco 104 B 4
Acarai, Serra 109 G 3
Acaraú 111 HJ 1
Acari 111 J 2
Acarigua 108 E 2
Accomac 103 L 4
Accra 90 DE 4
Achao 113 B 7
Achar 112 E 5
Achayvayam 69 VW 3
Achelóos 58 B 3
Achinsk 68 F 4
Acklins Island 105 H 3
Aconcagua, Cerro 112 BC 5
Acorizal 110 E 3–4
Acre (Brazil) 108 D 5
Acre (Brazil) 110 C 3
Acre (Israel) 60 B 2
Acri 57 G 4
Adaba 93 F 3
Adak (AK, U.S.A.) 98 B 5
Adak (Sweden) 54 G 2
'Adale 93 H 4
Adam, Mount 113 DE 9
Adamantina 111 F 5
Adamaoua 91 G 4
Adams Bridge 72 CD 6
Adamstown 83 G 4
Adana 60 B 1
Adapazari 58 D 2
Adare, Cape 115
Adavale 79 GH 4
Aḑ Ḑafrah 61 F 5
Ad Dahnā' 61 DE 4
Ad Dammām 61 EF 4
Ad Dār al Hamrā' 66 B 5
Ad Darb 89 G 5
Ad Dawādimī 60 D 4
Ad Dawḩah 61 F 4
Ad Dawr 60 D 2
Ad Dayr 60 A 4
Ad Dibdibah 61 E 3

Ad Dilam 61 E 5
Ad Dindar 88 E 6
Addis Ababa 93 F 3
Addis Zemen 93 F 2
Ad Diwanīyah 61 D 3
Ad Duwaym 88 E 6
Adelaide Island 115
Adelaide Peninsula 99 S 2
Adelaide River 78 E 1
Adélie Coast 115
Aden 89 H 6
Adige 57 F 2
Adıgüzel Barajı 58 C 3
Adirondack Mountains
    103 M 3
Adi Ugri 93 F 2
Adıyaman 59 E 3
Admiralty 98 L 4
Admiralty Islands 80 E 2
Admiralty Mountains 115
Ado 90 E 4
Ado Ekiti 91 F 4
Adok 92 E 3
Adrano 57 F 4
Adrar 86 E 3
Adrar des Iforas 90 E 1–2
Adré 91 J 3
Adriatic Sea 57 FG 3
Adwa 93 F 2
Adzhar 59 F 2
Adzopé 90 D 4
Aegean Sea 58 C 3
Afao, Mont 87 G 3
Afghanistan 67 GH 4
Afif 60 D 4–5
Afikpo 91 F 4
Afmadōw 93 G 4
Afognak 98 G 4
African Islands 93 J 5
Afyonkarahisar 58 D 3
Agabah, Khalij al 60 B 3
Agadez 91 F 2
Agadir 86 CD 2
Agana 82 A 2
Agapitovo 63 R 2
Agartala 73 F 3
Agata 68 F 2
Agats 75 J 5
Agattu 98 A 5
Agawa Bay 100 L 6
Agboville 90 CD 4
Agdary 68 L 3
Agen 56 D 3
Agepsta 59 F 2
Agha Jārī 61 EF 3
Agordat 93 F 1
Agra 72 C 2
Ağrı 59 F 3
Agrigento 57 F 4
Agrihan 82 A 1

Agrinion 58 B 3
Agto 101 R 2
Água Clara 111 F 5
Aguadulce 108 BC 2
Águas Formosas 111 HJ 4
Agulhas, Cape 94 C 6
Aguscalientes 104 B 3
Ahaggar 87 FG 4
Ahe 83 F 3
Ahmadabad 72 B 3
Ahmadnagar 72 BC 4
Ahome 102 E 6
Ähtävänjoki 54 H 3
Ahvāz 61 E 3
Ahvenanmaa 55 GH 3
Ahwar 89 H 6
Aihui 69 N 6
Ailinginae 82 BC 2
Ailinglapalap 82 C 2
Aillik 101 Q 4
Ailuk 82 C 2
Aim 69 O 4
Ain Amenas 87 G 3
Ain Amguel 87 FG 4
Aïn Beïda 87 G 1
Aïn Ezzane 87 H 4
Aïn Tiguelguemine 87 F 3
Aïoun el Atrouss 86 D 5
Aïr 91 F 2
Airao 109 F 4
Aitape 80 D 2
Aitutaki 83 E 4
Aix-en-Provence 57 DE 3
Aiyaion Pélagos 58 C 3
Aizuwakamatsu 71 M 3
Ajaccio 57 E 3
Aj Bogd Uul 70 BC 2
'Ajmān 61 G 4
Ajmer 72 B 2
Ajo, Cabo de 56 C 3
Akademii, Zaliv 69 P 5
Ak Dağ 58 C 3
Akespe 66 G 1
Akharnai 58 B 3
Akhisar 58 C 3
Akhtubinsk 62 J 6
Akhtyrka 62 FG 5
Akimiski 101 L 5
Akita 71 L 3
Akkabok 67 G 1
Akkajaure 54 G 2
'Akko 60 B 2
Aklavik 98 K 2
Akmenrags 55 H 4
Akobo 92 E 3
Akola 72 C 3
Akosombo Dam 90 E 4
Akpatok 101 O 3
Åkra Akritas 58 B 3
Akra Arnauti 60 A 2

Ákra Maleás **58** B 3
Ákra Spátha **58** B 3
Ákra Taínaron **58** B 3
Akritas, Ákra **58** B 3
Akron **103** K 3
Aksaray **59** D 3
Aksay Kazakzu Zizhixian **70** B 3
Aksehir **58** D 3
Aksha **68** K 5
Akshiy **67** G 1
Aksu (China) **67** L 2
Aksu (Turkey) **58** D 3
Aktash **67** H 3
Aktasty **63** M 5
Aktogay **63** P 6
Aktyubinsk **63** L 5
Akure **91** F 4
Akureyri **54** B 2
Ala, Monti di **57** E 3
Alabama **103** J 5
Alabama River **103** J 5
Al Abyaḍ, Ra's **87** G 1
Alaçam Dağları **58** C 3
Alachakh **69** P 4
Aladağ **59** F 3
Alagoas **111** J 2
Alagoinhas **111** J 3
Alagon **56** C 3
Alajuela **104** F 5
Alakurtti **54** K 2
Al 'Alamayn **88** D 2
Al Amādīyah **60** D 1
Alamagan **82** A 1
Al 'Amārah **61** E 3
Alamogordo **102** E 5
Alamos **102** E 6
Ålands hav **55** G 3–4
Alanya **59** D 3
Alaotra, Lac **95** H 3
Alapayevsk **63** M 4
Al' Aqabah **60** B 3
Al 'Aqaylah **87** J 2
Al 'Arabiyah as Su'udiyah **60** CD 4
Al'Arabiyah as Su'udiyah **89** GH 4
Al 'Arīsh **60** A 3
Al 'Armah **61** DE 4
Al Arṭāwīyah **61** D 4
Al 'Āshūrīyah **66** C 4
Alaska **98** FH 2
Alaska Peninsula **98** E 4
Alaska Range **98** GH 3
Alatyr' **62** J 5
Al 'Awaynāt **87** H 3
Al'Awsajīyah **60** D 4
Al 'Ayn **61** G 4
Alazani **59** G 2
Alba **57** E 3
Al Bāb **60** B 1
Albacete **56** C 4
Al Badi' **89** H 4
Al Bahrah **61** E 3
Al Baḥr al Mayyit **60** B 3
Alba Iulia **58** B 1
Albanel, Lac **101** N 5
Albania **58** AB 2

Albano Laziale **57** F 3
Albany (Australia) **78** B 5
Albany (GA, U.S.A.) **103** K 5
Albany (N.Y., U.S.A.) **103** M 3
Albany (Ontario, Can.) **100** L 5
Al Barkāt **87** H 4
Al Basrah **61** E 3
Al Batin **61** E 3
Al Bāṭinah **89** K 4
Albatross Point **81** Q 8
Al Bayḍā' **87** K 2
Alberta **99** OP 5
Albert Nile **92** E 4
Albertville **57** E 2
Albi **56** D 3
Al Bid' **60** B 3
Albina **109** H 2
Al Bi'r **60** B 3
Al Birkah **66** C 6
Alborán **56** C 4
Ålborg **55** F 4
Al Brayqah **87** JK 3
Albu Ali **59** F 4
Al Buḥayrah al Murrah al Kubrā **60** A 3
Albuquerque **102** E 4–5
Albury **79** H 6
Alcalá **56** C 3
Alcalá **56** B 4
Alcántara **109** K 4
Alcántara, Embalse de **56** B 4
Alcaraz, Sierra de **56** C 4
Alcázar de San Juan **56** C 4
Alciéni **91** G 6
Alcira **56** C 4
Alcolea del Pinar **56** C 3
Alcoy **56** C 4
Aldabra Islands **93** H 6
Aldan **69** O 3
Aldan **69** N 4
Aldanskoye Nagor'ye **69** MN 4
Aleg **86** C 5
Alegrete **112** E 4
Aleksandriya (Ukraine, U.S.S.R.) **62** FG 6
Aleksandrovsk **63** M 4
Aleksandrovskiy **68** L 5
Aleksandrovsk-Sakhalinskiy **69** Q 5
Alekseyevka (Kazakhstan, U.S.S.R.) **63** O 5
Alekseyevo **69** R 1
Alençon **56** D 2
Aleppo **60** B 1
Aléria **57** E 3
Alès **56** D 3
Alessandria **57** E 3
Ålestrup **55** E 4
Ålesund **54** E 3
Aleutian Islands **98** AC 4
Aleutian Islands **98** AC 5
Aleutian Range **98** F 4
Alexander Archipelago **98** K 4
Alexander Island **115**
Alexandra **80** PQ 10
Alexandra Falls **99** O 3
Alexandria (Egypt) **88** DE 2

Alexandria (LA, U.S.A.) **103** H 5
Alexandria (MD, U.S.A.) **103** L 4
Alexandria (Romania)**58** BC 2
Alexandroúpolis **58** C 2
Aleysk **63** Q 5
Al Fāshir **88** D 6
Al Fathah **66** C 3
Al Fayyūm **88** DE 3
Al Fuḥayhil **61** E 3
Al Fujayrah **61** G 4
Al Furat **59** F 3–4
Al Fuwayrit **61** F 4
Algama **69** N 4
Alganskaya **69** WX 3
Algarve **56** B 4
Algeciras **56** B 4
Algeria **86–87** EF 3
Al Ghazālah **60** C 4
Alghero **57** E 3
Algiers **87** F 1
Al Hadhālil **60–61** D 3
Al Hadithah **60** CD 2
Al Hamād **60** C 2–3
Al Hamrā' **60** C 5
Al Hanākīyah **60** C 4
Al Haniṣh al Kabir **89** G 6
Al Harrah **60** BC 2
Al Harrah **60** C 3
Al Hasa **60** B 3
Al Hasā' **61** E 4
Al Hasakah **60** C 1
Al Hasan **60** D 2
Al Hawwārī **87** K 4
Al Hayy **61** DE 2
Al Hijāz **88** F 3
Al Hijaz (Saudi Arabia) **60** B 4
Al Hillah **61** D 2
Al Hillah **61** E 5
Al Hudaydah **89** G 6
Al Hufrah **60** BC 3–4
Al Hufūf **61** E 4
Al Hūj **60** C 3
Al Husayhiṣah **88** E 6
Al Huwaymī **89** H 6
Aliābād **61** G 3
Aliákmon **58** B 2
Ali Bayramly **66** DE 3
Alicante **56** C 4
Alice River **79** H 3
Alice Springs **78** E 3
Aligarh **72** C 2
Al Iglim al Janūbīyah **92** DE 3
Aligüdarz **61** E 2
Alijūq, Kūh-e **61** F 3
Al 'Iraq **60** D 2
Al 'Irq **87** K 3
Ali Sabjeh **93** G 2
Al 'Isāwīyah **60** B 3
Al Iskandarīyah **88** DE 2
Aliskerovo **69** U 2
Al Ismā'īlīyah **60** A 3
Aliwal North **94** D 6
Al Jafr **60** B 3
Al Jāfūrah **61** F 4–5
Al Jaghbūb **87** K 3
Al Jahrah **61** E 3

Al Jalāmīd **60** C 3
Al Jawf **60** C 3
Al Jaylī **88** E 5
Al Jazā'ir **87** F 1
Al Jazīrah **59** F 3–4
Al Jiwā' **61** FG 5
Al Jizah **88** DE 2
Al Jubayl **66** DE 5
Al Jubaylah **61** E 4
Al Jumaymah **66** C 5
Al Junaynah **88** C 6
Al Karak **60** B 3
Al Karnak **88** E 3
Al Kāzimīyah **60** D 2
Al Khalīl **60** B 3
Al Khāliṣ **61** D 2
Al Kharijah **88** DE 3
Al Kharj **61** E 5
Al Kharṭūm **88** EF 5
Al Kharṭūm Bahrī **88** EF 5
Al Khaṣab **61** G 4
Al Khidr **61** D 3
Al Khubar **61** F 4
Al Khufayfiyah **61** D 4
Al Khunfah **60** C 3
Al Kir'ānah **61** F 4
Al Kūfah **60** D 2
Al Kumayt **61** E 2–3
Al Kuntillah **60** B 3
Al Kūt **61** D 2
Al Kuwayt **61** E 3
Al Labbah **60** C 3
Al Lādhiqīyah **88** EF 1
Al Lagowa **88** D 6
Allahabad **72** D 2
Allakh-Yun' **69** P 3
Allentown **103** L 3
Alleppey **72** C 6
Al Lifīyah **66** C 4
Al Liṣāfah **66** D 5
Al Lussuf **66** C 4
Alma-Ata **67** K 2
Almada **56** B 4
Al Madīnah **60** C 4
Al Mafraq **60** B 2
Al Mahallah al Kubrā **88** E 2
Al Mahrah **89** J 5
Al Majann **61** F 5
Al Makhaylī **87** K 2
Al Manadir **61** G 5
Al Manāmah **61** F 4
Al Manāqil **88** E 6
Al Manṣūrah **88** E 2
Al Maqṭā' **61** G 4
Al Marj **87** K 2
Al Mawṣil **60** D 1
Al Mayyāh **60** D 4
Almeirim **109** H 4
Almenara **111** HJ 4
Almendra, Embalse de **56** B 3
Almería **56** C 4
Al'met'yevsk **62** K 4–5
Al Minyā **88** DE 3
Almirante Brown **115**
Almoustarat **90** D 2
Al Mubarraz **61** E 4
Al Mudawwarah **60** B 3
Al Mughayrā' **66** B 5

Al Muharraq 61 F 4
Al Mukallā 89 HJ 6
Al Murabbā' 60 D 4
Al Musayjid 66 BC 6
Al Musayyib 60 D 2
Al Muwaylih 60 B 4
Al Nasser 60 A 4
Alofi 82 D 4
Alongshan 69 M 5
Alor, Pulau 75 F 5
Alor Setar 74 AB 2
Alpena 103 K 2
Alphonse 93 J 6
Alpi Carniche 57 F 2
Alpi Dolomitiche 57 F 2
Alpine 102 F 5
Al Qaḍārif 88 F 6
Al Qadimah 89 F 4
Al Qāhirah 88 E 2
Al Qalībah 60 B 3
Al Qāmishli 60 C 1
Al Qanṭarah 60 A 3
Al Qatif 61 E 4
Al Qaṭrāni 60 B 3
Al Qatrūn 87 H 3
Al Qay'īyah 60 D 4
Al Qayrawān 87 GH 1
Al Qaysūmah (Saudi Arabia)
   66 C 5
Al Qaysūmah (Saudi Arabia)
   66 D 5
Al Qunaytirah 60 B 2
Al Qunfudhah 89 FG 5
Al Qurayyah 88 F 3
Al Qurnah 61 E 3
Al Qusayr 60 B 4
Al Qūṣūrīyah 60 D 5
Al Quṭayfah 60 B 2
Al Quwārah 66 C 5
Al Quwayīyah 61 D 4
Al Shagra 61 F 4
Altamira 109 H 4
Altamont 102 B 3
Alta Shany 67 M 1
Altay (China) 67 M 1
Altay (Mongolia) 68 G 6
Altay (U.S.S.R.) 63 RS 5
Altiplanicie Mexicana
   104 AB 2
Altmark 53 F 4
Alto - Alentejo 56 B 4
Alto Garças 111 F 4
Alton 103 H 4
Alto Parnaíba 109 J 5
Alto Río Senguerr 113 BC 7–8
Alto Turi 109 J 4
Altun Shan 70 AB 3
Alturas 102 B 3
Altus 102 FG 5
Altynasar 67 G 1
Al Ubayyid 88 DE 6
Al Uqsur 60 A 4
Al Urayq (Saudi Arabia)
   60 C 3
Al Urdun 60 B 3
Al 'Uwayqilah 60 CD 3
Al 'Uzayr 61 E 3
Alva (OK, U.S.A.) 102 G 4

Alvano, Küh-e 61 E 2
Alvorado 111 G 3
Älvsbyn 54 H 2
Al Wajh 60 B 4
Alwar 72 C 2
Al Warī'ah 89 H 3
Al Widyān 60 C 3
Alxa Zuoqi 70 DE 3
Alygdzher 68 G 5
Alys-Khaya 69 P 2
Alytus 55 H 5
Amada 88 E 4
Amadjuak Lake 101 NO 2–3
Amakinskiy 68 K 1
Amambaí 111 EF 5
Amami-ō-shima 71 JK 5
Amangel'dy 63 N 5
Amanzimtoti 95 E 6
Amapá 109 H 3
Amarillo 102 F 4
Amaro Leite 111 G 3
Amarti 93 G 2
Amasya 59 E 2
Amazar 68 LM 5
Amazonas 108–109 EF 4
Amazonas 109 H 4
Ambala 72 C 1
Ambam 91 G 5
Ambarchik 69 U 2
Ambato 108 C 4
Ambikapur 72 D 3
Ambilobe 95 H 2
Ambohitralanana 95 J 3
Ambon 75 G 4
Ambositra 95 H 4
Ambovombe 95 H 5
Ambre, Cap d' 95 HJ 2
Ambrim 82 C 4
Ambrym 81 J 5
Ambur 72 C 5
Amchitka Pass 98 AB 5
Amdo 70 B 4
American Highland 115
American Samoa 82 D 3
Amery Ice Shelf 115
Ames 103 H 3
Amga 69 O 3
Amguema 98 B 2
Amguid 87 G 3
Amhara 93 F 2
Amiens 56 D 2
Amindivi Islands 72 B 5
Amirante Islands 93 J 6
Amlia 98 C 5
'Amman 60 B 3
Ammarfjället 54 G 2
Amo 68 H 3
Åmol 61 F 1
Amorgos 58 C 3
Amos 101 M 6
Amoy 71 G 6
Amravati 72 C 3
Amritsar 72 C 1
Amsa'ad 87 K 2
Amsterdam (Netherlands)
   52 DE 4
Amsterdam (N.Y., U.S.A.)
   103 M 3

Amu-Dar'ya 67 G 2
Amukta Pass 98 C 5
Amundsen Gulf 99 N 1
Amundsen-Scott 115
Amundsen Sea 115
Amuntai 74 E 4
Amur 69 P 5
Amysakh 68 L 2
Anabarskoye Ploskogor'ye
   68 J 1–2
Anaco 109 F 2
Anadoli 58–59 CD 3
Anadyr 69 WX 3
Anadyr 98 A 3
Anadyrskaja Nizmennost
   69 X 2
Anadyrskiy Zaliv 69 Y 3
Anadyrskoye Ploskogor'ye
   69 VW 2
Ånah 60 C 2
Anaimalai Hills 72 C 5
Anakapalle 72 D 4
Anamur 60 A 1
Anamur Burun 60 A 2
Anamuryum 59 D 3
Anantapur 72 C 5
Anapa 59 E 2
Anápolis 111 G 4
Anār 61 G 3
Añatuya 112 D 4
Anchorage 98 H 3
Ancohuma 110 C 4
Ancona 57 F 3
Ancud 113 B 7
Anda 71 J 1
Andalucía 56 BC 4
Andaman Islands 73 F 5
Andaman Sea 73 G 5–6
Andarab 67 H 3
Andenes 54 G 2
Anderson (IN, U.S.A.)
   103 J 3–4
Anderson (N.W.T., Can.)
   98 M 2
Anderson (S.C., U.S.A.)
   103 K 5
Andes Mountains 107 C 2–6
Andfjorden 54 G 2
Andhra Pradesh 72 C 4
Andimeshk 61 E 2
Andiria Burun 59 D 3
Andirlangar 67 L 3
Andiyskiy Khrebet 59 G 2
Andizhan 67 J 2
Andkhui 67 GH 3
Andong 71 J 3
Andorra 56 D 3
Andorra la Vella 56 D 3
Andøya 54 G 2
Andradina 111 F 5
Andreanof Islands 98 BC 5
Andriba 95 H 3
Andropov 62 G 4
Ándros 58 BC 3
Andros Island 105 G 3
Andújar 56 C 4
Andyngda 68 L 2
Anéfis 90 E 2

Anegada Passage 105 K 4
Aneto, Pico de 56 D 3
Angar 75 H 4
Angara 68 F 4
Angarsk 68 H 5
Angatau 83 F 4
Angaul 68 GH 5
Angeles 75 HJ 1
Angel Falls 109 F 2
Ängelholm 55 F 4
Ångermanälven 54 G 3
Angers 56 C 2
Angical 111 GH 3
Angijak Island 101 P 2
Angikuni Lake 99 RS 3
Angkor 73 H 5
Anglesey 52 BC 4
Angmagssalik 114
Angoche 95 G 3
Angol 113 B 6
Angola 94 BC 2
Angoulême 56 D 2
Angu 92 C 4
Anguilla 105 K 4
Anhua 70 F 5
Anhui 71 G 4
Aniak 98 F 3
Aniakchak National
   Monument and Preserve
   98 F 4
Animas Peak 102 E 5
Anjou 56 CD 2
Anjouan 95 GH 2
Ankang 70 E 4
Ankara 59 D 2
Ankazobe 95 H 3
Anlong 70 E 5–6
Anlu 70 F 4
Ann, Cape 115
Annaba 87 G 1
An Nabk 60 B 2
An Nabk Abū Qasr 66 BC 4
An Nafūd 60 C 3
An Nāhiyah 89 G 2
Annai 109 G 3
An Najaf 60 D 2–3
An' Nakhi 60 AB 3
Annam 73 J 4–5
Annandale 79 H 3
Anna Plains 78 C 2
Annapolis 103 L 4
Annapurna 72 D 2
Ann Arbor 103 K 3
An Nāsiriyah 61 E 3
Annecy 57 E 2
Annobón 91 F 6
An Nu'ayrīyah 61 E 4
An Nuhūd 88 D 6
Anori 109 F 4
Anqing 71 G 4
Anshan 71 H 2
Anshun 70 DE 5
Ansongo 90 DE 2
Anta 110 B 3
Antakya 59 E 3
Antalya Körfezi 58 D 3
Antananarivo 95 H 3
Antarctic Peninsula 115

Antequera 56 C 4
Antigua and Barbuda 105 K 4
Antillas Mayores 105 HJ 4
Antiope 82 D 4
Antipodes Islands 115
Antlåt 87 K 2
Antofagasta 110 B 5
Antofagasta de la Sierra 112 C 4
Antongil, Baie d' 95 HJ 3
Antonio de Biedma 113 CD 8
Antonovo 66 E 1
Antsirabe 95 H 3
Antsiranana 95 HJ 2
Antsohihy 95 H 2
Antwerpen 52 D 4
Anuradhapura 72 D 6
Anxi 70 C 2
Anxiang 70 F 5
Anyang 70 FG 3
Anzhero-Sudzhensk 63 RS 4
Aomori 71 M 2
Aosta 57 E 2
Aoudaghost 86 CD 5
Aouinat Legraa 86 D 3
Aoulef el Arab 86–87 F 3
Apaporis 108 DE 3–4
Apataki 83 F 4
Apatity 54 K 2
Apatzingán 104 B 4
Apeldoorn 52 E 4
Api, Tanjung 74 C 3
Apia 82 D 3
Aporé 111 F 4
Appalachian Mountains 103 KM 2–4
Appenno Lucano 57 G 3–4
Appenno Tosco-Emiliano 57 F 3
Appleton 103 J 3
Apsheronsk 59 E 2
Apucarana 111 F 5
Apure 108 E 2
Apurimac 110 B 3
Aqâr 'Atabah 87 H 3
Aqdâ 61 F 2
Aquidauana 110 E 5
'Arabah, Wâdi al 60 B 3
Arabestân 61 E 3
Arabian Sea 117
Aracaju 111 J 3
Aracati 111 J 1
Araçatuba 111 FG 5
Aracena, Sierra de 56 B 4
Araçuai 111 H 4
Arad 58 B 1
Arada 91 J 2
'Arâdah 61 F 5
Arafura Sea 75 HJ 5
Aragarças 111 F 4
Aragon 56 C 3
Araguacema 109 HJ 5
Aragua de Maturín 109 F 2
Araguaia 109 J 5
Araguaiana 111 F 4
Araguaína 109 J 5
Araguari 111 G 4
Araguatins 109 J 5

Arak (Algeria) 87 F 3
Aråk (Iran) 61 E 2
Arakaka 109 G 2
Arakan Yoma 73 FG 3–4
Aral Sea 66 F 2
Aral'sk 67 G 1
Aral'skoye More 66–67 FG 2
Aramac 79 H 3
Arandai 75 H 4
Aranjuez 56 C 3–4
Aranos 94 B 4
Aranuka 82 C 3
Araouane 90 D 2
Arapiraca 111 J 2–3
Araquara 111 G 5
Arauá 111 J 3
Arauca 108 D 2
Arauco 113 B 6
Aravalli Range 72 B 2–3
Araxá 111 G 4
Arbatax 57 E 4
Archer River National Park 79 G 1
Archipelago Kerimbas 95 G 2
Archipiélago de Colón 108 B 6
Archipiélago de la Reina Adelaida 113 A 9
Archipiélago de los Chonos 113 AB 7–8
Arco 102 D 3
Arcos 56 B 4
Arctic Ocean 114
Arctic Red River 98 L 2
Arctowski 115
Ardabil 66 D 3
Ardakân 61 F 2
Årdal 54 E 3
Ard as Sawwân 60 B 3
Ardennes 52 E 4
Ardestan 61 F 2
Arecibo 105 J 4
Areia Branca 111 J 1
Arenápolis 110 E 3
Arendal 55 E 4
Arequipa 110 B 4
Arere 109 H 4
Arezzo 57 F 3
Arga 69 R 2
Argan 70 A 2
Argentina 113 CD 6
Arges 58 C 2
Argolikós Kólpos 58 B 3
Argungu 91 EF 3
Argyle, Lake 78 D 2
Ar Horqin Qi 71 H 2
Århus 55 F 4
Arica (Chile) 110 B 4
Arica (Colombia) 108 D 4
Ariguaní 108 C 1
Arihâ 60 B 2
Arinos 110 E 3
Aripuanã 109 F 5
Aripuanã 109 FG 5
Ariquemes 109 F 5
Ariripina 111 HJ 2
Arizona (Argentina) 113 C 6
Arizona (U.S.A.) 102 D 5

Arjona 108 C 1
Arka 69 Q 3
Arkalyk 63 N 5
Arkansas 103 H 4
Arkansas City 103 G 4
Arkansas River 102–103 FH 4–5
Arkhangel'sk 62 H 3
Arkhara 69 O 6
Arklow 52 B 4
Arles 57 D 3
Arlington (OR, U.S.A.) 102 C 2
Arlington (TX, U.S.A.) 103 G 5
Arlington (VA, U.S.A.) 103 L 4
Arlit 91 F 2
Arly 90 E 3
Armant 88 E 3
Amavir 59 F 1
Armenia 108 C 3
Armeniya 59 F 2
Armidale 79 J 5
Armstrong 100 K 5
Armyansk 59 D 1
Arnauti, Akra 60 A 2
Arnawai 67 J 3
Arnhem 52 E 4
Arnhem, Cape 79 F 1
Aroab 94 B 5
Arorae 82 C 3
Arquipélago dos Bijagós 90 A 3
Ar Radisiyah Bahri 60 A 4
Ar Rahad 88 E 6
Arraias 111 G 3
Ar Ramâdi 60 D 2
Ar Ramlah 60 B 3
Arran 52 B 3
Ar Raqqah 60 C 2
Arras 56 D 1
Ar Rass 60 D 4
Ar Rawdatayn 61 E 3
Ar Rayhâni 61 G 5
Ar Rifâ'i 66 D 4
Ar Rimâl 89 J 4
Ar Riyâd 61 E 4
Ar Rub' al Khâli 89 HJ 4–5
Ar Rusâfah 66 B 3
Ar Rusayris 88 E 6
Ar Rutbah 60 C 2
Ar Ruways (Qatar) 61 F 4
Ar Ruways (United Arab Emirates) 61 F 4
Års 55 E 4
Arsen'yev 71 K 2
Årskogen 54 G 3
Arsuk 101 S 3
Arteaga 104 B 4
Artem 71 K 2
Artemisa 104 F 3
Artic Circle 54 AB 2
Artigas 112 E 5
Artoli 88 E 5
Artybash 63 R 5
Artyk 69 R 3
Arua 92 E 4
Aruanã 111 F 3
Aruba, Isla 108 E 1
Arunachal 73 F 2

Arun Qi 69 M 6
Aruppukkottai 72 C 6
Arusha 93 F 5
Arvada 102 E 4
Arvayheer 70 D 1
Arvika 55 F 4
Arys' 67 H 2
Arzamas 62 H 4
Asahikawa 71 LM 2
Asamakka 91 F 2
Asansol 72 E 3
Asba Tafari 93 G 3
Ascensión 110 D 4
Ascoli Piceno 57 F 3
Aselle 93 F 3
Asha 63 L 5
Ashdod 60 B 3
Asheville 103 K 4
Ashgelon 60 B 3
Ashkhabad 66 FG 3
Ash Shabakah 60 D 3
Ash Sharqât 60 D 2
Ash Shatrah 61 E 3
Ash Shihr 89 HJ 6
Ash Shinafiyah 61 D 3
Ash Shu'aybah 66 C 5
Ash Shu'bah 61 D 3
Ash Shumlûl 61 E 4
Ash Shwayrif 87 H 3
Ashtabula 103 KL 3
Ashuanipi 101 O 5
Ashuanipi Lake 101 O 5
Asinara 57 E 3
Asino 63 RS 4
Asir, Ra's 93 J 2
Asmara 93 F 1
Aspermont 102 F 5
Aspiring, Mount 80 P 9
Assab 93 G 2
Aş Şadr 61 G 4
Aş Şahrâ' al Gharbiyah 88 D 3
Aş Şahrâ' al Janûbiyah 88 DE 4
Aş Şahrâ' an Nûbiyah 88 EF 4
Aş Şahrâ' ash Sharqiyah 60 AB 4
As Salamiyah 61 E 4
Aş Sâlihiyah 60 C 2
As Sâlimiyah 61 E 3
As Salmân 61 D 3
As Salt 60 B 2
Assam 73 F 2
As Samâwah 61 D 3
As Sarir 87 K 3
As Silâ 61 F 4
Assiniboia 99 Q 6
Assis 111 F 5
Assisi 57 F 3
As Subû' 88 E 4
Aş Şulb 61 E 4
Aş Şummân 61 DE 4
Assur 60 D 2
As Suwaydâ' 60 B 2
As Suways 60 A 3
Astakh 69 P 2
Astipálaia 58 C 3
Astrakhan 66 DE 1

128

Asturias **56** B 3
Asuncion (Mariana Is.) **82** A 1
Asunción (Paraguay) **112** E 3–4
Aswān **60** A 4
Aswan High Dam **60** A 5
Asyūt **88** E 3
Atacama, Desierto de **110** C 5
Atacama, Salar de **110** C 5
Atafu **82** D 3
Atambua **75** F 5
Atangmik **101** R 3
Atar **86** C 4
Atas Bogd Uul **70** C 2
Atasu **63** O 6
'Atbarah **88** E 5
Atbarah **88** EF 5
Atbasar **63** N 5
Athens (GA, U.S.A.) **103** K 5
Athens (Greece) **58** B 3
Athínai **58** B 3
Ath Thumāmī **61** D 4
Ati **91** H 3
Atico **110** B 4
Atikokan **100** J 6
Atikonak Lake **101** P 5
Atka **98** C 5
Atka (U.S.S.R.) **69** S 3
Atkarsk **62** H 5
Atlanta **103** JK 5
Atlantic City **103** M 4
Atlantic Ocean **116**
Atlas el Kebir **86** DE 2
Atlas Mountains **86** DF 2
Atlin **98** L 4
Atran **55** F 4
Atrato **108** C 2
Atsy **75** J 5
At Tafilah **60** B 3
At Tā'if **89** G 4
Attawapiskat **100** KL 5
Attawapiskat **100** L 5
At Tawil **60** C 3
At Taysīyah **60** D 3–4
At Tīb, Ra's **87** H 1
Attikamagen Lake **101** O 5
Attu **98** A 5
At Turayf **60** C 3
At Turbah **89** G 6
Atuel **113** C 6
Atura **92** E 4
Aua **82** A 3
Auas Mountains **94** B 4
Auburn **103** LM 3
Auckland **81** Q 8
Auckland Islands **115**
Aude **56** D 3
Augathella **79** H 4
Augsburg **53** F 5
Augusta (AR, U.S.A.) **103** H 4
Augusta (GA, U.S.A.) **103** K 5
Augusta (ME, U.S.A.) **103** N 3
Augustus, Mount **78** B 3
Auki **82** B 3
Aur **82** C 2
Aurangabaand **72** C 4
Aurillac **56** D 3
Aurora **102** F 4

Aus **94** B 5
Ausangate, Nevado **110** B 3
Aust-Agder **55** E 4
Austin (MN, U.S.A.) **103** H 3
Austin (TX, U.S.A.) **102** G 5
Austin, Lake **78** B 4
Australia **78–79** CG 3
Australian Alps **79** H 6
Australian Capital Territory **79** H 6
Austria **57** F 2
Austvågøy **54** F 2
Auvézère **56** D 2
Auxerre **56** D 2
Auyuittuq National Park **101** OP 2
Avalon Peninsula **101** R 6
Avanavero **109** G 3
Avarua **83** E 4
Avaz **66** FG 4
Avdhira **58** C 2
Ávej **61** E 2
Avellaneda **112** E 5
Averøya **54** E 3
Avesta **55** G 3
Avignon **57** DE 3
Ávila **56** C 3
Avilés **56** B 3
Avola **57** G 4
Awara Plain **93** G 4
Awash **93** G 2
Awash **93** G 3
'Awaynat Wanīn **87** H 3
Awbārī **87** H 3
Awjilah **87** K 3
Axel Heiberg Island **114**
Axios **58** B 2
Ayabaca **108** BC 4
Ayacucho **110** AB 3
Ayaguz **63** Q 6
Ayan **69** P 4
Ayanaka **69** V 3
Ayava **68** H 4
Ayaviri **110** BC 3
Aydın **58** C 3
Ayers Rock – Mount Olga National Park **78** E 4
Áyion Óros **58** B 2
Aylmer Lake **99** Q 3
'Aynabo **93** H 3
'Ayn al Baydā' **60** BC 2
'Ayn al Ghazāl **87** K 4
Ayni **67** H 3
'Ayn Sukhnah **60** A 3
Ayon **69** V 1
Ayr (Australia) **79** H 2
Ayr (U.K.) **52** C 3
Aysary **63** O 5
Āzādshahr **61** G 1
Azamgarh **72** D 2
Azare **91** G 3
Azbine **91** F 2
Azerbaydzhan **66** D 2
Aznā **61** E 2
Azores **86** A 1
Azoum **91** J 3
Azov **59** E 1
Azovskoye More **59** E 1

Aztec ruins **102** E 4
Azul **113** E 6
Az Zallāq **61** F 4
Az Zarqā' **61** F 4
Az Zarqā' **60** B 2
Az Zāwiyah **87** H 2
Az Zilfi **61** D 4
Az Zugar **89** G 6

B

Baba Burnu **58** D 2
Baba Burun **58** C 3
Bābā Heydar **61** F 2
Babahoyo **108** BC 4
Babai Gaxun **70** D 2
Bāb al Mandab **89** G 6
Babanūsah **88** D 5
Babar, Kepulauan **75** G 5
Babine Lake **99** M 5
Babo **75** H 4
Bābol **61** F 1
Babol Sar **61** F 1
Babushkin **68** J 5
Babylon **60** D 2
Bacabal **111** GH 1
Bacan, Pulau **75** G 4
Bacău **58** C 1
Back **99** S 2
Bäd **61** F 2
Badajoz **56** B 4
Badalona **56** D 3
Badanah **60** C 3
Baden-Baden **53** E 5
Badiyat ash Shām **60** BC 2
Badoumbé **90** B 3
Badr Hunayn **60** C 5
Badulla **72** D 6
Badzhal **69** OP 5
Bafatá **90** B 3
Baffin Bay **114**
Baffin Island **101** NO 2
Bafia **91** G 5
Bafoussam **91** G 4
Bāfq **61** G 3
Bafra **59** E 2
Bāft **61** G 3
Bagadzha **68** L 3
Bagalkot **72** C 4
Baga Sola **91** GH 3
Bagdarin **68** K 5
Bagé **112** F 5
Baghdād **60** D 2
Bāghin **61** G 3
Baghlan **67** H 3
Bagua **108** C 5
Baguio **75** J 1
Baguirmi **91** H 3
Bahama Islands **105** H 3
Bahar Dar **93** F 2
Bahawalpur **67** J 5
Bahía (Argentina) **113** C 8
Bahía (Brazil) **111** H 3
Bahía Blanca **113** D 6
Bahía Blanca **113** D 6
Bahía de Campeche **104** CD 4
Bahía de Caráquez **108** B 4
Bahía Grande **113** C 9
Bahía Kino **102** D 6

Bahía Laura **113** CD 8
Bahía Rosario **102** C 6
Bahías, Cabo dos **113** CD 8
Bahía Sebastián Vizcaíno **102** D 6
Bahrain **61** F 4
Bahr al Abyad **88** E 6
Bahr al Azraq **88** E 6
Bahr al Jabal **92** E 3
Bahr ar Rimāl al 'Azīm **88** CD 3
Baía de Setúbal **56** B 4
Baia Mare **58** B 1
Baião **109** J 4
Baicheng (Man. China) **71** H 1
Baicheng (Sink. Uig. China) **67** L 2
Baie aux Feuilles **101** O 4
Baie d'Antongil **95** HJ 3
Baie-des-Moutons **101** Q 5
Bailang **68** M 6
Baile Átha Cliath **52** B 4
Bailundo **94** B 2
Baimuru **80** D 3
Baing **75** F 6
Baingoin **72** E 1
Baiquan **69** N 6
Bairiki **82** C 2
Bairin Zuoqi **71** GH 2
Baixo-Alentejo **56** B 4
Baiyü **70** C 4
Baja **58** A 1
Baja California Norte **102** C 5
Baja California Sur **102** CD 6
Bakadzhitsite **58** C 2
Bakel **90** B 3
Baker **82** D 2
Baker Lake (N.W.T., Can.) **99** S 3
Baker Lake (N.W.T., Can.) **99** S 3
Bakersfield **102** C 4
Bakhta **63** RS 3
Bakhtegān, Daryācheh-ye **61** FG 3
Bakony **58** A 1
Bakouma **92** C 3
Baku **66** DE 2
Balabac Strait **74** E 2
Balabakk, Ra's **60** B 2
Baladīyat 'Adan **89** H 6
Balaghat **72** D 3
Balakhta **68** F 4
Balakovo **62** J 5
Bala Murghāb **67** G 3
Balasore **72** E 3
Balaton **58** A 1
Balclutha **80** PQ 10
Balde **112** C 5
Bald Head **78** B 6
Baldy Peak **102** E 5
Bale **93** G 3
Balearic Islands **56** D 3
Baleia, Ponta da **111** J 4
Baley **68** L 5
Bali **74** D 5
Balıkesir **58** C 3
Balintang Channel **75** J 1

Bal – Baz

Balkan Mountains **58** C 2
Balkhash **63** OP 6
Balkhash, Ozero **63** P 6
Balladonia **78** C 5
Ballarat **79** G 6
Ballard, Lake **78** C 4
Balleny Islands **115**
Ballina **79** J 4
Balranald **79** G 5
Balsas **109** J 5
Balsas, Rio **104** B 4
Baltic Sea **55** GH 4
Baltimore **103** L 4
Baltiskaja Grjada **55** HJ 4–5
Baluchistan **66–67** G 5
Bam **66** F 5
Bamako **90** C 3
Bamba **90** D 2
Bambari **92** C 3
Bambesa **92** D 4
Bambesi **92** E 3
Bamenda **91** FG 4
Bamingui **92** C 3
Bamiyan **67** H 4
Bampūr **67** G 5
Banaba **81** J 2
Banalia **92** D 4
Banana **79** J 3
Banās, Ra's **60** B 5
Banās, Ra's **88** F 4
Bancroft **101** M 6
Banda **72** D 2
Banda Aceh **74** A 2
Bandar Abbas **61** G 4
Bandar-e-Anzalī **66** DE 3
Bandar-e Chārak **66** E 5
Bandar-e Deylam **66** E 4–5
Bandar-e Khomeynī **61** E 3
Bandar-e Lengeh **61** G 4
Bandar-e Māqām **61** F 4
Bandar-e Moghūyeh **61** FG 4
Bandar-e Rig **61** F 3
Bandarlampung **74** C 5
Bandarpunch **72** C 1
Bandar Seri Begawan **74** D 3
Bandar Shāh **61** E 1
Banda Sea **75** GH 5
Bandau **74** E 2
Band Boni **66** F 5
Bandeira **111** H 5
Bandeirante **111** FG 3
Bandırma **58** C 2
Bandundu **92** B 5
Bandung **74** C 5
Banes **105** GH 3
Banff National Park **99** O 5
Banfora **90** CD 3
Bangalore **72** C 5
Bangassou **92** C 4
Bangeta, Mount **80** E 3
Banggai, Kepulauan **75** F 4
Bangko **74** B 4
Bangkok **73** H 5
Bangladesh **73** F 3
Bangor (ME, U.S.A.) **103** N 3
Bangor (N. Ireland, U.K.) **52** B 4
Bangui **92** B 4

Banhine National Park **95** E 4
Banihal Pass **67** K 4
Banī Mazār **88** DE 3
Banī Suwayf **88** E 3
Bāniyās (Lebanon) **60** B 2
Bāniyās (Syria) **60** B 2
Banja Luka **57** G 3
Banjarmasin **74** DE 4
Banjul **90** A 3
Ban Kniet **73** J 5
Banks Island (N.W.T., Can.) **99** N 1
Banks Island (Queensland, Austr.) **79** G 1
Banks Islands **81** J 4
Banks Peninsula **81** Q 9
Banks Strait **80** L 9
Ban Me Thuot **73** J 5
Bannu **67** J 4
Banská Bystrica **53** G 5
Banyo **91** G 4
Banyuwangi **74** D 5
Banzare Coast **115**
Banzart **87** GH 1
Baoding **70** FG 3
Baoji **70** E 4
Baoqing **71** K 1
Baoshan **70** CD 5
Baotou **70** E 2
Baqen **70** B 4
Ba' qūbah **61** D 2
Barabinsk **63** P 4
Barabinskaya Step' **63** P 5
Baracaldo **56** C 3
Bārah **88** E 6
Barahona **105** H 4
Barakkul' **63** N 5
Baramula **67** J 4
Baran **72** C 2
Barangbarang **75** EF 5
Baranof **98** K 4
Baranovichi **55** J 5
Barão de Capanema **110** E 3
Barão de Melgaco **110** D 3
Barbados **105** K 5
Barcaldine **79** H 3
Barcellona **57** FG 4
Barcelona (Spain) **56** D 3
Barcelona (Venezuela) **109** F 2
Barcelos **109** F 4
Bardawil, Sabkhat al **60** A 3
Bārdère **93** G 4
Bardeskan **66** F 3
Bardufoss **54** G 2
Barēda **93** J 2
Bareilly **72** C 2
Barentsovo More **62** GJ 1
Barents Sea **114**
Barentu **93** F 1
Bårgå **54** G 2
Barga **72** D 1
Barguzin **68** J 5
Barhaj **72** D 2
Bari **57** G 3
Barīdi, Ra's **60** B 4
Barīm **89** G 6
Barinas **108** E 2
Baring, Cape **99** O 2

Barisal **73** F 3
Barisan, Pegunungan **74** B 4
Barito, Sungai **74** D 4
Barkā' **89** K 4
Barkam **70** D 4
Barkly Tableland **79** F 2
Barlee, Lake **78** B 4
Barletta **57** G 3
Barmer **72** B 2
Barnaul **63** Q 5
Barnes Ice Cap **101** N 1–2
Barong **70** C 4
Barotseland **94** C 3
Barquisimeto **108** DE 1
Barra (Bahía, Brazil) **111** H 3
Barra (U.K.) **52** B 3
Barracão do Barreto **109** G 5
Barra do Corda **109** J 5
Barragem da Rocha de Galé **56** B 4
Barra Head **52** B 3
Barranca **108** C 4
Barrancabermeja **108** D 2
Barrancas **109** F 2
Barranquilla **108** C 1
Barreiras **111** G 3
Barreirinhas **111** H 1
Barreiro **56** B 4
Barreiros **111** JK 2
Barren **73** F 5
Barren Lands **99** QS 2
Barretos **111** G 5
Barrie **101** LM 7
Barrow (AK, U.S.A.) **98** F 1
Barrow (Argentina) **113** E 6
Barrow (Rep. of Ireland) **52** B 4
Barrow, Point **98** FG 1
Barrow Island **78** A 3
Barsi **72** C 4
Bartica **109** G 2
Bartlesville **103** G 4
Bāruni **72** E 2
Bāsa'idū **61** G 4
Basauri **56** C 3
Basel **57** E 2
Bashi Haixia **71** H 6
Basilan City **75** F 2
Basílio **112** F 5
Baskol' **63** P 5
Basra **61** E 3
Bassas da India **95** FG 4
Bassein **73** F 4
Basse Terre **105** K 4
Bassinde Rennes **56** C 2
Bass Strait **80** KL 8
Bastak **61** G 4
Bastia **57** E 3
Bata **91** F 5
Batagay-Alyta **69** NO 2
Batama (U.S.S.R.) **68** H 5
Batamshinskiy **63** L 5
Batang **70** C 4
Batangas **75** F 1
Batang Hari **74** B 4
Bataysk **59** EF 1
Batemans Bay **79** J 6
Batha **91** H 3

Bathalha **56** B 4
Bathurst (Canada) **101** OP 6
Bathurst (N.S.W., Austr.) **79** H 5
Bathurst, Cape **98** LM 1
Bathurst Inlet **99** PQ 2
Bathurst Inlet **99** Q 2
Bathurst Island (N.T., Austr.) **78** D 1
Bathurst Island (The Arctic) **114**
Batin, Wadi al **61** DE 3
Batkanu **90** B 4
Bātlā q-e Gavkhūnī **61** F 2
Batman **59** F 3
Batna **87** G 1
Batoka **94** D 3
Batomga **69** P 4
Baton Rouge **103** H 5
Båtsfjord **54** J 1
Battambang **73** H 5
Battle Creek **103** J 3
Batu **93** F 3
Batui **75** F 4
Batumi **59** F 2
Batu Puteh, Gunung **74** B 3
Baturité **111** J 1
Baubau **75** F 5
Bauchi **91** F 3
Baures **110** D 3
Bauru **111** FG 5
Baús **111** F 4
Bavaria **53** F 5
Bavispe **102** E 5
Bawdwin **73** G 3
Baxoi **70** C 4
Bayamo **105** G 3
Bayan-Adraga **68** K 6
Bayan-Aul **63** P 5
Bayanbulag **68** G 6
Bayandzurh **68** J 6
Bayanga **92** B 4
Bayan Har Shankou **70** C 4
Bayanhongor **68** H 6
Bayan Obo **70** E 2
Bayāz **66** F 4
Bayāzeh **61** G 2
Bayburt **59** EF 2
Bay City (MI, U.S.A.) **103** K 3
Baydaratskaya Guba **63** N 2
Bay de Verde **101** R 6
Bayern **53** F 5
Bayji **60** D 2
Baykal'skiy Khrebet **68** J 4–5
Baykit **68** G 3
Bay of Bengal **72–73** EF 4
Bay of Biscay **56** C 2–3
Bay of Fundy **101** O 6–7
Bay of Plenty **82** C 5
Bayonne **56** C 3
Bayovar **108** B 5
Bayram-Ali **67** G 3
Bayreuth **53** F 5
Bayrūt **60** B 2
Baytown **103** H 6
Bazarnyy Syzgan **62** J 5
Bazaruto National Park **95** F 4
Bazhong **70** E 4

Bear Island **114**
Beata, Cabo **105** H 4
Beatton River **99** NO 4
Beatty **102** C 4
Beaufort (Malaysia) **74** E 2
Beaufort (U.S.A.) **103** K 5
Beaufort Sea **98** JL 1
Beaufort West **94** C 6
Beaumont **103** H 5
Beausejour **99** S 5
Beauvais **56** D 2
Beaver (Sask., Can.)**99** Q 5
Beaver (UT, U.S.A.) **102** D 4
Beawar **72** BC 2
Beberibe **111** J 1
Béchar **86** E 2
Bedourie **79** F 3
Be'er Sheva **60** B 3
Beeville **102** G 6
Bega **79** HJ 6
Begejski Kanal **58** B 1
Begna **55** E 3
Behbehän **61** F 3
Behshar **61** F 1
Bei'an **69** N 6
Beibu Wan **73** J 3
Beida **87** K 2
Beihai **70** E 6
Beijing **71** G 2
Beipiao **71** H 2
Beira **95** F 3
Beirut **60** B 2
Bei Shan **70** C 2
Beitbridge **94** DE 4
Beitstad **54** F 3
Beitun **67** M 1
Beja **56** B 4
Bejaïa **87** FG 1
Bekdash **66** E 2
Békéscsaba **58** B 1
Bekopaka **95** G 3
Bela **67** H 5
Belau **75** HJ 2
Bela Vista (Brazil) **110** E 5
Bela Vista (Mozambique) **95** E 5
Belaya Kalitva **59** F 1
Belaya Tserkov **62** F 5–6
Belcher Islands **101** L 4
Belebey **62** K 5
Belém (Amazonas, Brazil) **108** E 4
Belém (Pará, Brazil) **109** J 4
Belén **108** C 3
Belep, Îles **82** B 4
Beleuli **66** F 2
Belfast **52** B 4
Belfield **102** F 2
Belfort **57** E 2
Belgaum **72** BC 4
Belgium **52** DE 4
Belgorod **62** G 5
Belgorod-Dnestrovskiy **58** CD 1
Belgrade **58** B 2
Beli **91** G 4
Belikh **60** C 1
Belitung, Pulau **74** C 4

Belize **104** E 4
Belize City **104** E 4
Bel'kachi **69** O 4
Bell **101** LM 5
Bella Bella **99** M 5
Bella Coola **99** M 5
Bellary **72** C 4
Belle Ile **56** C 2
Belleville (IL, U.S.A.) **103** J 4
Belleville (KS, U.S.A.) **102** G 4
Belleville (Ontario, Can.) **101** M 7
Bellevue **102** B 2
Bellin **101** N 3
Bellingham **102** B 2
Bellingshausen **115**
Bellingshausen Sea **115**
Bello **108** C 2
Belluno **57** F 2
Bell Ville **112** D 5
Bellyk **68** F 5
Belmonte **111** J 4
Belmopan **104** E 4
Belogorsk (U.S.S.R.) **69** N 5
Belogor'ye **63** N 3
Belo Horizonte (Minas Gerais, Brazil) **111** H 4–5
Belo Horizonte (Pará, Brazil) **109** H 5
Beloit **103** J 3
Belo Monta **109** H 4
Belorechensk **59** FG 2
Belorussiya **55** J 5
Belorusskaya **55** J 5
Belovo **63** R 5
Beloyarovo **69** NO 5
Beloye More **62** G 2
Belt'sy **58** C 1
Belush'ya Guba **62** KL 1
Belush'ya Guba **114**
Belyy **62** F 4
Bemidji **103** G 2
Bena Dibile **92** C 5
Benalla **79** H 6
Benares **72** D 2
Bend **102** B 3
Bender Bäyla **93** J 3
Bendery **58** C 1
Bendigo **79** GH 6
Benevento **57** FG 3
Bengal **72** E 3
Bengbu **71** G 4
Benghazi **87** J 2
Bengkulu **74** B 4
Benguela **94** A 2
Beni (Bolivia) **110** C 3
Benidorm **56** CD 4
Beni Mellal **86** D 2
Benin **90** E 3–4
Benin City **91** EF 4
Beni Ounif **86** E 2
Benjamin Constant **108** D 4
Ben Nevis **52** BC 3
Benson **102** D 5
Bentiaba **94** A 2
Benue **91** F 4
Benxi **71** HJ 2

Beograd **58** B 2
Beraketa **95** H 4
Berati **58** A 2
Berau, Teluk **75** H 4
Berbera **93** H 2
Berbérati **92** B 4
Berchogur **66** FG 1
Berdichev **55** J 6
Berdigestyakh **69** MN 3
Berdyansk **59** E 1
Berekum **90** D 4
Berens River **99** S 5
Berezniki **62** KL 4
Berezovka (Russia, U.S.S.R.) **63** Q 4
Berezovo **63** N 3
Berezovskiy **63** LM 5
Bergamo (Italy) **57** EF 2
Bergamo (Turkey) **58** C 3
Bergen (F.R.G.) **53** F 4
Bergen (Norway) **55** DE 3
Bergerac **56** D 3
Bergö **54** H 2
Bergviken **54** G 3
Berhampore **72** E 3
Berhampur **72** DE 4
Bering Land Bridge National Preserve **98** E 2
Beringovskiy **69** XY 3
Bering Sea **65** UV 3–4
Bering Sea **114**
Bering Strait **98** CD 2–3
Berkakit **69** M 4
Berkeley **102** B 4
Berkner Island **115**
Berlevåg **54** J 1
Bermejo (Argentina) **112** D 4
Bermejo (Argentina) **112** C 5
Bermuda Islands **105** K 1
Bern **57** E 2
Bernasconi **113** D 6
Bernburg **53** F 4
Berne **57** E 2
Berner Alpen **57** E 2
Bernina **57** E 2
Bertolínia **111** H 2
Bertoua **91** G 5
Besalampy **95** G 3
Besançon **57** E 2
Besar, Gunung **74** E 4
Beskidy Zachodny **53** GH 5
Beslan **59** F 2
Besna Kobila **58** B 2
Bessarabiya **58** C 1
Bestobe **63** O 5
Beswick **78** E 1
Bethlehem **94** D 5
Béthune **56** D 1
Betong **73** H 6
Bet-Pak-Dala **63** NO 6
Betroka **95** H 4
Beyänlü **61** E 1
Bey Dağları **58** CD 3
Beyla **90** C 4
Beyra **93** H 3
Beyşehir Gölü **58** D 3
Béziers **56** D 3
Bhadrakh **72** E 3

Bhadravati **72** C 5
Bhagalpur **72** E 3
Bhamo **73** G 3
Bhandara **72** CD 3
Bharuch **72** B 3
Bhatinda **72** BC 2
Bhatpara **72** E 3
Bhavnagar **72** B 3
Bhilwara **72** BC 2
Bhopal **72** C 3
Bhopalpatnam **72** D 4
Bhuban **72** E 3
Bhubaneswar **72** E 3
Bhumiphol Dam **73** GH 4
Bhusawal **72** C 3
Bhutan **73** F 2
Biak (Indonesia) **75** F 4
Biak (New Guinea) **75** J 4
Biak, Pulau **75** J 4
Biała Podlaska **53** H 4
Białystok **53** H 4
Biankouma **90** C 4
Biaora **72** C 3
Biarritz **56** C 3
Biberach **53** EF 5
Bicuari National Park **94** AB 3
Bida **91** F 4
Bidar **72** C 4
Bidzhan **69** O 6
Bié **94** B 2
Biebrza **53** H 4
Biel **57** E 2
Bielefeld **53** E 4
Bielsko-Biała **53** G 5
Bien Hoa **73** J 5
Bienville, Lac **101** N 4
Bifoum **91** G 6
Big Bend National Park **102** F 6
Biger **68** G 6
Bighorn River **102** E 2
Bight of Bangkok **73** H 5
Bight of Benin **90** E 4
Bigi **92** C 4
Big Spring **102** F 5
Big Trout Lake **100** K 5
Bihač **57** G 3
Bihar **72** DE 2
Bijapur **72** C 4
Bijeljina **57** G 3
Bijiang **70** C 5
Bikaner **72** B 2
Bikar **82** C 2
Bikin **69** O 6
Bikini **82** B 2
Bilaspur **72** D 3
Bilbao **56** C 3
Bili **92** D 4
Billings **102** E 2
Bilma, Grand Erg de **91** GH 2
Biloela **79** J 3
Bilogora **57** G 2
Biloxi **103** J 5
Binaïya, Gunung **75** G 4
Binder **68** K 6
Bindura **95** E 3
Bingara **79** J 4
Binghamton **103** L 3

Bin – Bou

Binjai 74 A 3
Binnaway 79 H 5
Bintan, Pulau 74 B 3
Bintulu 74 D 3
Bira 69 P 6
Birao 92 C 2
Biratnagar 72 E 2
Bi'r Bū Zurayyq 87 K 3
Bi'r Fu'ād 88 D 2
Birjand 66 F 4
Birkat Nasser 60 A 5
Birkenhead 52 C 4
Birksgate Range 78 DE 4
Bīrlad 58 C 1
Birmingham (AL, U.S.A.) 103 J 5
Birmingham (U.K.) 52 C 4
Bir Moghreim 86 C 3
Bi'r Nasif 60 C 4
Birnie 82 D 3
Birnin Kebbi 91 EF 3
Birnin Kudu 91 F 3
Birobidzhan 69 O 6
Bir Ounane 90 D 1
Bir Rhoraffa 87 G 2
Bi'r Safājah 60 AB 4
Bi'r Shalatayn 88 F 4
Birsilpur 72 B 2
Birsk 62 L 4
Biru 70 B 4
Biscoe Islands 115
Bishop's Falls 101 Q 6
Biskra 87 G 2
Bismarck 102 F 2
Bismarck Archipelago 80–81 EF 2
Bismarck Range 80 DE 2–3
Bismarck Sea 80 EF 2
Bissau 90 A 3
Bistriţa 58 BC 1
Bitchana 93 F 2
Bitkiné 91 H 3
Bitlis 59 F 3
Bitola 58 B 2
Bitterfontein 94 B 6
Bitter Lake (Egypt) 60 A 4
Bitterroot Range 102 D 2–3
Biu 91 G 3
Biyang 70 F 4
Biysk 63 R 5
Bizerta 87 GH 1
Bjelašnica 58 A 2
Bjerkvik 54 G 2
Björkö 54 H 3
Björnöya 114
Blackall 79 GH 3
Blackburn, Mount 98 HJ 3
Black Hills 102 F 3
Blackpool 52 C 4
Black River Falls 103 H 3
Black Sea 59 DE 2
Blackwell 102 G 4
Blåfjellhatten 54 F 3
Blagoevgrad 58 B 2
Blagoveshchensk 69 NO 5
Blaine 103 H 2
Blantyre 95 E 3
Blåskavlen 54 E 3

Blåvands Huk 55 E 4
Blekinge 55 FG 4
Blenheim 82 C 5
Blida 87 F 1
Bloemfontein 94 CD 5
Blois 56 D 2
Blönduós 54 AB 2
Bloomington (IL, U.S.A.) 103 J 3
Bloomington (IN, U.S.A.) 103 J 4
Bloomington (MN, U.S.A.) 103 H 3
Blosseville Coast 114
Bluefields 104 F 5
Blue Ridge 103 KL 4
Bluff Knoll 78 B 5
Blumenau 112 FG 4
Blythe 102 D 5
Blytheville 103 J 4
Bo 90 B 4
Boa Vista (Cape Verde) 90 B 6
Boa Vista (Roraima, Brazil) 109 F 3
Bobai 70 EF 6
Bobo Dioulasso 90 D 3
Bobruysk 55 J 5
Boby, Pic 95 H 4
Boca del Rio 102 E 6
Bôca do Acre 108 E 5
Bocage Vendéen 56 C 2
Bocaiúva 111 H 4
Boca Raton 103 L 6
Bochum 53 E 4
Bodaybo 68 K 4
Bodélé 91 H 2
Boden 54 H 2
Bodensee 57 E 2
Bodö 54 F 2
Bo Duc 73 J 5
Boende 92 C 5
Boffa 90 B 3
Boggeragh Mountains 52 B 4
Bogor 74 C 5
Bogoroditsk 62 G 5
Bogotá 108 D 3
Bogra 72 E 2–3
Boguchany 68 G 4
Bogué 86 C 5
Bo Hai 71 GH 3
Bohemia 53 F 5
Böhmerwald 53 F 5
Bohol 75 F 2
Bohol Sea 75 F 2
Boiaçu 109 F 4
Boise 102 C 3
Boise City 102 F 4
Bojnürd 66 F 3
Bojuro 112 F 5
Bokatola 92 B 5
Boké 90 B 3
Boknafjorden 55 E 4
Bokora Game Reserve 92 E 4
Bokpyin 74 A 1
Bokungu 92 C 5
Bolan Pass 67 H 5
Bole (China) 67 L 2
Bole (Ghana) 90 D 4

Bolesławiec 53 G 4
Bolgatanga 90 D 3
Boli 71 K 1
Bolia 92 B 5
Bolívar (Argentina) 113 D 6
Bolívar (Colombia) 108 C 3
Bolivia 110 CD 4
Bollon 79 H 4
Bologna 57 F 3
Bologoye 62 F 4
Bologur 69 O 3
Bolombo 92 C 5
Bolsena, Lago di 57 F 3
Bol'shaya Glushitsa 62 K 5
Bol'sheretsk 69 T 5
Bol'shezemel'skaya Tundra 62 KM 2
Bolshoy Kavkaz 59 F 2
Bol'shoy Nimnyr 69 MN 4
Bol'shoy Shantar, Ostrov 69 P 4–5
Bolsón de Mapimi 104 B 2
Bolton 52 C 4
Bolu 59 D 2
Bolzano 57 F 2
Boma 91 G 7
Bombay 72 B 4
Bomberai 75 H 4
Bom Jesus 111 H 2
Bom Jesus da Lapa 111 H 3
Bömlo 55 DE 4
Bomongo 92 B 4
Bom Retiro 112 G 4
Bona, Mount 98 J 3
Bonaparte Archipelago 78 C 1
Bonavista Bay 101 R 6
Bondo 92 C 4
Bondowoso 74 D 5
Bonete, Cerro 112 C 4
Bongor 91 H 3
Bonifacio, Strait of 57 E 3
Bonin Islands 65 R 7
Bonito 110 E 5
Bonn 53 E 4
Bonners Ferry 102 C 2
Bonobono 74 E 2
Boola 90 C 4
Boothby, Cape 115
Boothia Peninsula 99 T 1
Bophuthatswana 94 C 5
Boquillagas del Carmen 104 B 2
Bor 58 B 2
Bora-Bora 83 EF 4
Borah Peak 102 D 3
Borås 55 F 4
Borasambar 72 D 3
Borāzjān 61 F 3
Borba 109 G 4
Bordeaux 56 CD 3
Bordertown 79 G 6
Bordj Fly Sainte Marie 86 E 3
Bordj Messouda 87 G 2
Börgefjellet 54 F 2
Borislav 53 H 5
Borisoglebsk 62 H 5
Borisov 55 J 5
Borispol 62 F 5

Bo River 92 D 3
Borja (Peru) 108 C 4
Borja (Yugoslavia) 58 A 2
Borkou 91 H 2
Borlänge 55 FG 3
Borneo 74 DE 3
Bornholm 55 F 5
Bornu 91 G 3
Borohoro Shan 67 L 2
Boroko 75 F 3
Borolgustakh 68 M 2
Borovichi 62 FG 4
Borroloola 79 F 2
Börselv 54 HJ 1
Borsippa 60 D 2
Boru 69 Q 1
Borüjen 61 F 3
Borüjerd 61 E 2
Borzya 68 L 5
Bösåso 93 H 2
Bose 70 E 6
Boshan 71 G 3
Boshnyakovo 69 Q 6
Boshuslän 55 F 4
Bosna 57 G 3
Bosporus 58 C 2
Bossangoa 92 B 3
Bossembele 92 B 3
Bossemptélé II 92 B 3
Bossier City 103 H 5
Bostandyk 62 J 6
Boston 103 MN 3
Botletle 94 C 4
Botoşani 58 C 1
Bo Trach 73 J 4
Botswana 94 CD 4
Botucatu 111 G 5
Bouaflé 90 C 4
Bouaké 90 D 4
Bouar 92 B 3
Bou Arfa 86 E 2
Boubandjida 91 GH 4
Boubandjida National Park 91 GH 4
Bou Djéhiba 90 D 2
Bougainville 81 G 3
Bougainville Reef 79 H 2
Bou Garfa 86 D 3
Bougouni 90 C 3
Bouïra 87 F 1
Bou Izakarn 86 D 3
Boulanouar 86 B 4
Boulder (U.S.A. Colorado) 102 E 3
Boulder (West Australia) 78 C 5
Boulia 79 F 3
Boulouli 90 C 2
Bouna 90 D 4
Boundiali 90 C 4
Boundou 90 B 3
Boun Neua 73 H 3
Bountiful 102 D 3
Bounty Islands 115
Bourem 90 D 2
Bourg 57 E 2
Bourges 56 D 2
Bourgogne 57 DE 2

Bou Rjeima **86** C 5
Bourke **79** H 4–5
Bournemouth **52** C 4
Bou Saâda **87** F 1
Bouvet Island **115**
Bowen (Argentina) **112** C 5
Bowen (Australia) **79** H 2
Bowling Green **103** J 4
Bowman **102** F 2
Bowman Bay **101** MN 2
Boxing **71** G 3
Boyabo **92** B 4
Boyne **52** B 4
Boyuibe **110** D 5
Bozok Platosu **59** DE 3
Brač **57** G 3
Bradenton **103** K 6
Bradford **52** C 4
Bradshaw **78** E 2
Brady **102** G 5
Braga **56** B 3
Bragança (Brazil) **109** J 4
Bragança (Portugal) **56** B 3
Bragina **69** X 3
Brahmaputra **73** F 2
Brai **101** M 2
Brăila **58** C 1
Bråk **87** H 3
Brampton **101** L 7
Brandberg **94** A 4
Brandenburg **53** F 4
Brandon **99** S 5–6
Brandvlei **94** BC 6
Brantford **101** L 7
Brasil, Planalto do **111** H 4
Brasiléia **110** C 3
Brasília **111** G 4
Braşov **58** C 1
Brassey, Mount **78** E 3
Bratislava **53** G 5
Bratsk **68** H 4
Bratskoye Vodokhranilishche **68** H 4
Bratslav **58** C 1
Bratul Chilia **58** C 1
Braunschweig **53** F 4
Brawley **102** CD 5
Brazil **110–111** EG 3
Brazo Casoquiare **108** E 3
Brazzaville **91** GH 6
Brčko **57** G 3
Brecknock, Península **113** B 9
Breda **52** D 4
Bredbyn **54** G 3
Breiðafjörður **54** A 2
Brejo **111** H 1
Brekken **54** F 3
Bremangerlandet **54** D 3
Bremen **53** E 4
Bremerhaven **53** E 4
Brenner **57** F 2
Brescia **57** F 2
Brest **56** C 2
Bretagne **56** C 2
Breves **109** H 4
Brevoort Island **101** P 3
Brewster, Kap **114**
Brewton **103** J 5

Brezhnev **62** K 4
Bridgeport **103** M 3
Bridger Peak **102** E 3
Bridgetown (Australia) **78** B 5
Bridgetown (Barbados) **105** KL 5
Brighton **52** D D 4
Brindisi **57** G 3
Brisbane **79** J 4
Bristol **52** C 4
Bristol Bay **98** EF 4
Bristol Channel **52** C D 4
British Columbia **99** MN 4–5
Britstown **94** C 6
Brive **56** D 2
Brno **53** G 5
Broadus **102** EF 2
Broadview **99** R 5
Brochet **99** R 4
Brokhovo **69** ST 4
Brokopondo **109** G 3
Brönnöysund **54** F 2
Brookings **103** G 3
Brooks Range **98** FH 2
Brookton **78** B 5
Broome **78** C 2
Browne Range Nature Reserve **78** CD 3
Brownfield **102** F 5
Brownsville **103** G 6
Brownwood **102** G 5
Bruce, Mount **78** B 3
Bruce Crossing **103** J 2
Brugge **52** D 4
Brumado **111** H 3
Brunei **74** D 2
Brusilovka **62** KL 5
Brusque **112** G 4
Bruxelles **52** D 4
Bryan **103** G 5
Bryan Coast **115**
Bryansk **62** F 5
Bryanskoye **59** G 2
Bryne **55** E 4
Brzeg **53** G 4
Bübiyãn **61** E 3
Bucaramanga **108** D 2
Buchanan **90** B 4
Bucharest **58** C 2
Buckingham Bay **79** F 1
Buckland **98** EF 2
Buco Zau **91** G 6
Bu Craa **86** C 3
Bucureşti **58** C 2
Budapest **58** AB 1
Budennovsk **59** F 2
Búðardalur **54** A 2
Buenaventura (Colombia) **108** C 3
Buenaventura (Mexico) **102** E 6
Buenavista **102** E 7
Buenos Aires **112** DE 5–6
Buenos Aires, Lago **113** B 8
Buffalo (N.Y., U.S.A.) **103** L 3
Buffalo (OK, U.S.A.) **102** G 4
Buffalo (S.D., U.S.A.) **102** F 2

Buffalo (WY, U.S.A.) **102** E 3
Buffalo Lake **99** OP 3
Buffalo Narrows **99** Q 4
Bug **53** H 4
Buga **108** C 3
Bugorkan **68** J 3
Bugöynes **54** J 2
Bugt **69** M 6
Bugul'ma **62** K 5
Buhayrat al Asad **59** E 3
Bujumbura **92** D 5
Buka **81** F 3
Bukadaban Feng **70** B 3
Bukavu **92** D 5
Bukhara **67** G 3
Bukit Gandadiwata **75** EF 4
Bukit Kambuno **75** EF 4
Bukit Masurai **74** B 4
Bukittinggi **74** AB 3–4
Bukoba **92** E 5
Bukukun **68** K 6
Bül, Küh-e **61** F 3
Bulawayo **94** D 3–4
Buldana **72** C 3
Bulgan **68** H 6
Bulgaria **58** C 2
Bullahãr **93** G 2
Bulo Berde **93** H 4
Bulungu **92** B 5
Bumba **92** C 4
Bumbulan **75** F 3
Bunbury **78** B 5
Bunda **92** E 5
Bundaberg **79** J 3
Bunda Bunda **79** G 3
Bundesrepublik Deutschland **53** EF 5
Bundooma **78** E 3
Bunia **92** DE 4
Buorkhaya, Guba **69** O 1
Buorkhaya, Mys **69** O 1
Buqayq **61** E 4
Buran **63** R 6
Bura'o **93** H 3
Burayda **60** D 4
Buraydah **89** G 3
Burdur **58** D 3
Burdwan **72** E 3
Bureinskiy, Khrebet **69** O 5
Bureya **69** O 5
Burgakhcha **69** Q 3
Burgas **58** C 2
Burgeo **101** O 6
Burgersdorp **94** D 6
Burgfjället **54** FG 3
Burgos (Mexico) **104** C 3
Burgos (Spain) **56** C 3
Burhanpur **72** C 3
Burin Peninsula **101** QR 6
Burkhala **69** RS 3
Burkina **90** DE 3
Burlington (CO, U.S.A.) **102** F 4
Burlington (IA, U.S.A.) **103** H 3
Burlington (N.Y., U.S.A.) **103** M 3

Burma **73** FG 3
Burmantovo **63** M 3
Burnie **80** L 9
Burns **102** C 3
Burnu **58** D 3
Burqin **67** M 1
Burra **79** F 5
Bursa **58** C 2
Bur Sa'id **60** A 3
Bür Südãn **88** F 5
Buru **75** G 4
Burundi **92** DE 5
Buşayrah **60** C 2
Büshehr **61** F 3
Bushman Land **94** BC 5
Businga **92** C 4
Busira **92** B 5
Buskerud **55** E 3
Busu Melo **92** C 4
Butang Group **73** G 6
Butaritari **82** C 2
Butembo **92** D 4
Butha Qi **69** M 6
Butte **102** D 2
Butt of Lewis **52** B 3
Button Bay **99** T 4
Button Islands **101** P 3
Butuan **75** G 2
Bu Tu Suay **73** J 5
Buy **62** H 4
Büyük Ağrı Daği **59** F 3
Buzachi, Poluostrov **66** E 1–2
Buzãu **58** C 1
Buzuluk **62** K 5
Byblos **60** B 2
Bydgoszcz **53** G 4
Bygdeå **54** H 3
Bygdeträsket **54** GH 3
Bykovo **62** J 3
Bykovskiy **69** NO 1
Bylot Island **114**
Byrd Station **115**
Byro **78** B 4
Byske **54** H 3
Byskeälven **54** GH 2
Bytom **53** G 4
Byuchennyakh **69** QR 3

C

Caaguazu **112** E 4
Cáatingas **111** GH 2–3
Caazapa **112** E 4
Cabanatuan **75** J 1
Cabezas **110** D 4
Cabimas **108** D 1
Cabinda **91** G 6–7
Cabo Barbas **86** B 4
Cabo Beata **105** H 4
Cabo Bojador **86** BC 3
Cabo Catoche **104** E 3
Cabo Corrientes **108** C 2
Cabo das Correntes **95** F 4
Cabo de Ajo **56** C 3
Cabo de Creus **56** D 3
Cabo de Finisterre **56** B 3
Cabo de Formentor **56** D 3
Cabo de Gata **56** C 4
Cabo de Hornos **113** CD 10

Cabo de la Nao 56 D 4
Cabo Delgado 95 G 2
Cabo de Palos 56 C 4
Cabo de Salinas 56 D 4
Cabo de Santa Maria
(Mozambique) 95 EF 5
Cabo de Santa Maria
(Portugal) 56 B 4
Cabo de São Roque 111 JK 2
Cabo de São Vicente 56 B 4
Cabo dos Bahías 113 CD 8
Cabo Frio 111 H 5
Cabo Gracias a Dios
104 F 4–5
Cabo Norte 109 J 3
Cabo Orange 109 H 3
Cabo Ortegal 56 B 3
Caborca 102 D 5
Cabo San Antonio
(Argentina) 113 E 6
Cabo San Antonio (Cuba)
104 EF 3
Cabo San Diego 113 C 9
Cabo San Lucas 102 E 7
Cabo Santa Elena 104 E 5
Cabo Trafalgar 56 B 4
Cabot Strait 101 Q 6
Cabo Verde 90 AB 6
Cabrera 56 D 4
Cabrera, Sierra de la 56 B 3
Cabruta 108 E 2
Caçador 112 F 4
Čačak 58 AB 2
Caceres (Brazil) 110 E 4
Cáceres (Spain) 56 B 4
Cachi, Nevado de 110 C 5
Cachimbo 109 H 5
Cachimbo, Serra do 109 G 5
Cachoeira 111 J 3
Cachoeira Alta 111 F 4
Cachoeira do Sul 112 F 5
Cachoeiro de Itapemirim
111 HJ 5
Caconda 94 B 2
Cacula 94 A 2
Cadi, Sierra del 56 D 3
Cadiz (Philippines) 75 F 1
Cádiz (Spain) 56 B 4
Cadiz, Golfo de 56 B 4
Caen 56 C 2
Caetite 111 H 3
Cagayan de Oro 75 F 2
Cagayan Islands 75 F 2
Cagliari 57 E 4
Caguas 105 J 4
Caia 95 EF 3
Caibarién 105 G 3
Caico 111 J 2
Caicos Islands 105 H 3
Cailloma 110 B 4
Cairns 79 H 2
Cairo 88 E 2
Caiundo 94 B 3
Cajamarca 108 C 5
Cajazeiras 111 J 2
Cajuapara 109 J 4
Calabar 91 F 4
Calabozo 108 E 2

Calabria 57 G 4
Calabro, Apennino 57 G 4
Calafate 113 B 9
Calais 52 D 4
Calama 110 C 5
Calamar 108 D 3
Calamian Group 75 E 1
Cala Ratjada 56 D 4
Calatayud 56 C 3
Calatrava, Campo de 56 C 4
Calbayog 75 FG 1
Calçoene 109 H 3
Calcutta 72 E 3
Caldas 108 C 2
Caldera 112 B 4
Caleta Olivia 113 C 8
Calgary 99 P 5
Cali 108 C 3
Calicut 72 BC 5
California 102 BC 4
Calilegua 110 CD 5
Callao 110 A 3
Caltanissetta 57 F 4
Calvi 57 E 3
Camagüey 105 G 3
Camaná 110 B 4
Camapuã 111 F 4
Camaquã 112 F 5
Camarat, Cap 57 E 3
Camargo 110 C 5
Camarones 113 CD 7
Camaxilo 94 B 1
Cambodia 73 HJ 5
Cambrai 56 D 1
Cambrian Mountains 52 C 4
Cambridge (MA, U.S.A.)
103 MN 3
Cambridge (U.K.) 52 D 4
Cambridge Bay 99 QR 2
Cameia National Park 94 C 2
Cameron 103 H 2
Cameroon 91 FG 4
Cameroon, Mont 91 F 5
Cametá 109 HJ 4
Camiranga 109 J 4
Camiri 110 D 5
Camocim 111 H 1
Camooweal 79 F 2
Camorta 73 F 6
Campana, Isla 113 A 8
Campbell Island 115
Campbellton 101 O 6
Camp Century 114
Campeche 104 D 4
Campeche, Bahia de
104 CD 4
Campeche 104 DE 4
Campidano 57 E 4
Campina Grande 111 J 2
Campinas 111 G 5
Campo 91 F 5
Campo Corral 108 DE 2
Campo de Calatrava 56 C 4
Campo Formoso 111 H 3
Campo Gallo 112 D 4
Campo Grande 111 F 5
Campo Maior 111 H 1
Campos (Brazil) 111 GH 3–4

Campos (Brazil) 111 H 5
Cam Ranh 73 JK 5
Camrose 99 P 5
Ca Na 74 C 1
Canada 98–101
Canadian River 102 F 4
Çanakkale 58 C 2
Çanakkale Boğazı 58 C 2–3
Canal de la Mona 105 J 4
Canal do Norte 109 H 3
Canal du Midi 56 D 3
Canale di Sicilia 57 F 4
Canale di Malta 57 F 4
Cananea 102 DE 5
Canary Islands 86 B 3
Canaveral, Cape 103 KL 6
Canavieiras 111 J 4
Canberra 79 H 6
Canchas 112 BC 4
Candeias 111 J 3
Candelaria 104 D 4
Canéla 111 H 3
Cangamba 94 C 2
Cangombé 94 B 2
Cangyuan 70 C 6
Cangzhou 71 G 3
Canindé 111 J 1
Çankırı 59 D 2
Cannanore 72 BC 5
Cannes 57 E 3
Canning Basin 78 C 2
Cann River 79 H 6
Canoas 112 F 4
Canora 99 R 5
Canosa 57 G 3
Canso 101 P 6
Cantabrian Mountains
56 BC 3
Cantaura 109 F 2
Canterbury Bight 82 C 5
Can Tho 73 J 6
Canto do Buriti 111 H 2
Canton 103 K 3
Canton (China) 70 F 6
Capanema 109 J 4
Capão Bonito 111 G 5
Cap Camarat 57 E 3
Cap Corse 57 E 3
Cap de Fer 87 G 1
Cap de Gaspé 101 P 6
Cap de la Hague 56 C 2
Cap-de-la-Madeleine 101 N 6
Cape Adare 115
Cape Agulhas 94 C 6
Cape Ann 115
Cape Arid 78 C 5
Cape Arid National Park
78 C 5
Cape Arnhem 79 F 1
Cape Baring 99 O 2
Cape Bathurst 98 LM 1
Cape Bauld 101 QR 5
Cape Boothby 115
Cape Breton Island 101 Q 6
Cape Canaveral 103 KL 6
Cape Catastrophe 79 F 5–6
Cape Chapman 99 U 2
Cape Charles 103 L 4

Cape Chelyuskin 114
Cape Chidley 101 P 3
Cape Churchill 99 T 4
Cape Coast 90 DE 4
Cape Cod 103 N 3
Cape Columbine 94 B 6
Cape Comorin 72 C 6
Cape Cretin 80 E 3
Cape Croker 78 E 1
Cape Cross 94 A 4
Cape d'Ambre,Cape
Bobraomby 95 HJ 2
Cape Darnley 115
Cape Dennison 115
Cape Dorchester 101 M 2
Cape du Couedic 79 F 6
Cape Dyer 101 P 2
Cape Engaño 75 J 1
Cape Farewell 81 Q 9
Cape Fear 103 L 5
Cape Finniss 78 E 5
Cape Flattery 102 AB 2
Cape Freels 101 R 6
Cape Fria 94 A 3
Cape Grim 80 K 9
Cape Harrison 101 Q 5
Cape Hatteras 103 LM 4
Cape Henrietta Maria 101 L 4
Cape Herluf Trolle 101 T 3
Cape Horn 113 CD 10
Cape Howe 79 J 6
Cape Jaffa 79 F 6
Cape Kellett 99 M 1
Cape Krusenstern National
Monument 98 E 2
Cape Lambert 81 F 2
Cape Lambton 99 MN 1
Cape Leeuwin 78 A 5
Cape Lévêque 78 C 2
Capelinha 111 H 4
Cape Lisburne 98 D 2
Cape Londonderry 78 D 1
Cape Lookout 103 L 5
Cape Low 99 UV 3
Cape Maria van Diemen
81 PQ 7
Cape Melville 79 GH 1
Cape Mendocino 102 AB 3
Cape Mercy 101 P 3
Cape Meredith 113 D 9
Cape Mohican 98 CD 3
Cape Morris Jesup 114
Cape Naturaliste 78 A 5
Cape Negrais 73 F 4
Cape Newenham 98 DE 4
Cape Norvegia 115
Cape of Good Hope 94 B 6
Cape Otway 79 G 6
Cape Palmas 90 C 5
Cape Poinsett 115
Cape Prince Alfred 99 M 1
Cape Prince of Wales 98 D 2
Cape Providence 80 OP 10
Cape Province 94 CD 6
Cape Race 101 R 6
Cape Raper 101 O 2
Cape Ray 101 Q 6
Cape Rodney 80 E 4

Cape Sable (Canada) **101** O 7
Cape Sable (FL, U.S.A.)
  103 K 6
Cape Saint Francis **94** CD 6
Cape Saint George **81** F 2–3
Cape Saint Lucia **95** E 5
Cape San Blas **103** J 6
Cape Scott **78** D 1
Cape Smith **101** LM 3
Cape Town **94** B 6
Cape Van Diemen **78** D 1
Cape Verde **90** AB 6
Cape Wessel **79** F 1
Cape Wrath **52** BC 3
Cape Yakataga **98** J 4
Cape York **79** G 1
Cape York Peninsula **79** G 1
Cape Zhelaniya **114**
Cap Ferret **56** C 3
Cap-Haïtien **105** H 3–4
Cap Hopes Advance **101** O 3
Capitán Arturo Prat **115**
Cap Lopez **91** F 6
Cap Masoala **95** J 3
Capo Carbonara **57** E 4
Capo Circeo **57** F 3
Capo Gallo **57** F 4
Capoompeta **79** J 4
Capo Palinuro **57** FG 4
Capo Passero **57** G 4
Capo San Marco **57** E 4
Capo Santa Maria di Leuca
  57 G 4
Capo Spartivento **57** E 4
Capo Testa **57** E 3
Capri **57** F 3
Capricorn Channel **79** J 3
Caprivi Game Park **94** C 3
Caprivi Strip **94** C 3
Cap Saint-André **95** G 3
Cap Sainte-Marie,Cap
  Vohimena **95** GH 5
Cap Timiris **86** B 5
Cap Vert **90** A 3
Cap Wolstenholme **101** M 3
Caquetá **108** D 4
Caracal **58** B 2
Caracarai **10** F 3
Caracas **108** E 1
Carahue **113** B 6
Carajás, Serra dos **109** H 4–5
Caratinga **111** H 4
Carauari **108** E 4
Carazinho **112** F 4
Carballo **56** B 3
Carbonara, Capo **57** E 4
Carbonia **57** E 4
Carcassonne **56** D 3
Cárdenas **105** F 3
Cardiff **52** C 4
Cardigan **52** C 4
Careiro **109** G 4
Carey, Lake **78** C 4
Caribbean Sea **105** GJ 4
Caribou Mountains **99** O 4
Carinhanha **111** H 3
Cariparé **111** G 3
Caritianas **109** F 5

Carletonville **94** D 5
Carlisle **52** C 4
Carnarvon (Australia) **78** A 3
Carnarvon (S. Africa) **94** C 6
Carnegie **78** C 4
Carnegie, Lake **78** C 4
Car Nicobar **73** F 6
Carnot **92** B 3
Carolina **109** J 5
Caroline **83** EF 3
Caroline Islands **82** AB 2
Carondelet **82** D 3
Carpathians **58** BC 1
Carpăţii Meridionali **58** B 1–2
Carpentaria Gulf of **79** F 1
Carpina **111** J 2
Carrick-on-Shannon **52** B 4
Carrillo **104** B 2
Carrizal **108** D 1
Carrizozo **102** E 5
Çarşamba **59** D 3
Carson City **102** C 4
Cartagena (Colombia) **108** C 1
Cartagena (Spain) **56** C 4
Cartago (Costa Rica) **104** F 6
Caruaru **111** J 2
Carvoeiro **109** F 4
Casablanca **86** D 2
Casbas **113** D 6
Cascade Range **102** B 2–3
Cascavel **111** F 5
Caserta **57** F 3
Casey **115**
Casino **79** J 4
Casma **108** C 5
Casper **102** E 3
Caspian Sea **66** DE 2–3
Cassiar Mountains **98** M 4
Cassino **57** F 3
Castanhal **109** J 4
Castaño **112** C 5
Castellón **56** CD 4
Castelo de Vide **56** B 4
Castelvetrano **57** F 4
Castilla (Chile) **112** B 4
Castilla (Peru) **108** BC 5
Castilla la Nueva **56** C 3–4
Castilla la Vieja **56** C 3
Castillos **112** F 5
Castlegar **99** O 6
Castor **99** P 5
Castres **56** D 3
Castries **105** K 5
Castro **113** B 7
Catalão **111** G 4
Cataluna **56** D 3
Çatalzeytin **59** D 2
Catamarca **112** CD 4
Catanduanes **75** FG 1
Catanduva **111** G 5
Catania **57** G 4
Catanzaro **57** G 4
Catastrophe, Cape **79** F 6
Catbalogan **75** FG 1
Cateel **75** G 2
Catinzaco **112** C 4
Cat Island **105** GH 3
Catoche, Cabo **104** E 3

Catrilo **113** D 6
Catrimani **109** F 3
Catwick Islands **73** J 5–6
Caucasus Mountains **59** F 2
Cauquenes **113** B 6
Caura **109** F 2
Cavalcante **111** G 3
Caxias (Amazonas, Brazil)
  108 D 4
Caxias (Maranhão, Brazil)
  111 H 1
Caxias do Sul **112** FG 4
Caxito **94** A 1
Cayenne **109** H 3
Cayman Islands **105** FG 4
Ceará **111** HJ 1
Ceballos **104** B 2
Cebollar **112** C 4
Cebu **75** F 2
Čechy **53** F 4
Cedar Falls **103** H 3
Cedar Lake **99** RS 5
Cedar Rapids **103** H 3
Cedros, Isla **102** C 6
Celaya **104** B 3
Celebes **75** EF 4
Celebes Sea **75** F 3
Celje **57** FG 2
Celle **53** F 4
Celtic Sea **52** B 4
Central, Cordilera (Colombia)
  108 C 2–3
Central, Cordillera (Peru)
  108 C 5
Central African Republic
  92 BC 3
Central Arctic District **99** PR 1
Central Kalahari Game
  Reserve **94** C 4
Central Makran Range
  67 GH 5
Centralno Tungusskoye Plato
  68 GH 3–4
Central Range **80** D 2–3
Central Siberian Plateau
  68 GK 3
Cereal **99** P 5
Ceres **111** FG 4
Cerf **93** J 6
Cerro Aconcagua **112** BC 5
Cerro Agua Caliente **104** A 2
Cerro Ángel **104** B 3
Cerro Blanco **102** E 6
Cerro Bonete **112** C 4
Cerro Champaquí **112** D 5
Cerro Chirripó **104** F 6
Cerro de la Encantada
  102 CD 5
Cerro del Toro **112** C 4
Cerro de Pasco **110** A 3
Cerro de Tocorpuri **110** C 5
Cerro Galán **112** C 4
Cerro Grande **104** B 3
Cerro Las Casilas **102** E 7
Cerro Las Minas **104** E 4–5
Cerro Marahuaca **108** E 3
Cerro Mariquita **104** C 3
Cerro Mohinora **102** E 6

Cerro Murallón **113** B 8
Cerro Nuevo Mundo **110** C 5
Cerro Ojos del Salado **112** C 4
Cerro San Valentín **113** B 8
Cerro Ventana **102** E 7
Cerro Yavi **108** E 2
Cerro Yucuyácua **104** C 4
Cerro Yumari **108** E 3
Cesano **57** F 3
České Budějovice **53** F 5
Českézemě **53** G 5
Ceuta **86** D 1
Ceva-i-Ra **82** C 4
Cévennes **56** D 3
Ceyhan (Turkey) **59** E 3
Ceyhan (Turkey) **59** E 3
Ceylanpınar **60** C 1
Ceylon **72** D 6
Chaca **110** B 4
Chachapoyas **108** C 5
Chad **91** HJ 3
Chädegän **61** F 2
Chadobets **68** GH 4
Chagai Hills **67** G 5
Chagda **69** O 4
Chagdo Kangri **72** D 1
Chaghcharän **67** GH 4
Chagos Archipelago **65** K 10
Chagyl **66** F 2
Chahah Burjak **67** G 4
Chah Bahâr **67** G 5
Chaiyaphum **73** H 4
Chakari **94** D 3
Chake Chake **93** FG 6
Chakhansur **67** G 4
Chala **110** B 4
Chalbi Desert **93** F 4
Chalhuanca **110** B 3
Challapata **110** C 4
Challenger Deep **77** D 1
Châlons-sur-Marne **57** D 2
Chalon-sur-Saône **57** DE 2
Châlûs **61** F 1
Chaman **67** H 4
Chamba **72** C 1
Chambery **57** E 2
Chamical **112** C 5
Chamoli **72** CD 1
Champagne **57** DE 2
Champaquí, Cerro **112** D 5
Champdoré, Lac **101** O 4
Chañaral **112** B 4
Chanco **113** B 6
Chandigarh **72** C 1
Chandler **101** P 6
Chandmanī **70** C 1
Chandpur **73** F 3
Chandrapur **72** C 3–4
Chanf **67** G 5
Changara **95** E 3
Changchun **71** J 2
Changde **70** F 5
Changji **67** M 2
Chang Jiang **70–71** EG 4
Changling **71** H 2
Changsha **70** F 5
Changwu **70** E 3
Changzhi **70** F 3

Channel Islands **102** C 5
Channel Islands (U.K.) **52** C 5
Chaoyang (Guangdoug, China) **70** G 6
Chaoyang (Liaoning, China) **71** GH 2
Chapayev-Zheday **68** L 3–4
Chapleau **100** L 6
Chapman, Cape **99** U 2
Chapoma **62** GH 2
Chapra **72** DE 2
Chara **68** L 4
Charagua **110** D 4
Charcot Island **115**
Chard **99** P 4
Chardzhou **67** G 3
Chari **91** H 3
Charity **109** G 2
Charkabozh **62** K 2
Charleroi **52** DE 4
Charlesbourg **101** N 6
Charles Peak **78** C 5
Charleston (S.C., U.S.A.) **103** L 5
Charleston (W.V., U.S.A.) **103** K 4
Charleville **79** H 4
Charlotte **103** KL 4
Charlottesville **103** L 4
Charlottetown **101** P 6
Charlton (Australia) **79** G 6
Charlton (Canada) **101** LM 5
Charters Towers **79** H 2–3
Chartres **56** D 2
Charyshskoye **63** Q 5
Chasel'ka **63** Q 2
Chatanga **68** K 6
Châteauroux **56** D 2
Châtellerault **56** CD 2
Chatham **81** S 9
Chatham (Ontario, Can.) **103** K 3
Chattanooga **103** J 5
Chaumont **57** DE 2
Chau Phu **73** HJ 5
Chaves (Brazil) **109** H 4
Chaves (Portugal) **56** B 3
Chayatyn, Khrebet **69** P 5
Chaykovskiy **62** KL 4
Chazhegovo **62** K 3
Cheb **53** F 4
Cheboksary **62** J 4
Cheduba **73** F 4
Chegga **87** G 2
Chegytun **98** C 2
Cheju **71** J 4
Cheju-do **71** J 4
Chekhov **69** Q 6
Chekunda **69** O 5
Chekuyevo **62** G 3
Chelforó **113** C 6
Chelkar **66** F 1
Chelm **53** H 4
Chelmuzhi **62** G 3
Chelyabinsk **63** M 4
Chenachane **86** E 3
Chengde **71** G 2
Chengdu **70** DE 4

Chenxi **70** EF 5
Chenzhou **70** F 5
Chepen **108** C 5
Chepes **112** C 5
Cherbourg **56** C 2
Cherchell **87** F 1
Cheremkhovo **68** H 5
Cherepovets **62** G 4
Cherkassy **62** EF 6
Cherkessk **59** F 2
Chernigov **62** EF 5
Chernovtsy **58** C 1
Chernyakhovsk **55** H 5
Chernyshevskiy **68** K 3
Chernyye Zemli **59** G 1
Chernyy Ostrov **68** F 3
Cherskiy Range **69** Q 2
Cherskogo, Khrebet **69** P 1–2
Chervonograd **55** H 5
Chervonoznamenka **58** CD 1
Chesapeake Bay Bridge-Tunnel **103** LM 4
Chesterfield Inlet **99** TU 3
Chesterfield Islands **82** B 4
Chetumal **104** E 4
Cheulik **69** P 2
Cheyenne **102** F 3
Chhatarpur **72** C 3
Chiang Kham **73** H 4
Chiang Mai **73** G 4
Chiang Rai **73** G 4
Chiang Saen **73** H 3
Chiapas **104** D 4
Chiavari **57** E 3
Chiayi **71** H 6
Chiba **71** M 3
Chibagalakh **69** PQ 2
Chibit **63** R 5
Chibougamau **101** N 6
Chicago **103** J 3
Chicapa **94** C 1
Chichagof **98** K 4
Chicheng **71** G 2
Chiclayo **108** B 5
Chico **113** C 7
Chicoutimi **101** N 6
Chidley, Cape **101** P 3
Chifeng **71** G 2
Chiganak **63** O 6
Chigorodó **108** C 2
Chigubo **95** E 4
Chihuahua **102** EF 6
Chik Ballapur **72** C 5
Chikhacheva **69** R 1
Chilabombwe **94** D 2
Childress **102** F 5
Chile **113** B 5–6
Chilete **108** C 5
Chilipa de Alvarez **104** C 4
Chillán **113** B 6
Chiloé, Isla de **113** B 7
Chilpancingo **104** BC 4
Chilwa, Lago **95** F 3
Chimbay **66** F 2
Chimborazo **108** C 4
Chimbote **108** C 5
Chimkent **67** H 2
Chin **73** F 3

China **70** DF 4
Chinandega **104** E 5
Chincha Alta **110** A 3
Chindu **70** C 4
Chindwin **73** FG 3
Chinese Wall **70** E 3
Chingola **94** D 2
Chinguetti **86** C 4
Chinju **71** J 4
Chipata **95** E 2
Chirchik **67** HJ 2
Chiriguaná **108** D 2
Chiriquí, Golfo de **108** B 2
Chishui **70** E 5
Chita **68** K 5
Chitado **94** A 3
Chitato **94** C 1
Chitina **98** HJ 3
Chitipa **95** E 1
Chitral **67** J 3
Chittagong **73** F 3
Chittaurgarh **72** BC 3
Chittoor **72** C 5
Chivasso **57** E 2
Chivay **110** B 4
Chizha **62** H 2
Chkalovo **63** O 5
Chobe National Park **94** C 3
Choele Choel **113** CD 6
Choggia **57** F 2
Choiseul **81** G 3
Chojnice **53** G 4
Cholet **56** C 2
Choluteca **104** E 5
Chomutov **53** F 4
Chona **68** J 3
Chon Buri **73** H 5
Ch'ŏngjin **71** JK 2
Ch'ŏngju **71** J 3
Chongqing **70** E 5
Chŏnju **71** J 3
Chonos, Archipiélago de los **113** AB 7–8
Chon Thanh **73** J 5
Chorzów **53** G 4
Chosica **110** A 3
Chos Malal **113** BC 6
Chotanagpur **72** DE 3
Chott Melrhir **87** G 2
Choum **86** C 4
Choybalsan **68** K 6
Christchurch **82** C 5
Christmas Island **74** C 6
Chubut **113** C 7
Chudskoye Ozero **55** J 4
Chukar **68** L 3
Chukchi Sea **114**
Chuken **69** P 6
Chukotsk Peninsula **114**
Chukotsk Range **114**
Chulak-Kurgan **67** HJ 2
Chulasa **62** J 3
Chula Vista **102** C 5
Chulym **63** QR 4
Chumikan **69** OP 5
Chumphon **73** GH 5
Ch'unch'ŏn **71** J 3
Chuquibamba **110** B 4

Chuquicamata **110** C 5
Chur **57** E 2
Churchill (Man., Can.) **99** ST 4
Churchill (Man., Can.) **99** T 4
Churchill, Cape **99** T 4
Churchill Falls **101** P 5
Churchill Lake **99** Q 4
Churchill Mountains **115**
Churu **72** C 2
Churuguara **108** E 1
Churún Merú **109** F 2
Chusovoy **63** L 4
Chusovskoy **62** L 3
Chute-des-Passes **101** NO 6
Chutes de Katende **92** C 6
Chutes de Livingstone **92** A 6
Chutes Ngaliema (Stanley Falls) **92** D 4
Chuxiong **70** D 5
Chuyengo **68** HJ 3
Cianjur **74** C 5
Cícero Dantas **111** J 3
Ciechanów **53** H 4
Ciego de Ávila **105** G 3
Ciénaga **108** D 1
Cienfuegos **105** F 3
Cieza **56** C 4
Cihanbeyli Platosu **59** D 3
Cilo Dağı **59** F 3
Cimarron River **102** G 4
Çimen Dağı **59** E 3
Cîmpia Bărăganului **58** C 1–2
Cîmpia Burnazului **58** C 2
Cîmpina **58** C 1
Cinca **56** D 3
Cincinatti **103** K 4
Cinto, Monte **57** E 3
Circeo, Capo **57** F 3
Circle **98** J 2
Cirebon **74** C 5
Cirque Mountain **101** P 4
Ciskei **94** D 6
Citta del Vaticano **57** F 3
Ciudad Acuña **104** B 2
Ciudad Bolívar **109** F 2
Ciudad Camargo **102** E 6
Ciudad del Carmen **104** D 4
Ciudad de Rio Grande **104** B 3
Ciudad Guayana **109** F 2
Ciudad Guzmán **104** B 4
Ciudad Hidalgo **104** BC 4
Ciudad Juárez **102** E 5
Ciudad Madero **104** C 3
Ciudad Mante **104** C 3
Ciudad Obregón **102** E 6
Ciudad Río Bravo **104** C 2
Ciudad-Rodrigo **56** B 3
Ciudad Valles **104** C 3
Ciudad Victoria **104** C 3
Civitanova Marche **57** F 3
Civitavecchia **57** F 3
Cizre **59** F 3
Claire, Lake **99** P 4
Claire Coast **115**
Clanwilliam **94** BC 6
Clarke Range **79** H 2–3
Clarksburg **103** KL 4

Clarksville **103** J 4
Clay Belt **100** LM 5
Clearwater **103** K 6
Clermont **79** H 3
Clermont-Ferrand **56** D 2
Cleveland (OH, U.S.A.)
 103 K 3
Cleveland, Mount **102** D 2
Clinton **99** N 5
Clinton-Colden Lake **99** Q 3
Cloncurry **79** FG 3
Clorinda **112** E 4
Cloud Peak **102** E 3
Clovis **102** F 5
Cluj-Napoca **58** B 1
Cmi Drim **58** B 2
Cnossus **58** C 3
Coahuila **104** B 2
Coal River **99** M 4
Coari **109** F 4
Coast Mountains
 98–99 LM 4–5
Coast of Labrador **101** QP 4–5
Coast Range (Queensland,
 Austr.) **79** J 4
Coast Range (U.S.A.)
 102 B 3–4
Coats Island **99** V 3
Coats land **115**
Coatzacoalcos **104** D 4
Cobar **79** H 5
Cobija **110** C 3
Cobquecura **113** B 6
Coburg **53** F 4
Cocachacra **110** B 4
Cochabamba **110** CD 4
Cochin **72** C 6
Cochrane **113** B 8
Cocklebiddy **78** D 5
Coco Islands **73** F 5
Codó **111** H 1
Cody **102** E 3
Coetivy **93** JK 6
Coeur d'Alene **102** C 2
Coff's Harbour **79** J 5
Coihaique **113** B 8
Coimbatore **72** C 5
Coimbra **56** B 3
Cojimies **108** B 3
Cojutepeque **104** E 5
Colatina **111** HJ 4
Cold Bay **98** E 5
Col de Perthus **56** D 3
Colesberg **94** D 6
Colima **104** B 4
Collier Bay **78** C 2
Collier Ranges National Park
 78 B 3
Collines du Perche **56** D 2
Collinson Peninsula **99** R 1–2
Cololo, Nevado **110** C 4
Colombia **108** D 3
Colombo **72** C 6
Colón (Cuba) **105** F 3
Colón (Panamá) **108** C 2
Colón, Archipiélago de
 108 B 6
Colona **78** E 5

Colonia Las Heras **113** C 8
Colorado (Argentina) **113** D 6
Colorado (U.S.A.) **102** EF 4
Colorado Plateau **102** DE 4
Colorado River (AZ, U.S.A.)
 102 D 5
Colorado River (TX, U.S.A.)
 103 G 5–6
Colorado Springs **102** F 4
Columbia (MO, U.S.A.)
 103 H 4
Columbia (S.C., U.S.A.)
 103 K 5
Columbia (WA, U.S.A.)
 102 BC 2
Columbia, Mount **99** O 5
Columbia Falls **102** D 2
Columbia Mountains **99** NO 5
Columbia Plateau **102** C 3
Columbine, Cape **94** B 6
Columbus (IN, U.S.A.) **103** J 4
Columbus (MS, U.S.A.)
 103 K 5
Columbus (OH, U.S.A.)
 103 K 4
Columbus (TX, U.S.A.)
 103 G 6
Colville Lake **99** MN 2
Comalcalco **104** DE 4
Comandante Luis
 Piedrabuena **113** CD 8–9
Combarbala **112** B 5
Combermere Bay **73** F 4
Commander Islands **114**
Committee Bay **99** U 2
Como **57** E 2
Comodoro Rivadavia **113** C 8
Comorin, Cape **72** C 6
Comoros **95** G 2
Compiègne **56** D 2
Conakry **90** B 4
Conceição do Araguaia
 109 HJ 5
Concepción (Bolivia) **110** D 4
Concepción (Chile) **113** B 6
Concepción (Paraguay)
 110 E 5
Concepción del Oro **104** B 3
Concepción del Uruguay
 112 E 5
Concord **103** M 3
Concórdia (Amazonas, Brazil)
 108 E 4
Concordia (Argentina) **112** E 5
Condon **102** C 2
Conejo **102** D 7
Congo **91** H 6
Connaught **52** B 4
Connecticut **103** M 3
Conrad **102** D 2
Conselheiro Lafaiete **111** H 5
Con Son **73** J 6
Constança **58** C 2
Constantine **87** G 1
Contamana **108** D 5
Contwoyto Lake **99** PQ 2
Conway Reef → Ceva-i-Ra
 82 C 4

Cook **78** E 5
Cook, Mount **82** C 5
Cook, Strait **82** C 5
Cookes Peak **102** E 5
Cook Inlet **98** G 3
Cook Islands **82** E 3
Cook Mountains **115**
Cook Strait **81** QR 9
Cooktown **79** H 2
Copenhagen **55** F 4
Copiapó **112** BC 4
Copperbelt **94** D 2
Coqên **72** E 1
Coquimbo **112** B 5
Coral Harbour **99** UV 3
Coral Sea **82** B 3–4
Coral Sea Islands Territory
 79 HJ 1–2
Corcaigh **52** B 4
Cordillera Cantábrica **56** BC 3
Cordillera Central (Colombia)
 108 C 2–3
Cordillera Central (Peru)
 108 C 5
Cordillera Central
 (Philippines) **75** J 1
Cordillera Occidental
 (Colombia) **108** C 2–3
Cordillera Occidental (Peru)
 110 BC 3–4
Cordillera Oriental (Bolivia)
 110 CD 3–5
Cordillera Oriental
 (Colombia) **108** CD 2–3
Cordillera Real (Ecuador)
 108 C 4
Córdoba (Argentina) **112** D 5
Córdoba (Mexico) **104** C 4
Córdoba (Spain) **56** BC 4
Corfu **58** AB 3
Corigliano Calabro **57** G 4
Corinth (Greece) **58** B 3
Corinto **111** H 4
Cork **52** B 4
Çorlu **58** C 2
Cornelio **102** D 6
Cornélio Procópio **111** F 5
Corner Brook **101** Q 6
Cornwall **101** M 6
Coro **108** DE 1
Coroatá **111** H 1
Corocoro **110** C 4
Coromandel Coast **72** D 5
Coromandel Peninsula **81** R 8
Coronation Gulf **99** P 2
Coronel **113** B 6
Coronel Fabriciano **111** H 4
Coronel Oviedo **112** E 4
Coronel Pringles **113** D 6
Coropuna, Nevado **110** B 4
Corpus Christi **103** G 6
Corrente **111** GH 3
Correntes, Cabo das **95** F 4
Correntina **111** GH 3
Corrientes **112** E 4
Corrientes, Cabo **108** C 2
Corse **57** E 3
Corse, Cap **57** E 3

Corsica **57** E 3
Çoruh **59** F 2
Çoruh Dağları **59** F 2
Çorum **62** E 2
Corumbá **110** E 4
Corunna **56** B 3
Corvallis **102** B 3
Cosenza **57** G 4
Cosmoledo Group **93** H 6
Costa Blanca **56** C 4
Costa Brava **56** D 3
Costa de la Luz **56** B 4
Costa del Azahar **56** D 3
Costa del Sol **56** C 4
Costa de Mosquitos **104** F 5
Costa Dorada **56** D 3
Costa Rica **104** EF 6
Costa Verde **56** B 3
Cotabato **75** F 2
Cotagaita **110** CD 5
Coteau du Missouri **102** FG 2
Côte d'Argent **56** C 3
Côte d'Azur **57** E 3
Cotonou **90** E 4
Cotopaxi **108** C 4
Cottbus **53** F 4
Cotulla **102** G 6
Council Bluffs **103** GH 3
Courland **55** H 4
Coventry **52** C 4
Covington **103** JK 4
Cowell **79** F 5
Cowra **79** H 5
Coxim **111** F 4
Cox's Bazar **73** F 3
Cracow **53** GH 4
Cradock **94** D 6
Craiova **58** B 2
Cranbrook **78** B 5
Crary Mountains **115**
Cratéus **111** HJ 2
Crato **111** J 2
Crawford **102** F 3
Creil **56** D 2
Cremona **57** F 2
Cres **57** F 3
Crescent City **102** AB 3
Crete **58** C 3
Creus, Cabo de **56** D 3
Creuse **56** D 2
Criciúma **112** G 4
Crimea **59** D 1
Cristmas Island **83** E 2
Cristóbal, Colón Pico **108** D 1
Croatia **57** G 2
Crockett **103** GH 5
Croker, Cape **78** E 1
Croker Island **78** E 1
Crooked Island **105** H 3
Crooked Island Passage
 105 GH 3
Crookston **103** G 2
Cross, Cape **94** A 4
Crotone **57** G 4
Crowell **102** G 5
Crown Prince Frederik Island
 99 U 2
Crowsnest Pass **99** OP 6

Cruz Alta 112 F 4
Cruz del Eje 112 CD 5
Cruzeiro do Oeste 111 F 5
Cruzeiro do Sul 108 D 5
Cruz Grande 104 C 4
Crystal Brook 79 F 5
Cuamba 95 F 2
Cuando Cubango 94 BC 3
Cuango 94 B 1
Cuanza 94 B 1–2
Cuanza Norte 94 AB 1
Cuanza Sul 94 AB 2
Cuauhtémoc 102 E 6
Cuba 105 FG 3
Cubango 94 B 3
Cucurpe 102 D 5
Cúcuta 108 D 2
Cuddalore 72 CD 5
Cuddapah 72 C 5
Cudi Dağı 59 F 3
Cuenca (Ecuador) 108 C 4
Cuenca (Spain) 56 C 3–4
Cuencamé de Ceniceros
    104 B 3
Cuiabá 110 E 4
Cuito Cuanavale 94 B 3
Cu Lao Hon 73 JK 5
Culiacán 102 E 7
Cumaná 109 F 1
Cumbal 108 C 3
Cumberland 103 L 4
Cumberland Peninsula
    101 OP 2
Cumberland Plateau 103 JK 4
Cumberland Sound
    101 OP 2–3
Cunani 109 H 3
Cunene (Angola) 94 A 3
Cunene (Angola) 94 B 3
Cuneo 57 E 3
Cunnamulla 79 H 4
Cupica 108 C 2
Curaçao, Isla 108 E 1
Curacautin 113 B 6
Curdimurka 79 F 4
Curicó 113 B 5–6
Curimatá 111 H 2–3
Curitiba 112 FG 4
Curtis 82 D 5
Curtis Island 79 J 3
Curuça 109 J 4
Curumu 109 H 4
Curupuru 109 K 4
Curvelo 111 H 4
Cushing, Mount 99 M 4
Cuttack 72 E 3
Cuvette 91 H 6
Cuxhaven 53 E 4
Cuya 110 B 4
Cuyo Islands 75 F 1
Cuzco 110 B 3
Cyangugu 92 D 5
Cyclades 58 BC 3
Cypress Hills 99 PQ 6
Cyprus 59 D 3
Cyrenaica 87 JK 3
Czechoslovakia 53 G 5
Częstochowa 53 GH 4

D

Dabat 93 F 2
Dabbāgh, Jabal 60 B 4
Dabola 90 B 3
Dacca 72 F 3
Dadali 82 B 3
Dadanawa 109 G 3
Daet 75 F 1
Dafeng 71 H 4
Dagabur 93 G 3
Dagana 91 H 3
Dagi 69 Q 5
Dagur 70 C 3
Dahabān 66 B 6
Da Hinggan Ling 71 GH 1–2
Dahlak Archipelago 93 FG 1
Dahongliutan 67 KL 3
Dahra 90 AB 2
Dahūk 60 D 1
Daintree River National Park
    79 G 2
Dairen 71 H 3
Daitō-shotō 71 K 5
Dajarra 79 F 3
Dakar 90 A 3
Dakha 72 F 3
Dakhla 86 B 4
Dakovica 58 B 2
Dala 94 BC 2
Dalälven 55 G 3
Dalaman 58 C 3
Dalandzadgad 70 DE 2
Dalarna 55 F 3
Da Lat 73 J 5
Dalby 79 J 4
Dali 70 D 5
Dalian 71 H 3
Dallas 103 G 5
Dall Lake 98 E 3
Dalmā' 61 F 4
Dal'negorsk 71 L 2
Dal'nerechensk 71 KL 1
Dal'nyaya 69 Q 6
Daloa 90 C 4
Dalsland 55 F 4
Dalstroy 69 P 3
Daltonganj 72 DE 3
Dalwallinu 78 B 5
Daly River 78 E 1
Daly Waters 78 E 2
Daman 72 B 3
Damanhūr 88 DE 2
Damara 92 B 3
Damaraland 94 B 4
Damascus 88 F 2
Damascus (Syria) 60 B 2
Damāvand 61 F 2
Damoh 72 C 3
Dampier 78 B 3
Danakil Plain 93 G 2
Danané 90 C 4
Da Nang 73 J 4
Danba 70 D 4
Dandarah 88 E 3
Dandong 71 H 2–3
Danghe Nanshan 70 CD 3
Dangjin Shankou 70 BC 3

Dangshan 71 G 4
Danmark 55 E 4
Danmarks Havn 114
Dan Sai 73 H 4
Danube 58 C 1
Danville 103 L 4
Dan Xian 70 E 7
Dao Xian 70 F 5
Dapoli 72 B 4
Da Qaidam 70 C 3
Dar'ā 60 B 2
Dārāb 66 E 5
Dāran 61 F 2
Darāw 60 A 4
Darband 66 F 4
Darbhanga 72 E 2
Dardanelles 58 C 3
Dar el Beida 86 C 2
Dar es Salaam 93 F 6
Dārfūr 88 C 6
Darganata 67 G 2
Dargaville 81 Q 8
Darién 108 C 2
Darjeeling 72 E 2
Darlag 70 CD 4
Darling Downs 79 H 4
Darling Range 78 B 5
Darling River 79 G 5
Darlington 52 C 4
Darmstadt 53 E 5
Darnah 87 K 2
Darnley, Cape 115
Dar Rounga 92 C 2–3
Dartmoor 52 C 4
Dartmouth 101 P 7
Darvaza 66 F 2
Darweshan 67 G 4
Darwin 78 E 1
Daryācheh-ye Bakhtegān
    61 FG 3
Daryācheh-ye Namak 61 F 2
Daryācheh-ye Orūmīyeh
    61 D 1
Daryācheh-ye Tashk 61 FG 3
Daryā-ye Māzandarān 66 E 3
Dasht-e Kavīr 61 FG 2
Dasht-e Lūt 61 G 2
Dasht-e Naomid 66–67 G 4
Date 71 M 2
Datia 72 C 2
Datong (Qin. China) 70 D 3
Datong (Ziz. China) 70 F 2
Datta 69 Q 6
Dāuarzan 66 F 3
Daugava 55 H 4
Daugav'pils 55 J 4
Daung Kyun 73 G 5
Dauphin 99 R 5
Dauphiné 57 E 3
Dauphin Lake 99 S 5
Daurskoye 68 F 4
Davangere 72 C 5
Davao 75 G 2
Dāvar Panāh 67 G 5
Dāvarzan 61 G 1
Davenport 103 HJ 3
David 108 B 2
Davis (Antarctica) 115

Davis (CA, U.S.A.) 102 B 4
Davis Inlet 101 P 4
Davis Sea 115
Davis Strait 101 Q 2
Dawhat as Salwā 61 F 4
Dawson 98 K 3
Dawson Creek 99 N 4
Dawu 70 D 4
Dayangshu 69 M 6
Dayong 70 EF 5
Dayrūt 88 DE 3
Dayton 103 K 4
Daytona Beach 103 KL 6
Dazhu 70 E 4
Dazjā 61 G 2
De Aar 94 C 6
Dead Sea 88 EF 2
Dead Sea (Jordan) 60 B 3
Deán Funes 112 CD 5
Dease Lake 98 L 4
Dease Strait 99 Q 2
Death Valley 102 C 4
Death Valley National
    Monument 102 C 4
Débo, Lac 90 D 2
Deboyne Island 81 F 4
Debra Birhan 93 F 3
Debra Markos 93 F 2
Debra Zeit 93 F 3
Debrecen 58 B 1
Decatur (AL, U.S.A.) 103 J 5
Decatur (IL, U.S.A.) 103 J 4
Deccan 72 CD 3–5
Decepción 115
Dechang 70 D 5
Dédougou 90 D 3
Dedza 95 E 2
Deering, Mount 78 D 3
Deer Lake 101 Q 6
Dêgê 70 C 4
de Gras, Lac 99 P 3
Deh Bīd 61 F 3
Dehdez 61 F 3
Dehlorān 66 D 4
Dehra Dun 72 C 1
Deh Shū 67 G 4
Dej 58 B 1
De Kalb 103 J 3
Delaware 103 M 4
Del Campillo 112 D 5
Del City 102 G 4
Delegate 79 H 6
Delgado, Cabo 95 G 2
Delgerhaan 68 HJ 6
Delgerhet 70 F 1
Delgertsogt 70 E 1
Delhi 72 C 2
Deličal Dağı 58 C 2–3
Delicias 102 E 6
Delijān 61 F 2
Delphi 58 B 3
Delta Dunării 58 CD 1
Delta Junction 98 HJ 3
Demba 92 C 6
Dembia 92 C 3
Dempo, Gunung 74 B 4
Dem'yanovka 63 N 5
Dem'yanskoye 63 N 4

Denali National Park and Preservative 98 GH 3
Denau 67 H 3
Den Helder 52 D 4
Denison 103 G 5
Denizli 58 C 3
Denkou 70 E 2
Denmark 55 E 4
Denmark Strait 114
Dennison, Cape 115
Denpasar 74 D 5
Denton 103 G 5
D'Entrecasteaux Islands 81 F 3
Denver 102 F 4
Deogarh 72 D 3
Deoghar 72 E 3
Deolali 72 B 4
Depósita 109 F 3
Deqing 70 F 6
Derbent 66 D 2
Derby (Australia) 78 C 2
Derby (U.K.) 52 C 4
Derdap 58 B 2
Dergachi 62 J 5
Dermott 103 H 5
Derudeb 88 F 5
Deryabino 63 Q 1
Derzhavinsk 63 N 5
Désappointement, Îles du 83 F 3
Desengaño, Punta 113 C 8
Desierto de Atacama 110 C 5
Desierto de Sechura 108 B 5
Des Moines 103 H 3
Desolación, Isla 113 AB 9
Desrouches, Île 93 J 6
Dessau 53 F 4
Dessye 93 FG 2
Detroit 103 K 3
Détroit de Jaques-Cartier 101 P 6
Détroit d'Honguedo 101 OP 6
Deutsche Bucht 53 E 4
Deutsche Demokratische Republik (D.D.R.) 53 F 4
Deva 58 B 1
Devil's Island 109 H 2
Devils Lake 102 G 2
Devon Island 114
Devonport 82 A 5
Devrez 59 D 2
Deyang 70 D 4
Dezfūl 61 E 2
Dez Gerd 61 F 3
Dezhou 71 G 3
Dhahab 60 B 3
Dhamār 89 G 6
Dhamtari 72 D 3
Dharwar 72 B 4
Dhaulagiri 72 D 2
Dhelfoí 58 B 3
Dhílavlos Zakínthou 58 B 3
Dhírfis Óros 58 B 3
Dhoraji 72 B 3
Dhule 72 B 3
Diable, Île du 109 H 2
Diaca 95 F 2

Diamantina (Minas Gerais, Brazil) 111 H 4
Diamantina (Queensland, Austr.) 79 G 3
Diamantina Lakes 79 G 3
Diamond Jenness Peninsula 99 OP 1
Dianjiang 70 E 4
Dibrugarh 73 FG 2
Dicle 66 C 3
Didiéni 90 C 3
Didyma 58 C 3
Diéma 90 C 3
Dieppe 56 D 2
Dihang 70 C 5
Dijlāh 61 D 2
Dijon 57 E 2
Dikmen Daği 59 D 2
Dikson 114
Dilaram 67 G 4
Di Linh 74 C 1
Dilj 57 G 2
Dilling 88 D 6
Dilolo 94 C 2
Dimashq 60 B 2
Dimbokro 90 D 4
Dimitrovgrad 58 C 2
Dimitrovgrad (U.S.S.R.) 62 JK 5
Dimona 60 B 3
Dinagat 75 G 1
Dinajpur 72 E 2
Dinara Planina 57 G 3
Dinder National Park 88 F 6
Dindigul 72 C 5
Dingbian 70 E 3
Dingxi 70 DE 3
Dingxian 70 FG 3
Dinokwe 94 D 4
Dionísio Cerqueira 112 F 4
Diourbel 90 A 3
Dipkarpas 60 B 2
Dipolog 75 F 2
Diré 90 D 2
Diredawa 93 G 3
Dirico 94 C 3
Dirk Hartog Island 78 A 4
Disappointment, Lake 78 C 3
Dishnā 60 A 4
Disko 114
Disko Bugt 114
Disna 55 J 4
District of Fort Smith 99 P 3
District of Inuvik 98 LM 2
District of Keewatin 99 SU 2–3
Distrito Federal 111 G 4
Diu 72 B 3
Divāndareeh 61 E 1
Divinopolis 111 GH 5
Divo 90 C 4
Dixon Entrance 98 L 5
Diyālā 61 D 2
Diyarbakır 59 F 3
Djanet 87 G 4
Djelfa 87 F 2
Djibouti 93 G 2
Djibouti 93 G 2

Djougou 90 E 4
Dneprodzerzhinsk 59 D 1
Dnepropetrovsk 59 E 1
Dneprovskiy Liman 58 D 1
Dnestr 58 C 1
Doba 91 H 4
Dobreta Turnu Severin 58 B 2
Dobrogea 58 C 2
Dobrowolski 115
Dobrudžansko Plato 58 C 2
Dodecanese 58 C 3
Dodge City 102 F 4
Dodoma 93 FG 6
Dogger Bank 52 D 4
Dogondoutchi 91 EF 3
Doguéraoua 91 F 3
Doğu Karadeniz Dağlari 59 EF 2
Doha 61 F 4
Dohad 72 B 3
Doi Inthanon 73 G 4
Doilungdêqen 73 F 1–2
Dôle 57 E 2
Dolo 93 G 4
Dolores 113 E 6
Dolphin and Union Strait 99 OP 2
Doma Peaks 80 D 3
Dom Aquino 111 F 4
Dombås 54 E 3
Dominica 105 K 4
Dominican Republic 105 J 3–4
Dompu 75 E 5
Don (U.S.S.R.) 62 H 6
Don Benito 56 B 4
Dondo 95 EF 3
Dondra Head 72 D 6
Donegal Bay 52 B 4
Donegal Mountains 52 B 4
Donetsk 59 E 1
Donetskiy Kryazh 59 EF 1
Dongara 78 B 4
Dongchuan 70 D 5
Dongfang 70 E 7
Dong Hai 71 HJ 5
Dongning 71 JK 2
Dongo 94 B 2
Dongoura 90 BC 3
Dongping 71 G 3
Dongsheng 70 EF 3
Dongting Hu 70 F 5
Dong Ujimqin Qi 71 G 1
Dongxiang 70 FG 5
Dönna 54 F 2
Doramarkog 70 C 4
Dordrecht 52 D 4
Dori 90 D 3
Dornogovĭ 70 EF 2
Döröö Nuur 68 F 6
Dortmund 53 E 4
Dosso 90 E 3
Dothan 103 J 5
Douala 91 FG 5
Douentza 90 D 3
Douglas (AZ, U.S.A.) 102 E 5
Douglas (U.K.) 52 C 4
Douglas (WY, U.S.A.) 102 EF 3

Doumbouene 91 J 3
Dourados 111 F 5
Douro 56 B 3
Dover 52 D 4
Dovrefjell 54 E 3
Dowlatābād 66 F 5
Dow Rüd 61 E 2
Dow Sar 61 E 2
Drakensberg 94 D 5–6
Drake Passage 115
Drake Strait 113 CD 10
Dráma 58 B 2
Drammen 55 F 4
Drau 57 F 2
Drava 57 G 2
Dresden 53 F 4
Dreux 56 D 2
Drini 58 B 2
Drogobych 53 H 5
Drumheller 99 P 5
Drummondville 101 N 6
Druzhnaya 115
Druzhnaya II 115
Dryden 100 J 6
Drysdale River National Park 78 D 2
Dschang 91 F 4
Duaringa 79 HJ 3
Dubawnt Lake 99 R 3
Dubayy 61 G 4
Dubbo 79 H 5
Dublin 52 B 4
Dubna 62 G 4
Dubno 55 J 5
Dubovskoye 59 F 1
Dubrovitsa 55 J 5
Dubrovnik 57 G 3
Dubrovnoye 63 NO 4
Dubuque 103 H 3
Duc de Gloucester, Îles du 83 F 4
Ducie 83 G 4
du Couedic, Cape 79 F 6
Dudhi 72 D 3
Dudinka 63 R 2
Dudley 52 C 4
Duékoué 90 C 4
Duero 56 C 3
Duff Islands 82 C 3
Dugi Otok 57 F 3
Duisburg 52 E 4
Duitama 108 D 2
Dukān 61 D 2
Dukhān 61 F 4
Dukou 70 D 5
Dukwe 94 D 4
Dulan 70 C 3
Dulga-Kyuyel' 68 K 3
Duluth 103 H 2
Dūmā 60 B 2
Dumaguete 75 F 2
Dumfries 52 C 3
Dumont d'Urville 115
Dumpu 82 A 3
Dumyât 88 E 2
Duna 58 A 1
Dunántúl 58 A 1
Dunaujváros 58 A 1

Dunav **58** B 2
Dunbar (Australia) **79** G 2
Dunbar (U.K.) **52** C 3
Dundalk **52** B 4
Dundalk Bay **52** B 4
Dundas Peninsula **99** P 1
Dundee **52** C 3
Dundgovĭ **70** E 1
Dunedin **81** Q 10
Dunhua **71** J 2
Dunhuang **70** B 2
Dunkerque **52** D 4
Dunkwa **90** D 4
Dún Laoghaire **52** B 4
Dunmarra **78** E 2
Dunqulah al 'Ordi **88** DE 5
Duolun **71** G 2
Durack Range **78** D 2
Dura Europos **60** C 2
Durance **57** E 3
Durango (CO, U.S.A.) **102** E 4
Durango (Mexico) **104** AB 3
Duratón **56** C 3
Durban **95** E 5
Durg **72** D 3
Durgapur **72** E 3
Durham **103** L 4
Durmã **61** E 4
Duroy **68** L 5
Durresi **58** A 2
D'Urville Sea **115**
Dushan **70** E 5
Dushanbe **67** H 3
Düsseldorf **52** E 4
Dutch Harbor **98** D 5
Duwayhin **66** E 6
Duye **92** D 4
Düzce **58** D 2
Dvina, Severnaya **62** H 3
Dwarka **72** A 3
Dyadmo **68** J 4
Dyrhólaey **54** B 3
Dyurmen'tobe **67** GH 1
Dzerzhinsk **62** H 4
Dzhagdy, Khrebet **69** O 5
Dzhalinda **69** M 5
Dzhambul **67** J 2
Dzhankoy **59** D 1
Dzhanybek **62** J 6
Dzhelinde **68** K 1
Dzhetygara **63** M 5
Dzhezkazgan **63** N 6
Dzhigudzhak **69** ST 3
Dzhirgatal' **67** J 3
Dzhugdzhur, Khrebet **69** OP 4
Dzhunkun **68** K 3
Dzhusaly **67** GH 1
Dzugdzhur Range **69** PQ 4

E

Eagle **98** J 3
Eagle Pass **102** FG 6
Eagle Peak **102** BC 3
East Antarctica **115**
East Cape **81** R 8
East China Sea **71** HJ 5
Easter Island **83** H 4
Eastern Ghats **72** CD 3–5

East Falkland **113** E 9
East London **94** CD 6
Eastmain **101** M 5
East Point **103** JK 5
Eastport **103** N 3
East Siberian Sea **114**
Eau Claire **103** H 3
Eauripik **82** A 2
Ebe **69** Q 3
Eberswalde **53** F 4
Eboli **57** G 3
Ebolowa **91** G 5
Ebon **82** C 2
Ebyakh **69** S 2
Ech Cheliff **87** F 1
Echmiadzin **59** F 2
Echo Bay **99** O 2
Écija **56** B 4
Ecuador **108** B 4
Edéa **91** FG 5
Edel Land **78** A 4
Edgeöya **114**
Edinburgh **52** C 3
Edirne **58** C 2
Edmonds **102** B 2
Edmonton **99** OP 5
Edremit **58** C 3
Edwards Plateau **102** FG 5–6
Efatē **81** J 5
Efes **58** C 3
Egersund **55** E 4
Egilsstaðir **54** C 2
Eglab Dersa **86** E 3
Egmont, Mount **81** Q 8
Eğridir Gölü **58** D 3
Egvekinot **98** B 2
Egypt **60** A 4
Egypt **88** DE 4
Eiao **83** F 3
Eidfjord **55** E 3
Eifel **52** E 4
Eights Coast **115**
Eighty Mile Beach **78** BC 2
Eire **52** B 4
Eirunepé **108** D 5
Eisenach **53** F 4
Eisenhüttenstadt **53** FG 4
Ejin Qi **70** D 2
Ekibastuz **63** P 5
Ekoli **92** C 5
Ekwan **100** L 5
El Aaiún **86** C 3
El Adeb Larache **87** G 3
El Alamo **102** C 5
Elat **60** B 3
Elâziğ **59** E 3
Elba **57** F 3
Elbeyli **59** E 3
Elblag **53** G 4
Elbrus **59** F 2
'El Bûr **93** H 4
Elburz Mountains **61** F 1
El Cajon **102** C 5

El Cerro **110** D 4
Elche **56** C 4
El Cuy **113** C 6
Elda **56** C 4
'El Dēre **93** H 4
El Difícil **108** D 2
El Diviso **108** C 3
El Djouf **86** CD 4
El Dorado (AR, U.S.A.)
  103 H 5
Eldorado (Argentina) **112** EF 4
El Dorado (KS, U.S.A.)
  103 G 4
El Dorado (Mexico) **102** E 7
El Dorado (Venezuela) **109** F 2
Eldoret **92** EF 4
Elektrostal' **62** GH 4
Elemi Triangle **92** EF 4
El Encanto **108** D 4
Elephant Island **115**
Elesbão Veloso **111** H 2
El Escorial **56** C 3
Eleuthera Island **105** G 2
El Fasher **88** CD 6
El Ferrol del Candillo **56** B 3
El'gakan **69** M 4
Elghena **93** F 1
El Goléa **87** F 2
Elgon, Mount **92** EF 4
'El Hamurre **93** H 3
El Homr **87** F 3
Elisenvaara **54** JK 3
Elista **59** F 1
Elizabeth **79** F 5
El Jadida **86** D 2
Elk **53** H 4
Elk City **102** G 4
Elkhart **103** J 3
Elko **102** C 3
Ellef Ringnes Island **114**
Ellensburg **102** BC 2
Ellesmere Island **114**
Ellice Islands **82** C 3
Elliot (Australia) **78** E 2
Elliot (South Africa) **94** D 6
Elliot, Mount **79** H 2
Ellsworth Land **115**
Ellsworth Mountains **115**
El Maestrazgo **56** CD 3
El Maitén **113** B 7
El Medo **93** G 3
El Messir **91** H 2
Elmhurst **103** J 3
Elmira **103** L 3
El Mirador **104** DE 4
El Mreiti **86** D 4
El Obeid **88** DE 6
El Oued **87** G 2
El Paso **102** E 5
El Progreso **104** E 4
El Puerto **102** D 6
El Puerto de Santa Maria
  56 B 4
El Salto **104** A 3
El Salvador **104** DE 5
El Sueco **102** E 6
El Tigre **109** F 2
El Tránsito **112** B 4

El Tunal **112** D 3–4
Eluru **72** D 4
El Valle **108** C 2
Elvas **56** B 4
Elvira **108** D 5
Ely **102** D 4
Emamrud **61** G 1
Emamshar **66** F 3
Emba **66** F 1
Embalse de Alcántara **56** B 4
Embalse de Almendra **56** B 3
Embalse del Ebro **56** C 3
Embalse de Mequinenza
  56 C 3
Embarcación **110** D 5
Embarras Portage **99** P 4
Emden **53** E 4
Emel'dzak **69** N 4
Emerald **79** H 3
Emi **68** G 5
Emi Koussi **91** HJ 2
Empalme **102** D 6
Empedrado **112** E 4
Ems **53** E 4
Encarnación **112** E 4
Enda Salassie **93** F 2
Ende **75** F 5
Enderbury **82** D 3
Enderby Land **115**
Endicott Mountains **98** GH 2
Engaño, Cape **75** J 1
Engel's **62** J 5
Enggano, Pulau **74** B 5
England **52** D 4
English Channel **52** BC 4–5
Engozero **54** K 2
Enid **102** G 4
Eniwetok **82** B 2
Enkan **69** Q 4
Enköping **55** G 4
Enmore **109** G 2
Ennadai **99** R 3
Ennedi **91** J 2
Enontekiö **54** H 2
Enrekang **75** EF 4
Enschede **53** E 4
Ensenada **102** C 5
Enshi **70** EF 4
Entebbe **92** E 4
Entre Rios **109** H 5
Enugu **91** F 4
Enugu Ezike **91** F 4
Enurmino **98** C 2
Envigado **108** CD 2
Envira **108** D 5
Épernay **52** D 3
Ephesus **58** C 3
Epi **81** J 5
Épinal **57** E 2
Équateur **92** BC 4
Equatoria **92** DE 3–4
Equatorial Guinea **91** F 5
Erbil **60** D 1
Érd **58** A 1
Erechim **112** F 4
Ereentsav **68** L 6
Ereğli **59** D 3
Erenhot **70** F 2

Eresma 56 C 3
Erfurt 53 F 4
Erg Brusset 91 FG 2
Erg Chech 86 E 3–4
Erg de Ténéré 91 FG 2
Erg Iguidi 86 DE 3
Ergun He 68 M 5
Ergun Zuoqi 69 M 5
Eriba 88 F 5
Eric 101 O 5
Erie 103 K 3
Erie, Lake 103 K 3
'Erigābo 93 H 2
Erikub 82 C 2
Erimbet 67 G 2
Eritrea 93 FG 2
Ermelo 94 DE 5
Ernest Legouvé 83 E 5
Erode 72 C 5
Erongo 94 B 4
Erongo Mountains 94 B 4
Erozionnyy 69 R 2
Errego 95 F 3
Erromanga 82 C 4
Erromango 81 J 5
Ertai 67 N 1
Erzgebirge 53 F 4
Erzincan 59 E 3
Erzurum 59 F 3
Erzurum-Kars Yaylâsı 59 F 2
Esbjerg 55 E 4
Escanaba 103 J 2
Eschan 69 R 3
Escondido 102 C 5
Escuintla 104 D 5
Esfahan 61 F 2
Eskilstuna 55 G 4
Eskimo Point 99 T 3
Eskişehir 58 D 3
Eslamabad 61 E 2
Eslöv 55 F 4
Esmeralda, Isla 113 A 8
Esmeraldas 108 BC 3
España 56 C 4
Esperance Bay 78 C 5
Esperanza (Antarctica) 115
Espinal (Bolivia) 110 E 4
Espinal (Colombia) 108 D 3
Espinar 110 B 3
Espírito Santo 111 HJ 4
Espiritu Santo 82 BC 4
Esplanada 111 J 3
Espoo (Esbo) 55 H 3–4
Esquel 113 B 7
Essaouira 86 CD 2
Essen 53 E 4
Essendon, Mount 78 C 3
Estados, Isla de los 113 D 9
Estância 111 J 3
Estelí 104 E 5
Esteros 110 D 5
Estevan 99 R 6
Estoniya 55 HJ 4
Estrecho de Gibraltar 56 B 4
Estrecho de le Maire
   113 CD 9–10
Estrecho de Magallanes
   113 B 9

Estrêla, Serra de 56 B 3
Estremadura 56 B 4
Estrondo, Serra do 109 J 5
Esztergom 58 A 1
Ethiopia 93 FG 3
Ethiopian Plateau 93 FG 3
Etna 57 FG 4
Etosha National Park 94 B 3
Etosha Pan 94 B 3
Eugene 102 B 3
Eugenia, Punta 102 C 6
Eugmo 54 H 3
Eungella National Park
   79 HJ 3
Euphrates 60 C 2
Eureka 102 B 3
Everest, Mount 72 E 2
Everett 102 B 2
Everett Mountains 101 O 3
Everglades National Park
   103 K 6
Évora 56 B 4
Evreux 56 D 2
Evvoia 58 B 3
Ewasse 81 F 3
Executive Committee Range
   115
Exeter 52 C 4
Exmouth 78 A 3
Extremadura 56 B 4
Eyre 78 D 5
Eyre Peninsula 79 F 5
Eysturoy 52 A 1
Ezop, Gora 69 S 3

F

Fabala 90 C 4
Fabriano 57 F 3
Fada 91 J 2
Faenza 57 F 3
Faeroe Islands 52 A 1
Făgăraș 58 BC 1
Fairbanks 98 GH 3
Fair Isle 52 C 3
Fairmont (W.V., U.S.A.)
   103 L 4
Fairview 79 G 2
Faisalabad 67 J 4
Faizabad (Afghanistan) 67 J 3
Faizabad (India) 72 D 2
Fakaina 83 F 4
Fakaofo 82 D 3
Fakarava 83 F 4
Faku 71 H 2
Falagh 92 E 3
Falkenberg 55 F 4
Falkland Islands 113 DE 9
Falkland Sound 113 DE 9
Fallon 102 C 4
Fall River 103 M 3
Falls City 103 G 3
Falmouth 52 B 4
Falster 55 G 4
Falun 55 G 3
Famagusta 59 D 3
Fana 90 C 3
Fangataufa 83 F 4
Fangzheng 71 JK 1

Faraday 115
Faradje 92 D 4
Farafangana 95 H 4
Farah 67 G 4
Farallon de Medinilla 82 A 1
Farallon de Pajaros 82 A 1
Faranah 90 B 3
Faraulep 82 A 2
Farewell, Cape 81 Q 9
Fargo (N.D., U.S.A.) 102 G 2
Faridpur 72 E 3
Färjestaden 55 G 4
Farmington (N.M., U.S.A.)
   102 E 4
Fårö 55 G 4
Faro (Brazil) 109 G 4
Faro (Portugal) 56 B 4
Farquhar Group 93 J 7
Färs 61 F 3
Fasā 61 F 3
Fasano 57 G 3
Fastov 62 E 6
Fataka 82 C 3
Fatehgarh 72 CD 2
Fāurei 58 C 1
Faxaflói 54 A 3
Faxälven 54 G 3
Faya-Largeau 91 HJ 2
Fayetteville (AR, U.S.A.)
   103 H 4
Fayetteville (N.C., U.S.A.)
   103 KL 5
Faysh Khābur 60 D 1
Fayu 82 B 2
Fazilka 72 B 1
Fdérik 86 C 4
Fear, Cape 103 L 5
Feathertop, Mount 79 H 6
Federal Republic of Germany
   53 E 4
Federated States of
   Micronesia 82 AB 2
Fehmarn 53 F 4
Feijó 108 D 5
Feira de Santana 111 J 3
Feklistova, Ostrov 69 P 4–5
Felipe Carrillo Puerto 104 E 4
Fengcheng 71 HJ 2
Fengjie 70 EF 4
Fengqing 70 CD 6
Fengshui Shan 69 M 5
Feni Islands 81 F 2
Fenoarivo Atsinanana
   95 HJ 3
Fensfjorden 54 DE 3
Fenyang 70 F 3
Feodosiya 59 DE 1
Fer, Cap de 87 G 1
Ferfer 93 H 3
Fergana 67 J 2
Fergus Falls 103 G 2
Fergusson 81 F 3
Ferjukot 54 A 3
Ferkéssédougou 90 C 4
Fernando de Noronha Island
   107 G 3
Fernandópolis 111 F 5

Fernando Póo → Bioko 91 F 5
Ferrara 57 F 3
Ferreira Gomes 109 H 3
Fès 86 E 2
Fethiye 58 C 3
Fezzan 87 HJ 3
Fianarantsoa 95 H 4
Fierras 54 G 2
Fiji 82 C 4
Fiji Islands 82 C 4
Filadélfia 110 E 5
Filchner Ice Shelf 115
Fimbul Ice Shelf 115
Fimi 92 B 5
Findlay 103 K 3
Finisterre, Cabo de 56 B 3
Finke 78 E 4
Finke, Mount 78 E 5
Finke Gorge National Park
   78 E 3
Finland 54 J 3
Finnmark 54 H 2
Finnmarksvidda 54 H 2
Finnsnes 54 G 2
Finnveden 55 F 4
Finspång 55 G 4
Fiordland National Park
   80 P 9–10
Firat 59 E 3
Firenze 57 F 3
Firminy 56 D 2
Firozabad 72 CD 2
Firth of Forth 52 C 3
Firūzābād 66 E 5
Firūz Kūh 61 F 2
Fisher Strait 99 UV 3
Fishguard 52 B 4
Fiskenæsset 101 R 3
Fitzcarrald 110 B 3
Fitzgerald River National Park
   78 B 5
Fitzroy Crossing 78 CD 2
Fitzroy River (Queensland,
   Austr.) 79 HJ 3
Fitzroy River (Western
   Australia) 78 C 2
Fizi 92 D 5
Flagstaff 102 D 4
Flamenco 112 B 4
Flåsjön 54 G 3
Flattery, Cape 102 AB 2
Flensburg 53 E 4
Flinders Chase National Park
   79 F 6
Flinders Passage 79 H 2
Flinders Range 79 F 5
Flinders Ranges National Park
   79 FG 5
Flinders River 79 G 2
Flin Flon 99 R 5
Flint (Kiribati) 83 E 3
Flint (MI, U.S.A.) 103 K 3
Flisa 55 F 3
Floraville (Queensland,
   Austr.) 79 F 2
Florence (AL, U.S.A.) 103 J 5
Florence (Italy) 57 F 3
Florencia 108 CD 3

Flo – Gar

Flores (Guatemala) **104** E 4
Flores (Indonesia) **75** F 5
Flores, Laut **75** E 5
Flores Sea **75** EF 5
Floriano **111** H 2
Floriano Pleixoto **108** E 5
Florianópolis **112** G 4
Florida (Cuba) **105** G 3
Florida (U.S.A.) **103** KL 6
Floridablanca **108** D 2
Florida Keys **103** L 6–7
Floró **54** E 3
Fluk **75** G 4
Fly River **80** D 3
Foci del Po **57** F 3
Focşani **58** C 1
Foggia **57** G 3
Fogo **90** B 7
Foleyet **100** L 6
Folkstone **52** D 4
Fond du Lac **103** J 3
Fonte Boa **108** E 4
Fonte do Pau-d'Agua **110** E 3
Fonualei **82** D 4
Forbes **79** H 5
Förde **54** E 3
Forêt d'Ecouves **56** C 2
Forín Linares **110** D 5
Forkas **90** E 3
Forli **57** F 3
Formentera **56** D 4
Formentor, Cabo de **56** D 3–4
Formosa **111** G 4
Formosa (Taiwan) **71** H 6
Formosa, Serra **111** EF 3
Formosa Strait **71** GH 5–6
Formoso **112** E 4
Fornæs **55** F 4
Forrest **78** D 5
Forsayth **79** G 2
Forsnäs **54** G 2
Forssa **55** H 3
Fortaleza **111** J 1
Fort Chimo **101** NO 4
Fort Chipewyan **99** PQ 4
Fort Collins **102** EF 3
Fort-de-France **105** K 5
Fort Dodge **103** H 3
Fort Frances **100** J 6
Fort Franklin **99** N 2
Fort George **101** M 5
Forth, Firth of **52** C 3
Fortín Coronel Eugenio Garay
110 D 5
Fortín Ingavi **110** DE 4
Fortín Madrejón **110** E 5
Fortín Ravelo **110** D 4
Fortín Suárez Arana **110** D 4
Fort Lauderdale **103** L 6
Fort Liard **99** N 3
Fort Mackay **99** P 4
Fort McMurray **99** P 4
Fort Miribel **87** F 3
Fort Morgan **102** F 3
Fort Myers **103** K 6
Fort Nelson **99** N 4
Fort Norman **99** M 3
Fort Peck Dam **102** E 2

Fort Peck Lake **102** E 2
Fort Pierce **103** KL 6
Fort Portal **92** DE 4
Fort Providence **99** O 3
Fort Randell Dam **102** FG 3
Fort Resolution **99** P 3
Fort Rupert **101** M 5
Fort Saint John **99** N 4
Fort Severn **100** K 4
Fort Shevchenko **66** E 2
Fort Simpson **99** N 3
Fort Smith **103** H 4–5
Fort Stockton **102** F 5
Fortune Bay **101** Q 6
Fort Vermilion **99** O 4
Fort Wayne **103** J 3
Fort Wellington **109** G 2
Fort William **52** BC 3
Fort Worth **102** G 5
Forveaux Strait **82** C 6
Foshan **70** F 6
Fosna **54** F 3
Foso **90** D 4
Fossano **57** E 3
Fossil Bluff **115**
Fougamou **91** G 6
Fougères **56** C 2
Fouladou **90** AB 3
Foumban **91** G 4
Fourmies **56** D 1
Four Mountains, Islands of
98 CD 5
Fouta Djallon **90** B 3
Fouta Ferlo **90** B 2
Foveaux Strait **80** P 10
Fowlers Bay **78** E 5
Foxe Basin **99** VW 2
Foxe Channel **101** M 3
Foxe Peninsula **101** M 3
Fox Islands **98** D 5
Foz do Breu **108** D 5
Franca **111** G 5
France **56** CD 2
Franceville **91** G 6
Francisco de Orellana
(Ecuador) **108** C 4
Francisco de Orellana (Peru)
108 D 4
Francisco Escárcega **104** D 4
Francistown **94** D 4
Francs Peak **102** E 3
Frankfurt am Main **53** E 4
Franklin Mountains
99 MN 2–3
Franklin Strait **99** S 1
Franz Josef Land **114**
Fraser **99** N 5
Fraser or Great Sandy Island
79 J 4
Fraser Plateau **99** N 5
Fredericia **55** EF 4
Fredericton **101** O 6
Frederik IX-Land **101** R 2
Frederiksdal **101** S 3
Frederikshåb **101** R 3
Frederikshavn **55** EF 4
Fredrika **54** G 3
Fredrikstad **55** F 4

Freetown **90** B 4
Freiburg **53** E 5
Fréjus **57** E 3
French Guiana **109** H 3
French Polynesia **83** EF 4
Fresnillo **104** B 3
Fresno **102** BC 4
Freycinet Peninsula **80** L 9
Fria, Cape **94** A 3
Friesland **52–53** E 4
Frio, Cabo **111** H 5
Frisian Islands **52** E 4
Frobisher Bay **101** O 3
Frobisher Lake **99** Q 4
Frolovo **62** H 6
Fronteiras **111** H 2
Front Range **102** E 3–4
Fröya **54** E 3
Frunze **67** J 2
Fu'an **71** G 5
Fuding **71** H 5
Fuerte Olimpo **110** E 5
Fuerteventura **86** C 3
Fujian **71** G 5
Fujin **69** O 6
Fukui **71** L 3
Fukuoka **71** JK 4
Fukushima (Japan) **71** LM 2
Fukushima (Japan) **71** M 3
Fukuyama **71** K 3–4
Funafuti **82** CD 3
Funchal **86** B 2
Funiu Shan **70** F 4
Funtua **91** F 3
Fuqing **71** GH 5
Furancungo **95** E 2
Furmanovka **67** J 2
Furmanovo **62** JK 6
Furneaux Group **82** A 5
Fürth **53** F 5
Fury and Hecla Strait **100** KL 1
Fusagasugá **108** D 3
Fushun **71** HJ 2
Fusong **71** J 2
Futuna (Vanuatu) **82** C 4
Futuna (Wallis and Futuna)
82 D 3
Fuxin **71** H 2
Fuyang **70** G 4
Fuyuan **70** D 5
Fuyun **67** M 1
Fuzhou **71** GH 5
Fyn **55** F 4

G

Gabela **94** A 2
Gabès **87** H 2
Gabon **91** FG 6
Gaborone **94** CD 4
Gabriel Strait **101** O 3
Gach Sārān **61** F 3
Gadag **72** C 4
Gadame **92** E 3
Gadsden **103** J 5
Gaeta **57** F 3
Gaferut **82** A 2
Gagnoa **90** C 4
Gagnon **101** O 5

Gahkom **61** G 3
Gaimán **113** C 7
Gainesville **103** K 6
Gairdner, Lake **79** F 5
Gakarosa **94** C 5
Gakona **98** H 3
Galán, Cerro **112** C 4
Galanino **68** F 4
Galápagos Islands **108** B 6
Galathea Deep **82** D 5
Galaţi **58** C 1
Galatina **57** G 3
Galdhöpiggen **54** E 3
Galena **98** F 3
Galesburg **103** HJ 3
Galicia (Poland) **53** H 5
Galicia (Spain) **56** B 3
Galimyy **69** ST 3
Gâlka'yo **93** H 3
Galle **72** CD 6
Gallinas, Punta **108** D 1
Gällivare **54** H 2
Gallo, Capo **57** F 4
Gallup **102** E 4
Galole **93** F 5
Galveston **103** H 6
Galvez **112** D 5
Galway **52** B 4
Gamba **91** F 6
Gambia **90** AB 3
Gambier Islands **83** FG 4
Gamboma **91** H 6
Gamboola **79** G 2
Ganäveh **61** F 3
Gandadiwata, Bukit **75** EF 4
Gandhi Sagar Dam **72** C 3
Gandía **56** CD 4
Ganetti **88** E 5
Ganga **72** E 2
Gangan **113** C 7
Gangapur **72** C 2
Gangdisê Shan **72** DE 1
Ganges **72** E 2
Ganina Gar' **68** F 4
Gannett Peak **102** E 3
Gansu **70** DE 3
Ganta **90** C 4
Ganzhou **70** FG 5
Gao **90** D 2
Gao'an **70** FG 5
Gaona **112** D 4
Gaoping **70** F 3
Gaoua **90** D 3
Gaoual **90** B 3
Gaozhou **70** EF 6
Gap **57** E 3
Garanhuns **111** J 2
Garbokaray **68** G 5
Garbosh, Küh-e **61** EF 2
Garda, Lago di **57** F 2
Gardaneh-ye Āvej **61** E 2
Gardaneh-ye Kandovān
61 F 1
Gardaneh-ye Khāneh Sorkh
61 G 3
Gardemoen **55** F 3
Gargano, Promontorio del
57 G 3

Garissa **93** FG 5
Garmisch-Partenkirchen **53** F 5
Garmsar **61** F 2
Garonne **56** D 3
Garoua **91** G 4
Garoua Boulai **91** GH 4
Garôwe **93** H 3
Garri, Kûh-e **61** E 2
Garry Lake **99** R 2
Garwa **72** D 3
Gary **103** J 3
Garze **70** C 4
Gascogne **56** CD 3
Gascoyne Junction **78** B 3–4
Gashagar **91** G 3
Gashua **91** G 3
Gaspé **101** OP 6
Gassi Touil **87** G 2
Gastello, Iméni **69** R 3
Gästrikland **55** G 3
Gata, Sierra de **56** B 3
Gatchina **55** JK 4
Gates of the Arctic National Park and Preserve **98** G 2
Gauhati **73** F 2
Gauja **55** H 4
Gausta **55** E 4
Gavanka **69** T 4
Gávdhos **58** B 4
Gave de Pau **56** C 3
Gävle **55** G 3
Gävlebukten **55** G 3
Gaya **72** E 3
Gayndah **79** J 4
Gaza Strip **60** AB 3
Gazelle Peninsula **81** F 2
Gaziantep **59** E 3
Gaziantep Yaylası **59** E 3
Gazimurskiy Zavod **68** L 5
Gazıpaşa **60** A 1
Gbarnga **90** C 4
Gdańsk **53** G 4
Gdynia **53** G 4
Gearhart Mountain **102** B 3
Gedi **93** F 5
Gediz **58** C 3
Geelong **79** G 6
Geigar **88** E 6
Geilo **55** E 3
Gejiu **70** D 6
Gela **57** F 4
Gelendzhik **59** E 2
Gelsenkirchen **53** E 4
Gemena **92** B 4
Gemsbok National Park **94** C 4–5
General Acha **113** D 6
General Alvear **113** C 6
General Belgrano II **115**
General Belgrano III **115**
General Bernardo O'Higgins **115**
General Madariaga **113** E 6
General Pico **113** D 6
General Roca **113** C 6
General San Martin **115**
General Santos **75** G 2

Genève **57** E 2
Gengma **70** C 6
Genoa **57** E 3
Genova **57** E 3
Genova, Golfo di **57** E 3
Gent **52** D 4
George **101** O 4
Georgetown (Gambia) **90** B 3
Georgetown (Guyana) **109** G 2
George Town (Malaysia) **74** AB 2
Georgetown (Queensland, Austr.) **79** G 2
George Town (Tasmania, Austr.) **82** A 5
George V Coast **115**
George VI Sound **115**
Georgia **103** K 5
Georgia (U.S.S.R.) **59** F 2
Georgian Bay **101** L 6
Georgiu-Dezh **62** G 5
Georgiyevka **63** Q 6
Georgiyevsk **59** F 2
Georg von Neumayer **115**
Gera **53** F 4
Geraldton **78** A 4
Gerâs, Serra do **56** B 3
Gerasimovka **63** O 4
German Democratic Republic **53** F 4
Germi **61** G 2
Gerona **56** D 3
Gêrzê **72** D 1
Gesoa **80** D 3
Getafe **56** C 3
Getz Ice Shelf **115**
Geyik Dağı **59** D 3
Ghadâmis **87** G 2
Ghana **90** D 4
Ghanzi **94** C 4
Ghardaïa **87** F 2
Gharib, Ra's **60** A 3
Gharyān **87** H 2
Ghazzah **60** B 3
Gheorghe Gheorghiu-Dej **58** C 1
Ghimbi **92** F 3
Ghudâf, Wâdi al **60** D 2
Gibraltar **56** B 4
Gibraltar, Estrecho de **56** BC 4
Gibson Desert **78** C 3
Gifu **71** L 3
Giglio **57** F 3
Gijon **56** B 3
Gila Bend **102** D 5
Gila River **102** D 5
Gilbert Islands **82** C 2–3
Gilbert River **79** G 2
Gilbués **109** J 5
Giles **78** D 4
Gilgandra **79** H 5
Gillam **99** T 4
Gillette **102** E 3
Gingin **78** B 5
Ginir **93** G 3
Gioia **57** G 3
Giresun **59** E 2

Girne **59** D 3
Gironde **56** C 2
Gisborne **81** R 8
Gitarama **92** DE 5
Giuba → Juba **93** G 4
Giza **88** DE 3
Gizhiga **69** U 3
Gizhiginskaya Guba **69** T 3
Gjiri i Vlorä **58** A 2
Gjögur **54** B 2
Gjövik **55** F 3
Glacier Bay National Park and Preserve **98** K 4
Gladstone **79** J 3
Glasgow **52** C 3
Glazov **62** K 4
Glen Canyon National Recreation Area **102** D 4
Glendale **102** D 5
Glendive **102** F 2
Glenhope **81** Q 9
Glennallen **98** H 3
Glenrothes **52** C 3
Glenwood Springs **102** E 4
Glittertind **54** E 3
Gliwice **53** G 4
Głogów **53** G 4
Gloucester (MA, U.S.A.) **103** MN 3
Gloucester (U.K.) **52** C 4
Glubokoye **55** J 4
Glukhov **62** F 5
Goa **72** B 4
Gobabis **94** B 4
Gobi **70** EF 2
Gochas **94** B 4
Godâr-e Sorkh **61** G 2
Godar-i-Shah **67** G 5
Godavari **72** D 4
Gods Lake **99** T 5
Godthâb **101** R 3
Godwar **72** B 2
Goéland, Lac au **101** M 5–6
Goiânia **111** FG 4
Goiás (Brazil) **111** G 3
Goiás (Brazil) **111** F 4
Goksu **59** D 3
Göksu **59** E 3
Golan Heights **60** B 2
Golcuk **58** C 2
Gold Coast (Australia) **79** J 4
Gold Coast (Ghana) **90** DE 5
Golden Hinde **99** M 6
Goldsboro **103** L 4
Goldsworthy **78** BC 3
Golets Skalistyy, Gora **69** O 4
Golf de Lion **56–57** D 2
Golfe de Saint-Malo **56** C 2
Golfito **104** F 6
Golfo de Cadiz **56** B 4
Golfo de California **102** DE 5–7
Golfo de Chiriquí **108** B 2
Golfo de Guayaquil **108** B 4
Golfo de Honduras **104** E 4
Golfo de los Mosquitos **108** B 2
Golfo de Panamá **108** C 2

Golfo de Penas **113** AB 8
Golfo de Tehuantepec **104** CD 4
Golfo de Valencia **56** D 4
Golfo de Venezuela **108** D 1
Golfo di Genova **57** E 3
Golfo di Salerno **57** F 3
Golfo di Squillace **57** G 4
Golfo di Taranto **57** G 3
Golfo San Jorge **113** C 8
Golfo San Matías **113** D 7
Gölgelı Dağları **58** C 3
Golmud **70** B 3
Golovin **98** E 3
Golovnino **71** MN 2
Golubovka **63** O 5
Goma **92** D 5
Gombe **91** G 3
Gomel **62** F 5
Gomera **86** B 3
Goméz Palacio **104** B 2
Gonâbâd **66** F 4
Gonaïves **105** H 4
Gonam **69** O 4
Gonâve, Ile de la **105** H 4
Gonbad-e Qâbus **66** EF 3
Gonda **72** D 2
Gondar **93** F 2
Gondia **72** CD 3
Gongbo' gyamda **70** BC 5
Gonghe **70** D 3
Gongpoquan **70** C 2
Goodnews Bay **98** E 4
Goondiwindi **79** HJ 4
Goose Bay **101** P 5
Gora Denezhkin Kamen' **63** LM 3
Gora Ezop **69** S 3
Gora Fisht **59** E 2
Gora Golets-Inyaptuk **68** K 4
Gora Golets-Skalistyy **68** LM 4
Gora Golets Skalistyy **69** O 4
Gora Kamen **68** FG 2
Gora Khil'mi **69** S 1
Gora Khoydype **63** N 2
Gorakhpur **72** D 2
Gora Konzhakovskiy Kamén **63** LM 4
Gora Kovriga **62** J 2
Gora Kuytun **63** R 6
Gora Medvezh'ya **69** P 6
Gora Munku-Sardyk **68** GH 5
Gora Narodnaya **63** LM 3
Gora Nelkuchan **69** P 3
Gora Pobeda **69** R 2
Gora Sokhor **68** J 5
Gora Syuge-Khaya **69** OP 2
Gora Taklaun **69** Q 3
Gora Tel'pos-Iz **63** LM 3
Gora Yamantau **63** L 5
Góra Zamkowa **53** H 4
Gorda **102** B 4
Gordion **59** D 3
Gordon **103** H 2
Gordon Downs **78** D 2
Gorgán **61** G 1
Gori **59** F 2

Gorki **63** N 2
Gor'kiy **62** H 4
Görlitz **53** F 4
Gorlovka **59** E 1
Gorna Oryakhovitsa **58** C 2
Gorno-Altaysk **63** QR 5
Gornozavodsk **69** Q 6
Gornyak **63** Q 5
Goroka **80** E 3
Goromay **69** Q 5
Gorongosa **95** E 3
Gorongosa National Park **95** EF 3
Gorontalo **75** F 3
Gory Byrranga **68** GH 1
Goryn' **55** J 5
Gory Putorana **68** FH 2
Gory Ulutau **67** H 1
Gorzów Wielkopolski **53** G 4
Goshogawara **71** LM 2
Gossi **90** D 2
Göta kanal **55** F 4
Götaland **55** FG 4
Göteborg **55** F 4
Gothenburg **55** F 4
Gotland **55** G 4
Gotska Sandön **55** GH 4
Göttingen **53** EF 4
Goulburn **79** H 5
Goulimime **86** C 3
Gouré **91** G 3
Gourma **90** E 3
Gourma-Rarous **90** D 2
Gouro **91** H 2
Gove Peninsula **79** F 1
Governador Valadares **111** H 4
Goya **112** E 4
Gozo **57** F 4
Graaff Reinet **94** C 6
Gračac **57** G 3
Gradaús, Serra dos **109** H 5
Grafton **79** J 4
Graham **98** L 5
Graham Land **115**
Grahamstown **94** D 6
Grain Coast **90** BC 4–C 5
Grajaú **109** J 5
Grampian Mountains **52** C 3
Granada (Nicaragua) **104** E 5
Granada (Spain) **56** C 4
Granby **101** N 6
Gran Canaria **86** BC 3
Gran Chaco **110** D 5
Grand Bassam **90** D 4
Grand Canyon **102** D 4
Grand Canyon National Park **102** D 4
Grand Coulee Dam **102** C 2
Grande, Bahía **113** C 9
Grande Comore **95** GH 2
Grande Prairie **99** NO 4
Grand Erg de Bilma **91** GI 2
Grand Erg Occidental **86–87** EF 2–3
Grand Erg Oriental **87** G 2–3
Grand Forks **102** G 2
Grandin, Lake **99** O 3

Grand Island **102** G 3
Grand Junction **102** E 4
Grand Marais **103** HJ 2
Grand Passage **81** H 5
Grand Rapids (Man., Can.) **99** S 5
Grand Rapids (MI, U.S.A.) **103** JK 3
Grand Rapids (MN, U.S.A.) **103** H 2
Grand Teton **102** D 3
Granite City **103** J 4
Granite Peak (MT, U.S.A.) **102** E 2
Granite Peakh (NV., U.S.A.) **102** C 3
Granja **111** H 1
Granön **54** G 3
Gran Sasso d'Italia **57** F 3
Grants Pass **102** B 3
Granville Lake **99** R 4
Gräsö **55** G 3
Grave, Pointe de **56** C 2
'S-Gravenhage **52** D 4
Gravina **57** G 3
Grayling **103** K 3
Graz **57** FG 2
Great Artesian Basin **79** G 3–4
Great Australian Bight **78** DE 5
Great Barrier **82** C 5
Great Barrier Island **81** R 8
Great Barrier Reef **79** H 1–2
Great Basin **102** C 3–4
Great Bear Lake **99** NO 2
Great Dividing Range **79** HJ 3–4
Greater Antilles **105** GH 4
Great Exuma Island **105** G 3
Great Falls **102** D 2
Great Fisher Bank **52** D 3
Great Inagua Island **105** H 3
Great Indian Desert **72** B 2
Great Karroo **94** C 6
Great Nicobar **73** F 6
Great Plains **102** FG 2–4
Great Salt Lake **102** D 3
Great Salt Lake Desert **102** D 3
Great Sandy Desert **78** C 3
Great Slave Lake **99** P 3
Great Victoria Desert **78** DE 4
Great Victoria Desert Nature Reserve **78** D 4
Greece **58** B 3
Greeley **102** F 3
Green Bay **103** J 3
Green Coast **115**
Green Islands **82** B 3
Greenland **114**
Greenland Sea **114**
Greenock **52** BC 3
Green River (Papua New Guinea) **80** D 2
Green River (UT, U.S.A.) **102** DE 4

Green River (WY, U.S.A.) **102** DE 3
Greensboro (GA, U.S.A.) **103** K 5
Greensboro (N.C., U.S.A.) **103** L 4
Greenvale **79** GH 2
Greenville (Liberia) **90** C 5
Greenville (MS, U.S.A.) **103** HJ 5
Greenville (S.C., U.S.A.) **103** K 5
Gregory, Lake **79** F 4
Gregory Range **79** G 2
Greifswald **53** F 4
Grenada **105** K 5
Grenoble **57** E 2
Greymouth **81** Q 9
Grey Range **79** G 4
Grim, Cape **80** K 9
Grimsby **52** CD 4
Grímsey **54** B 2
Grimshaw **99** O 4
Grímsstaðir **54** B 2
Grimstad **55** E 4
Grindavik **54** A 3
Griquatown **94** C 5
Grmeč **57** G 3
Grodno **55** H 5
Gröndalen **54** F 3
Grong **54** F 3
Groningen **52** E 4
Groote Eylandt **79** F 1
Grootfontein **94** B 3
Groot Vloer **94** BC 5
Groot Winter Berg **94** D 6
Grosseto **57** F 3
Group, Actaeon **83** F 4
Groznyy **59** G 2
Grudziądz **53** G 4
Grünau **94** B 5
Gruñidera **104** B 3
Gruziya **59** F 2
Grytviken **115**
Guadalajara (Mexico) **104** B 3
Guadalajara (Spain) **56** C 3
Guadalcanal **81** G 3
Guadalquivir **56** C 4
Guadalupe **56** B 4
Guadalupe **104** C 2
Guadalupe, Isla de **102** C 6
Guadalupe, Sierra de **56** B 4
Guadeloupe **105** KL 4
Guadeloupe Passage **105** K 4
Guadiana **56** B 4
Guajará Mirim **110** CD 3
Gualeguaychú **112** E 5
Guam **82** A 2
Guaminí **113** D 6
Guanare **108** E 2
Guandacol **112** C 4
Guangde **71** GH 4
Guanghua **70** F 4
Guangshan **70** G 4
Guangxi Zhuangzu Zizhiqu **70** EF 6
Guangyuan **70** E 4

Guangzhou **70** F 6
Guantánamo **105** H 3
Guan Xian **70** D 4
Guapí **108** C 3
Guaporé **110** D 3
Guaqui **110** C 4
Guarapuava **112** F 4
Guarda **56** B 3
Guardal **56** C 4
Guarenas **108** E 1
Guasave **102** E 6
Guasipati **109** F 2
Guatemala **104** DE 4
Guatemala City **104** DE 5
Guaviare **108** E 3
Guayabal **108** E 2
Guayaquil **108** C 4
Guayaquil, Golfo de **108** B 4
Guayaramerin **110** C 3
Guaymallén **112** C 5
Guba **94** D 2
Guba (U.S.S.R.) **62** F 3
Guba Buorkhaya **69** NO 1
Gubakha **63** L 4
Gubkin **62** G 5
Gudbrandsdalen **54** F 3
Gudermes **59** G 2
Gudur **72** CD 5
Guelta Zemmur **86** C 3
Guéné **90** E 3
Güera **86** B 4
Guéra **91** H 3
Guéréda **91** J 3
Guernsey **52** C 5
Guerrero **104** BC 4
Gügerd, Küh-e **61** F 2
Gughe **93** F 3
Guguan **82** A 1
Guiana Highlands **109** FH 3
Guiding **70** E 5
Guidjiba **91** G 4
Guijá **95** E 4
Guildford **52** C 4
Guilin **70** F 5
Guinan **70** D 3
Guinea **90** BC 3
Guinea-Bissau **90** AB 3
Güines **105** F 3
Guiratinga **111** F 4
Guisanbourg **109** H 3
Guixi **71** G 5
Gui Xian **70** EF 6
Guiyang **70** E 5
Guizhou **70** E 5
Gujarat **72** B 3
Gujranwala **67** J 4
Gujrat **67** J 4
Gulbarga **72** C 4
Gulf of Aden **89** H 6
Gulf of Alaska **98** HJ 4
Gulf of Boothia **99** T 1
Gulf of Bothnia **54** GH 3
Gulf of Carpentaria **79** F 1
Gulf of Chihli **71** GH 3
Gulf of Finland **55** H 4
Gulf of Guinea **91** EF 5
Gulf of Khambhat **72** B 3–4
Gulf of Kutch **72** A 3

Gulf of Maine **103** N 3
Gulf of Mannar **72** C 6
Gulf of Martaban **73** G 4
Gulf of Mexico **104** DE 2
Gulf of Ob **63** O 2
Gulf of Oman **89** K 4
Gulf of Papua **80** DE 3
Gulf of Riga **55** H 4
Gulf of Saint Lawrence **101** P 6
Gulf of Sirt **87** J 2
Gulf of Suez **60** A 3
Gulf of Thailand **73** H 5
Gulf of Tonkin **73** J 3–4
Gulf of Venice **57** F 2–3
Gulfport **103** J 5
Gulf Saint Vincent **79** F 5–6
Gulgong **79** HJ 5
Gulin **70** E 5
Gulistan **67** H 2
Gulu **92** E 4
Guna **72** C 3
Güneydoğu Toros lar **59** EF 3
Gungu **92** B 6
Guntur **72** CD 4
Gunung Abong Abong **74** A 3
Gunung Besar **74** E 4
Gunung Binaiya **75** G 4
Gunung Dempo **74** B 4
Gunung Kerinci **74** B 4
Gunung Kinabalu **74** E 2
Gunung Kwoka **75** H 4
Gunung Leuser **74** A 3
Gunung Lokilalaki **75** F 4
Gunung Maling **75** F 3
Gunung Mulu **74** DE 3
Gunung Mutis **75** F 5
Gunung Saran **74** D 4
Gunung Sorikmerapi **74** A 3
Gunung Tahan **74** B 3
Guoyang **70** G 4
Gurban Obo **70** F 2
Gurbantünggüt Shamo **67** M 1–2
Gurgan **61** G 1
Gürlevik Dağı **59** E 3
Gurskoye **69** P 5
Gurupá **109** H 4
Gurupí **111** G 3
Gurvanbulag **68** HJ 6
Gur'yev **66** E 1
Gusau **91** F 3
Guyana **109** G 3
Guyenne **56** C 3
Guzar **67** H 3
Güzelhisar **58** C 3
Gwalior **72** C 2
Gwelo **94** D 3
Gya La **72** DE 2
Gyangzê **72** E 2
Gydanskiy Poluostrov **63** P 1–2
Gympie **79** J 4
Gyöngyös **58** B 1
Győr **57** G 2
Gypsum Point **99** OP 3
Gyula **58** B 1

H

Haanja Kõrgustik **55** J 4
Ha'apai Group **82** D 4
Haapsalu **55** H 4
Haarlem **52** D 4
Habana **105** F 3
Habay **99** O 4
Hābbāniyah **60** D 2
Hachinohe **71** M 2
Hadd, Ra's al **89** KL 4
Hadejia **91** F 3
Hadejia **91** G 3
Hadera **60** B 2
Hadilik **67** M 3
Hadley Bay **99** Q 1
Hadramawt **89** H 5
Hafar al Bāṭin **89** H 3
Hafirat al 'Aydā **60** C 4
Hafit **61** G 4–5
Hāfūn, Ra's **93** J 2
Hagemeister **98** E 4
Hagfors **55** F 3
Hague, Cap de la **56** C 2
Haicheng **71** H 2
Haifa **60** B 2
Haifeng **70** G 6
Haikang **70** EF 6
Haikou **70** F 6–7
Hā'il **60** C 4
Hailar **68** L 6
Hailin **71** J 2
Hailun **69** N 6
Hailuoto **54** H 2
Hainan Dao **70** F 7
Haines **98** K 4
Haines Junction **98** K 3
Hai Phong **73** J 3
Haïti **105** H 4
Hajārah, Sahrā' al **89** GH 2–H 3
Hājjiābād **66** F 5
Hājjiābād-e Māsileh **61** F 2
Hakkâri Dağları **59** F 3
Hakodate **71** M 2
Halab **60** B 1
Ḥalā'ib **88** F 4
Ḥalbā **60** B 2
Halden **55** F 4
Hale, Mount **78** B 4
Halī **89** G 5
Halifax **101** P 7
Hall **98** C 3
Halland **55** F 4
Hallat' Ammār **60** B 3
Hall Beach **99** V 2
Halle **53** F 4
Halley Bay **115**
Hallingskarvet **55** E 3
Hall Islands **82** B 2
Hall Peninsula **101** O 3
Halls Creek **78** D 2
Halmahera, Laut **75** G 4
Halmstad **55** F 4
Hälsingeskogen **54** G 3
Hälsingland **54** G 3
Halti **54** H 2
Hālūl **61** F 4

Hamadān **61** E 2
Hamāh **60** B 2
Hamamatsu **71** L 4
Hamar **55** F 3
Hamburg **53** F 4
Häme **54** HJ 3
Hämeenlinna **54** HJ 3
Hamelin Pool **78** A 4
Hamersley Range **78** B 3
Hamersley Range National Park **78** B 3
Hamhŭng **71** J 2–3
Hami **70** B 2
Hamilton (New Zealand) **81** R 8
Hamilton (Ontario, Can.) **101** M 7
Hamilton (Victoria, Austr.) **79** G 6
Hamm **53** E 4
Hammar, Hawr al **61** E 3
Hammerfest **54** H 1
Hammond **103** J 3
Hammur Koke **93** F 3
Hampden **81** Q 10
Hamrīn, Jabal **60–61** D 2
Hamuku **75** HJ 4
Hanak **60** B 4
Hanang **92** EF 5
Hanceville **99** N 5
Hanchuan **70** F 4
Handan **70** F 3
Handeni **93** F 6
Hanegev **60** B 3
Hanggin Houqi **70** E 2
Hangu **71** G 3
Hangzhou **71** H 4
Hankoniemi **55** H 4
Hannover **53** E 4
Hanöbukten **55** FG 4
Ha Noi **73** HJ 3
Hanover **94** C 6
Hanover, Islas **113** AB 9
Hanstholm **55** E 4
Hao **83** F 4
Haparanda **54** H 2
Hara **68** J 6
Ḥaraḍh **61** E 4
Harar **93** G 3
Harare **95** E 3
Hararge **93** GH 3
Harazé **91** J 4
Harbin **71** J 1
Hardangerfjorden **55** E 3–4
Hardangerjøkulen **55** E 3
Hardangervidda **55** E 3
Hardin **102** E 2
Hargeysa **93** G 3
Hari, Batang **74** B 4
Harib **89** H 6
Hari Kurk **55** H 4
Hārim **60** B 1
Härjedalen **54** F 3
Harlingen **103** G 6
Härnösand **54** G 3
Harrat al 'Uwayrid **60** B 4
Harrat Ithnayn **60** C 4
Harrington Harbour **101** Q 5

Harrisburg **103** L 3
Harrismith **94** DE 5
Harrison, Cape **101** Q 5
Harrison Bay **98** G 1
Harstad **54** G 2
Hartford **103** M 3
Hartlepool **52** C 4
Hartz Mountains National Park **80** KL 9
Har Us Nuur **68** F 6
Harvey **102** G 2
Haryana **72** C 2
Harz **53** F 4
Hasalbag **67** K 3
Hassan **72** C 5
Hassi Bel Guebbour **87** G 3
Hassi Messaoud **87** G 2
Hastings (NE, U.S.A.) **102** G 3
Hastings (New Zealand) **81** R 8
Hat Hin **73** H 3
Ha Tinh **73** J 4
Hattiesburg **103** J 5
Hatutu **83** F 3
Hat Yai **73** H 6
Hauberg Mountains **115**
Haugesund **55** DE 4
Haukipudas **54** J 2
Hauraki Gulf **81** QR 8
Hauterive **101** O 6
Haut-Zaïre **92** CD 4
Havana **105** F 3
Havern **54** G 3
Havre **102** E 2
Havre-Saint-Pierre **101** P 5
Hawaii **83** E 1
Hawaiian Islands **83** E 1
Hawalli **61** E 3
Hawke Harbour **101** Q 5
Hawr al Hammar **61** E 3
Hawrān, Wādī **60** C 2
Hawr as S'adīyah **61** E 2
Hay **79** G 5
Hay River **99** O 3
Hayyā **88** F 5
Hazarajat **67** H 4
Hazar Gölü **59** E 3
Hearst **100** L 6
Hebei **71** G 3
Hebel **79** H 4
Hebi **70** F 3
Hebron **101** P 4
Hecate Strait **98** L 5
Hechi **70** E 6
Hechuan **70** E 4–5
Hedmark **54** F 3
Hefa **60** B 2
Hefei **71** G 4
Hegang **69** O 6
Heidelberg **53** E 5
Heidenheim **53** F 5
Heilbronn **53** E 5
Heilong Jiang **69** O 6
Heilongjiang **71** JK 1
Heimaey **54** A 3
Heimahe **70** C 3
Hejaz **60** B 4
Hekla **54** B 3

145

Helagsfjället 54 F 3
Helena 102 D 2
Hellas 58 B 3
Hells Canyon 102 C 2
Helmeringhausen 94 B 5
Helong 71 JK 2
Helsingborg 55 F 4
Helsingfors 55 J 3–4
Helsingör 55 F 4
Helsinki 55 J 3–4
Henan 70 F 4
Henbury 78 E 3
Henderson 83 G 4
Hendijan 61 E 3
Hengduan Shan 70 CD 5
Heng Xian 70 E 6
Hengyang 70 F 5
Henik Lakes 99 S 3
Henrietta Maria, Cape 101 L 4
Henryetta 103 G 4
Henzada 73 FG 4
Heraklia 60 C 1
Herat 67 G 4
Herberton 79 H 2
Hereford 52 C 4
Herlen He 68 L 6
Herluf Trolle, Cape 101 T 3
Hermiston 102 C 2
Hermit Islands 82 A 3
Hermon, Mount 60 B 2
Hermosillo 102 DE 6
Herning 55 E 4
Herzliyya 60 B 2
He Xian 70 F 6
Heydarābād 61 D 1
Heze 70 FG 3
Hialeah 103 K 6
Hidalgo 104 C 3
Hidalgo del Parral 102 EF 6
Hidcolândia 111 FG 4
Hierro 86 B 3
High Level 99 O 4
High Prairie 99 O 4
Higuerote 108 E 1
Hiiumaa 55 H 4
Hillsboro 103 G 5
Hilo 83 E 1
Himachal Pradesh 72 C 1
Himā Dariyah, Jabal 60 C 4
Himalayas 72 CE 1–2
Hims 60 B 2
Hinchinbrook Island 79 H 2
Hindu Kush 67 HJ 3–4
Hinganghat 72 C 3
Hingol 67 H 5
Hinnöya 54 G 2
Hinton 99 O 5
Hirara 71 J 6
Hirfanlı Barajı 59 D 3
Hirhafok 87 G 4
Hirosaki 71 LM 2
Hiroshima 71 K 4
Hirtshals 55 E 4
Hismā 60 B 3
Hispaniola 105 HJ 4
Hitachi 71 M 3
Hitra 54 E 3
Hiva Oa 83 F 3

Hjälmaren 55 G 4
Hjelmsöya 54 H 1
Hmeenselk 54 H 3
Ho 90 E 4
Hoa Binh 73 HJ 3
Hoachanas 94 B 4
Hoare Bay 101 P 2
Hobart 80 L 9
Hobbs 102 F 5
Hoburgen 55 G 4
Hobyä 93 H 3
Ho Chi Minh 73 J 5
Hodda 93 J 2
Hodeida 89 G 6
Hodh 86 D 5
Hofsá 54 B 2
Hofsjökull 54 B 2
Hofu 71 K 4
Hoggar 87 F 4
Hohhot 70 F 2
Hoima 92 E 4
Hokitika 82 C 5
Hokkaidö 71 M 2
Hokmäbäd 66 F 3
Holanda 110 C 3
Holguín 105 G 3
Holland 103 J 3
Hollick-Kenyon Plateau 115
Hollywood (CA, U.S.A.)
   102 C 5
Hollywood (FL, U.S.A.)
   103 L 6
Holstebro 55 E 4
Holyhead 52 C 4
Homäyünshahr 61 F 2
Hombori Tondo 90 D 3
Home Bay 101 O 2
Homosassa 103 K 6
Honavar 72 B 5
Honduras 104 E 5
Hönefoss 55 F 3
Hong Kong 70 FG 6
Hongliuhe 70 BC 2
Hongor 70 F 1
Hongyuan 70 D 4
Honiara 81 G 3
Honningsvåg 54 J 1
Honolulu 83 E 1
Hon Panjang 73 H 6
Honshü 71 KL 3
Hood Point 78 BC 5
Hoover Dam 102 D 4
Hope, Point 98 D 2
Hopes Advance, Cap 101 O 3
Hopin 73 G 3
Hordaland 55 E 3
Horizon Deep 82 D 4
Horlick Mountains 115
Hormuz, Strait of 61 G 4
Horn, Cape 113 CD 10
Hornavan 54 G 2
Hörnefors 54 G 3
Horn Islands 82 D 3
Hornos, Cabo de 113 CD 10
Horn Plateau 99 O 3
Horqin Youyi Qianqi 71 H 1
Horsens 55 EF 4
Horsham 79 G 6

Hosalay 59 D 2
Hose Mountains 74 D 3
Hoseynïyeh 61 E 3
Hospet 72 C 4
Hospitalet 56 D 3
Hoste, Isla 113 C 10
Hotagen 54 F 3
Hotan 67 K 3
Hotazel 94 C 5
Hoting 54 G 3
Hot Springs 103 H 5
Hottah Lake 99 O 2
Houma (China) 70 F 3
Houma (LA, U.S.A.) 103 H 6
Houston 103 G 5
Hovd (Mongolia) 68 F 6
Hovd (Mongolia) 70 D 2
Hövsgöl Nuur 68 H 5
Howe, Cape 79 J 6
Howland 82 D 2
Howrah 72 E 3
Hoxud 70 A 2
Hox Xil Shan 70 AB 3–4
Hoy 52 C 3
Hrvatska 57 G 2
Hsinchu 71 H 6
Huacho 108 C 6
Hua Hin 73 GH 5
Huaibin 70 FG 4
Huainan 71 G 4
Huairen 70 F 3
Huajuapan de León 104 C 4
Huallaga 108 C 5
Huambo (Angola) 94 B 2
Huambo (Angola) 94 B 2
Huanan 71 K 1
Huancabamba 108 C 5
Huancavelica 110 A 3
Huancayo 110 A 3
Huangchuan 70 G 4
Huang Hai 71 H 3
Huangshi 70 F 4
Huang Xian 71 GH 3
Huangyan 71 H 5
Huangzhong 70 D 3
Huánuco 108 C 5–6
Huara 110 C 4
Huaral 110 A 3
Huaraz 108 C 5
Huarmey 108 C 6
Huascarán, Nevado 108 C 5
Huasco 112 B 4
Huashixia 70 C 3
Huayllay 110 A 3
Hubei 70 F 4
Hubli 72 C 4–5
Huckitta 78 F 3
Hudat 93 F 4
Huddur Hadama 93 G 4
Huder 69 M 6
Hudiksvall 54 G 3
Hudson Bay 99 R 5
Hudson Bay 100 KL 3–4
Hudson River 103 M 3
Hudson's Hope 99 N 4
Hudson Strait 101 NO 3
Hue 73 J 4
Huelva 56 B 4

Huesca 56 C 3
Hughenden 79 G 3
Hugo 103 GH 5
Hüich'on 71 J 2
Huihe 68 L 6
Huila (Angola) 94 AB 2
Huila (Colombia) 108 C 3
Huilai 70 G 6
Huili 70 D 5
Huimin 71 G 3
Huize 70 D 5
Hulayfä' 60 C 4
Huld 70 E 1
Hull 101 M 6
Huma 69 N 5
Humaitá (Amazonas, Brazil)
   109 F 5
Humaitá (Paraguay) 112 E 4
Humay 110 A 3
Húnaflói 54 A 2
Hunan 70 F 5
Hunchun 71 K 2
Hunedoara 58 B 1
Hungary 58 A 1
Hüngnam 71 J 3
Hunjiang 71 J 2
Hunsur 72 C 5
Hunter 82 C 4
Huntington 103 K 4
Huntsville (AL, U.S.A.) 103 J 5
Huntsville (Ontario, Can.)
   101 M 6
Huntsville (TX, U.S.A.)
   103 GH 5
Hunyuan 70 F 3
Huocheng 67 KL 2
Huon 82 B 4
Huon Gulf 80 E 3
Huo Xian 70 F 3
Huron 102 G 3
Hurst 103 G 5
Husum 53 E 4
Hutag 68 H 6
Hutchinson 102 G 4
Hvar 57 G 3
Hveragerði 54 A 3
Hyargas Nuur 68 F 6
Hyden 78 B 5
Hyderabad (India) 72 CD 4
Hyderabad (Pakistan) 67 H 5
Hyères, Iles d' 57 E 3
Hyesan 71 J 2
Hyvinkää 55 H 3

I

Iaçu 111 H 3
Ialomiţa 58 C 2
Iaripo 109 H 3
Iaşi 58 C 1
Ibadan 91 E 4
Ibagué 108 C 3
Ibaiti 111 FG 5
Ibarra 108 C 3
Iberville, Lac d' 101 N 4
Ibestad 54 G 2
Ibi 91 F 4
Ibitiara 111 H 3
Ibiza (Spain) 56 D 4

Íbiza (Spain) **56** D 4
Ibotirama **111** H 3
Ibrim **88** E 4
Icá (Amazonas, Brazil) **108** E 4
Ica (Peru) **110** A 3
Icana **108** E 3
Içel **59** D 3
Iceland **54** A 2
Iceland **54** A 3
Ichera **68** J 4
Ichinskaya Sopka **69** ST 4
Ico **111** J 2
Icy Cape **98** E 1
Idaho **102** CD 3
Idaho Falls **102** D 3
Idfú **88** E 4
Idhán Awbári **87** H 3
Idhán Murzuq **87** H 4
Ídhi Óros **58** BC 3
Ídhra **58** B 3
Idlib **60** B 2
Idre **54** F 3
Ifalik **82** A 2
Ifanadiana **95** H 4
Ife **91** E 4
Igarka **63** R 2
Iglesias **57** E 4
Ignace **100** J 6
Ignashino **69** M 5
Igneada **58** C 2
Iguaçu **112** F 4
Iguala **104** C 4
Iguassú Falls **112** F 4
Iguatu **111** J 2
Ihosy **95** H 4
Ihtamir **68** H 6
Iivaara **54** J 2
Ijebu Ode **91** EF 4
Ijsselmeer **52** E 4
Ijuí **112** F 4
Ikaría **58** C 3
Ikerre **91** F 4
Ikot Ekpene **91** F 4
Ilaferh **87** F 4
Ilagan **75** J 1
Ilam **61** E 2
Ilbenge **69** M 3
Ile-à-la-Crosse **99** Q 4
Ilebo **92** C 5
Île d'Anticosti **101** P 6
Ile de France **56** D 2
Ile de la Gonâve **105** H 4
Île de la Madeleine **101** P 6
Ile de Ré **56** C 2
Ile des Noefs **93** J 6
Ile des Pins **81** J 6
Ile d'Oléron **56** C 2
Ile d'Ouessant **56** B 2
Île du Diable **109** H 2
Ile d'Yeu **56** C 2
Iles Chesterfield **82** B 4
Îles de Los **90** B 4
Iles d'Hyères **57** E 3
Îles du Désappointement
  83 F 3
Îles du Duc de Gloucester
  83 F 4
Îles du Roi Georges **83** F 3

Iles Glorienses **95** H 2
Îles Palliser **83** F 4
Ile Tidra **86** B 5
Ilha de Maracá **109** HJ 3
Ilha de Marajó **109** HJ 4
Ilha Grande **108** E 4
Ilha Santa Carolina **95** F 4
Ilhéus **111** J 3
Iliamna **98** G 4
Iliamna Lake **98** F 4
Ilichevsk **58** D 1
Ilimsk **68** H 4
Ilinskiy **69** Q 6
Illapel **112** B 5
Illimani, Nevado **110** C 4
Illinois **103** J 3–4
Illizi **87** G 3
Ilo **110** B 4
Iloilo **75** F 1
Ilots de Bass **83** F 4
Ilubabor **92** EF 3
Ilyichovsk **58** D 1
Ima **68** L 4
Imám al Hamzah **61** D 3
Imandra, Ozero **54** K 2
Imatra **54** J 3
Imbituba **112** G 4
Iméni Gastello **69** R 3
Iméni Mariny **69** QR 3
Imgytskoye Boloto **63** O 4
Imperatriz **109** J 5
Imphal **73** F 3
Imtonzha **69** NO 2
Inagua Island, Great **105** H 3
Inarijarvi **54** J 2
In Azaoua **91** F 1
In Bogd Uul **70** CD 1
Ince Burnu **59** D 2
Inch'ón **71** J 3
Inchôpe **95** E 3
Independence **103** H 4
India **72** CD 3
Indiana **103** J 3
Indianapolis **103** J 4
Indian Harbour **101** Q 5
Indian Ocean **117**
Indias Occidentales **105** H 3
Indigirka **69** R 2
Indigirskaya Nizmennost'
  69 QR 2
Indispensable Reefs **82** B 3
Indispensable Strait **81** H 3–4
Indonesia **74–75** OG 4
Indore **72** C 3
Indus **67** H 6
İnegöl **58** C 2
In Gall **91** F 2
Ingoda **68** K 5
Ingrid Christensen Coast **115**
Ingul **59** D 1
Inhambane **95** F 4
Inharrime **95** F 4
Inhumas **111** FG 4
Inírida **108** E 3
Inkerman **79** G 2
Inn **53** F 5
Inner Hebrides **52** B 3
Inner Mongolia **70** E 2–3

Innisfail **79** H 2
Innokent'yevka **69** P 6
Innsbruck **57** F 2
Inoucdjouac **101** M 4
In Salah **87** F 3
Insulá Sacalin **58** CD 2
Inta **63** L 2
Intletovy **63** P 3
Inuvik **98** L 2
Invercargill **80** P 10
Inverness **52** C 3
Investigator Strait **79** F 6
Inya **63** R 5
Iolotan **67** G 3
Iona National Park **94** A 3
Ionian Islands **58** A 3
Ionian Sea **58** A 3
Ionioi Nísoi **58** A 3
Iónion Pélagos **58** AB 3
Íos **58** C 3
Iowa **103** H 3
Iowa City **103** H 3
Ipameri **111** G 4
Ipatinga **111** H 4
Ipiales **108** C 3
Ipiaú **111** J 3
Ípiros **58** B 3
Ipixuna **108** D 5
Ipoh **74** B 3
Iporá **111** F 4
Ipswich (Australia) **79** J 4
Ipswich (U.K.) **52** D 4
Ipu **111** H 1
Iquapé **111** G 5
Iquique **110** B 5
Iquitos **108** D 4
Iracoubo **109** H 2
Irafshan **67** G 5
Iráklion **58** C 3
Iran **66** EF 4
Iran, Pegunungan **74** D 3
Irapuato **104** B 3
Iraq **60** D 2
Irbid **60** B 2
Irbit **63** M 4
Irebu **92** B 5
Irecê **111** H 3
Irgiz **67** G 1
Irian Jaya **75** HJ 4
Iriba **91** J 2
Iringa **93** F 6
Iriomote-jima **71** HJ 6
Iriona **104** EF 4
Iriri **109** H 4
Irish Sea **52** BC 4
Irkutsk **68** HJ 5
Iron Gate **58** B 2
Iron Knob **79** F 5
Írq al Idrísí **87** K 4–5
'Irq al Mazhur **60** D 4
Irrawaddy **73** G 3–4
Irrawaddy, Mouths of the
  73 FG 4
Irtuia **109** J 4
Irtysh **63** N 4
Irtysh **63** O 5
Irún **56** C 3
Isa, Mount **79** F 3

Isabela **108** B 6
Isangi **92** C 4
Ischia **57** F 3
Iscia Baidoa → Isha Baydabo
  93 G 4
Iseyin **90** E 4
Isfendiyar Dağlari **59** D 2
Isherton **109** G 3
Ishigaki **71** HJ 6
Ishikhly **66** D 3
Ishim **63** N 4
Ishim **63** O 4
Ishimskaya Step' **63** O 5
Ishinomaki **71** M 3
İšiklar Dağı **58** C 2
Isil'kul **63** O 5
Isinga **68** K 5
Isiro **92** D 4
İskenderun **59** E 3
İskenderun Kẞrfezi **59** E 3
Iskitim **63** Q 5
Isla Ángel de la Guarda
  102 D 6
Isla Aruba **108** E 1
Isla Campana **113** A 8
Isla Cedros **102** C 6
Isla Curaçao **108** DE 1
Isla de Chiloé **113** B 7
Isla de Cozumel **104** E 3
Isla de Guadelupe **102** C 6
Isla de la Juventud **104** F 3
Isla del Maíz **104** F 5
Isla de los Estados **113** D 9
Isla Desolación **113** AB 9
Isla Esmeralda **113** A 8
Isla Grande de Tierra del
  Fuego **113** C 9
Isla Hoste **113** C 10
Islamabad **67** J 4
Isla Malpelo **108** B 3
Ísland **54** A 3
Island Lake **99** T 5
Islands of Four Mountains
  98 CD 5
Isla Santa Inés **113** B 9
Islas Baleares **56** D 3–4
Islas Canarias **86** B 3
Islas Hanover **113** AB 9
Isla Tiburon **102** D 6
Isla Tobago **109** F 1
Isla Trinidad **109** F 1
Islay **52** B 3
Isle of Man **52** C 4
Isle of Wight **52** C 4
Isles of Scilly **52** B 5
Isole Eolie o Lipari **57** F 4
Isole Ponziane **57** F 3
Isosyöte **54** J 2
Ísparta **58** D 3
Israel **60** B 3
Israel **88** E 2
Issano **109** G 2
Istanbul **58** C 2
İstanbul Boğazı **58** C 2
Isteren **54** F 3
Isthmus of Kra **73** G 5
Istmo de Tehuantepec
  104 D 4

Isto, Mount **98** J 2
Istra **57** F 2
Itaberaba **111** H 3
Itabira **111** H 4
Itabuna **111** J 3
Itaguí **108** C 2
Itaituba **109** G 4
Itajaí **112** G 4
Italia **57** FG 3
Italy **57** F 3
Itambé **111** H 4
Itaperucu Mirim **111** H 1
Itaperuna **111** H 5
Itapetinga **111** J 4
Itapipoca **111** J 1
Itapiranga **109** G 4
Itapiúna **111** J 1
Itarsi **72** C 3
Itaúnas **111** J 4
Itbäy **60** AB 4
Itbäy **88** EF 3–4
Itchen Lake **99** P 2
Iténez **110** D 3
Ithaca **103** L 3
Itháki **58** B 3
Ithnayn, Harat **60** C 4
Itivdleg **101** R 2
Ituberá **111** J 3
Ituiutaba **111** FG 4
Itumbiara **111** FG 4
Iturama **111** F 4
Iturbe **110** C 5
Itzehoe **53** EF 4
Iul'tin **98** B 2
Ivalojoki **54** J 2
Ivanhoe **79** GH 5
Ivano-Frankovsk **62** D 6
Ivanovo **62** H 4
Ivigtut **101** S 3
Ivory Coast **90** CD 4
Ivory Coast **90** CD 5
Ivrea **57** E 2
Iwaki **71** M 3
Iwo **91** E 4
Iwo Jima **65** R 7
Iwón **71** J 2
Ixiamas **110** C 3
İzmir **58** C 3
İzmir Körfezi **58** C 3
Izmit **58** CD 2
Izu-shotō **71** M 4–5

J

Jabal Abadab **88** EF 5
Jabal al Bishri **88** F 1
Jabal al Humara **88** E 5
Jabal al Lawz **88** F 3
Jabal an Nabī Shu'ayb **89** G 5
Jabal as Hasāwinah **87** H 3
Jabal ash Shaykh **60** B 2
Jabal at Tubayq **60** B 3
Jabal Dabbāgh **60** B 4
Jabal Hajhir **93** J 2
Jabal Hamātah **60** B 4
Jabal Hamoyet **88** F 5
Jabal Hamrin **60–61** D 2
Jabal Himā Ḍariyah **60** C 4
Jabal Ibrāhīm **89** G 4

Jabal Kātrīna **60** AB 3
Jabal Katul **88** D 6
Jabal Lotuke **92** E 4
Jabal Lubnān **60** B 2
Jabal Marrah **88** CD 6
Jabal Oda **88** F 4
Jabalpur **72** CD 3
Jabal Ṣabir **89** G 6
Jabal Shā'ib al Banāt **60** A 4
Jabal Shammar **60** CD 4
Jabal Tuwayq **61** D 4
Jabālyah **60** B 3
Jablah **60** B 2
Jablanica **57** G 3
Jabung, Tanjung **74** B 4
Jacareacanga **109** G 5
Jaciara **111** F 4
Jaciparaná **109** F 5
Jackpot **102** D 3
Jackson (MS, U.S.A.)
103 HJ 5
Jackson (TX, U.S.A.) **103** J 4
Jackson, Mount **115**
Jacksonville (FL, U.S.A.)
103 K 5
Jacksonville (TX, U.S.A.)
103 GH 5
Jacobabad **67** H 5
Jacobina **111** H 3
Jacona **104** B 3–4
Jadal **91** E 2
J.A.D. Jensens Nunatakker
101 S 3
Jādū **87** H 2
Jaén **56** C 4
Jaffa, Cape **79** F 6
Jaffa → Tel Aviv-Yafo
88 E 2
Jaffna **72** D 6
Jagdalpur **72** D 4
Jaguarão **112** F 5
Jaguarari **111** J 3
Jaguariaíva **111** FG 5
Jaguaribe **111** J 2
Jahrom **61** F 3
Jaina **104** D 3
Jaipur **72** C 2
Jakarta **74** C 5
Jakobshavn **114**
Jakobstad **54** H 3
Jalaid Qi **71** H 1
Jalapa Enríquez **104** CD 4
Jalgaon **72** BC 3
Jalibah **61** E 3
Jalisco **104** B 3
Jalón **56** C 3
Jaluit **82** C 2
Jalūlā' **61** D 2
Jama **108** B 4
Jamaica **105** G 4
Jamāme **93** G 4
Jamari **109** F 5
Jambi **74** B 4
James **102** G 3
James Bay **101** L 5
James Ross Strait **99** S 1–2
Jamestown (N.D., U.S.A.)
102 G 2

Jamestown (N.Y., U.S.A.)
103 L 3
Jamiltepec **104** C 4
Jammu **67** K 4
Jammu and Kashmir **67** K 4
Jamnagar **72** AB 3
Jamsah **60** A 4
Jamshedpur **72** DE 3
Jämtland **54** F 3
Jandaia **111** FG 4
Jandaq **66** EF 4
Janesville **103** J 3
Janjira **72** B 4
Jan Mayen Island **114**
Janos **102** E 5
Januária **111** H 4
Japan **71** L 3
Japurá **108** E 4
Jarabulus **60** C 1
Jaramillo **113** C 8
Jarbah **87** H 2
Jardine River National Park
79 G 1
Jarrahdale **78** B 5
Jarud Qi **71** H 2
Jarvis **83** E 3
Jasikan **90** E 4
Jasper **103** H 5
Jasper National Park **99** O 5
Jastrzebie Zdrój **53** G 5
Jászberény **58** AB 1
Jataí **111** F 4
Jatobal **109** HJ 4
Jaú **111** G 5
Jauja **110** A 3
Java **74** C 5
Java Sea **74** CD 5
Jawa **74** CD 5
Jaya, Puncak **75** J 4
Jayapura **80** D 2
Jaza'ir Farasān **89** G 5
Jazā'ir Khuriyā Muriyā **89** K 5
Jazirat **60** B 4
Jbel Toubkal **86** D 2
Jeci **95** F 2
Jefferson, Mount (NV, U.S.A.)
102 C 4
Jefferson City **103** H 4
Jēkabpils **55** J 4
Jekkevarre **54** GH 2
Jelenia Góra **53** G 4
Jelgava **55** H 4
Jelow Gir **61** E 2
Jequié **111** H 3
Jequitinhonha **111** HJ 4
Jerada **86** E 2
Jeremoabo **111** J 3
Jerez de la Frontera **56** B 4
Jerome **102** CD 3
Jersey **52** C 5
Jerusalem **60** B 3
Jeypore **72** D 4
Jhang Sadar **67** J 4
Jhansi **72** C 2
Jhelum **67** J 4
Jiamusi **71** K 1
Jiang'an **70** DE 5
Jianghua **70** F 5

Jiangmen **70** F 6
Jiangsu **71** GH 4
Jiangxi **70** FG 5
Jiangyou **70** D 4
Jianyang **71** G 5
Jiaozuo **70** F 3
Jiayu **70** F 5
Jiayuguan **70** C 3
Jiddah **89** FG 4
Jieyang **70** G 6
Jigzhi **70** D 4
Jijiga **93** G 3
Jilib **93** G 4
Jilin **71** HJ 2
Jimāl, Wādi **60** B 4
Jimma **93** F 3
Jinan **71** G 3
Jincheng **70** F 3
Jingdezhen **71** G 5
Jingning **70** E 3
Jing Xian **70** F 5
Jingyuan **70** DE 3
Jinhua **71** GH 5
Jining **71** G 3
Jinja **92** E 4
Jinkouhe **70** D 5
Jinping **70** D 6
Jinsha **70** E 5
Jinsha Jiang **70** D 5
Jinshan **71** H 4
Jin Xian **71** H 3
Jinxiang **71** G 3–4
Jinzhou **71** H 2
Jiparaná **109** F 5
Jipijapa **108** B 4
Jishou **70** F 5
Jisr ash Shughūr **60** B 2
Jiu **58** B 2
Jiujiang **70** G 5
Jiuquan **70** C 3
Jixi **71** K 1
João Pessoa **111** K 2
Jodhpur **72** B 2
Joensuu **54** JK 3
Jöetsu **71** L 3
Johannesburg **94** DE 5
John O'Groat's **52** C 3
Johnsons Crossing **98** L 3
Johnston **82** D 1
Johnstown **103** L 3
Johor Baharu **74** B 3
Joinvile **112** G 4
Joinville Island **115**
Jokkmokk **54** H 2
Jolo **75** F 2
Jonesboro **103** HJ 4
Jonglei **92** E 3
Jönköping **55** FG 4
Jonquière **101** N 6
Joplin **103** H 4
Jordan **60** B 2–3
Jordan **60** B 3
Jordan **88** F 2
Jorhat **73** F 2
Jos **91** F 4
Joseph Bonaparte Gulf
78 D 1
Joseph Lake **101** O 5

Jos Sodarso, Pulau **75** J 5
Jostedalsbreen **54** E 3
Jotunheimen **54** E 3
Juan de Nova **95** G 3
Juan Fernández Islands
  107 B 6
Juárez **113** E 6
Juàzeiro **111** H 2
Juàzeiro do Norte **111** J 2
Jûba **92** E 4
Jubayl **60** B 2
Jubayt **88** F 5
Júcar **56** C 4
Juchitan de Zaragoza **104** D 4
Juiz de Fora **111** H 5
Juktån **54** G 2
Juliaca **110** B 4
Julia Creek **79** G 3
Julianatop **109** G 3
Julianehåb **101** S 3
Jumanggoin **70** C 4
Junagadh **72** B 3
Jun Bulen **71** G 1
Junction **102** G 5
Jundiaí **111** G 5
Juneau **98** L 4
Junee **79** H 5
Junggar Pendi **67** M 1
Junín **112** D 5
Jûniyah **60** B 2
Jun Xian **70** F 4
Juoksengi **54** H 2
Jura **52** B 3
Jurado **108** C 2
Jurien Bay **78** A 5
Jürmala **55** H 4
Juruá **108** E 4
Juruena **110** E 3
Juruti **109** G 4
Jutaí **108** E 4
Jutland **55** E 4
Juva **54** J 3
Juventud, Isla de la **104** F 3
Ju Xian **71** G 3
Jüyom **61** F 3
Juzur Qarqannah **87** H 2
Jylland **55** EF 4
Jyväskylä **54** J 3

K

Kabaena, Pulau **75** F 5
Kabalo **92** D 6
Kaban'ya **69** P 6
Kabba **91** F 4
Kåbdalis **54** G 2
Kabinda **92** CD 6
Kabir Küh **61** E 2
Kabo **92** B 3
Kabompo **94** C 2
Kabondo Dianda **92** D 6
Kabud Råhang **61** E 2
Kabul **67** HJ 4
Kabwe **94** D 2
Kachikattsy **69** NO 3
Kachin **73** G 2
Kachug **68** J 5
Kadirli **59** E 3
Kadiyevka **59** E 1

Kadoma **94** D 3
Kådugli **88** D 6
Kaduna **91** F 3
Kaédi **86** C 5
Kafue **94** D 2
Kafue **94** D 3
Kafue National Park **94** D 3
Kafura **92** E 5
Kagoshima **71** JK 4
Kagul **58** C 1
Kahemba **92** B 6
Kahoolawe **83** E 1
Kahramanmaras **59** E 3
Kai, Kepulauan **75** H 5
Kaifeng **70** FG 4
Kaikoura **81** Q 9
Kaili **70** E 5
Kailu **71** H 2
Kaimur Range **72** D 3
Kainantu **80** E 3
Kainji Dam **91** EF 4
Kainji Reservoir **91** E 3
Kaintragarh **72** DE 3
Kairouan → Al Qayrawân
  87 GH 1
Kaiserslautern **53** E 5
Kai Xian **70** E 4
Kaiyuan **70** D 6
Kajaki Dam **67** H 4
Kakhovka **59** D 1
Kakhovskoye
  Vodokhranilishche **59** DE 1
Käki **61** F 3
Kakinada **72** D 4
Kakisa **99** O 3
Kaktovik **98** J 1
Kalabagh **67** J 4
Kalach **62** H 5
Kalachinsk **63** OP 4
Kalahari **94** C 4
Kalahari Gemsbok National
  Park **94** BC 5
Kalai-Khumb **67** J 3
Kalajoki **54** H 3
Kalámai **58** B 3
Kalaong **75** F 2
Kalbarri National Park **78** A 4
Kaldbakur **54** A 2
Kalehe **92** D 5
Kalemie **92** CD 6
Kalevala **54** K 2
Kalewa **73** F 3
Kalga **68** L 5
Kalgoorlie **78** C 5
Kalimantan **74** DE 3
Kalinin **62** FG 4
Kaliningrad **55** H 5
Kalisz **53** G 4
Kalixälven **54** H 2
Kallsjön **54** F 3
Kalmar **55** G 4
Kalmykovo **66** E 1
Kaloko **92** D 6
Kalole **92** D 5
Kalsubai **72** B 4
Kaltag **98** F 3
Kaluga **62** FG 5
Kamaishi **71** M 3

Kamanjab **94** B 3
Kamarän **89** G 5
Kamaria Falls **109** FG 2
Kambal'naya Sopka **69** T 5
Kamchatka **69** T 4
Kamchatka Peninsula **114**
Kamenets-Podolskiy **58** C 1
Kamenjak, Rt **57** F 3
Kamen-na-Obi **63** PQ 5
Kamensk-Ural'skiy **63** M 4
Kamet **72** D 1
Kamina **92** D 6
Kamkaly **67** J 2
Kamloops **99** N 5
Kamnrokan **68** K 4
Kampala **92** E 4–5
Kampar **74** B 3
Kampar, Sungai **74** B 3
Kampot **74** B 1
Kamsack **99** R 5
Kamyshin **62** HJ 5
Kanaaupscow **101** M 5
Kanaga **98** B 5
Kananga **92** C 6
Kanangra Boyd National Park
  79 HJ 5
Kanazawa **71** KL 3
Kanchipuram **72** CD 5
Kandagach **66** F 1
Kandahar **67** H 4
Kandalaksha **54** K 2
Kandalakshskaya Guba
  54 K 2
Kandangan **74** DE 4
Kandavu **82** C 4
Kande **90** E 4
Kandi **90** E 3
Kandy **72** D 6
Kandychan **69** RS 3
Kanem **91** GH 3
Kangalassy **69** N 3
Kangan **61** F 4
Kangar **74** B 2
Kangaroo Island **79** F 6
Kangävar **61** E 2
Kangchenjunga **72** E 2
Kangding **70** D 5
Kangean, Kepulauan
  74 E 5
Kangeeak Point **101** P 2
Kanggye **71** J 2
Kangmar **72** DE 1
Kangnüng **71** JK 3
Kango **91** G 5
Kangping **71** H 2
Kangynin **98** B 2
Kaniama **92** C 6
Kaniet Islands **82** A 3
Kankan **90** C 3
Kankesanturai **72** D 5–6
Kankossa **86** C 5
Kanmaw Kyun **73** G 5
Kannapolis **103** K 4
Kano **91** F 3
Kanovlei **94** B 3
Kansas **102** G 4
Kansas City **103** H 4
Kansk **68** FG 4

Kantang **73** G 6
Kantaralak **73** HJ 5
Kantchari **90** E 3
Kanye **94** CD 4
Kaohsiung **71** GH 6
Kaolack **90** A 3
Kaoma **94** C 2
Kaouar **91** G 2
Kapanga **92** C 6
Kapatu **95** E 1
Kap Brewster **114**
Kapchagay **67** K 2
Kapchagayskoye
  Vodokhranilishche **67** K 2
Kap Farvel **101** T 4
Kapfenberg **57** G 2
Kapingamarangi **82** B 2
Kapiri Moposhi **94** DE 2
Kapisigdlit **101** RS 3
Kapona **92** D 6
Kaposvár **58** A 1
Kapsukas **55** H 5
Kapustoye **54** K 2
Karabekaul **67** GH 3
Karabük **59** D 2
Karabutak **66** F 1
Karachi **67** H 6
Kara Dağ **59** D 3
Karaga **69** U 4
Karaganda **63** OP 6
Karagüney Dağları **59** DE 2
Karaikkudi **72** C 6
Karaj **61** F 2
Kara-Kala **66** F 2
Karakelong, Pulau **75** G 3
Karakoram **67** JK 3–4
Karakorum Shankou
  67 JK 3–4
Karaköse **59** F 3
Karalundi **78** B 4
Karam **68** J 4
Karamagay **67** M 1
Karaman **59** D 3
Karamay **67** LM 1
Karasburg **94** B 5
Kara Sea **114**
Karasjåkka **54** H 2
Karasu (Turkey) **59** F 2–3
Karasu-Aras Dağları **59** F 3
Karasuk **63** P 5
Karatal **63** P 6
Karatau **67** J 2
Karathuri **73** G 5
Karaton **66** E 1
Karaul **63** Q 1
Karaulkel'dy **66** EF 1
Karazhingil **63** O 6
Karbalä' **60** D 2
Kardhítsa **58** B 3
Kärdla **55** H 4
Kareliya **54** K 3
Karen **73** G 4
Karesuando **54** H 2
Karganay **69** X 2
Kargat **63** Q 4
Kargopol'**62** G 3
Kari **91** G 3

Kar – Kha

Kariba Dam **94** D 3
Karibib **94** B 4
Karikal **72** CD 5
Karimata, Selat **74** C 4
Karimganj **73** F 2
Karisimbi **92** D 5
Karjala **54** K 3
Karkâr **80** E 2
Karkas, Küh-e **61** F 2
Karkinitskiy Zaliv **59** D 1
Karleby **54** H 3
Karlik Shan **70** BC 2
Karl-Marx-Stadt **53** F 4
Karlovac **57** G 2
Karlovy Vary **53** F 4
Karlshamn **55** FG 4
Karlskoga **55** FG 4
Karlskrona **55** G 4
Karlsruhe **53** E 5
Karlstad (MN, U.S.A.) **103** G 2
Karlstad (Sweden) **55** F 4
Karmöy **55** DE 4
Karnataka **72** BC 4
Karong **73** F 2
Karonga **95** E 1
Kárpathos **58** C 3
Kars **59** F 2
Karsakpay **67** H 1
Karshi **67** H 3
Karskiye Vorota, Proliv
  62–63 L 1
Karskoye More **63** LM 1
Kars Platosu **59** F 2
Kartal **58** C 2
Kartaly **63** LM 5
Karufa **75** H 4
Karwar **72** B 5
Kasai **92** B 5
Kasai Occidental **92** C 6
Kasai Oriental **92** C 5–6
Kasaji **94** C 2
Kasama **95** E 2
Kasba Lake **99** R 3
Kâshân **61** F 2
Kashi **67** K 3
Kashken Teniz **63** O 6
Kâshmar **66** F 3
Kasimov **62** H 5
Kaskelen **67** K 2
Kas Kong **73** H 5
Kasongo **92** D 5
Kásos **58** C 3
Kaspiyskiy **59** G 1
Kaspiyskoye More **66** D 1
Kassalâ **88** F 5
Kassándra **58** B 2
Kassel **53** E 4
Kastamonu **59** D 2
Kasungu **95** E 2
Katako-Kombe **92** CD 5
Katangli **69** Q 5
Katawaz **67** H 4
Katende Falls **92** C 6
Katerini **58** B 2
Katherine **78** E 1
Katherine Gorge National
  Park **78** E 1
Kathiawar **72** B 3

Kathīri **89** H 5
Kathmandu **72** E 2
Katihar **72** E 2
Katmai National Park and
  Preserve **98** G 4
Katowice **53** G H 4
Kātrīna, Jabal **60** AB 3
Katrineholm **55** G 4
Katsina **91** F 3
Kattegat **55** F 4
Katyl'ga **63** P 4
Kauai **83** E 1
Kaufbeuren **53** F 5
Kaunas **55** H 5
Kauno Marios **55** H 5
Kavalerovo **71** KL 2
Kaválla **58** B 2
Kavar **61** F 3
Kavendou, Mont **90** B 3
Kavīr, Dasht-e **61** FG 2
Kavir-e Abarqu **61** F 3
Kavir-e Namak **61** G 1
Kawa **88** E 5
Kawich Peak **102** CD 4
Kawm Umbū **88** E 4
Kaya **90** D 3
Kayah **73** G 4
Kayak **98** J 4
Kayala **54** K 3
Kayan **74** E 3
Kayes **90** B 3
Kaynar **63** P 6
Kayseri **59** DE 3
Kazachinskoye **68** J 4
Kazakhskiy Melkosopochnik
  63 NP 6
Kazakhstan **67** FH 1
Kazan'**62** JK 4
Kazan Islands **65** QR 7
Kazanlük **58** C 2
Kazanskoye **63** NO 4
Kazbek **59** F 2
Kaz Daği **58** C 3
Kāzerün **61** F 3
Kazymskaya **63** N 3
Kazymskiy Mys **63** MN 3
Kazzân ar Ruşayriş **88** E 6
Keams Canyon **102** D 4
Keban Gölü **59** E 3
Kebbi **91** E 3
Kebnekaise **54** G 2
Kediat Idjil **86** C 4
Kediri **74** D 5
Kédougou **90** B 3
Keetmanshoop **94** B 5
Kefa **93** F 3
Kefallinia **58** B 3
Keimoes **94** C 5
Keitele **54** J 3
Keith **79** FG 6
Keketa **80** D 3
Kelang **74** B 3
Keli Hâji Ibrâhîm **61** D 1
Kelkit **59** E 2
Kellett, Cape **99** M 1
Kellog (U.S.S.R.) **63** R 3
Kellogg **102** C 2
Kelloselkä **54** J 2

Kelsey **99** S 4
Kelsey Bay **99** MN 5
Keluang **74** B 3
Kem' **54** K 3
Ké Macina **90** CD 3
Kemerovo **63** QR 4
Kemi **54** HJ 2
Kemijärvi **54** J 2
Kemijoki **54** J 2
Kemkra **69** P 4
Kempendyayi **68** LM 3
Kemps Bay **105** G 3
Kempsey **79** J 5
Kenai **98** G 3–4
Kenai Fjords National Park
  98 H 4
Kenai Mountains **98** G 3–4
Kenai Peninsula **98** GH 4
Kencha **69** PQ 3
Kendari **75** F 4
Kenhardt **94** C 5
Kenitra **86** D 2
Keniut **69** X 3
Kenmare **102** F 2
Kennedy Range National Park
  78 B 3
Keno Hill **98** L 3
Kenora **100** KJ 6
Kentau **67** H 2
Kent Peninsula **99** Q 2
Kentucky **103** J 4
Kentucky Lake **103** J 4
Kenya **93** F 4–5
Kenya, Mount **93** F 5
Kepe **54** K 2
Kepulauan Anambas **74** C 3
Kepulauan Aru **75** HJ 5
Kepulauan Babar **75** GH 5
Kepulauan Banggai **75** F 4
Kepulauan Kai **75** H 5
Kepulauan Kangean **74** E 5
Kepulauan Leti **75** G 5
Kepulauan Lingga **74** BC 3–4
Kepulauan Mentawai **74** AB 4
Kepulauan Natuna **74** C 3
Kepulauan Riau **74** B 3
Kepulauan Sangihe **75** G 3
Kepulauan Sula **75** FG 4
Kepulauan Talaud **75** G 3
Kepulauan Tanimbar **75** H 5
Kepulauan Tenggara **75** G 5
Kepulauan Togian **75** F 4
Kepulauan Tukangbesi **75** F 5
Kerama-rettō **71** J 5
Kerch **59** E 1
Kerchenskiy Proliv **59** E 1–2
Kerekhtyakh **69** N 3
Kerema **80** E 3
Kerempe Burnu **59** D 2
Keren **93** F 1
Keret', Ozero **54** K 2
Keriske **69** O 2
Kerki **67** GH 3
Kérkira **58** A 3
Kermadec Islands **82** D 4–5
Kermân **66** F 4
Kermanshâh **61** E 2
Kermânshâhân **61** G 3

Kerme Körfezi **58** C 3
Kerzaz **86** E 3
Kestenga **54** K 2
Ketoy, Ostrov **69** S 6
Keul' **68** H 4
Keurusselkä **54** HJ 3
Kewanee **103** J 3
Keyano **101** N 5
Key West **103** L 7
Kezhma **68** H 4
Khabarovsk **69** P 6
Khabr, Küh-e **61** G 3
Khabūr **60** C 1
Khachmas **66** D 2
Khafjī, Ra's al **61** E 3
Khaipur **67** H 5
Khairpur **67** J 5
Khakhea **94** C 4
Khakriz **67** GH 4
Khalesavoy **63** PQ 3
Khalīj al 'Aqabah **60** B 3
Khalīj al 'Aqabah **88** E 3
Khalīj as Suways **60** A 3
Khalīj Maşirah **89** K 5
Khalīj Qâbis **87** H 2
Khálki **58** C 3
Khalkidhiki **58** B 2
Khalkis **58** B 3
Khambhat, Gulf of **72** B 3–4
Khamgaon **72** C 3
Khampa **68** L 3
Khampa **69** M 3
Khamseh **61** E 1
Khanabad **67** HJ 3
Khandwa **72** C 3
Khandyga **69** P 3
Khanglasy **63** M 3
Khanh Hung **73** HJ 6
Khani **68** M 4
Khánia **58** B 3
Khanpur **67** J 5
Khân Shaykhūn **60** B 2
Khantau **67** J 2
Khanty-Mansiysk **63** NO 3
Khanyangda **69** Q 4
Khanyardakh **69** N 3
Khao Lang **73** G 6
Khao Luang **73** G 6
Khao Sai Dao Tai **73** H 5
Khappyrastakh **69** M 4
Khara **68** G 5
Kharagpur **72** E 3
Kharan **67** GH 5
Kharânaq **61** G 2
Kharânaq, Küh-e **61** G 2
Kharik **68** H 5
Khärk **61** F 3
Kharkov **62** G 5
Kharoti **67** H 4
Kharstan **69** Q 1
Khash (Afghanistan) **67** G 4
Khâsh (Iran) **67** G 5
Khash Desert **67** G 4
Khashm Mishrag **66** D 6
Khaskovo **58** C 2
Khatanga **68** H 1
Khatangskiy Zaliv **68** JK 1

Khataren **69** T 3
Khatyrka **69** X 3
Khawr al Fakkān **61** G 4
Khaybar **60** C 4
Khaybar, Harrat **60** C 4
Khazzān Jabal al Awliyá'
 88 E 5–6
Khe Bo **73** HJ 4
Khenifra **86** D 2
Kherpuchi **69** P 5
Khersan **61** F 3
Kherson **59** D 1
Kheta **68** G 1
Kheta **68** H 1
Kheyrābād **66** EF 5
Khibiny **54** K 2
Khíos **58** C 3
Khíos **58** C 3
Khirbat Isriyah **60** BC 2
Khmel'nitskiy **62** E 6
Khodzheyli **66** F 2
Khoe **69** P 6
Khok Kloi **73** G 6
Kholmsk **69** Q 6
Khomeyn **61** F 2
Khongo **69** S 3
Khon Kaen **73** H 4
Khor Anghar **93** G 2
Khorāsān **66** F 4
Khorat Plateau **73** H 4
Khordogoy **68** L 3
Khoronnokh **68** LM 2
Khorramābād **61** E 2
Khorramshahr **61** E 3
Khorsābād **60** D 1
Khosrowābād **61** E 3
Khrebet Bureinskiy **69** O 5
Khrebet Chayatyn **69** P 5
Khrebet Cherskogo **69** P 1–2
Khrebet Dzhagdy **69** O 5
Khrebet Dzhugdzhur **69** OP 4
Khrebet Khugdyungda **68** G 2
Khrebet Kolymskiy **69** SU 3
Khrebet Koryakskiy **69** VW 3
Khrebet Nuratau **67** H 2
Khrebet Pay-Khoy **63** M 2
Khrebet Sette Daban
 69 PQ 3–4
Khrebet Suntar Khayata
 69 PQ 3
Khrebet Turana **69** O 5
Khudzhakh **69** R 3
Khugdyungda, Khrebet
 68 G 2
Khulkhuta **59** G 1
Khulna **72** E 3
Khurays **61** E 4
Khurayt **88** D 6
Khurr, Wādi al **60** C 3
Khurramshahr **61** E 3
Khursanīyah **61** E 4
Khuzdar **67** H 5
Khūzestān **61** E 3
Khvaf **66** FG 4
Khvojeh, Kūh-e **61** E 2
Khvor **61** G 2
Khvormūj **61** F 3
Khvoy **66** D 3

Kiambi **92** D 6
Kiantajärvi **54** J 2
Kibangou **91** G 6
Kibwezi **93** F 5
Kichi Kichi **91** H 2
Kidal **90** E 2
Kidira **90** B 3
Kiel **53** F 4
Kielce **53** H 4
Kieta **81** G 3
Kiffa **86** C 5
Kigali **92** E 5
Kigilyakh **69** P 1
Kigoma **92** D 5
Kihnu **55** H 4
Kikiakki **63** Q 3
Kikladhes **58** BC 3
Kikori **82** A 3
Kikwit **92** B 6
Kilambé **104** E 5
Kilbuck Mountains **98** F 3
Kilchu **71** J 2
Kil'din, Ostrov **54** K 2
Kili **82** C 2
Kılıç Dağları **58** C 3
Kilimanjaro **93** F 5
Kilindini **93** F 5
Kilis **59** E 3
Kiliya **58** C 2
Killarney **52** AB 4
Killeen **102** G 5
Killinek **101** O 3
Killini Óros **58** B 3
Kilmarnock **52** C 3
Kilmez **62** K 4
Kil'mez' **62** K 4
Kilosa **93** F 6
Kilpisjärvi **54** H 2
Kilp-Javr **54** K 2
Kilwa **92** D 6
Kilwa Masoko **93** F 6
Kimball, Mount **98** J 3
Kimbe Bay **81** F 3
Kimberley (South Africa)
 94 CD 5
Kimberley (Western
 Australia) **78** D 2
Kimberley Plateau **78** D 2
Kimch'aek **71** JK 2
Kimito **55** H 3
Kimparana **90** CD 3
Kinabalu, Gunung **74** E 2
Kinchega National Park
 79 G 5
Kinda **92** C 6
Kindia **90** B 4
Kindu **92** D 5
King **80** K 8
King Christian IX Land **114**
King Christian X Land **114**
King Frederik VI-Coast **114**
King Frederik VIII Land **114**
Kingissepp (Estoniya,
 U.S.S.R.)**55** H 4
King Leopold Ranges **78** CD 2
Kingman (AZ, U.S.A.) **102** D 4
Kingman (Pacific Ocean,
 U.S.A.) **82** E 2

Kingoonya **79** F 5
Kingsmill Group **82** C 3
King Sound **78** C 2
Kings Peak **102** DE 3
Kingsport **103** K 4
Kingston (Canada) **101** M 7
Kingston (Jamaica) **105** G 4
Kingston (Norfolk Is., Austr.)
 82 C 4
Kingston-upon-Hull **52** C 4
Kingstown **105** K 5
Kingsville **102** G 6
King William Island **99** S 2
King Williams Town **94** D 6
Kinkala **91** G 6
Kinmaw **73** F 4
Kinnairds Head **52** C 3
Kinoosao **99** R 4
Kinshasa **92** B 5
Kipaka **92** D 5
Kipushi **94** D 2
Kirakira **82** B 3
Kirbey **68** H 2
Kirbey **68** K 2
Kirensk **68** J 4
Kirghiz Steppe **63** LM 6
Kirgiziya **67** JK 2
Kirgiz Step' **66–67** FH 1
Kiribati **82** DE 3
Kırıkhan **59** E 3
Kırıkkale **59** D 3
Kirillovka **59** E 1
Kirimati **83** E 2
Kirishi **55** K 4
Kirkjubæjarklaustur **54** B 3
Kırklareli **58** C 2
Kirkpatrick, Mount **115**
Kirksville **103** H 3
Kirkük **60** D 2
Kirkwall **52** C 3
Kirkwood **103** H 4
Kirov **62** JK 4
Kirov **62** FG 5
Kirovabad **66** D 2
Kirovakan **59** FG 2
Kirovo Chepetsk **62** K 4
Kirovograd **59** D 1
Kirovsk **54** K 2
Kırşehir **59** D 2–3
Kiruna **54** H 2
Kisangani **92** D 4
Kishinev **58** C 1
Kisii **92** E 5
Kısılırmak **59** D 2
Kiska **98** A 5
Kislovodsk **59** F 2
Kismāyu **93** G 5
Kisoro **92** DE 5
Kissidougou **90** BC 4
Kisumu **92** E 5
Kita **90** C 3
Kitakyushū **71** JK 4
Kitale **92** F 4
Kitami **71** M 2
Kitchener **101** L 7
Kitgum **92** E 4
Kíthira **58** B 3

Kithnos **58** B 3
Kitwe **94** D 2
Kiunga **80** D 3
Kivak **98** C 3
Kivijärvi **54** HJ 3
Kiviõli **55** J 4
Kivu **92** D 5
Kiyev **62** F 5
Kizel **63** L 4
Kızıl Dağ **59** D 3
Kızılırmak **62** E 3
Kizlyar **59** G 2
Kizlyarskiy Zaliv **59** G 2
Kizyl-Arvat **66** F 3
Kizyl-Atrek **66** E 3
Kjöllefjord **54** J 1
Klagenfurt **57** FG 2
Klaipéda **55** H 4
Klamath Falls **102** B 3
Klarälven **55** F 3
Klerksdorp **94** D 5
Klintsy **62** F 5
Klit **55** E 4
Kłodzko **53** G 4
Klotz, Lac **101** NO 3
Kluane National Park **98** K 3
Klukhorskiy Pereval **59** F 2
Klyuchr **69** U 4
Knosós **58** C 3
Knox Coast **115**
Knoxville **103** K 4
Knud Rasmussen Land **114**
Köbe **71** KL 3–4
Köbenhavn **55** F 4
Kobenni **86** CD 5
Koblenz **53** E 4
Koboldo **69** O 5
Kobrin **55** H 5
Kobroor, Pulau **75** H 5
Kobuk **98** F 2
Kobuk Valley National Park
 98 F 2
Koca Çal **59** D 3
Kocaeli **58** CD 2
Kocasu **58** C 3
Koch **101** M 2
Ko Chang **73** H 5
Kōchi **71** K 4
Kochikha **68** G 1
Kodi **75** E 5
Kodiak **98** G 4
Kodiak Island **98** G 4
Kodima **62** H 3
Kodža Balkan **58** C 2
Köes **94** B 5
Koforidua **90** D 4
Kohistan **67** J 3
Kohlu **67** H 5
Kohtla-Järve **55** J 4
Kokalaat **67** GH 1
Kokand **67** HJ 2
Kokchetav **63** N 5
Kokkola **54** H 3
Kokomo **103** J 3
Kokpekty **63** Q 6
Koksoak **101** O 4
Kokstad **94** D 6
Koktuma **63** Q 6

Ko K – Kun

Ko Kut **73** H 5
Kola **54** K 2
Kolai **67** J 3
Kola Peninsula **62** G 2
Kolar **72** C 5
Kolar Gold Fields **72** C 5
Kolbachi **69** M 5
Kolbio **93** G 5
Kolding **55** E 4
Kolesovo **69** S 1
Kolhapur **72** B 4
Koli **54** J 3
Kolkasrags **55** H 4
Kollumúli **54** C 2
Köln **53** E 4
Kołobrzeg **53** G 4
Kolombangara **81** G 3
Kolomna **62** GH 4
Kolomyya **58** C 1
Kolpakovsky **69** T 5
Kolpashevo **63** QR 4
Koluton **63** N 5
Kolwezi **94** D 2
Kolyma **69** TU 2
Kolyma Range **69** U 3
Kolymskaya **69** UV 2
Kolymskaya Nizmennost'
  69 ST 2
Kolymskiy, Khrebet **69** SU 3
Kolymskoye Nagor'ye **69** S 3
Kolyvan' **63** Q 5
Komárno **53** G 5
Komba **92** C 4
Kombolchia **93** FG 2
Komelek **69** O 3
Kommunarsk **59** E 1
Komotini **58** C 2
Kompas Berg **94** C 6
Kompong Cham **73** J 5
Kompong Chhnang **73** HJ 5
Kompong Som **73** H 5
Kompot **75** F 3
Komsomol'sk-na-Amure
  69 P 5
Kona **90** D 3
Kondakova **69** T 2
Kondinin **78** B 5
Kondoa **93** F 5
Kondon **69** P 5
Kondut **78** B 5
Konevo **62** GH 3
Kong Frederik VI-Kyst **101** T 3
Kongola **94** C 3
Kongolo **92** D 6
Kongor **92** E 3
Kongsvinger **55** F 3
Konin **53** G 4
Konkan **72** B 4
Konkudera **68** K 4
Konosha **62** H 3
Konotop **62** F 5
Konstantinovka **59** E 1
Konstanz **53** E 5
Kontagora **91** F 3
Kontcha **91** G 4
Kontiomäki **54** J 3
Konya **59** D 3
Konya Ovası **59** D 3

Kooch Bihar **72** E 2
Kootenay National Park
  99 OP 5
Kópasker **54** B 2
Kopeysk **63** M 5
Ko Phangan **73** H 6
Ko Phuket **73** G 6
Köping **55** G 4
Korba **72** D 3
Korça **58** B 2
Korčula **57** G 3
Kordestān **61** E 2
Kord Küy **61** G 1
Korea Strait **71** J 4
Korenovsk **59** E 1
Korfovskiy **69** P 6
Korhogo **90** C 4
Korinthiakos Kólpos **58** B 3
Kórinthos **58** B 3
Koriolei **93** G 4
Kōriyama **71** M 3
Korkodon **69** ST 3
Korla **67** M 2
Kormakiti Bur **60** A 2
Koro **82** C 4
Köroğlu Dağları **59** D 2
Korosten **55** J 5
Koro Toro **91** H 2
Korovin Volcano **98** C 5
Korsakov **69** Q 6
Korsfjorden **55** DE 3
Korshunovo **68** K 4
Koryakskiy Khrebet **69** VW 3
Kos **58** C 3
Kosa Fedotova **59** E 1
Košice **53** H 5
Kosŏng **71** J 3
Kosovska Mitrovica **58** B 2
Kossou, Lac de **90** CD 4
Kostino **63** R 2
Kostroma **62** H 4
Koszalin **53** G 4
Kota **72** C 2
Kotabumi **74** BC 4
Kota Kinabalu **74** DE 2
Kotel'nich **62** J 4
Kotel'nikovo **59** F 1
Kotel'nyy, Ostrov **69** P 1
Kotikovo **69** QR 6
Kotka **55** J 3
Kotlas **62** J 3
Kotlik **98** E 3
Kotovsk **58** CD 1
Kotu Group **82** D 4
Kotuy **68** H 1
Kotzebue Sound **98** E 2
Koudougou **90** D 3
Koulen **73** HJ 5
Koumac **81** H 6
Koumbi-Saleh **86** D 5
Koundara **90** B 3
Koundian **90** B 3
Koungheul **90** AB 3
Kourou **109** H 2
Koutous **91** FG 3
Kouvola **54** J 3
Kova **68** H 4
Kovac **58** A 2

Kovel' **55** H 5
Kovrizhka **69** U 3
Kovrov **62** GH 4
Kowloon **70** FG 6
Kowt-e-Ashrow **67** H 4
Koyuk **98** E 2
Koyukuk **98** F 2
Kozáni **58** B 2
Kozlu **59** D 2
Kozyrevsk **69** TU 4
Kragujevac **58** B 2
Krakow **53** GH 4
Kraljevo **58** B 2
Kramfors **54** G 3
Kranj **57** F 2
Krasino **62** K 1
Krasnaya Yaranga **98** C 2
Kraśnik **53** H 4
Krasnodar **59** EF 1–2
Krasnogorsk **69** Q 6
Krasnoje Selo **55** JK 4
Krasnokamsk **62** KL 4
Krasnotur'insk **63** M 4
Krasnoural'sk **63** M 4
Krasnovodsk **66** E 2
Krasnoyarsk **68** F 4
Krasnoyarskiy **63** L 5
Krasnyy Chikoy **68** J 5
Krasnyy Luch **59** E 1
Kremenchug **62** FG 6
Kresti **62** F 4
Krestovka **62** K 2
Kresty **68** E 1
Kribi **91** F 5
Krichev **62** F 5
Krishna **72** C 4
Kristiansand **55** E 4
Kristianstad **55** F 4
Kristiansund **54** E 3
Kristineberg **54** G 2
Kristinehamn **55** F 4
Kristinestad **54** H 3
Krifti **58** B 3
Kritikón Pélagos **58** BC 3
Krivoy Rog **59** D 1
Krk **57** F 2
Krnov **53** G 4
Krokom **54** F 3
Kronotski **69** U 5
Kronotskaya Sopka **69** TU 5
Kronshtadt **55** J 4
Kroonstad **94** D 5
Kropotkin **59** F 1
Krosno **53** H 5
Krotoszyn **53** G 4
Kruger National Park **95** E 4
Krugersdorp **94** D 5
Krung Thep **73** H 5
Kruševac **58** B 2
Krutinka **63** O 4
Kryazh Kula **69** O 2
Krym (Ukraine, U.S.S.R.)
  59 D 1
Krymsk **59** E 1
Krymskiye Gory **59** D 2
Ksabi **86** E 3
Ksar Chellala **87** F 1
Ksar el Boukhari **87** F 1

Ksar Torchane **86** C 4
Ksen'yevka **68** L 5
Kuala Lumpur **74** B 3
Kuala Terengganu **74** B 2
Kuamut **74** E 2
Kuantan **74** B 3
Kuban' **59** E 1–2
Kubenskoye, Ozero **62** G 4
Kudus **74** D 5
Kudymkar **62** KI 4
Kufstein **57** F 2
Kūh-e 'Alīābād **61** F 2
Kūh-e Alījūq **61** F 3
Kūh-e Alvano **61** E 2
Kūh-e Būl **61** F 3
Kūh-e Dīnār **61** F 3
Kūh-e Garbosh **61** EF 2
Kūh-e Garri **61** E 2
Kūh-e Gügerd **61** F 2
Kūh-e Karkas **61** F 2
Kūh-e Khabr **61** G 3
Kūh-e Khāiz **61** F 3
Kūh-e Kharānaq **61** G 2
Kūh-e Khvojeh **61** E 2
Kūh-e Kükalär **61** F 3
Kūh-e Masāhim **61** G 3
Kūh-e Safid **61** E 2
Kūh-e Sorkh **61** G 2
Kūhestak **66** F 5
Kūh-e Tābask **61** F 3
Kūhhā-ye Qorūd **61** F 2–3
Kūhhā-ye-Sabalān **66** D 3
Kūhhā ye Zagros **61** EF 2–F 3
Kuikkavaara **54** J 3
Kui Nua **74** AB 1
Kuito **94** B 2
Kuivaniemi **54** J 2
Kujani Game Reserve **90** D 4
Kuji **71** M 2
Kula Kangri **73** F 2
Kulakshi **66** EF 1
Kulaneh **67** G 5
Kul'chi **69** P 5
Kulgera **78** E 4
Kulinda **68** J 3
Kullen **55** F 4
Kul'sary **66** E 1
Kulundinskaya Step' **63** P 5
Kulyab **67** HJ 3
Kuma (Russia, U.S.S.R.)
  59 G 2
Kumai, Teluk **74** D 4
Kumamoto **71** K 4
Kumanovo **58** B 2
Kumasi **90** D 4
Kumba **91** F 5
Kumbakonam **72** CD 5
Kumdah **89** H 4
Kumertau **62** KL 5
Künas **67** L 2
Kunashir **71** N 2
Kunda Hills **72** C 5
Kunduz **67** H 3
Kunene **94** A 3
Kungälv **55** F 4
Kungrad **66** F 2
Kungu **92** B 4
Kungur **62** L 4

Kunlun Shan **67** KM 3
Kunlun Shankou **70** B 3
Kunming **70** D 5
Kunsan **71** J 3
Kuntuk **69** R 4
Kununurra **78** D 2
Kuop **82** B 2
Kuopio **54** J 3
Kuoqiang **70** A 3
Kuorboaivi **54** J 2
Kuoyka **68** LM 1
Kupang **75** F 6
Kupreanof **98** L 4
Kupyansk **62** G 6
Kuqa **67** L 2
Kura **59** G 2
Kurashiki **71** K 3–4
Kurdufân **88** DE 6
Kürdžhali **58** C 2
Kure **71** K 4
Kurgan **63** N 4
Kurgan-Tyube **67** H 3
Kuria **82** C 2
Kuria Muria Islands **89** K 5
Kuril Islands **69** S 6
Kurilovka **62** J 5
Kuril'skiye Ostrova (U.S.S.R)
  69 RS 6
Kurmuk **88** E 6
Kurnool **72** C 4
Kursk **62** G 5
Kurşunlu Dağı **59** E 3
Kuruman (South Africa)
  94 C 5
Kuruman (South Africa)
  94 C 5
Kurunegala **72** D 6
Kurupka **98** C 3
Kurzeme **55** H 4
Kuşada Körfezi **58** C 3
Kusaie **82** B 2
Kushchevskaya **59** E 1
Kushiro **71** MN 2
Kushka **67** G 3
Kushmurun **63** MN 5
Kuskokwim **98** E 3
Kuskokwim Bay **98** E 4
Kuskokwim Mountains
  98 FG 3
Kustanay **63** M 5
Küsti **88** E 6
Kut **61** E 3
Kütahya **58** C 3
Kutai, Sungai **74** E 4
Kutaisi **66** C 2
Kutch **72** AB 3
Kutch, Gulf of **72** A 3
Kutch, Rann of **72** AB 3
Kutno **53** G 4
Kuvango **94** B 2
Kuwait **61** E 3
Kuwait **61** E 3
Kuybyshev **62** K 5
Kuybyshev **63** PQ 4
Kuybyshevo **69** R 6
Kuybyshevskoye
  Vodokhranilishche **62** J 5
Kuygan **63** O 6

Küysanjaq **66** C 3
Kuytun, Gora **63** R 6
Kuyucuk Dağı **58** D 3
Kuyumba **68** G 3
Kuznetsk **62** J 5
Kvænangen **54** H 1
Kvalöy **54** G 2
Kvalöya **54** H 1
Kvarner **57** F 2–3
Kvarnerič **57** F 3
Kverkfjol **54** B 3
Kvichak Bay **98** F 4
Kvikkjokk **54** G 2
Kwajalein **82** C 2
Kwakoegron **109** G 2
Kwangju **71** J 3
Kwethluk **98** E 3
Kwoka, Gunung **75** H 4
Kyakhta **68** J 5
Kyancutta **79** F 5
Kyaukme **73** G 3
Kyeintali **73** F 4
Kyle of Lochalsh **52** B 3
Kynnefjell **55** F 4
Kyōto **71** KL 3
Kyrbykan **69** N 3
Kyren **68** H J 5
Kyrgyday **69** M 3
Kyrta **62** L 3
Kyrynniky **68** L 3
Kyshtovka **63** P 4
Kyshtym **63** M 4
Kystatam **68** M 2
Kytalyktakh **69** OP 2
Kyushe **66** F 1
Kyūshū **71** K 4
Kyustendil **58** B 2
Kyusyur **69** N 1
Kyzas **63** RS 5
Kyzultau **63** O 6
Kyzyl **68** FG 5
Kyzyldyykan **67** H 1
Kyzylkum, Peski **67** G 2
Kyzyluy **67** H 1
Kzyl-Orda **67** H 2
Kzyltu **63** O 5

L

La Banda **112** D 4
Labbezenga **90** E 2
Labé **90** B 3
Labengke, Pulau **75** F 4
Labinsk **59** F 2
Labrador **101** NP 4
Labrador City **101** O 5
Labrador Sea **101** QR 4
Lábrea **109** F 5
Labuhanbajo **75** EF 5
Labytnangi **63** N 2
Lac Alaotra **95** H 3
Lac Albanel **101** N 5
Lac à l'Eau-Claire **101** MN 4
La Carlota **112** D 5
Lac au Goéland **101** M 5–6
Lac Bienville **101** N 4
Laccadive Islands **72** B 5
Lac Caniapiscau **101** O 5

Lac Champdoré **101** O 4
Lac Débo **90** CD 2
Lac de Gras **99** P 3
Lac de Kossou **90** CD 4
Lac d'Iberville **101** N 4
La Ceiba **104** E 4
Lacepede Bay **79** F 6
Lachlan River **79** GH 5
La Chorrera **108** BC 2
Lac Klotz **101** NO 3
Lac la Martre **99** O 3
Lac la Ronge **99** R 4
Lac Léman **57** E 2
Lac Mai-Ndombe **92** B 5
Lac Maunoir **99** MN 2
Lac Minto **101** N 4
Lac Mistassini **101** N 5
Lac Moero **92** D 6
Lac Naococane **101** N 5
La Coronilla **112** F 5
La Coruña **56** B 3
La Crosse **103** H 3
La Cruz **102** E 7
Lac Sakami **101** M 5
Lac Seul **100** J 5
Lac Upemba **92** D 6
La Digue **93** K 5
Ladoga, Lake **54** K 3
La Dorada **108** D 2
Ladozhskoye Ozero **54** K 3
Ladysmith **94** D 5
Lae (Marshall Is.) **82** C 2
Lae (Papua New Guinea)
  80 E 3
Læsö **55** F 4
La Estrada **56** B 3
Lafayette (IN, U.S.A.) **103** J 3
Lafayette (LA, U.S.A.)
  103 H 5–6
Lafia **91** F 4
Lafiagi **91** EF 4
La Fría **108** D 2
Lagarto **111** J 3
Laghouat **87** F 2
Lagoa dos Patos **112** F 5
Lago Agrio **108** C 4
Lagoa Mangueira **112** F 5
Lagoa Mirim **112** F 5
Lago Buenos Aires **113** B 8
Lago Cabora Bassa **95** E 3
Lago Chilwa **95** F 3
Lago de Maracaibo **108** D 1–2
Lago de Nicaragua **104** EF 5
Lago de Poopó **110** C 4
Lago di Bolsena **57** F 3
Lago Maggiore **57** E 2
Lago O'Higgins **113** B 8
Lago Posadas **113** B 8
Lago Rogagua **110** C 3
Lagos **90** E 4
Lago Titicaca **110** C 4
Lago Viedma **113** B 8
La Grande **102** C 2
La Gran Sabana **109** F 2–3
Laguna **112** G 4
Laguna Madre **103** G 6
Laguna Mar Chiquita **112** D 5
Laguna Merín **112** F 5

Lagunas (Chile) **110** BC 5
Lagunas (Peru) **108** C 5
Lagune Ndogo **91** G 6
Lagune Nkomi **91** F 6
Lagunillas **110** D 4
La Habana **105** F 3
Lähïjän **66** E 3
Lahore **67** J 4
Lahti **54** J 3
Lai **91** H 4
Lainioälven **54** H 2
Lajes **112** FG 4
La Junta (Bolivia) **110** D 4
La Junta (Mexico) **102** E 6
Lake Abaya **93** F 3
Lake Abitibi **101** M 6
Lake Albert (Zaire/Uganda)
  92 E 4
Lake Amadeus **78** E 3
Lake Argyle **78** D 2
Lake Athabasca **99** Q 4
Lake Austin **78** B 4
Lake Baikal **68** J 5
Lake Ballard **78** C 4
Lake Bangweulu **94** D 2
Lake Barlee **78** B 4
Lake Carey **78** C 4
Lake Carnegie **78** C 4
Lake Chad **91** G 3
Lake Charles **103** H 5
Lake City **103** K 5
Lake Claire **99** P 4
Lake Clark National Park and
  Preserve **98** FG 3
Lake Dall, **98** E 3
Lake Disappointment **78** C 3
Lake Edward **92** D 5
Lake Erie **103** K 3
Lake Eyasi **92** E 5
Lake Eyre **79** F 4
Lake Eyre Basin **79** F 4
Lake Francis Case **102** FG 3
Lake Gairdner **79** F 5
Lake Grandin **99** O 3
Lake Gregory **79** FG 4
Lake Huron **103** K 3
Lake Itchen, **99** P 2
Lake Kariba **94** D 3
Lake Kivu **92** D 5
Lake Kyoga **92** E 4
Lakeland **103** K 6
Lake Lefroy **78** C 5
Lake Mackay **78** D 3
Lake Malawi **95** EF 2
Lake Manitoba **99** S 5
Lake Maurice **78** E 4
Lake Mc Leod **78** A 3
Lake Melville **101** Q 5
Lake Michigan **103** J 3
Lake Moore **78** B 4
Lake Mweru **92** D 6
Lake Nash **79** F 3
Lake Nasser **60** A 5
Lake Nasser (Egypt) **88** E 4
Lake Natron **92** E 5
Lake Nipigon **100** K 6
Lake Nipissing **101** LM 6
Lake Nyasa **95** EF 2

Lak – Lia

Lake Oahe **102** FG 2
Lake of the Ozarks **103** H 4
Lake of the Woods **100** H 6
Lake Okeechobee **103** K 6
Lake Onega **62** FG 3
Lake Ontario **103** L 3
Lake Powell **102** DE 4
Lake Rebecca **78** C 4–5
Lake River **101** L 5
Lake Rukwa **92** E 6
Lake Saint Lucia **95** E 5
Lake Sakakawea **102** F 2
Lake Stefanie **93** F 4
Lake Superior **103** J 2
Lake Tana **93** F 2
Lake Tanganyika **92** DE 6
Lake Taupo **81** R 8
Lake Torrens **79** F 5
Lake Turkana (Lake Rudolf) **93** F 4
Lake Victoria **92** E 5
Lake Volta **90** DE 4
Lake Winnipeg **99** S 5
Lake Winnipegosis **99** RS 5
Lakewood **102** E 4
Lakon **81** J 4
Lakonikos Kólpos **58** B 3
Lakselv **54** J 1–2
Lakshadweep **72** B 5
Lalara **91** G 5
Láleli Geçidi **59** E 3
La Ligua **112** B 5
La Linea **56** B 4
Lalitpur **72** C 3
La Loche **99** Q 4
La Mancha **56** C 4
La Manche **52** C 5
Larnar **102** F 4
La Mariscala **112** F 5
La Marmora **57** E 4
Lamarque **113** C 6
Lamas **108** C 5
Lambaréné **91** F 6
Lambayeque **108** B 5
Lambert, Cape **81** F 2
Lambert Glacier **115**
Lamberts Bay **94** B 6
La Merced **112** C 4
Lamezia Terme **57** G 4
Lamía **58** B 3
Lamington National Park **79** J 4
La Montaña **110** B 2–3
La Mosquitia **104** F 4–5
Lamotrek **82** A 2
Lampang **73** G 4
Lamu **93** G 5
Lancang Jiang **70** C 6
Lancang Jiang **70** D 6
Lancaster (CA, U.S.A.) **102** C 5
Lancaster (U.K.) **52** C 4
Lanciano **57** F 3
Land's End **52** B 4
Landshut **53** F 5
Landskrona **55** F 4
Landsort **55** G 4
Landsortsdjupet **55** G 4

Langjökull **54** AB 3
Langkon **74** E 2
Langöya **54** F 2
Langry **69** Q 5
Lang Son **73** J 3
Langzhong **70** E 4
Lansing **103** JK 3
Lanzarote **86** C 3
Lanzhou **70** DE 3
Laoag **75** J 1
Laon **56** D 2
La Oroya **110** A 3
Laos **73** HJ 4
Laouni **87** G 4
Lapa **112** G 4
La Palma (Canary Islands) **86** B 3
La Palma (Panama) **108** C 2
La Paragua **109** F 2
La Paz (Argentina) **112** C 5
La Paz (Bolivia) **110** C 4
La Paz (Mexico) **102** D 7
La Piedad **104** B 3
Lapland **54** H 2
La Plata **112** E 5–6
Lappajärvi **54** H 3
Lappi **54** J 2
Laptev Sea **114**
Lapua **54** H 3
L'Aquila **57** F 3
Lär **61** G 4
Larache **86** D 1
Laramie Mountains **102** E 3
Larantuka **75** F 5
Laredo **102** G 6
Lärestän **61** G 4
La Ribera **56** C 3
La Rioja (Argentina) **112** C 4
La Rioja (Spain) **56** C 3
Lárisa **58** B 3
Larkana **67** H 5
Larlomkriny **63** O 4
Larnaca **60** A 2
Larne **52** B 4
La Rochelle **56** C 2
La Roche-sur-Yon **56** C 2
La Romana **105** J 4
La Ronge **99** Q 4
Larrey Point **78** B 2
Larsen Ice Shelf **115**
La Salina **102** D 5
Lås 'Ánöd **93** H 3
Las Cejas **112** D 4
Lås Dåred **93** H 2
La Serena (Chile) **112** B 4
La Serena (Spain) **56** B 4
La Seyne-sur-Mer **57** E 3
Las Flores **113** E 6
Läsh-e Joveyn **67** G 4
Lashio **73** G 3
Lashkar Gäh **67** GH 4
Las Lajas **113** BC 6
Las Palmas **86** BC 3
La Spezia **57** EF 3
Las Plumas **113** C 7
Las Tablas **108** B 2
Las Vegas **102** C 4
Latady Island **115**

Latakia **60** B 2
Lätäseno **54** H 2
Latgales Augstiene **55** J 4
Latviya **55** J 4
Laughlin Peak **102** F 4
Lau Group **82** D 4
Lauhanvuori **54** H 3
Launceston **82** A 5
La Unión **113** B 7
Laurentian Scarp **101** M 6
Lauria **57** G 3
Lausanne **57** E 2
Laut, Pulau **74** E 4
Laut Arafura **75** HJ 5
Laut Bali **74** E 5
Laut Banda **75** GH 5
Laut Flores **75** E 5
Laut Halmahera **75** G 4
Laut Jawa **74** CD 4
Laut Maluku **75** G 3
Laut Seram **75** G 4
Laut Sulawesi **75** EF 3
Laut Timor **75** GH 5
Laval (France) **56** C 2
Laval (Quebec, Can.) **101** N 6
Lävän **61** F 4
La Vega **105** H 4
Lavka Integralsoyuza **69** VW 2
Lawra **90** D 3
Lawton **102** G 5
Laydennyy, Mys **62** J 2
La Zarca **104** B 2
Lazarev **69** Q 5
Läzeh **61** F 4
Leavenworth **103** GH 4
Lebanon **88** EF 2
Lebanon (Lebanon) **60** B 2
Lebanon (PA, U.S.A.) **103** L 3
Lebedin **62** F 5
Lebu **113** B 6
Lebyazh'ye **63** P 5
Lecce **57** G 3
Lechang **70** F 5
Le Creusot **57** D 2
Leeds **52** C 4
Leeuwarden **52** DE 4
Leeward Islands (French Polynesia) **83** E 4
Leeward Islands (West Indies) **105** K 4
Leganés **56** C 3
Legaspi **75** F 1
Legnago **57** F 2
Legnano **57** E 2
Legnica **53** G 4
Legune **78** D 2
Le Havre **56** CD 2
Leicester **52** C 4
Leichardt River **79** F 2
Leiden **52** DE 4
Leipzig **53** F 4
Leirvik **55** E 4
Leiyang **70** F 5
Leka **54** F 2
Lékana **91** G 6
Leksozero, Ozero **54** K 3
Leleque **113** B 7

Le Maire, Estrecho de **113** CD 9–10
Léman, Lac **57** E 2
Le Mans **56** D 2
Le Mars **103** G 3
Lemieux Islands **101** P 3
Lemmenjoki **54** J 2
Lemmon **102** F 2
Lemoro **75** F 4
Lena **68** J 4
Lendery **62** F 3
Leninabad **67** HJ 2–3
Leninakan **59** F 2
Leningrad **55** K 4
Leningradskaya **115**
Leninogorsk **62** K 5
Leninogorsk **63** Q 5
Leninsk-Kuznetskiy **63** QR 5
Len'ki **63** Q 5
Lenkoran' **66** D 3
Lensk **68** K 3
Lentini **57** G 4
Leon (Mexico) **104** B 3
León (Nicaragua) **104** E 5
León (Spain) **56** B 3
Leonardville **94** B 4
Leonora **78** C 4
Leopold and Astrid Coast **115**
Lepsy **63** P 6
Le Puy **56** D 2
Lerfroy, Lake **78** C 5
Lérida (Colombia) **108** D 3
Lérida (Spain) **56** D 3
Léros **58** C 3
Lerum **55** F 4
Lerwick **52** C 2
Leskovac **58** B 2
Les Landes **56** C 3
Lesnaya **69** U 4
Lesosibirsk **68** F 4
Lesotho **94** D 5
L'Esperance Rock **82** D 5
Lesser Antilles **105** K 4–5
Lesser Slave Lake **99** OP 4
Lesser Sunda Islands **75** FG 5
Lestijoki **54** H 3
Lésvos **58** C 3
Leszno **53** G 4
Lethbridge **99** P 6
Lethem **109** G 3
Leti, Kepulauan **75** G 5
Leticia **108** D 4
Letsok-aw Kyun **73** G 5
Leuser, Gunung **74** A 3
Levante, Riviera di **57** E 3
Levis **101** N 6
Levkás **58** B 3
Lewis **52** B 3
Lewiston (ID, U.S.A.) **102** C 2
Lewiston (ME, U.S.A.) **103** N 3
Lexington **103** K 4
Lhari **70** B 4
Lhasa **73** F 2
Lhazhong **72** E 1
Liancheng **70** G 5
Lianjiang **70** EF 6
Lian Xian **70** F 6

Lianyin 69 M 5
Lianyungang 71 GH 4
Liao He 71 H 2
Liaoning 71 H 2
Liaoyuan 71 HJ 2
Liard 99 N 3
Liard River 99 M 4
Liberal 102 F 4
Liberia 90 BC 4
Liberia 104 E 5
Libya 87 HK 3
Libyan Desert 88 CD 3–4
Licata 57 F 4
Lichinga 95 F 2
Lida (U.S.S.R.) 55 J 5
Lidköping 55 F 4
Liechtenstein 57 EF 2
Liege 52 E 4
Lieksa 54 K 3
Lienart 92 D 4
Lienz 57 F 2
Liepäja 55 H 4
Lievestuoreenjärvi 54 J 3
Lifou 81 J 6
Ligurian Sea 57 E 3
Lihir Group 82 B 3
Lihou Reef and Cays 79 J 2
Lijiang 70 D 5
Likasi 94 D 2
Likiep 82 C 2
Likouala 91 H 5
Lille 56 D 1
Lilongwe 95 E 2
Lima (OH, U.S.A.) 103 K 3
Lima (Peru) 110 A 3
Lima (Portugal) 56 B 3
Limassol 59 D 4
Limay Mahuida 113 C 6
Limerick 52 B 4
Limfjorden 55 E 4
Limningen 54 F 3
Limnos 58 C 3
Limoeiro 111 JK 2
Limoges 56 D 2
Limon (CO, U.S.A.) 102 F 4
Limón (Costa Rica) 104 F 5
Limousin 56 D 2
Limpopo 95 E 4
Linakhamari 54 K 2
Linares (Chile) 113 B 6
Linares (Mexico) 104 C 3
Linares (Spain) 56 C 4
Lincang 70 CD 6
Lincoln (NE, U.S.A.) 103 G 3
Lincoln (U.K.) 52 C 4
Lincoln Sea 114
Lindau 53 EF 5
Linden 109 G 2
Lindesnes 55 E 4
Lindi 93 F 6–7
Line Islands 83 E 2–3
Linfen 70 F 3
Lingayen 75 H 1
Lingga, Kepulauan 74 B 3–4
Lingomo 92 C 4
Lingyuan 71 G 2
Linhares 111 J 4
Linhe 70 E 2

Linhpa 73 G 2
Linjanti 94 C 3
Linköping 55 G 4
Linkou 71 JK 1
Linosa 57 F 4
Lins 111 G 5
Lintao 70 D 3
Linxi 71 G 2
Linxia 70 D 3
Linyi 71 G 3
Linz 57 F 2
Lipa 75 F 1
Lipari 57 G 4
Lipetsk 62 GH 5
Lipin Bor 62 G 3
Lisala 92 C 4
Lisboa 56 B 4
Lisbon (Portugal) 56 B 4
Lisburn 52 B 4
Lisburne, Cape 98 D 2
Lishui 71 GH 5
Lisichansk 62 G 6
Lisieux 56 D 2
Lithinon, Ákra 58 B 4
Lithuania 55 H 4
Litke 69 Q 5
Litovko 69 P 6
Little Abaco Island 105 G 2
Little Andaman 73 F 5
Little Colorado River 102 D 4
Little Desert National Park
　　79 G 6
Little Grand Rapids 99 ST 5
Little Nicobar 73 FG 6
Little Rock 103 H 5
Litva 55 H 4
Liuzhou 70 EF 6
Livengood 98 H 2
Liverpool 52 C 4
Livingston (MT, U.S.A.)
　　102 DE 2
Livingstone 94 D 3
Livingstone Falls 91 G 7
Livoniya 55 J 4
Livorno 57 EF 3
Liwale 93 F 6
Liwonde 95 F 2–3
Li Xian (Hunan China) 70 F 5
Li Xian (Sichuan China)
　　70 D 4
Lizard 52 BC 5
Lizarda 109 J 5
Ljubeli 57 F 2
Ljungby 55 F 4
Ljusnan 54 F 3
Llallagua 110 C 4
Llano Estacado 102 F 5
Llanos 108 DE 2–3
Llanos de Moxos 110 CD 4
Llullaillaco, Volcán 110 C 5
Lobito 94 A 2
Locarno 57 E 2
Loch Lomond 52 C 3
Loch Ness 52 C 3
Lockhart River Mission 79 G 1
Lod 60 B 3
Lodja 92 C 5
Lodwar 92 F 4

Łodz 53 G 4
Lofoten 54 F 2
Logan, Mount 98 J 3
Logroño 56 C 3
Lohjanjärvi 55 H 3
Lohjanselkä 55 H 3
Loholoho 75 F 4
Loire, Val de 56 D 2
Loja 108 C 4
Lokan tekojärvi 54 J 2
Lokilalaki, Gunung 75 F 4
Lökken 54 E 3
Lokshak 69 O 5
Loks Land 101 P 3
Lolland 55 F 5
Lomami 92 C 4–5
Loma Mountains 90 B 4
Lomas 110 B 4
Lomas de Zamora 112 DE 6
Lomblen, Pulau 75 F 5
Lombok 74 E 5
Lomé 90 E 4
Lomonosov 55 J 4
Lompoc 102 B 5
Łomz'a 53 H 4
Loncoche 113 B 6
London (Canada) 101 L 7
London (U.K.) 52 CD 4
Londonderry (Chile) 113 B 10
Londonderry (U.K.) 52 B 3
Londonderry, Cape 78 D 1
Londrina 111 F 5
Long Beach (CA, U.S.A.)
　　102 C 5
Long Beach (WA, U.S.A.)
　　102 AB 2
Long Island (Papua New
　　Guinea) 80 E 3–2
Long Island (The Bahamas)
　　105 GH 3
Longjiang 69 M 6
Longlac 100 K 6
Longmont 102 E 3
Long Range Mountains
　　101 Q 5–6
Longreach 79 G 3
Long Valley 102 D 5
Longview (TX, U.S.A.)
　　103 GH 5
Longview (WA, U.S.A.)
　　102 B 2
Longxi 70 D 3
Long Xian 70 E 4
Long Xuyen 73 J 5
Longyan 70 G 5
Longzhou 70 E 6
Lookout, Cape 103 L 5
Lopatka 69 T 5
Lop Buri 73 H 5
Lopcha 69 M 4
Lop Nur 70 B 2
Lopphavet 54 H 1
Lopydino 62 K 3
Lorca 56 C 4
Lord Howe Island 79 K 5
Lordsburg 102 E 5
Lorestan 61 E 2
Loreto (Colombia) 108 D 4

Loreto (Maranhão, Brazil)
　　109 JK 5
Loreto (Mexico) 102 D 6
Lorient 56 C 2
Lorraine 57 E 2
Los Alamos 102 E 4
Los Ángeles (Chile) 113 B 6
Los Angeles (U.S.A.) 102 BC 5
Losap 82 B 2
Los Blancos 110 D 5
Los Gatos 102 B 4
Lošinj 57 F 3
Los Lagos 113 B 6
Los Lavaderos 104 C 3
Los Mochis 102 E 6
Lospalos 75 G 5
Los Teques 108 E 1
Lost Trail Pass 102 D 2
Los Vilos 112 B 5
Lot 56 D 3
Lota 113 B 6
Lotta 54 J 2
Loubomo 91 G 6
Louga 90 A 2
Louisiade Archipelago 79 J 1
Louisiana 103 H 5
Louis Trichardt 94 D 4
Louisville 103 J 4
Loukhi 62 F 2
Loum 91 FG 5
Lövånger 54 H 3
Lovech 58 B 2
Lovelock 102 C 3
Loviisa 55 J 3
Lovozero 54 L 2
Low, Cape 99 UV 3
Lowa 92 D 5
Lowell 103 M 3
Lower California 102 D 6
Lowestoft 52 D 4
Loyalty Islands 81 J 6
Loyalty Islands 82 C 4
Loyoro 92 E 4
Luacano 94 C 2
Lualaba 92 D 5
Luanda 94 A 1
Luando (Angola) 94 B 2
Luando (Angola) 94 B 2
Luando Reserve 94 B 2
Luang Prabang 73 H 4
Luangwa 95 E 2
Luangwa Valley Game
　　Reserve 95 E 2
Luanshya 94 D 2
Luapala 94 D 2
Luba 91 F 5
Lubalo 94 B 1
Lubang Islands 75 EF 1
Lubango 94 A 2
Lubao 92 D 6
Lubbock 102 F 5
Lübeck 53 F 4
Lubefu 92 CD 5
Lublin 53 H 4
Lubnān, Jabal 60 B 2
Lubny 62 F 5
Lubumbashi 94 D 2
Lucas 110 E 3

155

Lucea 105 G 4
Lucena 56 C 4
Lučenec 53 G 5
Lucera 57 G 3
Lucero 102 E 5
Lüchun 70 D 6
Lucknow 72 D 2
Lucusse 94 C 2
Ludhiana 72 BC 1
Ludogorie 58 C 2
Ludvika 55 G 3
Ludwigshafen 53 E 5
Luebo 92 C 6
Lüeyang 70 E 4
Lufeng 70 G 6
Luga 55 J 4
Lugano 57 E 2
Luganville 82 C 4
Lugenda 95 F 2
Lugnvik 54 G 3
Lugo 56 B 3
Lugoj 58 B 1
Lugovoy 67 J 2
Luhuo 70 D 4
Luiana 94 C 3
Luimneach 52 B 4
Luís Correia 111 H 1
Luiza 92 C 6
Lukashkin Yar 63 PQ 3
Lukolela 92 B 5
Luleå 54 H 2
Luleälven 54 H 2
Lüleburgaz 58 C 2
Lumbala Kaquengue 94 C 2
Lumbala N'guimbo 94 C 2
Lumding 73 F 2
Lumsden 80 P 10
Lunda Norte 94 BC 1
Lunda Sul 94 C 2
Lundazi 95 E 2
Lüneburg 53 EF 4
Lunkho 67 J 3
Luntai 67 L 2
Luochuan 70 E 3
Luofu 92 D 5
Luoisiade 82 B 3
Luoyang 70 F 4
Luoyuan 71 GH 5
Lupane 94 D 3
Lupeni 58 B 1
Luputa 92 C 6
Lüq 93 G 4
Lusaka 94 D 3
Lusambo 92 C 5
Lushui 70 C 5
Lusk 102 F 3
Lüt, Dasht-e 61 G 2
Luton 52 C 4
Lutsk 55 J 5
Luxembourg 52 DE 5
Luxi (Junnan China) 70 C 6
Luxi (Junnan China) 70 D 6
Luxor 60 A 4
Luza 62 J 3
Luzern 57 E 2
Luzhai 70 E 6
Luzhou 70 E 5

Luzhskaya Vozvyshennost' 55 HJ 4
Lvov 53 H 5
L'vovka 63 P 4
Lyakhovskiye Ostrova 69 P 1
Lynchburg 103 L 4
Lynd 79 G 2
Lynn Lake 99 RS 4
Lynx Lake 99 Q 3
Lyon 57 E 2
Łyso Gory 53 H 4
Lyubertsy 62 G 4

M

Ma'ân 60 B 3
Maarianhamina (Mariehamn) 55 H 3–4
Ma'arrat an Nu'mān 59 E 3–4
Maastricht 52 E 4
Mabaruma 109 G 2
Mabote 95 E 4
Ma'bùs Yüsuf 87 K 3
Macadam Plains 78 B 4
Macaíba 111 J 2
Macao 70 F 6
Macapá 109 H 3
Macará (Peru) 108 C 4
Macas 108 C 4
Macau 111 J 2
Macauley 82 D 4–5
Macdonnell Ranges 78 E 3
Maceió 111 JK 2
Macerata 57 F 3
Machala 108 C 4
Machevna 69 W 3
Machilipatnam 72 D 4
Machupicchu 110 B 3
Macia 95 E 5
Mackay, Lake 78 D 3
Mackenzie 98 LM 2
Mackenzie Bay 98 K 2
Mac Kenzie Bay 115
Mackenzie King Island 114
Mackenzie Mountains 98–99 LM 2–3
Mackenzie River 79 H 3
Mackinaw City 103 K 2
Macocola 94 B 1
Macomia 95 FG 2
Mâcon (France) 57 DE 2
Macon (GA, U.S.A.) 103 K 5
Macquarie Island 115
Mac Robertson Land 115
Madagascar 95 H 3
Madā'in Şāliḥ 66 B 5
Madang 80 E 3
Madaoua 91 F 3
Madd, Ra's Abū 60 B 4
Madeira (Brazil) 109 F 4–5
Madeira (Portugal) 86 B 2
Madeleine, Île de la 101 P 6
Madeniyet 63 P 6
Madetkoski 54 J 2
Madhya Pradesh 72 CD 3
Madimba 92 B 5
Madingo-Kayes 91 G 6
Madison 103 HJ 3
Madiun 74 D 5

Madoi 70 C 4
Madrakah 66 BC 6
Madrakah, Ra's al 89 K 5
Madras 72 D 5
Madre de Dios 110 C 3
Madre Oriental, Sierra 104 BC 2–3
Madrid 56 C 3
Madrona, Sierra 56 C 4
Madura, Pulau 74 D 5
Madurai 72 C 6
Madyan 60 B 4
Maebashi 71 L 3
Maevatanana 95 H 3
Maéwo 81 J 5
Mafeteng 94 D 5
Mafia Island 93 G 6
Magadan 69 S 4
Magallanes, Estrecho de 113 B 9
Magangue 108 D 2
Magaria 91 F 3
Magdagachi 69 N 5
Magdalena 108 D 1–2
Magdeburg 53 F 4
Magellan, Strait of 113 BC 9
Mageröya 54 J 1
Maggiore, Lago 57 E 2
Magnitogorsk 63 L 5
Magyarország 58 A 1
Mahābād 66 D 3
Mahabharat Range 72 E 2
Mahabo 95 GH 4
Mahadday Wèyne 93 H 4
Mahajan 72 B 2
Mahajanga 95 H 3
Mahalapye 94 D 4
Mahanoro 95 H 3
Maharashtra 72 BC 4
Maha Sarakham 73 H 4
Mahatsanary 95 G 5
Mahbés 86 CD 3
Mahbubnagar 72 C 4
Mahd adh Dhahab 66 C 6
Mahḍah 61 G 4
Mahdia 109 G 2
Mahenge 93 F 6
Mahesana 72 B 3
Mahia Peninsula 81 R 8
Mahkene 54 F 3
Mahmūdābād 61 F 1
Mahmud-Raqi 67 H 4
Mahón 56 D 4
Mahuva 72 B 3
Maiana 82 C 2
Maiduguri 91 G 3
Maimana 67 GH 3
Mai-Ndombe, Lac 92 B 5
Maine 103 N 2
Mainland (Orkney Is., U.K.) 52 C 3
Mainland (Shetland Is., U.K.) 52 C 2
Maintirano 95 G 3
Mainz 53 E 5
Maio 90 B 6
Maipú 113 E 6
Maipuco 108 D 4

Maitengwe 94 D 4
Maitland 79 J 5
Maíz, Isla del 104 F 5
Majuro 82 C 2
Makale 93 FG 2
Makambako 92 EF 6
Makarikari 94 CD 4
Makarikha 63 LM 2
Makarov 69 Q 6
Makat 66 E 1
Makaw 70 C 5
Makedhonía 58 B 2
Makedonija 58 B 2
Makeyevka 59 E 1
Makgadikgadi Pan 94 CD 4
Makhachkala 66 D 2
Makinsk 63 O 5
Makkah 89 G 4
Makó 58 B 1
Makokou 91 G 5
Makran 66–67 G 5
Makri 72 D 4
Maksimovka 71 L 1
Mäkü 59 F 3
Makurdi 91 F 4
Makushino 63 N 4
Makuyuni 93 F 5
Makwa 82 BC 3
Malabar Coast 72 BC 5–6
Malabo 91 F 5
Málaga 56 C 4
Malagasy Republic 95 H 3
Malaimbandy 95 H 4
Malaita 81 H 3
Malakäl 92 E 3
Malakula 81 J 5
Malang 74 D 5
Malanje 94 B 1
Malao 81 J 5
Mälaren 55 G 4
Malargue 113 C 6
Malaspina 113 C 7
Malatya 59 E 3
Malatya Dağları 59 E 3
Malåwi 61 E 2
Malawi 95 E 2
Malawi National Park 95 E 2
Malaybalay 75 FG 2
Malåyer 61 E 2
Malaysia 74 BD 2
Malden 83 E 3
Maldives 72 B 6
Maldonado 112 F 5
Malegaon 72 BC 3
Malei 95 F 3
Malek 92 E 3
Malekula 82 C 4
Maleyevo 68 G 4
Malhada 111 H 3
Mali 90 CD 2–3
Mali Kyun 73 G 5
Malindi 93 G 5
Maling, Gunung 75 F 3
Malin Head 52 B 3
Mallaig 52 B 3
Mallani 72 B 2
Mallery Lake 99 S 3
Mallorca 56 D 4

Malmö 55 F 4
Maloelap 82 C 2
Malozemel'skaya Tundra
  62 JK 2
Malpelo, Isla 108 B 3
Malta 57 F 4
Malta 102 E 2
Maluku 75 G 4
Malung 55 F 3
Maly Kavkaz 59 FG 2
Malyy Lyakhovskiy, Ostrov
  69 Q 1
Malyy Yenisey 68 FG 5
Mama 68 K 4
Mamagota 81 FG 3
Mambasa 92 D 4
Mambéré 92 B 3–4
Mamoré 110 C 3
Mamou 90 B 3
Mamuju 75 E 4
Mamuno 94 C 4
Man 90 C 4
Manacapuru 109 F 4
Manado 75 F 3
Managua 104 E 5
Manaka 81 Q 9
Manakara 95 H 4
Manama 61 F 4
Mananara 95 H 3
Manapouri 82 C 6
Manas 67 M 2
Manaus 109 FG 4
Manchester 52 C 4
Manchuria 71 HJ 2
Máncora 108 B 4
Mand 61 F 3
Mandal 55 E 4
Mandalay 73 G 3
Mandal-Ovoo 70 D 2
Mandasor 72 B 3
Mandera 93 G 4
Mandeville 105 G 4
Mandiana 90 C 3
Mandimba 95 F 2
Mandji 91 G 6
Mandla 72 CD 3
Mandor 74 C 3
Mandvi 72 A 3
Manfredonia 57 G 3
Manga (Minas Gerais, Brazil)
  111 H 3
Manga (Niger/Chad) 91 GH 3
Mangaia 83 E 4
Mangalore 72 B 5
Mangnai 70 B 3
Mangoky 95 G 4
Mangole, Pulau 75 G 4
Mangueira, Lagoa 112 F 5
Mangut 68 K 6
Manhan 68 F 6
Manhattan 103 G 4
Manicaland 95 E 3
Manicore 109 F 5
Manicouagan 101 O 5
Maniganggo 70 CD 4
Manihi 83 F 3
Manipur 73 F 3
Manisa 58 C 3

Manistique 103 J 2
Manitoba 99 S 5
Manitoba, Lake 99 S 5
Manitowoc 103 J 3
Manizales 108 C 2
Manjil 61 E 1
Mankato 103 H 3
Manlay 70 E 2
Manmad 72 BC 3
Mannheim 53 E 4–5
Manning 99 O 4
Manoa 108 E 5
Manono 92 D 6
Manra 82 D 3
Manresa 56 D 3
Mansa 94 D 2
Mansel Island 101 L 3
Mansfield 103 K 3
Manta 108 B 4
Mantecal 108 E 2
Mantova 57 F 2
Manú 110 B 3
Manuae 83 E 4
Manuangi 83 F 4
Manuel Urbano 108 DE 5
Manukau 82 C 5
Manus 80 E 2
Manychskaya Vpadina 59 F 1
Manyoni 92 E 6
Manzanillo (Cuba) 105 G 3
Manzanillo (Mexico) 104 B 4
Manzhouli 68 L 6
Manzil Bū Ruqaybah 87 G 1
Manzurka 68 J 5
Mao 105 H 4
Maoke, Pegunungan 75 J 4
Maoming 70 F 6
Mapaga 75 EF 4
Mapai 95 E 4
Mapi 75 J 5
Maple Creek 99 Q 6
Mapuera 109 G 4
Maputo 95 E 5
Maquela do Zombo 94 B 1
Maquinchao 113 C 7
Maraá 108 E 4
Marabá 109 HJ 5
Maracá, Ilha de 109 HJ 3
Maracaibo 108 D 1
Maracaibo, Lago de
  108 D 1–2
Maracaju 111 F 5
Maracay 108 E 1
Marādah 87 J 3
Maradi 91 F 3
Marāgheh 66 D 3
Marahuaca, Cerro 108 E 3
Marajó, Ilha de 109 HJ 4
Maramba 94 D 3
Maränd 66 D 3
Maranhão 111 GH 2
Marañón 108 C 4
Marão, Serra do 56 B 3
Marathon 100 K 6
Marawi 88 E 5
Marbella 56 C 4
March 57 G 2
Marche 57 F 3

Marche, Plateaux de la 56 D 2
Mar Chiquita, Laguna 112 D 5
Mar del Plata 113 E 6
Mardin 59 F 3
Mardin Eşigi 59 F 3
Maré 81 J 6
Marëg 93 H 4
Marganets 59 D 1
Margaret River 78 A 5
Margaritovo 71 KL 2
Margilan 67 J 2
Margyang 72 E 1–2
Mari (Burma) 73 G 2
Mari (Papua New Guinea)
  80 D 3
Maria (Tuamotu Is.) 83 F 4
Maria (Tubai Is.) 83 E 4
Mariana Islands 82 A 1
Marianao 105 F 3
Maria Theresa 83 F 5
Mariato, Punta 108 B 2
Maria van Diemen, Cape
  81 Q 7
Maribor 57 FG 2
Maricourt 101 N 3
Marie Byrd Land 115
Mariental 94 B 4
Mariestad 55 F 4
Marietta 103 JK 5
Mariinsk 63 R 4
Mariinskoye 69 Q 5
Marília 111 G 5
Maringa 111 F 5
Mariny, Iméni 69 R 3
Marion (IN, U.S.A.) 103 J 3
Marion (OH, U.S.A.) 103 K 3
Marion Reef 79 J 2
Mariu 80 D 3
Mariyyah 61 F 5
Märjamaa 55 HJ 4
Marka 93 GH 4
Markha 68 M 3
Marko 54 G 2
Markovo 63 R 3
Marlin 103 G 5
Marmara 58 C 2
Marmara Denizi 58 C 2
Marmaris 58 C 3
Marne 56 D 2
Maroa 108 E 3
Maroni 109 H 3
Maroua 91 GH 3
Marovoay 95 H 3
Marowijne 109 H 3
Marqadah 59 F 3
Marquesas Islands 83 F 3
Marquette 103 J 2
Marrakech 86 D 2
Marree 79 F 4
Marrero 103 HJ 6
Marrupa 95 F 2
Marsa al' Alam 60 B 4
Marsabit National Reserve
  93 F 4
Marsala 57 F 4
Marsa 'Umm Ghayj 60 B 4
Marseille 57 E 3
Marsfjllet 54 G 2

Marshall Islands 82 BC 2
Marshalltown 103 H 3
Marsh Harbour 105 G 2
Marta 57 F 3
Martaban, Gulf of 73 G 4
Martigues 57 DE 3
Martinique 105 K 5
Martinique Passage 105 K 5
Martin Vaz Islands 107 H 5
Martre, Lac la 99 O 3
Marutea 83 F 4
Mary 67 G 3
Maryborough 79 J 4
Maryland 103 L 4
Marystown 101 QR 6
Maryville 103 H 3
Masāhīm, Kūh-e 61 G 3
Masai Steppe 93 F 5
Masaka 92 E 5
Masåkin 87 H 1
Masan 71 J 3
Masasi 95 F 2
Masaya 104 E 5
Masbate 75 F 1
Mascarene Islands 95 K 6
Maseru 94 D 5
Mashhad 66 FG 3
Mashiz 61 G 3
Mashonaland 95 E 3
Masindi 92 E 4
Maşirah 89 K 4
Masjed Soleymän 61 E 3
Maskanah 60 B 2
Masoala, Cap 95 J 3
Masohi 75 G 4
Mason City 103 H 3
Masqat 89 K 4
Massachusetts 103 M 3
Massafra 57 G 3
Massangena 95 E 4
Massau 81 EF 2
Massava 63 M 3
Massawa 93 FG 1
Masset 98 L 5
Massif Central 56 D 2–3
Massif du Pelvoux 57 E 2
Massif du Tsaratanana 95 H 2
Massinga 95 F 4
Masteksay 66 E 1
Mastuj 67 J 3
Mastung 67 H 5
Mastūrah 66 B 6
Masvingo 95 E 4
Maşyāf 60 B 2
Matabeleland 94 D 3–4
Matadi 92 A 6
Matagalpa 104 E 5
Matagami 101 M 6
Matagorda Island 103 G 6
Mataiva 83 F 3
Matam 90 B 2
Matara 72 CD 6
Matarani 110 B 4
Mataranka 78 E 1
Matatiele 94 D 6
Matatila Dam 72 C 2
Mata-Utu 82 D 3
Matay 63 P 6

Matehuala **104** B 3
Matera **57** G 3
Mathura **72** C 2
Matla **72** E 3
Mato Grosso **110–111** EF 3
Mato Grosso (Mato Grosso, Brazil) **110** E 3
Matozinhos **56** B 3
Mátra **58** A 1
Matrûh **88** D 2
Matsudo **71** M 3
Matsue **71** K 3
Matsuyama **71** K 4
Matterhorn (NV, U.S.A.) **102** CD 3
Matterhorn (Switzerland) **57** E 1
Matthew **82** C 4
Matu **74** D 3
Matua, Ostrov **69** S 6
Maturín **109** F 2
Matyushkinskaya **63** PQ 4
Maubeuge **56** D 1
Maués **109** G 4
Maui **83** E 1
Mauke **83** E 4
Maun **94** C 4
Mauna Kea **83** E 1
Maunoir, Lac **99** MN 2
Maupihaa **83** E 4
Mauralasan **74** E 3
Maurice, Lake **78** E 4
Mauritania **86** BD 5
Mauritius **95** K 5
Mavasjaure **54** G 2
Mawson **115**
Mawson Coast **115**
Maxcanu **104** D 3
Mayaguana Island **105** H 3
Mayagüez **105** J 4
Mayámey **61** G 1
Mayd **93** H 2
Maydān **61** D 2
Maykop **59** F 2
Maymakan **69** P 4
Mayna **68** F 5
Maynas **108** C 4
Mayo, Mountains of **52** B 4
Mayor-Krest **69** Q 2
Mayotte **95** H 2
May Pen **105** G 4
Maysk **63** P 4
Mayumba **91** FG 6
Mayya **69** O 3
Mazabuka **94** D 3
Mazar **67** K 3
Mazar-i-Sharif **67** H 3
Mazatenango **104** D 5
Mazatlán **104** A 3
Mazomeno **92** D 5
Mazong Shan **70** C 2
Mazowsze **53** H 4
Mazury **53** H 4
Mbabane **95** E 5
Mbakaou Reservoir **91** G 4
Mbala **95** E 1
Mbale **92** E 4

Mbalmayo **91** G 5
Mbamba Bay **95** E 2
Mbandaka **92** B 4
Mbanga **91** FG 5
M'banza Congo **94** AB 1
Mbanza-Ngungu **92** B 6
Mbeya **92** E 6
Mbinda **91** G 6
Mbini **91** F 5
Mbokou **92** D 3
Mbour **90** A 3
Mbuji-Mayi **92** CD 6
McAllen **102** G 6
McCammon **102** D 3
McComb **103** H 5
McCook **102** F 3
McKean **82** D 3
McKeesport **103** L 3
McKinley, Mount **98** G 3
Mc Leod, Lake **78** A 3
M'Clintock Channel **99** R 1
M'Clure Strait **99** O 1
Mc Murdo **115**
Mc Murdo Sound **115**
Meadow Lake **99** Q 5
Meaux **56** D 2
Mecca **89** G 4
Mecklenburg **53** F 4
Mecklenburger Bucht **53** F 4
Medan **74** A 3
Medanosa, Punta **113** CD 8
Medellín **108** CD 2
Medelpad **54** G 3
Medford **102** B 3
Medgidia **58** C 2
Mediaş **58** B 1
Medicine Bow **102** E 3
Medicine Hat **99** P 5
Medigan **63** R 5
Medina **60** C 4
Mediterranean Sea **56** CE 4
Mednogorsk **63** L 5
Medvezhiy Var **68** F 1
Meekatharra **78** B 4
Meerut **72** C 2
Mega (Ethiopia) **93** F 4
Mega (Indonesia) **75** H 4
Megasani Hill **72** E 3
Meghalaya **73** F 2
Megra **62** H 2
Meguinenza, Embalse de **56** CD 3
Mehrizi **61** G 3
Mehtar-Lam **67** J 4
Meiganga **91** G 4
Meissen **53** F 4
Mei Xian **70** G 6
Mejillones **110** BC 5
Mékambo **91** G 5
Meknès **86** D 2
Mekong **73** HJ 4–5
Mekongga, Gunung **75** F 4
Melaka **74** B 3
Melanesia **81** FJ 2–3
Melbourne (Australia) **79** G 6
Melbourne (FL, U.S.A.) **103** KL 6
Melchor Ocampo **104** B 4

Melendiz Dağı **59** D 3
Meletsk **68** F 4
Meleuz **62** KL 5
Melfort **99** QR 5
Melilla **86** E 1
Melimoyo, Monte **113** B 7
Melitopol' **59** E 1
Melo **112** F 5
Meltaus **54** H 2
Melun **56** D 2
Melville **99** R 5
Melville, Cape **79** G 1
Melville, Lake **101** Q 5
Melville Bay **114**
Melville Hills **99** N 2
Melville Island (Australia) **78** E 1
Melville Island (Canada) **96** G 2
Melville Peninsula **99** UV 2
Melyuveyem **69** W 3
Memmingen **53** EF 5
Memphis (Egypt) **88** E 3
Memphis (TN, U.S.A.) **103** J 4
Mena **62** F 5
Ménaka **90** E 2
Mendoza (Argentina) **112** C 5
Mendoza (Peru) **108** C 5
Mengcheng **71** G 4
Mengene Dağı **59** F 3
Menghai **70** CD 6
Mengzi **70** D 6
Menihek Lakes **101** O 5
Meningie **79** FG 6
Menkere **68** M 2
Menongue **94** B 2
Menorca **56** D 3
Mentawai, Kepulauan **74** A 4
Mentese **58** C 3
Menyuan **70** D 3
Menza **68** J 6
Menzies **78** C 4
Menzies, Mount **115**
Mepistskaro **59** F 2
Meppen **53** E 4
Meråker **54** F 3
Merano **57** F 2
Merced **102** BC 4
Mercedes (Argentina) **112** E 4
Mercedes (Argentina) **112** C 5
Mercedes (Uruguay) **112** E 5
Merchants Bay **101** P 2
Mercy, Cape **101** P 3
Meredith, Cape **113** D 9
Merefa **62** G 6
Merenga **69** ST 3
Mergui **73** G 5
Mergui Archipelago **73** G 5
Meriç **58** C 2
Mérida (Mexico) **104** DE 3
Mérida (Spain) **56** B 4
Mérida (Venezuela) **108** D 2
Meridian **103** J 5
Mérignac **56** C 2
Merikarvia **54** H 3
Merín, Laguna **112** F 5
Merredin **78** B 5
Merritt Island **103** KL 6

Merseburg **53** F 4
Mersin **59** D 3
Meru Game Reserve **93** F 4–5
Merzifon **59** E 2
Mesabi Range **103** H 2
Mesopotamia **60–61** D 2–3
Messina **57** FG 4
Messiniakós Kolpós **58** B 3
Messo **63** P 2
Mesters Vig **114**
Meta **108** DE 2
Meta Incognita Peninsula **101** O 3
Metairie **103** H 5–6
Metán **112** D 4
Metangula **95** EF 2
Metemma **92** F 2
Metéora-monastery **58** B 3
Metlakatla **98** L 4
Metu **92** F 3
Metz **57** E 2
Meuse **57** E 2
Mexicali **102** CD 5
Mexican Hat **102** E 4
Mexico **104** AB 2
México City **104** BC 4
Meymeh **61** F 2
Mezen' **62** H 2
Mezhdurechenskiy **63** N 4
Miami **103** K 6
Miami Beach **103** L 6
Miändowäb **61** D 1
Mianeh (Iran) **61** E 1
Mianyang **70** DE 4
Miarinarivo **95** H 3
Miazz **63** LM 5
Michigan **103** JK 2–3
Michigan, Lake **103** J 3
Michoacán **104** B 4
Michurinsk **62** G 5
Micronesia **82** BC 2
Middelburg **94** DE 5
Middle Andaman **73** F 5
Midi, Canal du **56** D 3
Midland (MI, U.S.A.) **103** JK 3
Midland (TX, U.S.A.) **102** F 5
Midżor **58** B 2
Miekojärvi **54** HJ 2
Mielec **53** H 4
Mieres **56** B 3
Migiurtinia **93** HJ 2
Mijdahah **89** H 6
Mikha Tskhakaya **59** F 2
Mikhaylovgrad **58** B 2
Mikhaylovka **62** H 5
Mikinai **58** B 3
Mikindani **95** FG 2
Mikino **69** U 3
Míkonos **58** C 3
Milagro **108** C 4
Milan **57** E 2
Milando Reserve **94** B 1
Milange **95** F 2
Milano **57** E 2
Milás **58** C 3
Milazzo **57** FG 4
Milcan Tepe **59** E 3
Mildura **79** G 5

Mile 70 D 6
Miles 79 HJ 4
Miles City 102 EF 2
Milford Haven 52 B 4
Milgun 78 B 3–4
Mili 82 C 2
Milk River 102 E 2
Millau 56 D 3
Millevaches, Plateau de
  56 D 2
Mílos 58 B 3
Milparinka 79 G 4
Milwaukee 103 J 3
Mina 68 F 5
Minā' 'Abd Allāh 61 E 3
Minahassa Peninsula 75 F 3
Minas 112 F 5
Minā' Sa'ūd 61 E 3
Minas Gerais 111 GH 4
Minas Novas 111 H 4
Minatitlán 104 D 4
Minbya 73 F 3
Mincha 112 B 5
Mindanao 75 FG 2
Mindelo 90 B 6
Mindoro 75 F 1
Mindoro Strait 75 EF 1
Mineiros 111 F 4
Mineral'nyye Vody 59 F 2
Minerva Reefs 82 D 4
Minfeng 67 L 3
Mingary 79 G 5
Mingechaur 66 D 2
Mingshui 71 J 1
Mingteke 67 K 3
Minho 56 B 3
Ministro João Alberto 111 F 3
Minna 91 F 4
Minneapolis (KS, U.S.A.)
  102 G 4
Minneapolis (MN, U.S.A.)
  103 GH 3
Minnesota 103 GH 2
Minot 102 F 2
Minqin 70 D 3
Minqing 71 G 5
Minsin 73 G 2
Minsk 55 J 5
Minto 82 B 2
Minto, Lac 101 N 4
Minusinsk 68 F 5
Min Xian 70 D 4
Miquelon 101 M 6
Mirabad 67 G 4
Miramichi Bay 101 P 6
Miranda 110 E 5
Miranda de Ebro 56 C 3
Miri 74 D 3
Miriam Vale 79 J 3
Mirim, Lagoa 112 F 5
Mirnyy 115
Mirpur Khas 67 H 5
Mirtóon Pélagos 58 B 3
Mirzapur 72 D 2–3
Mish'āb, Ra's al 61 E 3
Mishan 71 K 1
Miskolc 58 AB 1
Misool, Pulau 75 H 4

Mişr 88 DE 4
Mişrātah 87 H 2
Mişrātah, Ra's 87 J 2
Mississippi 103 HJ 5
Mississippi Delta 103 J 6
Mississippi River 103 H 5
Missoula 102 D 2
Missouri 103 H 4
Missouri River
  102–103 GH 3–4
Mistassini, Lac 101 MN 5
Misti, Volcán 110 B 4
Misty Fjords National
  Monument 98 L 4
Mitchell 102 G 3
Mitchell River 79 G 2
Mitilini 58 C 3
Mitra 91 F 5
Mitú 108 D 3
Mitumba, Monts 92 D 5–6
Miyako 71 M 3
Miyakonojō 71 K 4
Miyako-rettō 71 H 6
Miyaly 66 E 1
Mizdah 87 H 2
Mizen Head 52 AB 4
Mizoram 73 F 3
Mizuho 115
Mizusawa 71 M 3
Mjölby 55 G 4
Mjösa 55 F 3
Mkata 93 F 6
Mkomazi 93 F 5
Mkomazi Game Reserve
  93 F 5
Mkushi 94 DE 2
Mladá Boleslav 53 FG 4
Mljet 57 G 3
Moab 102 E 4
Moamba 95 E 5
Moba 92 D 6
Mobaye 92 C 4
Mobile 103 J 5
Mobridge 102 F 2
Moçambique 95 G 3
Mochudi 94 D 4
Mocímboa da Praia 95 G 2
Moctezuma (Mexico) 102 E 6
Moctezuma (Mexico) 104 B 3
Mocuba 95 F 3
Modena (Italy) 57 F 3
Modena (NV., U.S.A.) 102 D 4
Moero, Lac 92 D 6
Mogadishu 93 H 4
Mogadouro, Serra do 56 B 3
Mogaung 73 G 2
Mogilev 55 JK 5
Mogilev Podol'skiy 58 C 1
Mogogh 92 E 3
Mogoyn 68 G 6
Mogoytui 68 KL 5
Moguqi 69 M 6
Mohe 69 M 5
Moheli 95 G 2
Mohikan, Cape 98 D 3
Mohon Peak 102 D 5
Mohoro 93 F 6
Mointy 63 O 6

Mo i Rana 54 F 2
Mojave Desert 102 C 4
Mojiang 70 D 6
Mokp'o 71 J 4
Mokra Gora 58 AB 2
Moldava 58 C 1
Moldava 58 C 1
Moldaviya 58 C 1
Molde 54 E 3
Moldefjorden 54 E 3
Mole Game Reserve 90 D 4
Molepolole 94 CD 4
Mollendo 110 B 4
Molodechno 55 J 5
Molodezhnaya 115
Molokai 83 E 1
Molopo 94 C 5
Mombasa 93 FG 5
Mombetsu 71 M 2
Momboyo 92 B 5
Momskiy Khrebet 69 QR 2
Monaco 57 E 3
Monaghan 52 B 4
Monapo 95 G 2
Monarch Mountain 99 M 5
Monasterio de Montserrat
  56 D 3
Monastery of Saint Catherine
  60 AB 3
Monchegorsk 54 K 2
Mönchen-Gladbach 52 E 4
Monclova 104 B 2
Moncton 101 O 6
Mondo 91 H 3
Mondragone 57 F 3
Monfalcone 57 F 2
Monga 92 C 4
Mong Hpayak 73 G 3
Monghyr 72 E 2–3
Mongolia 68 GJ 6
Mongolo 68 J 2
Mongu 94 C 3
Mönhhaan 70 F 1
Monkira 79 G 3
Monou 91 J 2
Monreal del Campo 56 C 3
Monroe (LA, U.S.A.) 103 H 5
Monroe (MI, U.S.A.) 103 K 3
Monrovia 90 B 4
Mons 52 D 4
Mont Afao 87 G 3
Montague 98 H 4
Montana 102 DE 2
Montauban 56 D 3
Montbeliard 57 E 2
Mont Blanc 57 E 2
Mont Cameroon 91 F 5
Montceau-les-Mines 56 D 2
Mont-de-Marsan 56 C 3
Monte Alegre 109 H 4
Monte Binga 95 E 3
Monte Carlo 57 E 3
Monte Cinto 57 E 3
Monte Claros 111 H 4
Montecristi 105 H 3–4
Montecristo 57 F 3
Monte Cristo 110 D 3
Monte d'Oro 57 E 3

Montego Bay 105 G 4
Montejinnie 78 E 2
Monte Melimoyo 113 B 7
Montemoreos 104 C 2
Monte Negro Falls 94 A 3
Montepuez 95 F 2
Monte Quemado 112 D 4
Monterado 74 C 3
Monterey 102 B 4
Monteria 108 C 2
Montero 110 D 4
Monterrey 104 B 2
Montes Altos 109 J 5
Montes de Toledo 56 C 4
Montesilvano 57 F 3
Montes Universales 56 C 3
Montevideo 112 EF 5–6
Montgomery 103 J 5
Monti di Ala 57 E 3
Mont Kavendou 90 B 3
Mont Lozére 56 D 3
Montluçon 56 D 2
Mont Panié 81 H 6
Mont Pelat 57 E 3
Montpelier (VT, U.S.A.)
  103 M 3
Montpéllier 56 D 3
Montréal 101 N 6
Montreux 57 E 2
Montrose 102 E 4
Monts d'Aubrac 56 D 3
Montserrat 105 K 4
Monts Mitumba 92 D 5–6
Monts Nimba 90 C 4
Monts Notre-Dame 101 O 6
Monts Otish 101 N 5
Monts Tamgak 91 F 2
Monts Timétrine 90 DE 2
Mont Tahat 87 G 4
Mont Tembo 91 G 5
Mont Ventoux 57 E 3
Monza 57 E 2
Moonie 79 J 4
Mooraberree 79 G 4
Moore, Lake 78 B 4
Moorhead 103 G 2
Moorlands 79 FG 6
Moose Jaw 99 Q 5
Moosonee 101 L 5
Mopti 90 D 3
Moquegua 110 BC 4
Mora 55 F 3
Moradabad 72 CD 2
Moramanga 95 H 3
Morane 83 F 4
Moratuwa 72 CD 6
Morava (Czechoslovakia)
  53 G 5
Morava (Western Australia)
  78 B 4
Morava (Yugoslavia) 58 B 2
Morawhanna 109 G 2
Moray Firth 52 C 3
Moree 79 H 4
More Laptevykh 68 MN 1
Morelia 104 B 4
Morena, Sierra 56 BC 4
Moreno 108 C 5

Mor – Mut

Möre og Romsdal **54** E 3
Moresby **98** L 5
Mori **70** B 2
Morioka **71** M 3
Mornington Island **79** F 2
Morobe **82** A 3
Morocco **86** D 2
Morogoro **93** F 6
Moro Gulf **75** F 2
Morombe **95** G 4
Mörön **68** H 6
Morón (Cuba) **105** G 3
Morón (Spain) **56** B 4
Morón (Venezuela) **108** E 1
Morondava **95** G 4
Moroni **95** G 2
Moroshechnoye **69** T 4
Morotai, Pulau **75** G 3
Morozovsk **59** F 1
Morro de Môco **94** AB 2
Mors **55** E 4
Morshansk **62** H 5
Mörsil **54** F 3
Mortlock Islands **82** B 2
Morwell **79** H 6
Moselle **57** E 2
Moshi **93** F 5
Mosjöen **54** F 2
Moskal'vo **69** Q 5
Moskenesöya **54** F 2
Moskva **62** FG 4
Mosquera **108** C 3
Mosquitos, Costa de **104** F 5
Mosquitos, Golfo de los **108** B 2
Moss **55** F 4
Mosselbaai **94** C 6
Mossendjo **91** G 6
Mossoró **111** J 2
Mostaganem **86** EF 1
Mostar **57** G 3
Mosul **89** G 1
Motala **55** G 4
Motihari **72** DE 2
Motril **56** C 4
Motykleyka **69** RS 4
Moudjéria **86** C 5
Moul **91** G 2
Moulins **56** D 2
Moulmein **73** G 4
Moundou **91** H 4
Mount Adam **113** DE 9
Mountains of Mayo **52** B 4
Mount Aspiring **80** P 9
Mount Augustus **78** B 3
Mount Balbi **81** F 3
Mount Bangeta **80** E 3
Mount Blackburn **98** HJ 3
Mount Bona **98** J 3
Mount Brassey **78** E 3
Mount Bruce **78** B 3
Mount Brukkaros **94** B 5
Mount Carter **79** G 1
Mount Cleveland **102** D 2
Mount Columbia **99** O 5
Mount Cook **81** Q 9
Mount Cushing **99** M 4
Mount Dalrymple **79** H 3

Mount Deering **78** D 3
Mount Demavend **61** F 2
Mount Douglas **79** H 3
Mount Egmont **81** Q 8
Mount Elbert **102** E 4
Mount Elgon **92** EF 4
Mount Elliot **79** H 2
Mount Essendon **78** C 3
Mount Everest **72** E 2
Mount Feathertop **79** H 6
Mount Finke **78** E 5
Mount Forel **114**
Mount Gambier **79** FG 6
Mount Godwin Austin **67** K 3
Mount Hale **78** B 4
Mount Hermon (Lebanon) **60** B 2
Mount Hood **102** B 2–3
Mount Hutton **79** H 4
Mount Isa **79** F 3
Mount Isto **98** J 2
Mount Jackson (Antarctica) **115**
Mount Jackson (Australia) **78** BC 5
Mount Jefferson **102** C 4
Mount Kenya **93** F 5
Mount Kimball **98** J 3
Mount Kirkpatrick **115**
Mount Livermore **102** F 5
Mount Logan **98** J 3
Mount Magnet **78** B 4
Mount Marcus Baker **98** H 3
Mount McKinley **98** G 3
Mount Menzies **115**
Mount Morgan **79** J 3
Mount Mowbullan **79** J 4
Mount Nurri **79** H 5
Mount Nyiru **93** F 4
Mount Oglethorpe **103** K 5
Mount Olympus **102** AB 2
Mount Omatako **94** B 4
Mount Ord **78** D 2
Mount Ossa **80** L 9
Mount Pulog **75** J 1
Mount Queen Bess **99** N 5
Mount Rainier **102** B 2
Mount Ratz **98** L 4
Mount Robson **99** NO 5
Mount Roosevelt **99** M 4
Mount Shasta **102** B 3
Mount Shenton **78** C 4
Mount Sir James MacBrian **98** M 3
Mount Sunflower **102** F 4
Mount Tama **94** A 2
Mount Taylor **102** E 4
Mount Victoria **73** F 3
Mount Victoria (Papua New Guinea) **82** A 3
Mount Vsevidof **98** D 5
Mount Waddington **99** MN 5
Mount Whitney **102** C 4
Mount Wilhelm **80** D 3
Mount Wilson **102** E 4
Mount Wrightson **102** D 5
Moura **109** F 4
Moussoro **91** H 3

Mouths of the Amazon **109** J 3
Mouths of the Danube **58** CD 1–2
Mouths of the Ganges **72–73** EF 3
Mouths of the Indus **67** H 6
Mouths of the Irrawaddy **73** FG 4
Mouths of the Mekong **73** J 5–6
Mouths of the Orinoco **109** FG 2
Movas **102** E 6
Mowbullan, Mount **79** J 4
Moxico **94** BC 2
Moxos, Llanos de **110** CD 4
Moyale **93** F 4
Moyobamba **108** C 5
Mozambique **95** EF 3
Mozambique Channel **95** FG 2–4
Mozdok **59** FG 2
Mozharka **68** F 5
Mozyr' **55** J 5
Mpanda **92** E 6
Mpika **95** E 2
Msata **93** F 6
Mtsensk **62** G 5
Mtwara **95** G 2
Muang Nan **73** H 4
Muang Ngao **73** GH 4
Muang Phrae **73** H 4
Muang Ubon **72** H 4
Muar **74** B 3
Muaraenim **74** B 4
Muara Teweh **74** D 4
Mubarak **61** G 4
Mubi **91** G 3
Muchinga Escarpment **95** E 2
Mucojo **95** G 2
Mudanjiang **71** JK 2
Muddy Gap **102** E 3
Mufulira **94** D 2
Muganskaya Step' **66** D 3
Muhagiriya **88** D 6
Muhammad, Ra's **60** B 4
Muhammad Qawl **88** F 4
Mühlhausen **53** F 4
Mühlig-Hofmann Mountains **115**
Muhulu **92** D 5
Mui Bai Bung **73** H 6
Muite **95** F 2
Mukachevo **58** B 1
Mukur **66** EF 1
Mukur **67** H 4
Mulan **71** J 1
Mulanje **95** F 3
Mulata **93** G 3
Mulchén **113** B 6
Mulegé **102** D 6
Mulgrave Island **80** D 4
Mulhacén **56** C 4
Mulhouse **57** E 2
Mull **52** B 3
Mullaittivu **72** D 6
Mullaley **79** HJ 5

Muller, Pegunungan **74** D 3
Mullet Peninsula **52** A 4
Mullewa **78** B 4
Mulligan River **79** F 4
Mulobezi **94** D 3
Multan **67** J 5
Multanovy **63** O 3
Mulu, Gunung **74** DE 3
Mulym'ya **63** N 3
Mumra **66** D 1
Muna, Pulau **75** F 5
München **53** F 5
Muncie **103** JK 3
Mundar **69** R 2
Munday **102** G 5
Münden **53** E 4
Munhango **94** B 2
Munich **53** F 5
Munkhafad al Qattārah **88** D 3
Munster **52** B 4
Münster **53** E 4
Muntii Rodnei **58** B 1
Munugudzhak **69** TU 3
Munzur Silsilesi **59** EF 3
Muojärvi **54** J 2
Muong Hiem **73** H 3
Muong Khoua **73** H 3
Muong Sing **73** H 3
Mupa National Park **94** B 3
Mura **57** G 2
Murallón, Cerro **113** B 8
Murana **75** H 4
Muranga **93** F 5
Murashi **62** J 4
Murat **59** F 3
Murchison River **78** AB 4
Murcia **56** C 4
Murdo **102** FG 3
Mureş **58** B 1
Muriaé **111** H 5
Murilo **82** B 2
Murjek **54** H 2
Murmansk **54** K 2
Murmashi **54** K 2
Murom **62** H 4
Muromtsevo **63** P 4
Muroran **71** M 2
Murray Bridge **79** F 6
Murray River **79** G 5
Murrumbidgee River **79** H 5
Murukta **68** H 2
Mururoa **83** F 4
Murwara **72** D 3
Muş **59** F 3
Musala **58** B 2
Musan **71** JK 2
Musandam Peninsula **61** G 4
Muscat **89** K 4
Musgrave **79** G 1
Musgrave Ranges **78** E 4
Mushäsh al 'Ashäwi **61** E 4
Müsiän **61** E 2
Muskegon **103** JK 3
Muskogee **103** GH 4
Mussende **94** B 2
Mustafa **69** P 3
Müt **88** D 3
Mutanda **94** D 2

Mutarara **95** F 3
Mutare **95** E 3
Mutoray **68** H 3
Mutshatsha **94** CD 2
Mutsu-wan **71** M 2
Mu Us Shamo **70** E 3
Muynak **66** F 2
Muzaffarnagar **72** CD 2
Muzaffarpur **72** DE 2
Muzhi **63** M 2
Muztag **67** L 3
Muztag **67** M 3
Mvomero **93** F 6
Mwanza **92** E 5
Mweka **92** C 5
Mwinilunga **94** CD 2
Myakit **69** S 3
Myaundzha **69** R 3
Mycenae **58** B 3
Myingyan **73** G 3
Myitkyina **73** G 2
Myitta **73** G 5
Myittha **73** G 3
Mymensingh **73** F 3
Mýrdalsjökull **54** B 3
Myrtle Beach **103** L 5
Mys Aniva **69** Q 6
Mys Buorkhaya **69** O 1
Mys Duga-Zapadnaya **69** R 4
Mys Kanin Nos **62** H 2
Mys Kril'on **69** Q 6
Mys Kronotskiy **69** U 4–5
Mys Kurgalskiy **55** J 4
Mys Laydennyy **62** J 2
Mys Lopatka **69** T 5
Mys Navarin **69** X 3
Mys Olyutorskiy **69** VW 4
Mysore **72** C 5
Mysovaya **69** T 2
Mys Peschanyy **66** E 2
Mys Pitsunda **59** F 2
Mys Sarych **59** D 2
Mys Shipunskiy **69** TU 5
Mys Svatoy Nos **69** P 1
Mys Svyatoy Nos **62** GH 2
Mys Taran **55** GH 4–5
Mys Taygonos **69** U 3
Mys Terpeniya **69** QR 6
Mys Tolstoy **69** T 4
Mys Uengan **63** MN 1
Mys Yelizavety **69** Q 5
Mys Yuzhnyy **69** ST 4
My Tho **73** J 5

N

Naandi **92** D 3
Naba **73** G 3
Na Baek **73** H 4
Nabk al Gharbi **60** B 3
Nābul **87** H 1
Nābulus **60** B 2
Nachana **72** B 2
Nadiad **72** B 3
Nador **86** E 1
Nadym **63** O 2
Næstved **55** F 4
Naftshahr **61** D 2

Nafuce **91** F 3
Nafūd al 'Urayq **60** D 4
Nafūd as Sirr **66** CD 5–6
Nafūd as Surrah **66** C 6
Naga **75** F 1
Naga Hills **73** FG 2
Nagaland **73** FG 2
Nagano **71** L 3
Nagaoka **71** L 3
Nagasaki **71** J 4
Nagaur **72** B 2
Nagda **72** C 3
Nagercoil **72** C 6
Nago **71** J 5
Nagornyy **69** N 4
Nagoya **71** L 4
Nagpur **72** C 3
Nagqu **70** B 4
Nagykanizsa **58** A 1
Naha **71** J 5
Nahanni National Park
  99 M, N 3
Naharīyya **60** B 2
Nahāvand **61** E 2
Nahr an Nīl **60** A 4
Nā'in **61** F 2
Nain **101** P 4
Nairobi **93** F 5
Najafābād **61** F 2
Najd **60** CD 4
Najin **71** K 2
Najrān **89** GH 5
Nakhichevan' **66** CD 3
Nakhodka **71** K 2
Nakhon Ratchasima **73** H 5
Nakhon Sawan **73** G 4
Nakhon Si Thammarat
  73 GH 6
Nakina **100** K 5
Nakuru **93** F 5
Nalayh **68** J 6
Nal'chik **59** F 2
Nālūt **87** H 2
Namak, Kavir-e **61** G 1
Namanga **93** F 5
Namangan **67** J 2
Namapa **95** G 2
Namaqualand **94** B 5
Namatanai **81** F 2
Nambour **79** J 4
Nam Can **73** J 6
Nam Dinh **73** HJ 3
Nametil **95** F 3
Namib Desert **94** AB 4–5
Namib Desert Park **94** AB 4
Namibe **94** A 3
Namibe Reserve **94** A 3
Namibia **94** AB 4
Namjagbarwa Feng **70** C 5
Namkham **73** G 3
Namlea **75** G 4
Namling **72** E 2
Namoi River **79** H 5
Namoluk **82** B 2
Namonuito **82** A 2
Namorik **82** C 2
Nampala **90** C 2
Nampula **95** FG 3

Namru **72** D 1
Namsang **73** G 3
Namsen **54** F 2–3
Namsos **54** F 3
Namtsy **69** NO 3
Namu **82** C 2
Namuli **95** F 3
Namur **52** E 4
Namy **69** O 2
Nancha **69** NO 6
Nanchang **70** G 5
Nanchong **70** E 4
Nancy **57** E 2
Nanda Devi **72** D 1
Nander **72** C 4
Nandyal **72** C 4
Nanfeng **70** G 5
Nanga Parbat **67** J 3–4
Nangatayap **74** D 4
Nangong **70** FG 3
Nang Xian **70** B 5
Nanjiang **70** E 4
Nanjing **71** GH 4
Nan Ling **70** EF 5
Nanning **70** E 6
Nanping (Fujian, China)
  71 G 5
Nanping (Gansu, China)
  70 DE 4
Nansei-shotō **71** J 5
Nantes **56** C 2
Nanton **99** P 5
Nantong **71** H 4
Nanumanga **82** C 3
Nanumea **82** C 3
Nanuque **111** HJ 4
Nanyang **70** F 4
Nanyuki **93** F 4
Nanzhang **70** F 4
Naococane, Lac **101** NO 5
Napata **88** E 5
Napier **81** R 8
Napier Mountains **115**
Naples **57** F 3
Napo **108** D 4
Napoli **57** F 3
Nara (Japan) **71** L 4
Nara (Mali) **90** C 2
Naranjos **104** C 3
Narasun **68** K 5
Narathiwat **73** H 6
Narayanganj **73** F 3
Narbonne **56** D 3
Nares Strait **114**
Narew **53** H 4
Narmada **72** C 3
Närpes **54** H 3
Narrabri **79** HJ 5
Narrogin **78** B 5
Narsinghgarh **72** C 3
Narssaq **101** S 3
Narva **55** J 4
Narvik **54** G 2
Narwietooma **78** E 3
Naryn **68** G 5
Näsåker **54** G 3
Nashville **103** JK 4
Näsijärvi **54** H 3

Nasik **72** B 3
Nâşir **92** E 3
Nassau **105** G 2
Nasser, Birkat **88** E 4
Nasser, Lake **88** E 4
Nässjö **55** FG 4
Nata **94** D 4
Natal (Brazil) **111** JK 2
Natal (South Africa) **94–95** E 5
Natashquan **101** P 5
Natchez **103** H 5
Natitingou **90** E 3
Natividade **111** G 3
Natkyizin **73** G 5
Natron, Lake **93** F 5
Natuna, Kepulauan **74** C 3
Naturaliste, Cape **78** A 5
Naupe **108** C 5
Nauru **81** J 2
Nauru **82** C 3
Naushki **68** J 5
Nauta **108** D 4
Navarino **113** C 10
Navarra **56** C 3
Navia **56** B 3
Navojoa **102** DE 6
Navolok **62** G 3
Nawabshah **67** H 5
Náxos **58** C 3
Nayarit **104** B 3
Nāy Band **61** F 4
Nāy Band, Ra's-e **61** F 4
Nayoro **71** M 2
Nazaré **56** B 4
Nazareth **108** C 5
Nazca **110** A 3
Naze **71** J 5
Nazerat **60** B 2
Nazilli **58** C 3
Ndali **90** E 4
Ndélé **92** C 3
Ndendé **91** G 6
Ndola **94** D 2
Neagh, Lough **52** B 4
Néapolis **58** B 3
Near Islands **98** A 5
Nebit-Dag **66** E 3
Nebolchi **62** F 4
Nebraska **102** FG 3
Nechako Reservoir **99** M 5
Necochea **113** E 6
Nédéley **91** H 2
Nedong **73** F 2
Neftelensk **68** J 4
Nefteyugansk **63** O 3
Negage **94** AB 1
Negelli **93** F 3
Negombo **72** C 6
Negonengo **83** F 4
Negra, Punta **108** B 5
Negrais, Cape **73** F 4
Negritos **108** B 4
Negros **75** F 1–2
Nehāvand **61** E 2
Nehe **69** MN 6
Neijiang **70** DE 5
Nei Monggol Zizhiqu **70** DG 2
Neiva **108** CD 3

Nej – Nor

Nejd (Saudi Arabia) 60 CD 5
Nekemt 93 F 3
Nelemnoye 69 S 2
Nel'kan 69 P 4
Nelkuchan, Gora 69 P 3
Nellore 72 D 5
Nel'ma 69 P 6
Nelson 81 Q 9
Nelson Island 98 D 3
Nelspruit 95 E 5
Néma 86 D 5
Nemunas 55 H 4
Nemuro 71 N 2
Nendo 81 J 4
Nenjiang 69 MN 6
Nepa 68 J 4
Nepal 72 DE 2
Nepeña 108 C 5
Nerchinsk 68 L 5
Nerekhta 62 H 4
Neringa-Nida 55 H 4
Neriquinha 94 C 3
Nesbyen 55 E 3
Néstos 58 B 2
Netanya 60 B 2
Netherlands 52 D–E 4
Netherlands Antilles 105 K 4
Nettiling Lake 101 NO 2
Nettuno 57 F 3
Neuchâtel 57 E 2
Neuquén 113 C 6
Nevada (U.S.A.) 102 C 4
Nevada, Sierra (Spain) 56 C 4
Nevado Ausangate 110 B 3
Nevado Cololo 110 C 4
Nevado Coropuna 110 B 4
Nevado de Cachi 110 C 5
Nevado de Colima 104 B 4
Nevado Huascarán 108 C 5
Nevado Illimani 110 C 4
Nevado Sajama 110 C 4
Nevado Salluyo 110 C 3
Nevado Yerupajá 110 A 3
Never 69 M 5
Nevers 56 D 2
Nevinnomyssk 59 F 2
Nevşehir 59 D 3
Nev'yansk 63 M 4
New Albany 103 J 4
New Amsterdam 109 G 2
Newark (N.J., U.S.A.) 103 M 3
Newark (OH, U.S.A.) 103 K 3
New Bedford 103 M 3
New Bern 103 L 4
New Britain 81 F 3
New Brunswick 101 O 6
Newburgh 103 LM 3
New Caledonia 81 H 6
Newcastle (N.S.W., Austr.)
   79 J 5
Newcastle (WY, U.S.A.)
   102 EF 3
Newcastle-upon-Tyne 52 C 3
Newcastle Waters 78 E 2
New England 103 MN 3
Newenham, Cape 98 DE 4
Newfoundland 101 PQ 5
Newfoundland 101 QR 6

New Georgia 81 G 3
New Glasgow 101 P 6
New Guinea 80 E 3
New Hanover 81 F 2
New Haven 103 M 3
New Hebrides 81 J 5
New Iberia 103 H 6
New Ireland 81 F 2
New Ireland 82 AB 3
New Liskeard 103 K 2
Newman 78 B 3
New Meadows 102 C 2
New Mexico 102 E 5
New Orleans 103 J 5–6
New Plymouth 81 Q 8
Newport (OR, U.S.A.)
   102 AB 3
Newport (U.K.) 52 C 4
Newport Beach 102 C 5
New Providence Island
   105 G 3
Newry 78 D 2
New Siberian Islands 114
New South Wales 79 GH 5
New Stuvahok 98 F 4
Newtonabbey 52 B 4
New York (N.Y., U.S.A.)
   103 M 3
New York (U.S.A.) 103 L 3
New Zealand 81 RS 9
Neya 62 H 4
Neyriz 61 G 3
Neyshābūr 66 F 3
Nezhin 62 F 5
Ngamiland 94 C 3
Ngamring 72 E 2
Ngangla Ringco 72 DE 1
Nganglong Kangri 72 D 1
Ngatik 82 B 2
Ngidinga 92 B 6
Ngoc Linh 73 J 4
Ngoko 91 H 5
Ngoring 70 C 3
Nguara 91 H 3
Ngwane 95 E 5
Nhambiquara 110 E 3
Nha Trang 73 JK 5
Niagara Falls 103 L 3
Niamey 90 E 3
Niamtougou 90 E 3
Niangara 92 D 4
Nia-Nia 92 D 4
Nianzishan 69 M 6
Nias, Pulau 74 AB 3
Niassa 95 F 2
Nicaragua 104 EF 5
Nicaragua, Lago de 104 EF 5
Nice 57 E 3
Nichalakh 69 QR 1
Nicobar Islands 73 F 6
Nicocli 108 C 2
Nicosia 59 D 3
Nicosia (Cyprus) 60 A 2
Nicoya, Península de 104 E 6
Nicuadala 95 F 3
Nidelva 55 E 4
Niedersachsen 53 EF 4
Niedre Tauern 57 F 2

Niellé 90 C 3
Niemba 92 D 6
Nieuw Amsterdam 109 H 2
Nieuw Nickerie 109 G 2
Nieuwoudtville 94 BC 6
Niğde 59 DE 3
Niger 91 FG 2
Niger 91 F 4
Niger Delta 91 F 5
Nigeria 91 EG 4
Nihau 83 E 1
Nihiru 83 F 4
Niigata 71 L 3
Nijmegen 52 E 4
Nikel 54 K 2
Nikk 90 E 4
Nikolayev 58 D 1
Nikolayevka 63 N 5
Nikolayevsk-na-Amure
   69 PQ 5
Nikoleyeva 55 JK 4
Nikol'sk 62 J 4
Nikol'skiy 67 H 1
Nikopol 59 D 1
Nikpey 61 E 1
Nikšic 58 A 2
Nikumaroro 82 D 3
Nile (Egypt) 60 A 4
Nimba, Monts 90 C 4
Nimbe 91 F 5
Nimes 56 D 3
Nimule 92 E 4
Nincheng 71 G 2
Ninety Mile Beach 79 H 6
Nineveh 60 D 1
Ningbo 71 H 5
Ningde 71 G 5
Ningdu 70 G 5
Ningxia Huizu Zizhiqu 70 E 3
Ninigo Group 82 A 3
Nioro du Sahel 90 C 2
Niort 56 C 2
Niout 86 D 5
Nipigon 100 K 6
Nipigon, Lake 100 K 6
Nipissing, Lake 101 LM 6
Nippur 89 H 2
Nis 58 B 2
Nisāb 89 H 6
Nísoi 58 B 3
Niterói 111 H 5
Nitiya 69 P 4
Nitra 53 G 5
Niuafo'ou 82 D 4
Niuato Putapu 82 D 4
Niue 82 D 4
Niulakita 82 C 3
Niutao 82 C 3
Nizamabad 72 C 4
Nizhneangarsk 68 JK 4
Nizhne-Ozernaya 69 UV 4
Nizhneudinsk 68 G 5
Nizhnevartovskoye 63 PQ 3
Nizhneye Karelina 68 J 4
Nizhniy Pyandzh 67 H 3
Nizhniy Tagil 63 M 4
Nizhnyaya Omka 63 O 4
Nizhnyaya Poyma 68 G 4

Nizhnyaya Tunguska 68 F 3
Nizhnyaya Voch' 62 K 3
Nizhnyaya Zolotitsa
   (Nizhnyaya) 62 H 2
Nizina Podlaska 53 H 4
Nizip 60 B 1
Njunes 54 G 2
Njutånger 54 G 3
Nkayi 91 G 6
Nkhata Bay 95 E 2
Nkolabona 91 G 5
Nkomi, Lagune 91 F 5
Nkongsamba 91 G 4–5
Nkurenkuru 94 B 3
Noatak National Preserve
   98 F 2
Noefs, Ile des 93 J 6
Nogales 102 DE 5
Nogayskiye Step' 59 G 2
Noginsk 62 G 4
Nokrek Peak 73 F 2
Nomad 82 A 3
Nome 98 D 3
Nonacho Lake 99 Q 3
Nong Khai 73 H 4
Nonouti 82 C 3
Nordaustlandet 114
Nordfriesische Inseln
   53 E 3–4
Norðoyar 52 A 1
Nordkapp 54 J 1
Nordkinn 54 J 1
Nord-Kvaloy 54 G 1
Nordland 54 EF 2
Nordostrundingen 114
Nordöyane 54 E 3
Nordreisa 54 H 2
Nordsjön 55 E 4
Nord-Tröndelag 54 F 3
Nordvik 68 K 1
Norfolk (NE, U.S.A.)
   102 G 3
Norfolk (VA, U.S.A.) 103 L 4
Norfolk Islands 82 C 4
Norge 54 EF 2
Nori 63 O 2
Noril'sk 63 R 2
Norman 102 G 4
Normanby Island 79 J 1
Normandie 56 CD 2
Normanton 79 G 2
Norra Storfjället 54 G 2
Norrbotten 54 GH 2
Norrköping 55 G 4
Norrland 54 FG 3
Norrtälje 55 G 4
Norseman 78 C 5
Norsjö 54 G 2
Norsk 69 O 5
Norte, Canal do 109 H 3
Northam 78 B 5
Northampton 52 C 4
North Andaman 73 F 5
North Battleford 99 Q 5
North Bay 101 M 6
North Bend 102 AB 3
North Cape 82 C 3
North Carolina 103 L 4

North Cascades National Park **102** BC 2
North Channel **52** B 3–4
North Dakota **102** FG 2
Northeast Cape **98** D 3
Northeast Providence
Channel **105** G 2
Northern Cook Islands **82** E 3
Northern Indian Lake **99** S 4
Northern Ireland **52** B 4
Northern Mariana Islands
82 B 1
Northern Territory **78** E 2–3
North Fork Pass **98** K 3
North Geomagnetic Pole **114**
North Highlands **102** BC 4
North Island **81** Q 8
North Korea **71** K 2
North Lakhimpur **73** F 2
North Las Vegas **102** C 4
North Little Rock **103** H 5
North Magnetic Pole **114**
North Minch **52** B 3
North Platte (Nebraska
U.S.A.) **102** F 3
North Platte (Nebraska
U.S.A.) **102** F 3
North Point **80** L 8
North Pole **114**
North Sea **52** D 3
North Slope **98** FH 2
North Uist **52** B 3
Northumberland Islands
79 J 3
Northumberland Strait
101 P 6
North West Cape **78** A 3
North West Highlands
52 BC 3
Northwest Territories
99 NT 2
Norton Sound **98** DE 3
Norway **54** F 2
Norwegian Sea **54** DE 2–3
Norwich **52** D 4
Noshiro **71** L 2
Nosovaya **62** K 2
Nosratābād **66** F 5
Nossob **94** BC 5
Nosy-Bé **95** H 2
Noteć **53** G 4
Nótioi Sporádhes **58** C 3
Notodden **55** E 4
Noto-hantō **71** L 3
Notre Dame Bay **101** QR 6
Nottingham (Canada)
101 MN 3
Nottingham (U.K.) **52** C 4
Nouadhibou **86** B 4
Nouakchott **86** B 5
Nouméa **81** J 6
Nouvelle-Calédonie **81** H 6
Nova Cruz **111** JK 2
Nova Iguaçu **111** H 5
Nova Mambone **95** F 4
Novara **57** E 2
Nova Scotia **101** OP 7
Nova Vida **110** D 3

Novaya Kakhovka **59** D 1
Novaya Kazanka **62** J 6
Novaya Zemlya **62** KL 1
Novgorod **55** K 4
Novgorodka **55** J 4
Novi Ligure **57** E 3
Novillero **104** A 3
Novi Pazar **58** AB 2
Novi Sad **58** A 1
Novoaltaysk **63** QR 5
Novobiryusinskiy **68** G 4
Novograd-Volynskiy **55** J 5
Novo Hamburgo **112** FG 4
Novokazalinsk **67** G 1
Novokocherdyk **63** M 5
Novokuznetsk **63** R 5
Novolazarevskaya **115**
Novomoskovsk **62** G 5
Novopavlovskoye **68** K 5
Novopokrovskaya **59** F 1
Novopolotsk **55** J 4
Novorossiysk **59** E 2
Novorybnoye **68** HJ 1
Novoshakhtinsk **62** H 6
Novosibirsk **63** QR 4
Novosibirskiye Ostrova →
New Siberian Islands
61 QR 2
Novotroitskoye **67** JK 2
Novoyeniseysk **68** FG 4
Novoye Ust'ye **69** Q 4
Novvy Bug **59** D 1
Novy Uzen' **66** E 2
Novyy Karymkary **63** N 3
Novyy Port **63** O 2
Novyy Tanguy **68** H 4
Nowa Sól **53** FG 4
Nowbarān **61** E 2
Nowdesheh **61** E 2
Nowgong **73** F 2
Nowra **79** J 5
Now Shahr **61** F 1
Nowy Sacz **53** H 5
Nsukka **91** F 4
Ntui **91** G 5
Nuatja **90** E 4
Nūbiyah **88** DE 5
Nueltin Lake **99** S 3
Nueva Esperanza **110** CD 4
Nueva Galia **113** CD 6
Nueva Gerona **104** F 3
Nueva León **104** BC 2
Nueva Lubecka **113** BC 7
Nueva Rosita **104** B 2
Nueve de Julio **113** D 6
Nuevo Casas Grandes
102 E 5
Nuevo Laredo **104** BC 2
Nuevo Mundo, Cerro **110** C 5
Nuevo Rocafuerte **108** C 4
Nugāl **93** H 3
Nuguria Islands **82** B 3
Nui **82** C 3
Nukey Bluff **79** F 5
Nukhayb **60** D 2
Nuku'alofa **82** D 4
Nukufetau **82** C 3
Nuku Hiva **83** F 3

Nukulaelae **82** D 3
Nukumanu Islands **82** B 3
Nukunau **82** C 3
Nukunonu **82** D 3
Nukuoro **82** B 2
Nukus **66** FG 2
Nullarbor Plain **78** DE 5
Numan **91** G 4
Numbulwar Mission **78** EF 1
Numfor, Pulau **75** H 4
Numto **63** O 3
Nungnain Sum **71** G 1
Nunivak Island **98** D 3–4
Nunlygran **98** B 2
Nuntherungie **79** G 5
Nunyamo **98** C 2
Nuoro **57** E 3
Nuqrah **60** C 4
Nuratau, Khrebet **67** H 2
Nuremberg **53** F 5
Nurhak Daği **59** E 3
Nūri **88** E 5
Nuristan **67** J 3
Nürnberg **53** F 5
Nurri, Mount **79** H 5
Nushki **67** H 5
Nutak **101** P 4
Nuupas **54** J 2
Nuwaybi'al Muzayyinah
60 B 3
Nyabéssan **91** G 5
Nyakanazi **92** E 5
Nyaksimvol' **63** M 3
Nyala **88** CD 6
Nyamlell **92** D 3
Nyandoma **62** H 3
Nyazepetrovsk **63** L 4
Nyda **63** O 2
Nyika Plateau **95** E 2
Nyima **72** E 1
Nyiregyháza **58** B 1
Nyiru, Mount **93** F 4
Nykøbing **55** F 5
Nyköping **55** G 4
Nylstroom **94** D 4
Nymagee **79** H 5
Nyurba **68** L 3
Nzega **92** E 5
Nzerékoré **90** C 4

O

Oahe, Lake **102** F 2
Oahe Dam **102** F 3
Oahu **83** E 1
Oakbank **79** G 5
Oakland **102** B 4
Oakley **102** F 4
Oak Ridge **103** K 4
Oates Coast **115**
Oaxaca **104** C 4
Oaxaca de Juárez **104** C 4
Oba **100** L 6
Obala **91** G 5
Oban **52** B 3
Obeh **67** G 4
Óbidos **109** GH 4
Obihiro **71** M 2
Obil'noye **59** FG 1

Obluch'ye **69** O 6
Obodovka **58** C 1
Obruk Platosu **59** D 3
Obshchiy Syrt **62** K 5
Obskaya Guba **63** O 1–2
Ocala **103** K 6
Ocaña **108** D 2
Occidental, Cordillera
108 C 2–3
Oconee River **103** K 5
Odawara **71** L 3–4
Ödemiş **58** C 3
Odendaalsrus **94** D 5
Odense **55** EF 4
Oder **53** F 4
Odessa **102** F 5
Odessa (U.S.S.R.) **58** D 1
Odienné **90** C 4
Odorheiu Secuiesc **58** C 1
Odra **53** FG 4
Odzala National Park **91** GH 5
Oeiras **111** H 2
Oeno **83** G 4
Offenbach **53** E 4–5
Oficina **109** F 2
Ogaden **93** GH 3
Ōgaki **71** L 3
Ogallala **102** F 3
Ogbomosho **91** EF 4
Ogden **102** D 3
Ogilvie Mountains **98** JK 2
Oglat Beraber **86** E 2
Ogoki **100** K 5
Ogooué **91** G 6
Ograzden **58** B 2
O'Higgins, Lago **113** B 8
Ohio **103** K 3
Ohio River **103** K 4
Ohopoho **94** A 3
Ohrid **58** B 2
Oiapoque **109** H 3
Ōita **71** K 4
Ojo de Agua **112** D 4
Ojos del Salado, Cerro
112 C 4
Okaba **75** J 5
Okahandja **94** B 4
Okak Islands **101** P 4
Okapa **80** E 3
Okara **67** J 4
Okavango **94** C 3
Okavango Swamp **94** C 3
Okavarumendu **94** B 4
Okayama **71** K 3–4
Okeanskoye **69** T 5
Okeechobee, Lake **103** K 6
Okha (U.S.S.R.) **69** Q 5
Okhotsk **69** Q 4
Okhotskiy Perevoz **69** P 3
Okhotskoye More **69** QS 4
Okinawa-jima **71** JK 5
Oki-shotō **71** K 3
Oklahoma **102–103** G 4
Oklahoma City **103** G 4
Okondja **91** G 6
Okstindan **54** F 2
Oktemberyan **59** F 2
Oktyabrskiy **62** KL 5

Oktyabr'skiy (U.S.S.R.) **68** F 5
Oktyabr'skiy (U.S.S.R.) **69** N 4
Oktyabr'skoye **63** N 3
Öland **55** G 4
Olanga **54** JK 2
Olavarría **113** DE 6
Olbia **57** E 3
Old Bahama Channel **105** G 3
Oldenburg **53** E 4
Olenegorsk **54** K 2
Olenëk **68** M 1
Olenëk **68** K 2
Olenëkskiy Zaliv **68** LM 1
Olenevod **69** WX 3
Oléron, Ile d' **56** C 2
Ölgiy **68** F 6
Olifants **95** E 4
Olimarao **82** A 2
Olimbia **58** B 3
Olimbia (Greece) **58** B 3
Olimbos **58** B 2–3
Olinda **111** K 2
Ollagüe, Volcán **110** C 5
Olmos **108** C 5
Olomouc **53** G 5
Olonets **54** K 3
Oloyskiye Gory **69** U 2
Olsztyn **53** H 4
Olt **58** B 2
Olympia **102** B 2
Olympia (Greece) **58** B 3
Olympus **58** B 3
Olympus, Mount **102** B 2
Olyutorka **69** V 3
Olyutorskiy **69** VW 3
Omaha **103** G 3
Oman **89** JK 4–5
Omatako, Mount **94** B 4
Omboué **91** F 6
Omchali **66** E 2
Ömnögovĭ **70** DE 2
Omolon **69** T 2
Omolon **69** U 2
Omsk **63** O 4
Omutinskiy **63** N 4
Omutninsk **62** K 4
Onawa **103** G 3
Ondangwa **94** B 3
Ondo **91** E 4
Öndörhaan **68** K 6
Onega **62** G 3
Ongole **72** D 4
Onilahy **95** G 4
Onitsha **91** F 4
Onkuchakh **68** KL 2
Ono-i-Lau Islands **82** CD 4
Onon **68** L 5
Onotoa **82** C 3
Onslow **78** B 3
Ontario **102** C 3
Ontario, Lake **103** L 3
Ontojärvi **54** J 3
Ontong Java **82** B 3
Oodnadatta **79** F 4
Ooldea **78** E 5
Oostende **52** D 4
Opasatika **100** L 6
Opis **60** D 2

Opobo **91** F 5
Opole **53** G 4
Oporto **56** B 3
Oppland **54** E 3
Oradea **58** B 1
Oran **86** E 1
Orange (France) **57** D 3
Orange (TX, U.S.A.) **103** H 5
Orange, Cabo **109** H 3
Orange Free State **94** D 5
Oranje **94** B 5
Orapa **94** D 4
Orcadas **115**
Ord, Mount **78** D 2
Ord River **78** D 2
Ordu **59** E 2
Ordynskoye **63** Q 5
Ordzhonikidze **59** FG 2
Örebro **55** FG 4
Oregon **102** BC 3
Orel **62** G 5
Orenburg **62** K 5
Orense **56** B 3
Öresund **55** F 4
Organ Peak **102** E 5
Orgeyev **58** C 1
Orhon Gol **68** HJ 6
Oriental, Cordillera (Bolivia)
  110 CD 3–5
Oriental, Cordillera
  (Colombia) **108** CD 2–3
Orihuela **56** C 4
Orillia **101** M 7
Orinduik **109** F 3
Orinoco (Colombia) **108** E 3
Orinoco (Venezuela) **108** E 2
Orissa **72** DE 3
Orissaare **55** H 4
Oristano **57** E 3–4
Orivesi **54** J 3
Oriximiná **109** G 4
Orizaba **104** C 4
Orkanger **54** E 3
Orkney **94** D 5
Orkney Islands **52** C 3
Orlando **103** K 6
Orléans **56** D 2
Ormara **67** GH 5
Ormoc **75** FG 1
Ornö **55** G 4
Örnsköldsvik **54** G 3
Oro, Monte d' **57** E 3
Orocué **108** D 3
Oroluk **82** B 2
Orona **82** D 3
Oroqen Zizhiqi **69** M 5
Oroquieta **75** F 2
Oroville **102** C 2
Orsa **54** F 3
Orsa Finnmark **54** F 3
Orsha **55** JK 5
Orsk **63** L 5
Ortegal, Cabo **56** B 3
Orto-Ayan **69** NO 1
Ortonville **103** G 2
Orümiyeh **59** F 3
Oruro **110** C 4

Osa **68** H 5
Ōsaka **71** L 4
Osakarovka **63** O 5
Osceola **103** H 3
Osh **67** J 2
Oshakati **94** AB 3
Oshkosh **103** J 3
Oshogbo **91** EF 4
Oshtoran Küh **61** E 2
Osijek **57** G 2
Osinovka **63** Q 6
Oskarshamn **55** G 4
Oskoba **68** H 3
Oslo **55** F 4
Oslofjorden **55** F 4
Osmanabad **72** C 4
Osmaneli **58** D 2
Osmaniye **59** E 3
Osnabrück **53** E 4
Osorno **113** B 7
Osoyoos **99** O 6
Ost Berlin **55** F 5
Ost Berlin **55** F 5
Österdalälven **54** F 3
Österdalen **54** F 3
Östergötland **55** G 4
Östersund **54** FG 3
Östhavet **54** JK 1
Ostrava **53** G 5
Ostroda **53** GH 4
Ostrołęka **53** H 4
Ostrov (Russia, U.S.S.R.)
  55 J 4
Ostrova Chernyye Brat'ya
  69 S 6
Ostrov Bol'shoy Begichev
  68 KL 1
Ostrov Bol'shoy Shantar
  69 P 4–5
Ostrov Feklistova **69** P 4–5
Ostrov Iturup **69** R 6–7
Ostrov Ketoy **69** S 6
Ostrov Kil'din Sal. **69** KL 2
Ostrov Kolguyev **62** J 2
Ostrov Kotel'nyy **69** P 1
Ostrov Malyy Lyakhovskiy
  69 Q 1
Ostrov Matua **69** S 6
Ostrovnoye (U.S.S.R.) **69** U 2
Ostrov Onekotan **69** ST 6
Ostrov Paramushir **69** ST 5
Ostrov Rasshua **69** S 6
Ostrov Shiashkotan **69** S 6
Ostrov Simushir **69** S 6
Ostrov Urup **69** S 6
Ostrov Vaygach **63** L 1–2
Ostrov Zav'yalova **69** RS 4
Ostrowiec Świetokrzyski
  53 H 4
Ostrów Wielkopolski **53** G 4
Ōsumi-shotō **71** JK 4
Otaru **71** M 2
Otavalo **108** C 3
Otavi **94** B 3
Otepää Kõrgustik **55** J 4
Otjozondu **94** B 3
Otradnoye **69** T 5
Otta **54** E 3

Ottawa **101** MN 6
Ottawa River **101** M 6
Ottumwa **103** H 3
Otway, Cape **79** G 6
Otwock **53** H 4
Ouachita Mountains
  103 GH 5
Ouadane **86** C 4
Ouadda **92** C 3
Ouaddaï **91** J 3
Ouad Naga **86** BC 5
Ouagadougou **90** DE 3
Ouahigouya **90** D 3
Oualam **90** E 3
Ouanda-Djallé **92** C 3
Ouangolodougou **90** D 4
Ouargla **87** G 2
Ouarzazate **86** D 2
Oubangui **91** H 5
Oudtshoorn **94** C 6
Oued Zem **86** D 2
Ouessant, Ile de **56** B 2
Ouesso **91** H 5
Ouezzane **86** DE 2
Ouham **91** H 4
Oujda **86** E 2
Oulu **54** J 2
Oulujärvi **54** J 3
Oum Chalouba **91** J 2
Oum Hadjer **91** H 3
Ounianga **91** J 2
Ouricuri **111** J 2
Ourinhos **111** G 5
Outapi **94** A 3
Outer Hebrides **52** B 3
Outjo **94** B 4
Outokumpu **54** J 3
Ouvéa **81** J 6
Ouyen **79** G 5–6
Ovalle **112** B 5
Ovamboland **94** AB 3
Oviedo **56** B 3
Owensboro **103** J 4
Owerri **91** F 4
Owo **91** F 4
Oxford **52** C 4
Oyem **91** G 5
Oyo **90** E 4
Oyón **110** A 3
Oysurdakh **69** S 2
Ozamiz **75** F 2
Ozark Plateau **103** H 4
Ózd **58** B 1
Ozernovskiy **69** T 5
Ozero Balkhash **63** OP 6
Ozero Baykal **68** J 5
Ozero Chany **63** P 5
Ozero Chervonoye **55** J 5
Ozero Dadynskoye **59** FG 1
Ozero Il'men **55** K 4
Ozero Imandra **54** K 2
Ozero Keret' **54** K 2
Ozero Kubenskoye **62** G 4
Ozero Leksozero **54** K 3
Ozero Manych Gudilo **59** F 1
Ozero Nyuk **54** K 3
Ozero Osvejskoje **55** J 4
Ozero Pyaozero **54** K 2

Ozero Sasykkol' **63** Q 6
Ozero Segozero **54** K 3
Ozero Seletyteniz **63** O 5
Ozero Sevan **59** G 2
Ozero Syamozero **54** K 3
Ozero Taymyr **68** H 1
Ozero Tengiz **63** N 5
Ozero Verkhneye Kuyto **54** K 3
Ozero Zaysan **63** Q 6

P

Paarl **94** B 6
Paavola **54** J 3
Pacaraima, Sierra **109** F 3
Pacasmayo **108** BC 5
Pachiza **108** C 5
Pachuca **104** C 3–4
Pacific Ocean **116**
Padang **74** B 4
Padang, Pulau **74** B 3
Padangpanjang **74** AB 4
Padangsidempuan **74** A 3
Paddle Prairie **99** O 4
Paderborn **53** E 4
Padilla **110** D 4
Padova **57** F 2
Padre Island **103** G 6
Paducah **103** J 4
Pag **57** FG 3
Pagan **82** A 1
Pago-Pago **82** D 3
Pagri **72** E 2
Päijänne **54** J 3
Paisley **52** BC 3
Paita **108** B 4–5
Pakin **82** B 2
Pakistan **67** H 5
Pakokku **73** FG 3
Pak Phanang **73** H 6
Pakse **73** J 4
Pakwach **92** E 4
Palacios **103** G 6
Palangkaraya **74** D 4
Palanpur **72** B 3
Palapye **94** D 4
Palatka **69** RS 3
Palauk **73** G 5
Palaw **73** G 5
Palawan **74–75** E 2
Palawan Passage **74–75** E 1–2
Palca **110** C 4
Palembang **74** BC 4
Palencia **56** C 3
Palenque **104** D 4
Palermo **57** F 4
Palestine **60** B 2–3
Paletwa **73** F 3
Pali **72** B 2
Paljakka **54** J 3
Palk Strait **72** C 5–6
Pallastunturit **54** H 2
Palliser, Cape **81** R 9
Palma **56** D 4
Pal Malmal **81** F 3
Palmares **111** JK 2
Palmar Sur **104** F 6
Palma Soriano **105** G 3

Palm Bay **103** KL 6
Palmeira dos Indios **111** J 2
Palmeirais **111** H 2
Palmer **115**
Palmer Archipelago **115**
Palmer Land **115**
Palmerston **82** E 4
Palmerston North **81** R 9
Palmira **108** C 3
Palmyra (Pacific Ocean, U.S.A.) **82** E 2
Palmyra (Syria) **60** C 2
Palmyras Point **72** E 3
Palo Alto **102** B 4
Paloich **88** E 6
Palopo **75** F 4
Palo Santo **112** E 4
Paltamo **54** J 3
Palu (Indonesia) **75** E 4
Palu (Turkey) **59** EF 3
Pamekasan **74** D 5
Pamir **67** JK 3
Pamlico Sound **103** L 4
Pampa **102** F 4
Pampas **112–113** D 5–6
Pamplona **56** C 3
Pan, Tierra del **56** B 3
Panaji **72** B 4
Panama **108** C 2
Panamá, Golfo de **108** C 2
Panama Canal **108** B 2
Panama City **103** J 5
Panay **75** F 1
Pandamatenga **94** D 3
Pandharpur **72** BC 4
Pandivere Kõrgustik **55** J 4
Panevežys **55** HJ 4
Panggoe **82** B 3
Panjao **67** H 4
Panjgur **67** G 5
Panorama **111** F 5
Pantanal de São Lourénço **110** E 4
Pantanal do Río Negro **110** E 4
Pantelleria **57** F 4
Pan Xian **70** DE 5
Paoua **92** B 3
Pápa **58** A 1
Papeete **83** F 4
Papenburg **53** E 4
Papey **54** C 3
Paphos **59** D 4
Papua, Gulf of **80** DE 3
Papua New Guinea **80** E 2–3
Papua New Guinea **82** AB 3
Pará **109** GH 5
Parabel **63** Q 4
Paracatu **111** G 4
Paracel Islands **73** K 4
Paraguai **110** E 5
Paraguarí **112** E 4
Paraguay **110** DE 5
Paraguay **112** E 4
Paraíba **111** J 2
Parakou **90** E 4
Paramaribo **109** GH 2
Paramirim **111** H 3

Paraná (Argentina) **112** DE 5
Paraná (Brazil) **111** F 5
Paranaguá **112** G 4
Paranam **109** G 2
Paranavai **111** F 5
Parangaba **111** J 1
Paraoa **83** F 4
Paratinga **111** H 3
Parbig **63** Q 4
Parc National de la Boucle De Baoule **90** C 3
Parc National de la Komoé **90** D 4
Parc National de Sinianka-Minia **91** H 3
Parc National de Taï **90** C 4
Parc National de Wonga Wongué **91** F 6
Parc National de Zakouma **91** H 3
Parc National du Bamingui-Ban-goran **92** BC 3
Parc National du Niokolo Koba **90** B 3
Parcs Nationaux du "W" **90** E 3
Pardo **111** H 4
Pardubice **53** G 4
Parecis, Serra dos **110** D 3
Parepare **75** E 4
Parima, Sierra **109** F 3
Parinari **108** D 4
Pariñas, Punta **108** B 4
Parintins **109** G 4
Paris (France) **56** D 2
Paris (TX, U.S.A.) **103** G 5
Parkano **54** H 3
Parker **102** D 5
Parkersburg **103** K 4
Parlakimidi **72** D 4
Parlakote **72** D 4
Parma **57** E 3
Parnaíba **111** H 1
Parnamirim **111** J 2
Parnarama **111** H 2
Parnassós Óros **58** B 3
Pärnu **55** H 4
Parpaillon **57** E 3
Parral **113** B 6
Parry Islands **114**
Parry Peninsula **99** MN 2
Partille **55** F 4
Partizansk **71** K 2
Paryang **72** D 2
Parys **94** D 5
Pasadena **102** C 5
Pascagoula **103** J 5
Pas de Calais **52** D 4
Pasni **67** G 5
Paso de Indios **113** C 7
Paso del Limay **113** BC 7
Paso de los Libres **112** E 4
Paso de los Vientos **105** H 3–4
Paso de San Francisco **112** C 4
Paso Río Mayo **113** B 8

Passau **53** F 5
Passo Fundo **112** F 4
Passos **111** G 5
Pasto **108** C 3
Pastos Bons **111** H 2
Patagonia **113** BC 7–9
Patan (India) **72** B 3
Patan (Nepal) **72** DE 2
Paterson **103** LM 3
Pathankot **72** C 1
Patiala **72** C 1–2
Pativilca **108** C 6
Patkaglik **67** M 3
Patna **72** E 2
Patnagarh **72** D 3
Patos **111** J 2
Patos, Lagoa dos **112** F 5
Patos de Minas **111** G 4
Pátrai **58** B 3
Patras **58** B 3
Patríkos Kólpos **58** B 3
Patrocínio **111** G 4
Pau **56** C 3
Pau d'Arco **109** J 5
Paulina Peak **102** B 3
Paulistana **111** H 2
Paulo Afonso **111** J 2
Pauls Valley **103** G 5
Pavlodar **63** P 5
Pavlof Volcano **98** E 4
Pavlovka **63** O 5
Paxson **98** H 3
Payakumbuh **74** B 3–4
Paynes Find **78** B 4
Paysandú **112** E 5
Payturma **68** F 1
Pazardžik **58** B 2
Peace River **99** P 4
Peaked Mountain **103** N 2
Pearl **103** J 5
Peary Land **114**
Pebane **95** F 3
Pebas **108** D 4
Peć **58** B 2
Pechora **62** K 2
Pechorskoye More **62** KL 2
Pecos **102** F 5
Pecos Plains **102** F 5
Pecos River **102** F 5
Pécs **58** A 1
Pedernales **109** F 2
Pedro Afonso **109** J 5
Pedro de Valdivia **110** BC 5
Pedro Juan Caballero **110** E 5
Peera Peera Poolanna Lake **79** F 4
Pegu **73** G 4
Pegunungan Barisan **74** B 4
Pegunungan Maoke **75** J 4
Pegunungan Muller **74** D 3
Pegunungan Schwaner **74** D 4
Pegu Yoma **73** G 3–4
Pehuajó **113** D 6
Peixe **111** G 3
Pekalongan **74** CD 5
Pekanbaru **74** B 3
Pekin **103** HJ 3

Peking **71** G 3
Pelat, Mont **57** E 3
Pelješac **57** G 3
Pelly **98** L 3
Pelly Bay **99** U 2
Pelly Crossing **98** K 3
Pelly Mountains **98** L 3
Peloponnese **58** B 3
Pelopónnisos **58** B 3
Pelotas **112** F 5
Pelvoux, Massif du **57** E 3
Pemangkat **74** C 3
Pematangsiantar **74** A 3
Pemba **95** G 2
Pemba Island **93** FG 6
Pembina **102** G 2
Penas, Golfo de **113** AB 8
Pendembu **90** B 4
Penedo **111** J 3
Penglai **71** GH 3
Península Brecknock **113** B 9
Península de Nicoya **104** E 6
Península de Taitao **113** AB 8
Península Valdés **113** D 7
Pénisule de Gaspé **101** OP 6
Peninsule d'Ungava
  101 MN 4
Penisola Salentina **57** G 3
Penninechain **52** C 4
Pennsylvania **103** L 3
Penny Ice Cap **101** O 2
Penong **78** E 5
Penrhyn **83** E 3
Pensacola **103** J 5
Pensacola Mountains **115**
Pentecoste **82** C 4
Pentecôte **81** J 5
Penza **62** H 5
Penzhinskaya Guba **69** U 3
Penzhinskiy Khrebet **69** U 3
Peoria **103** J 3
Perche, Collines du **56** D 2
Pereira **108** C 3
Pereval Yablonitse **58** BC 1
Pergamino **112** D 5
Pergamon **58** C 3
Périgueux **56** CD 2
Perm **62** L 4
Pernambuco **111** J 2
Perpignan **56** D 3
Perryville **98** F 4
Persepolis **61** F 3
Persevarancia **110** D 3
Persia **66** EF 4
Persian Gulf → The Gulf
  61 F 4
Perth (Australia) **78** B 5
Perth (U.K.) **52** C 3
Perthus, Col de **56** D 3
Peru **108** C 5
Perugia **57** F 3
Pervomaysk (Ukraine,
  U.S.S.R.) **58** D 1
Pervomayskiy **62** H 3
Pervoural'sk **63** L 4
Pesaro **57** F 3
Pescara **57** F 3
Peschanyy, Mys **66** E 2

Peshawar **67** J 4
Peski Karakumy **66–67** FG 3
Peski Kyzylkum **67** GH 2
Peski Sary Ishikotrau **63** P 6
Peski Taukum **67** JK 2
Pessac **56** C 3
Petaluma **102** B 4
Petare **108** E 1
Petauke **95** E 2
Petén **104** DE 4
Peterborough (Ontario, Can.)
  101 M 7
Peterborough (South
  Australia) **79** F 5
Peter I Island **115**
Petersburg (VA, U.S.A.)
  103 L 4
Petites Pyrénées **56** D 3
Petorca **112** B 5
Petra **88** F 2
Petra Azul **111** H 4
Petrel **115**
Petrila **58** B 1
Petrodvorets **55** J 4
Petrolina **111** H 2
Petropavlovsk **63** NO 4–5
Petropavlovsk-Kamchatskiy
  69 ST 5
Petrópolis **111** H 5
Petrova Gora **57** G 2
Petrovsk **62** J 5
Petrovsk-Zabaykal'skiy **68** J 5
Petrozavodsk **62** FG 3
Peureulak **74** A 3
Pevek **114**
Pforzheim **53** E 5
Phalodi **72** B 2
Phaltan **72** BC 4
Phatthalung **73** H 6
Phenix City **103** J 5
Phet Buri **73** G 5
Philadelphia **103** M 4
Philae **88** E 4
Philippines **75** G 1
Philippine Trench **75** G 1–2
Phillipsburg **102** G 4
Phitsanulok **73** H 4
Phnom Aural **74** B 1
Phnom Penh **73** H 5
Phoenix **102** D 5
Phoenix Islands **82** D 3
Phuket **73** G 6
Phuoc Le **73** J 5
Phu Set **73** J 4
Phu Vinh **73** J 5–6
Piacenza **57** EF 2–3
Piara Açu **109** H 5
Piatra Neamţ **58** C 1
Piauí **111** H 2
Pibor Post **92** E 3
Picardie **56** D 2
Pic Boby **95** H 4
Pichanal **110** D 5
Pichilemu **113** B 5
Pickle Lake **100** J 5
Pico Cristóbal Colón **108** D 1
Pico de Aneto **56** D 3
Pico Rondón **109** F 3

Picos **111** H 2
Pico Tamacuarí **108** E 3
Pidurutalagala **72** D 6
Piedras Negras **104** B 2
Piedra Sola **112** E 5
Pielinen **54** J 3
Pierre **102** FG 3
Piešť'ány **53** G 5
Pietarsaari **54** H 3
Pietermaritzburg **94** DE 5
Pietersburg **94** D 4
Pigué **113** D 6
Pihtipudas **54** J 3
Pikelot **82** A 2
Pikhtovka **63** Q 4
Pik Kommunizma **67** J 3
Pik Pobedy **67** KL 2
Piła **53** G 4
Pilão Arcado **111** H 3
Pilar (Alagoas, Brazil) **111** J 2
Pilar (Paraguay) **112** E 4
Pilcomayo **110** DE 5
Pilot Peak **102** D 3
Pil'tun **69** Q 5
Pim **63** O 3
Pimenta Bueno **110** D 3
Pimental **109** G 4
Pimentel **108** B 5
Pinaki **83** F 4
Pinar del Rio **104** EF 3
Pindaíba **111** F 3
Pindaré Mirim **109** J 4
Pindhos Óros **58** B 2–3
Pine Bluff **103** H 5
Pine Island Bay **115**
Pine Pass **99** N 4
Pinerolo **57** E 2–3
Pinetown **95** E 5
Pingdingshan **70** FG 4
Pingdu **71** H 3
Pingelap **82** B 2
Pingle **70** EF 6
Pingliang **70** E 3
Pingluo **70** E 3
Pingquan **71** G 2
Pingtung **71** H 6
Pingwu **70** DE 4
Pingxiang (China) **70** E 6
Pingxiang (Jiangxi, China)
  70 F 5
Pingyang **71** H 5
Pingyao **70** F 3
Pinheiro **109** J 4
Pinnaroo **79** G 6
Pinrang **75** E 4
Pins, Ile des **82** C 4
Pinsk **55** J 5
Pinyug **62** J 3
Piotrków Trybunalski **53** G 4
Piracicaba **111** G 5
Piracuruca **111** H 1
Piraiévs **58** B 3
Pirapora **111** H 4
Pires do Río **111** G 4
Pirin **58** B 2
Piripiri **111** H 1
Pirot **58** B 2
Piru **75** G 4

Pisa **57** F 3
Pisac **110** B 3
Pisagua **110** B 4
Pisco **110** A 3
Písek **53** F 5
Pishan **67** K 3
Pitalito **108** C 3
Pitcairn **83** G 4
Piteå **54** H 2
Piteşti **58** B 2
Pit-Gorodoko **68** FG 4
Pitkyaranta **54** K 3
Pitt **82** D 5
Pittsburgh **103** L 3
Pium **111** G 3
Pjórsá **54** B 3
Placentia Bay **101** QR 6
Placetas **105** G 3
Plaine des Flandres **56** D 1
Planalto Central **111** G 4
Planalto do Brasil **111** H 4
Planalto do Mato Grosso
  110–111 EF 3–4
Plasencia **56** B 3–4
Plateau de Millevaches **56** D 2
Plateau du Djado **91** G 1
Plateau du Tademaït **87** F 3
Plateau Laurentien **101** NQ 5
Plateau of Tibet **72** DE 1
Plateaux **91** GH 6
Plateaux de la Marche **56** D 2
Plato Ustyurt **66** EF 2
Platte River **102** FG 3
Plaza Huincul **113** C 6
Pleasanton **102** G 6
Pleiku **73** J 5
Plentywood **102** EF 2
Pleven **58** BC 2
Ploče **57** G 3
Płock **53** GH 4
Ploieşti **58** C 2
Plovdiv **58** B 2
Plymouth **52** C 4
Plzeň **53** F 5
Po **57** F 3
Pobedy, Pik **67** KL 2
Pocatello **102** D 3
Pocklington Reef **81** G 4
Poconé **110** E 4
Poços de Caldas **111** G 5
Podgornoye **63** Q 4
Podgornyy **69** R 6
Podol'sk **62** G 4
Podosinovets **62** J 3
Podresovo **63** N 4
Pod'yelanka **68** H 4
Pofadder **94** BC 5
Pogibi **69** Q 5
Pohjanmaa **54** J 3
Poinsett, Cape **115**
Point Arena **102** B 4
Point Barrow **98** FG 1
Point Conception **102** B 5
Point Culver **78** D 5
Point D'Entrecasteaux
  78 AB 5
Pointe-à-Pitre **105** K 4
Pointe de Grave **56** C 2

Pointe de Penmarch **56** BC 2
Pointe Louis-XIV **101** L 5
Pointe Noire **91** G 6
Point Hope **98** D 2
Point Lake **99** P 2
Poitiers **56** D 2
Poitou **56** CD 2
Pojeierze Pomorskie **53** G 4
Pojezierze Mazurskie **53** H 4
Pokrovsk **69** N 3
Pola de Siero **56** B 3
Poland **53** G 4
Polar Plateau **115**
Polatlı **59** D 3
Pole of Inaccessibility **115**
Polesie Lubelskie **53** H 4
Polesye **55** J 5
Polgovskoye **63** N 4
Polist' **55** K 4
Pollensa **56** D 4
Polotsk **55** J 4
Polska **53** G 4
Polson **102** D 2
Poltava **62** FG 6
Poluostrov Buzachi **66** F 1
Poluostrov Kamchatka
  69 S 4–5
Poluostrov Kanin **62** HJ 2
Poluostrov Kol'skiy **62** G 2
Poluostrov Koni **69** S 4
Poluostrov Rybachiy **54** K 2
Poluostrov Taymyr **68** FH 1
Poluostrov Yamal **63** NO 1
Polyarnik **98** B 2
Polyarnyy Ural **63** MN 2
Polynesia **83** EG 2–4
Pombal **111** J 3
Pomerania **53** FG 4
Pomio **82** B 3
Pommersche Bucht **53** F 4
Pomona **102** C 5
Pompei **57** F 3
Pompeyevka **69** O 6
Ponape **82** B 2
Ponca City **103** G 4
Ponce **105** J 4
Pondicherry **72** CD 5
Ponente, Rivera di **57** E 3
Ponferrada **56** B 3
Ponoy **62** H 2
Ponta da Baleia **111** J 4
Ponta Grossa **112** F 4
Ponta Porã **111** EF 5
Ponte Nova **111** H 5
Pontevedra **56** B 3
Pontianak **74** C 4
Pontine Mountains **59** EF 2
Poochera **78** E 5
Pool **91** H 6
Poole **52** C 4
Poopó **110** C 4
Poopó, Lago de **110** C 4
Poorman **98** F 3
Popayán **108** C 3
Poplar Bluff **103** H 4
Popokabaka **92** B 6
Popondetta **80** E 3

Porangatu **111** FG 3
Porbandar **72** A 3
Porco **110** C 4
Pori **54** H 3
Porirua **81** R 9
Porjus **54** H 2
Porlamar **109** F 1
Porpoise Bay **115**
Porsangerhalvöya **54** HJ 1
Porsgrunn **55** EF 4
Portage la-Prairie **99** S 5
Port Alberni **99** N 6
Port Alice **99** M 5
Port Arthur (Tasmania,
  Austr.) **80** L 9
Port Arthur (TX, U.S.A.)
  103 H 6
Port Augusta **79** F 5
Port au Prince **105** H 4
Port Blair **73** F 5
Port Blandford **101** R 6
Port Darwin (Falkland Is.,
  U.K.) **113** E 9
Port Darwin (N.T., Austr.)
  78 DE 1
Port Elizabeth **94** D 6
Port Gentil **91** F 6
Port Harcourt **91** F 4–5
Port Hardy **99** M 5
Port Hedland **78** B 3
Port Hope Simpson **101** QR 5
Port Huron **103** K 3
Portile de Fier **58** B 2
Port Keats **78** DE 1
Port Láirge **52** B 4
Portland (ME, U.S.A.) **103** N 3
Portland (OR, U.S.A.) **102** B 2
Portland (Victoria, Austr.)
  79 G 6
Portlaoise **52** B 4
Port Lincoln **79** F 5
Port Loko **90** B 4
Port-Louis **95** K 6
Port Moller **98** E 4
Port Moresby **80** E 3
Port Nelson **99** T 4
Port Nolloth **94** B 5
Port-Nouveau-Québec
  101 OP 4
Pôrto Alegre **112** FG 5
Porto Amboim **94** A 2
Pôrto Artur **111** F 3
Pôrto de Moz **109** H 4
Pôrto Esperidião **110** E 4
Port of Spain **109** F 1
Pôrto Grande **109** H 3
Pôrto Jofre **110** E 4
Pörtom **54** H 3
Pôrto Murtinho **110** E 5
Pôrto Nacional **111** G 3
Porto Novo **90** E 4
Pôrto Santana **109** H 4
Pôrto Santo **86** B 2
Pôrto Seguro **111** J 4
Pôrto Valter **108** D 5
Porto-Vecchio **57** E 3
Pôrto Velho **109** F 5
Portoviejo **108** BC 4

Portree **52** B 3
Port Said **60** A 3
Port Saint Johns **94** DE 6
Port Saunders **101** Q 5
Portsmouth (N.H., U.S.A.)
  103 MN 3
Portsmouth (OH, U.S.A.)
  103 K 4
Portsmouth (U.K.) **52** C 4
Portsmouth (VA, U.S.A.)
  103 L 4
Portugal **56** B 3
Portugalete **56** C 3
Port Wakefield **79** F 5
Porvenir **113** BC 9
Posadas **112** E 4
Posht-e Badam **61** G 2
Positos **110** D 5
Posse **111** G 3
Postavy **55** J 4
Poste-de-la-Baleine **101** M 4
Poste Maurice Cortier **87** F 4
Postmasburg **94** C 5
Posto Cunambo **108** CD 4
Potapovo **63** R 2
Potenza **57** G 3
Potgietersrus **94** D 4
Poti (Gruziya, U.S.S.R.) **59** F 2
Potiskum **91** G 3
Potosi **110** C 4
Potrerillos **112** BC 4
Potsdam **53** F 4
Pou Bia **73** H 4
Povenets **62** F 3
Póvoa de Varzim **56** B 3
Powell, Lake **102** D 4
Požarevac **58** B 2
Poza Rica de Hidalgo **104** C 3
Poznan **53** G 4
Pozo Almonte **110** C 5
Prado **111** J 4
Prague **53** FG 4–5
Praha **53** FG 4–5
Praia **90** B 7
Prainha **109** FG 5
Praslin **93** K 5
Prato **57** F 3
Praya **74** E 5
Prepansko jezero **58** B 2
Presidencia Roque Sáenz-
  Peña **112** D 4
Presidente Dutra **111** H 2
Presidente Prudente **111** F 5
Presnogor'kovka **63** N 5
Preston **52** C 4
Pretoria **94** D 5
Priazovskaya Vozvyshennost'
  59 E 1
Pribilof Islands **98** D 4
Příbram **53** F 5
Prichernomorskaya
  Nizmennost' **59** D 1
Prieska **94** C 5
Prikaspiyskaya Nizmennost
  66 DE 1
Prikubanskaya Nizmennost'
  59 E 1
Prilep **58** B 2

Priluki **62** H 3
Primavera **115**
Primeira Cruz **111** H 1
Primorsk **55** J 3
Primorsko-Akhtarsk **59** E 1
Prince Albert **99** Q 5
Prince Albert Mountains **115**
Prince Albert National Park
  99 Q 5
Prince Albert Peninsula
  99 O 1
Prince Albert Sound **99** OP 1
Prince Charles Island
  101 LM 2
Prince Charles Mountains **115**
Prince Edward Island
  (Canada) **101** P 6
Prince Edward Islands
  (Antarctica) **115**
Prince George **99** N 5
Prince of Wales Island (AK,
  U.S.A.) **98** L 4
Prince of Wales Island
  (Canada) **99** S 1
Prince of Wales Island
  (Queensland, Austr.) **79** G 1
Prince of Wales Strait **99** O 1
Prince Patrick Island **114**
Prince Rupert **98** L 5
Princess Astrid Coast **115**
Princess Charlotte Bay **79** G 1
Princess Martha Coast **115**
Princess Ragnhild Coast **115**
Princess Royal Island **98** M 5
Prince William Sound **98** H 3
Príncipe **91** F 5
Pripet Marshes **55** J 5
Pripyat' **55** J 5
Pristina **58** B 2
Prizren **58** B 2
Prokhladnyy **59** F 2
Prokhorkino **63** P 4
Prokop'yevsk **63** R 5
Proliv Karskiye Vorota
  62–63 L 1
Proliv Nevel'skogo **69** Q 5
Prome **73** G 4
Promontoire Portland
  101 LM 4
Promontorio del Gargano
  57 G 3
Propria **111** J 3
Protochnoye **63** N 3
Provence **57** E 3
Providence **103** M 3
Providence, Cape **80** P 10
Provideniya **98** C 3
Prudhoe Bay **98** H 1
Prut **58** C 1
Prydz Bay **115**
Przheval'sk **67** K 2
Pshish **59** E 2
Pskov **55** J 4
Pskovskoye Ozero **55** J 4
Ptich **55** J 5
Pucallpa **108** D 5
Pucheng **71** G 5
Pudasjärvi **54** J 2

Puebla **104** C 4
Pueblo **102** F 4
Pueblo Hundido **112** C 4
Puelches **113** CD 6
Puente Alto **112** BC 5
Puente-Genil **56** C 4
Puerto Aisén **113** B 8
Puerto Angel **104** C 4
Puerto Asis **108** C 3
Puerto Ayacucho **108** E 2
Puerto Baquerizo Moreno **108** B 6
Puerto Barrios **104** E 4
Puerto Cabello **108** E 1
Puerto Cabezas **104** F 5
Puerto Carreño **108** E 2
Puerto Chicama **108** BC 5
Puerto Coig **113** C 9
Puerto Colombia **108** C 1
Puerto Cortés **104** E 4
Puerto Cumarebo **108** E 1
Puerto Deseado **113** CD 8
Puerto de Somport **56** C 3
Puerto de Villatoro **56** B 3
Puerto Escondido **104** C 4
Puerto Esperanza **112** F 4
Puerto Estrella **108** D 1
Puerto Heath **110** C 3
Puerto Juárez **104** E 3
Puerto la Cruz **109** F 1
Puerto Leguizamo **108** D 4
Puerto Lempira **104** F 4
Puerto Limón **108** D 3
Puertollano **56** C 4
Puerto Madryn **113** C 7
Puerto Magdalena **102** D 7
Puerto Maldonado **110** C 3
Puerto Montt **113** B 7
Puerto Natales **113** B 9
Puerto Nuevo **108** E 2
Puerto Padilla **110** B 3
Puerto Páez **108** E 2
Puerto Patillos **110** B 5
Puerto Patiño **110** C 4
Puerto Plata **105** HJ 4
Puerto Portillo **108** D 5
Puerto Princesa **75** E 2
Puerto Rico (Argentina) **112** F 4
Puerto Rico (U.S.A.) **105** J 4
Puerto Rondón **108** D 2
Puerto Siles **110** C 3
Puerto Suárez **110** E 4
Puerto Vallarta **104** AB 3
Puerto Varas **113** B 7
Puerto Verlarde **110** D 4
Puerto Villamizar **108** D 2
Puerto Villazón **110** D 3
Puerto Wilches **108** D 2
Puerto Williams **113** BC 9–10
Pugachev **62** JK 5
Pukapuka (Cook Is.) **82** DE 3
Pukapuka (French Polynesia) **83** F 3
Pukaruha **83** FG 4
Pukatawagan **99** RS 4
Pukch'ŏng **71** J 2
Puksoozero **62** H 3

Pula **57** F 3
Pulap **82** A 2
Pulau Alor **75** F 5
Pulau Bacan **75** G 4
Pulau Bangka **74** C 4
Pulau Belitung **74** C 4
Pulau Biak **75** J 4
Pulau Bintan **74** B 3
Pulau Enggano **74** B 5
Pulau Jos Sodarso **75** J 5
Pulau Kabaena **75** F 5
Pulau Kai Besar **75** H 5
Pulau Karakelong **75** G 3
Pulau Kobroor **75** H 5
Pulau Labengke **75** F 4
Pulau Laut **74** E 4
Pulau Lomblen **75** F 5
Pulau Madura **74** D 5
Pulau Mangole **75** G 4
Pulau Misool **75** H 4
Pulau Morotai **75** G 3
Pulau Muna **75** F 5
Pulau Nias **74** A 3
Pulau Numfor **75** H 4
Pulau Padang **74** B 3
Pulau Roti **75** F 6
Pulau Salawati **75** H 4
Pulau Selaru **75** H 5
Pulau Selayar **75** F 5
Pulau Siberut **74** A 4
Pulau Simeulue **74** A 3
Pulau Taliabu **75** F 4
Pulau Trangan **75** H 5
Pulau Waigeo **75** H 3
Pulau Wetar **75** G 5
Pulau Wokam **75** H 5
Pulau Yamdena **75** H 5
Pulau Yapen **75** J 4
Pulawy **53** H 4
Pullman **102** C 2
Pulog, Mount **75** J 1
Pulozero **54** K 2
Pulusuk **82** A 2
Puna de Atacama **110** C 5–6
Puncak Jaya **75** J 4
Pune **72** B 4
Punjab **67** J 4
Punkaharju **54** J 3
Puno **110** B 4
Punta Alta **113** D 6
Punta Arenas **113** B 9
Punta Desengaño **113** C 8
Punta Eugenia **102** C 6
Punta Fijo **108** D 1
Punta Gallinas **108** D 1
Punta Gorda (Belize) **104** E 4
Punta Gorda (Nicaragua) **104** F 5
Punta Mariato **108** B 2
Punta Medanosa **113** CD 8
Punta Negra **108** B 5
Punta Pariñas **108** B 4
Punta Prieta **102** D 6
Puntarenas **104** EF 6
Punta Rieles **110** E 5
Puqi **70** F 5
Pur **63** P 2
Purdy Islands **82** A 3

Purnia **72** E 2
Purus **109** F 4
Puruvesi **54** J 3
Pusan **71** JK 3
Pushchino **69** T 5
Pushkin **55** K 4
Pushkino **62** J 5
Pustoretsk **69** U 3
Putao **73** G 2
Putorana, Gory **68** FH 2
Putumayo **108** D 4
Puulavesi **54** J 3
Puyang **70** G 3
Puy de Sancy **56** D 2
Puyo **108** C 4
Pweto **92** D 6
Pyaozero, Ozero **54** K 2
Pyatigorsk **57** E 2
Pyatistennoy **69** TU 2
Pyawbwe **73** G 3
Pyhäjoki **54** HJ 3
Pyhätunturi **54** J 2
Pyinmana **73** G 4
P'yŏngyang **71** HJ 3
Pyrénées **56** CD 3
Pyshchug **62** J 4

Q

Qābis **87** H 2
Qā'emshahr **61** F 1
Qafşah **87** G 2
Qagcaka **72** D 1
Qahremānshahr **61** E 2
Qaidam Pendi **70** BC 3
Qala-Nau **67** G 3
Qālat **67** H 4
Qal'at Dizah **61** D 1
Qal'at Şāliḥ **61** E 3
Qal'at Sukkar **61** E 3
Qalib ash Shuyūkh **61** E 3
Qamalung **70** CD 4
Qamdo **70** C 4
Qaminis **87** J 2
Qanāt as Suways **60** A 3
Qapqal **67** L 2
Qarah Dagh **59** F 3
Qardo **93** H 3
Qasr-e Shīrīn **61** DE 2
Qaşr Farāfirah **88** D 3
Qatar **61** F 4
Qatrūyeh **61** G 3
Qāyen **66** F 4
Qayyārah **60** D 2
Qazvīn **66** DE 3
Qeshm **61** G 4
Qeshm **61** G 4
Qeys **61** F 4
Qezel Owzan **61** E 1
Qezi'ot **60** B 3
Qian'an **71** H 2
Qiaowan **70** C 2
Qidong **71** H 4
Qiemo **67** M 3
Qift **60** A 4
Qijiang **70** E 5
Qijiaojing **70** B 2
Qila Saifullah **67** H 4
Qilian Shan **70** CD 3

Qimen **71** G 5
Qinā **60** A 4
Qina, Wādi **60** A 4
Qingdao **71** H 3
Qinggang **71** HJ 1
Qinghai **70** C 3
Qinghai Hu **70** D 3
Qingjiang (Jiangsu, China) **71** GH 4
Qingjiang (Jiangxi, China) **70** FG 5
Qing Zang Gaoyuan **72** DE 1
Qinhuangdao **71** GH 3
Qinling Shan **70** E 4
Qinzhou **70** E 6
Qionghai **70** F 7
Qionglai **70** D 4
Qiqiar **68** M 5
Qiqihar **69** MN 6
Qira **67** L 3
Qirjat Yam (Israel) **60** B 2
Qitai **70** AB 2
Qitaihe **71** K 1
Qiyang **70** F 5
Qog Ui **71** G 2
Qolleh-ye Damāvand **61** F 2
Qom **61** F 2
Qomsheh **61** F 2–3
Qorud, Kuhha-ye **61** F 2–3
Qoşbeh-ye Naşşār **61** E 3
Qotbābād **61** G 4
Quang Ngai **73** J 4
Quanhov **70** E 5
Quan Phu Quoc **73** H 5
Quanzhou **71** GH 6
Qu'Appelle **99** R 5
Quartu Sant' Elena **57** E 4
Qūchān **66** F 3
Québec **101** MO 5
Québec **101** N 6
Quebracho Coto **112** D 4
Queen Charlotte Islands **98** KL 5
Queen Charlotte Sound **98** LM 5
Queen Elizabeth Islands **114**
Queen Fabiola Mountains **115**
Queen Mary Coast **115**
Queen Maud Gulf **99** R 2
Queen Maud Land **115**
Queen Maud Mountains **115**
Queensland **79** GH 3
Queenstown (South Africa) **94** D 6
Queenstown (Tasmania, Austr.) **80** L 9
Quelimane **95** F 3
Quembo **94** B 2
Que Que **94** D 3
Querétaro **104** BC 3
Queshan **70** F 4
Quesnel **99** N 5
Quetta **67** H 4
Quevedo **108** C 4
Quezaltenango **104** DE 5
Quibala **94** B 2
Quibdó **108** C 2

Quiçama National Park 94 A 1–2
Quiculungo 94 B 1
Quillabamba 110 B 3
Quillacollo 110 C 4
Quillaicillo 112 B 5
Quillota 112 B 5
Quilon 72 C 6
Quimilí 112 D 4
Quimper 56 C 2
Quincy 103 H 4
Quines 112 C 5
Qui Nhon 73 JK 5
Quintana Roo 104 E 3–4
Quito 108 C 4
Quixadá 111 J 1
Qujing 70 D 5
Qulansiyah 93 J 2
Qulbān Layyah 61 E 3
Qurnat aş Şawdā' 60 B 2
Qūs 60 A 4
Qusaybah 66 C 4
Qusum 70 B 5
Qu Xian 71 GH 5

R

Raab 57 G 2
Raahe 54 H 3
Rába (Hungary) 58 A 1
Raba (Indonesia) 75 E 5
Rabak 88 E 6
Rabat 86 D 2
Rabaul 82 B 3
Rabyānah 87 K 4
Rach Gia 73 HJ 5–6
Racine 103 J 3
Radhanpur 72 B 3
Radisson 101 M 5
Radom 53 H 4
Radomsko 53 G 4
Rae 99 O 3
Ra's-e Nāy Band 61 F 4
Raevavae 83 F 4
Rafaela 112 D 5
Rafah 60 B 3
Rafha' 60 D 3
Rafsanjān 61 G 3
Raga 92 D 3
Rahimyar Khan 67 J 5
Raiatea 83 E 4
Raichur 72 C 4
Raiganj 72 E 2
Raigarh 72 D 3
Rainbow Peak 102 C 3
Rainier, Mount 102 B 2
Rainy Lake 100 J 6
Raipur 72 D 3
Rajada 111 H 2
Rajahmundry 72 D 4
Rajakoski 54 J 2
Rajapalaiyam 72 C 6
Rajasthan 72 BC 2
Rajgarh 72 C 3
Rajkot 72 AB 3
Raj Nandgaon 72 D 3
Rajshahi 72 E 3
Rakahanga 82 E 3
Rakitnoye 55 J 5

Rakulka 62 HJ 3
Raleigh 103 L 4
Ralik Chain 82 C 2
Ramādah 87 H 2
Ramapo Deep 65 R 6
Ramea 101 Q 6
Rāmhormoz 61 E 3
Ramlat Hagolan 60 B 2
Ramlat Rabyānah 87 JK 4
Rampur 72 CD 2
Ramree 73 F 4
Ramsgate 52 D 4
Rancagua 112 B 5
Ranchi 72 DE 3
Randers 55 F 4
Randijaure 54 G 2
Rangoon 73 FG 4
Rangpur 72 E 2
Rankin Inlet 99 T 3
Rann of Kutch 72 AB 3
Rantauprapat 74 AB 3
Ranua 54 J 2
Raoul 82 D 4
Rapa 83 F 4
Rapa Nui 83 H 4
Rapid City 102 F 3
Raraka 83 F 4
Rarotonga 83 E 4
Ra's Abū Madd 60 B 4
Ra's Abū Qumayyis 61 F 4
Ra's al Abyad 60 BC 5
Ra's al Abyad 87 G 1
Ra's al Khafji 61 E 3
Ra's al Khaymah 61 G 4
Ra's al Madrakah 89 K 5
Ra's al Mish'āb 61 E 3
Ra's ash Shaykh 60 B 3
Ra's Asir 93 J 2
Ra's as Saffānīyah 61 E 3
Ra's aţ Ţīb 87 H 1
Ra's az Zawr 61 E 4
Ra's Ba'labakk 60 B 2
Ra's Banās 60 B 5
Ra's Barīdī 60 B 4
Ras Dashan 93 F 2
Ra's Fartak 89 J 5
Ra's Ghārib 60 A 3
Ra's Hāfūn 93 J 2
Rasht 66 D 3
Raskoh 67 GH 5
Ra's Mişrātah 87 J 2
Ra's Muhammad 60 B 4
Rasshua, Ostrov 69 S 6
Rasskazovo 62 H 5
Rastigaissa 54 J 1
Råstojaure 54 H 2
Ratak Chain 82 C 2
Ratangarh 72 B 2
Rat Buri 73 G 5
Rat Islands 98 A 5
Ratlam 72 BC 3
Ratnagiri 72 B 4
Ratnapura 72 D 6
Ratta 63 Q 3
Raufarhöfn 54 BC 2
Raukela 72 DE 3
Raúl Leoni, Represa 109 F 2
Rauma 54 H 3

Raupelyan 98 C 2
Ravahere 83 F 4
Ravänsar 61 E 2
Rāvar 61 G 3
Ravenna 57 F 3
Ravenshoe 79 GH 2
Rāwah 66 C 4
Rawaki 82 D 3
Rawalpindi 67 J 4
Rawāndūz 66 C 3
Rawlinna 78 D 5
Rawlins 102 E 3
Rawson 113 D 7
Raychikhinsk 69 NO 6
Raymond 102 B 2
Rāzān 61 E 2
Razdan 59 F 2
Razgrad 58 C 2
Ré, Ile de 56 C 2
Reading 52 C 4
Real, Cordillera 108 C 4
Realico 112 D 5
Reao 83 G 4
Rebbenesöy 54 G 1
Rebecca, Lake 78 C 5
Reboly 62 F 3
Recife 111 K 2
Récifs d'Entrecasteaux 82 B 4
Reconquista 112 DE 4
Red Bluff 102 B 3
Red Deer 99 P 5
Red Deer River 99 P 5
Redding 102 B 3
Redenção da Gurguéia 111 H 2
Red Lake 100 J 5
Redoubt Volcano 98 G 3
Red River (LA, U.S.A.) 103 H 5
Red River (MN, U.S.A.) 103 G 2
Red Sea 60 B 4
Red Sea 89 FG 4–5
Red Water 99 P 5
Reef Islands 82 BC 3
Regensburg 53 F 5
Reggane 86 EF 3
Reggio di Calabria 57 G 4
Reggio nell'Emilia 57 EF 3
Reghin 58 B 1
Regina (Brazil) 109 H 3
Regina (Canada) 99 R 5
Registan 67 GH 4
Rehoboth 94 B 4
Reims 56 D 2
Reina Adelaida, Archipiélago de la 113 A 9
Reindeer Lake 99 R 4
Reinoksfjellet 54 G 2
Reitoru 83 F 4
Rekinniki 69 U 3
Reliance 99 Q 3
Remansão 109 HJ 4
Remanso 111 H 2
Rembang 74 D 5
Renascença 108 E 4
Renfrew 101 M 6
Rengo 112 B 5
Rennell 81 H 4

Rennes 56 C 2
Rennie Lake 99 Q 3
Reno 102 BC 4
Renton 102 B 2
Replot 54 H 3
Represa Raúl Leoni 109 F 2
Republic of Ireland 52 B 4
Republic of South Africa 94 BD 6
Repulse Bay 99 U 2
Requena 108 D 5
Réservoir Baskatong 101 MN 6
Réservoir Cabonga 101 M 6
Réservoir Decelles 101 M 6
Réservoir Gouin 101 MN 6
Réservoir Pipmouacan 101 N 6
Reshteh-ye Kūhhā-ye Alborz 61 F 1
Resistencia 112 DE 4
Reşiţa 58 B 1
Resolution Island 101 P 3
Réunion 95 HK 6
Reus 56 D 3
Revilla Gigedo Islands 97 G 8
Rewari 72 C 2
Rey 61 F 2
Reykjahlð 54 B 2
Reykjanes 54 A 3
Reykjavik 54 A 3
Reynosa 104 C 2
Rezé 56 C 2
Rēzekne 55J 4
Rhein 52 E 4
Rhinelander 103 J 2
Rhinmal 72 B 2
Rhodes 58 C 3
Rhodope Mts 58 BC 2
Rhondda 52 C 4
Rhône 57 D 3
Rías Altas 56 B 3
Rías Bajas 56 B 3
Riau, Kepulauan 74 B 3
Ribeirão Prêto 111 G 5
Riberalta 110 C 3
Richard's Bay 95 E 5
Richland 102 C 2
Richmond (Queensland, Austr.) 79 G 3
Richmond (VA, U.S.A.) 103 L 4
Richmond Hill 101 LM 7
Riding Mountain National Park 99 RS 5
Rietavas 55H 4
Riga 55 H 4
Rihand Dam 72 D 3
Riiser-Larsen Ice Shelf 115
Riiser-Larsen Peninsula 115
Rijau 91 F 3
Rijeka 57 F 2
Riley 102 CD 3
Rimatara 83 E 4
Rimini 57 F 3
Rîmnicu Sărat 58 C 1
Rîmnicu Vîlcea 58 B 1–2
Rimouski 101 O 6

Rinchinlhümbe **68** G 5
Rinconada **110** C 5
Ringgold Isles **82** D 4
Ringvassöy **54** G 2
Ríobamba **108** C 4
Rio Branco (Acre, Brazil) **108** E 5
Río Branco (Roraima, Brazil) **109** F 3
Río Bravo del Norte **102** EF 5–6
Río Chico **113** C 8
Río Claro **111** G 5
Río Colorado **113** D 6
Río Cuarto **112** CD 5
Rio das Mortes **111** F 3
Rio de Janeiro **111** H 5
Río de la Plata **112** E 5–6
Rio de Oro **86** BC 4
Río Gallegos **113** C 9
Río Grande (Argentina) **113** C 9
Río Grande (Bahía, Brazil) **111** H 3
Río Grande (Brazil) **111** G 4–5
Río Grande (Río Grande do Sul, Brazil) **112** F 5
Rio Grande (TX, U.S.A.) **102** G 6
Rio Grande de Santiago **104** B 3
Río Grande do Norte **111** J 2
Río Grande do Sul **112** EF 4
Río Grande o'Guapay **110** D 4
Rioja **108** C 5
Río Lagartos **104** E 3
Riom **56** D 2
Río Mulatos **110** C 4
Rio Negro (Argentina) **113** D 6–7
Río Negro (Brazil) **109** F 4
Ríosucio **108** C 2
Río Turbio Mines **113** B 9
Río Verde **111** F 4
Río Verde de Mato Grosso **111** F 4
Rissa **54** E 3
Ritzville **102** C 2
Rivadavia **112** BC 4
Rivas **104** E 5
Rivera (Argentina) **113** D 6
Rivera (Uruguay) **112** E 5
Riverside **102** C 5
Riviera di Levante **57** E 3
Riviera di Ponente **57** E 3
Rivoli **57** E 2
Riwoqê **70** C 4
Riyādh **61** E 4
Rize **59** F 2
Rizhao **71** GH 3
Rizhskiy Zaliv **55** H 4
Rjuven **55** E 4
Rkiz **86** B 5
Roanne **56** D 2
Roan Plateau **102** E 4
Robât-e Khān **61** G 2
Robert Butte **115**
Robinson River **79** F 2

Robore **110** E 4
Robson, Mount **99** NO 5
Rocha **112** F 5
Rocha de Galé, Barragem da **56** B 4
Rochefort **56** C 2
Rocher River **99** P 3
Rocher Thomasset **83** F 3
Rochester (MN, U.S.A.) **103** H 3
Rochester (N.Y., U.S.A.) **103** L 3
Rockefeller Plateau **115**
Rockford **103** J 3
Rockhampton **79** HJ 3
Rock Hill **103** K 5
Rock Island **103** H 3
Rockport **102** B 4
Rock Springs **102** E 3
Rocky Mount **103** L 4
Rocky Mountains **99** MP 4–6
Rodeo **104** B 2
Rodez **56** D 3
Ródhos **58** C 3
Rodina **68** FG 4
Rodney, Cape **80** E 4
Rodopi **58** BC 2
Roebourne **78** B 3
Roebuck Bay **78** C 2
Roes Welcome Sound **99** U 2–3
Rogagua, Lago **110** C 3
Rogaland **55** E 4
Rogers Peak **102** D 4
Rohtak **72** C 2
Rolla **102** G 2
Rolleston **79** H 3
Roma (Italy) **57** F 3
Roma (Queensland, Austr.) **79** H 4
Romaine **101** P 5
Roman **58** C 1
Romania **58** BC 1
Romanovka **68** K 5
Romans-sur-Isère **57** E 2
Rome **102** C 3
Rome (Italy) **57** F 3
Romny **62** F 5
Romsdal **54** E 3
Roncador, Serra do **111** F 3
Ronda **56** C 4
Rondane **56** EF 3
Rondón, Pico **109** F 3
Rondonia (Brazil) **110** D 3
Rondônia (Brazil) **110** D 3
Rondonópolis **111** F 4
Rongan **70** E 5
Ronge, Lac la **99** R 4
Rongelap **82** C 2
Rongerik **82** C 2
Rongjiang **70** E 5
Rong Xian **70** F 6
Rönne **55** F 4
Ronneby **55** G 4
Ronne Ice Shelf **115**
Roosevelt, Mount **99** M 4
Roosevelt Island **115**
Roper River **78** E 1

Roraima (Brazil) **109** F 3
Roraima (Venezuela) **109** F 2
Röros **54** F 3
Rosario (Argentina) **112** D 5
Rosário (Maranhão, Brazil) **111** H 1
Rosario (Mexico) **104** A 3
Rosario, Bahía **102** C 6
Rosario de Lerma **112** C 4
Roseau **105** K 4
Roseburg **102** B 3
Rosenheim **53** F 5
Rosetown **99** Q 5
Rosignol **109** G 2
Roşiori de Vede **58** C 2
Roskilde **55** F 4
Roslavl' **62** F 5
Rossano **57** G 4
Ross Ice Shelf **115**
Ross Island **115**
Rosslare **52** B 4
Rosso **86** B 5
Rossosh **62** GH 5
Ross River **98** L 3
Ross Sea **115**
Rostock **53** F 4
Rostov **62** G 4
Rostov-na-Donu **59** EF 1
Roswell **102** EF 5
Rota **82** A 2
Rothera **115**
Roti, Pulau **75** F 6
Rotorua **81** R 8
Rotterdam **52** D 4
Rotuma **82** C 3
Rouen **56** D 2
Rovaniemi **54** J 2
Rovdino **62** H 3
Rovereto **57** F 2
Rovigo **57** F 2
Rovno **55** J 5
Rowley **101** M 2
Roxas **75** F 1
Roy Hill **78** C 3
Röyrvik **54** F 3
Rozhdestvenskoye **62** J 4
Roztocze **53** H 4
Rtishchevo **62** H 5
Rt Ploča **57** G 3
Ruacana Falls **94** AB 3
Ruaha National Park **92** E 6
Ruapehu **81** R 8
Rubtsovsk **63** Q 5
Ruby **98** G 3
Rudall River National Park **78** C 3
Rudbar **67** G 4–5
Rudnyy **63** M 5
Rufiji **93** F 6
Rufino **112** D 5
Rufisque **90** A 3
Rügen **53** F 4
Ruijin **70** G 5
Rujm al Mudhari **66** B 4
Rumädah **89** G 6
Rum Jungle **78** E 1
Rumphi **95** E 2

Rundu **94** B 3
Rungwa **92** E 6
Ruoqiang **70** A 3
Rupert **101** M 5
Rurrenabaque **110** C 3
Rurutu **83** E 4
Rusakovo **69** U 4
Ruse **58** C 2
Rushan (U.S.S.R.) **67** J 3
Russas **111** J 1
Russkaya (Antarctica) **115**
Russkaya (U.S.S.R.) **71** L 1
Rustavi **59** G 2
Rustenburg **94** D 5
Rutenga **95** E 4
Ruvuma **95** FG 2
Ruwenzori National Park **92** DE 5
Ruzayevka **62** H 5
Ružomberok **53** GH 5
Rwanda **92** DE 5
Ryazan' **62** GH 5
Ryazhsk **62** H 5
Rybachiy, Poluostrov **54** K 2
Rybach'ye **67** K 2
Rybnik **53** G 4
Rybnitsa **58** C 1
Ryn Peski **62** J 6
Ryukyu Islands **71** J 5
Rzeszów **53** H 4

S

Sa'ādatābād **61** F 3
Saalfeld **53** F 4
Saarbrücken **53** E 5
Saaremaa **55** H 4
Saariselkä **54** J 2
Šabac **58** A 2
Sabadell **56** D 3
Sabah **74** E 2
Sabanalarga **108** C 1
Sabaya **110** C 4
Sabhā **87** H 3
Sabinas **104** B 2
Sabkhat al Bardawil **60** A 3
Sable, Cape (Canada) **101** O 7
Sable, Cape (FL., U.S.A.) **103** K 6
Sable Island **101** P 7
Sabonkafi **91** F 3
Sabrina Coast **115**
Sabzevār **66** F 3
Sachsen **53** F 4
Sachs Harbour **99** N 1
Sacramento **102** BC 4
Sacramento Mountains **102** E 5
Sacramento Valley **102** B 3–4
Şa'dah **89** G 5
Sad Bi'Ar **60** B 2
Saddlede **54** F 3
Sa Dec **74** C 1
Sadiya **73** G 2
Sad Kharv **61** G 1
Sadon **66** C 2
Sado-shima **71** L 3
Sæböl **54** A 2
Şafāqis **87** GH 2

Saffāniyah, Ra's as **61** E 3
Safi **86** D 2
Safid, Kūh-e **61** E 2
Safonovo (U.S.S.R.) **62** J 2
Safonovo (U.S.S.R.) **62** F 4
Şafwān **61** E 3
Saga **72** DE 2
Sagaing **73** FG 3
Sagar **72** C 3
Sagastyr **69** N 1
Sage **102** D 3
Saglouc **101** M 3
Sagres **56** B 4
Sagua la Grande **105** G 3
Sagunto **56** C 4
Sagwon **98** GH 2
Sahagún **108** CD 2
Sahara **86–87** HK 4
Saharanpur **72** C 2
Sahiwal **67** J 4
Sahlābad **66** F 4
Saḥraʾ al Hajārah **60–61** D 3
Sahuayo de Diaz **104** B 4
Saʿidābād **61** G 3
Said Bundas **92** CD 3
Saigon **73** JK 5
Saihan Toroi **70** CD 2
Saiki **71** KL 4
Saimaa **54** J 3
Saindak **67** G 5
Sāin Dezh **61** E 1
Saint Alban's **101** QR 6
Saint-André, Cap **95** G 3
Saint Anthony **101** QR 5
Saint Arnaud **79** G 6
St. Austell **52** BC 4
Saint-Brieuc **56** C 2
Saint Cloud **103** GH 2
Saint Croix **105** JK 4
Saint-Denis (France)
  56 D 2
Saint-Denis (Réunion)
  95 HK 6
Saint-Dizier **57** E 2
Saint-Elie **109** H 3
Saintes **56** C 2
Sainte-Thérèse **101** N 6
Saint-Étienne **56** D 2
Saint Francis, Cape **94** CD 6
St. Gallen **57** E 2
Saint George (Queensland,
  Austr.) **79** H 4
Saint George (UT, U.S.A.)
  102 D 4
Saint George, Cape **81** F 2
Saint-Georges **101** NO 6
Saint George's **105** K 5
Saint George's Channel
  (Papua New Guinea)
  81 F 2–3
Saint George's Channel (Un.
  Kingdom) **52** B 4
Saint Helena **84** B 6
Saint Jean **101** N 6
Saint Jérôme **101** N 6
Saint-John **101** O 6
Saint John's (Antigua)
  105 K 4

Saint Johns (AZ, U.S.A.)
  102 E 5
Saint John's (Canada) **101** R 6
Saint Joseph **103** H 4
Saint Kitts-Nevis **105** K 4
Saint Lawrence Island **98** C 3
Saint Lawrence River **101** O 6
Saint Léonard **101** O 6
Saint Louis (MO, U.S.A.)
  103 HJ 4
Saint-Louis (Senegal) **90** A 2
Saint Lucia **105** K 5
Saint Lucia, Lake **95** E 5
Saint-Malo **56** C 2
Saint Marys **80** L 9
St. Marys (AK, U.S.A.) **98** E 3
Saint Matthias Group **81** EF 2
St. Moritz **57** F 2
Saint-Nazaire **56** C 2
Saint Paul (MN, U.S.A.)
  103 H 3
Saint-Paul (Réunion) **95** HK 6
St. Peter and St. Paul Rocks
  107 G 2
Saint Petersburg **103** K 6
Saint Pierre et Miquelon
  101 Q 6
Saint-Quentin **56** D 1–2
Saint-Thomas **101** L 7
Saint Vincent **105** K 5
Saint Vincent, Gulf **79** F 6
Saint Vincent Passage
  105 K 5
Saipan **82** A 1
Sajama, Nevado **110** C 4
Sakākah **60** C 3
Sakami, Lac **101** M 5
Sakaraha **95** G 4
Sakarya **58** D 2
Sakata **71** L 3
Săkevare **54** G 2
Sakhalin **69** QR 5
Sakhalinskiy Zaliv **69** Q 5
Sakht Sar **61** F 1
Saksaulʾskiy **67** G 1
Salaca **55** HJ 4
Salada **104** B 2
Salado **112** D 4
Salado **113** C 6
Salaga **90** D 4
Salālah **89** J 5
Salamá **104** D 4
Salamanca **56** B 3
Salamat **91** J 3
Salar de Atacama **110** C 5
Salar de Uyuni **110** C 5
Salavat **62** KL 5
Salaverry **108** C 5
Salawati, Pulau **75** H 4
Sala y Gómes **83** H 4
Saldanha **94** B 6
Sale (Australia) **79** H 6
Salé (Morocco) **86** D 2
Şālehābād **61** E 2
Salekhard **63** N 2
Salem (India) **72** C 5
Salem (OR, U.S.A.) **102** B 3
Salerno **57** F 3

Saletekri **72** D 3
Salida **102** E 4
Salihli **58** C 3
Salina (KS, U.S.A.) **102** G 4
Salina (UT, U.S.A.) **102** D 4
Salinas (CA, U.S.A.) **102** B 4
Salinas (Ecuador) **108** B 4
Salinas de Hidalgo **104** B 3
Salinas Grandes **112** CD 4–5
Salinópolis **109** J 4
Salisbury **101** MN 3
Salling **55** E 4
Salluyo, Nevado **110** C 3
Salmas **59** F 3
Salmon Mountains **102** B 3
Salon-de-Provence **57** E 3
Salonga National Park **92** C 5
Salonica **58** B 2
Salpausselkä **54** J 3
Salʾsk **59** F 4
Salso **57** F 4
Salta **110** CD 5
Saltdalselva **54** G 2
Saltillo **104** B 2–3
Salt Lake **79** F 3
Salt Lake City **102** D 3
Salto **112** E 5
Salt Range **67** J 4
Salumbar **72** B 3
Salvador **111** J 3
Salwā **61** F 4
Salwā Bahri **60** A 4
Salween **73** G 4
Salzach **57** F 2
Salzburg **57** F 2
Salzgitter **53** F 4
Samagaltay **68** G 5
Samak, Tanjung **74** C 4
Samangan **67** H 3
Samar **75** G 1
Samarkand **67** H 3
Sämarrā' **60** D 2
Samarskoye **63** Q 6
Samaúma **108** E 5
Sambaliung **74–75** E 3
Sambalpur **72** DE 3
Sambava **95** J 2
Sambor **74** C 1
Sambor (Russia, U.S.S.R.)
  53 H 5
S. Ambrosio Island **107** C 5
Samfya **94** DE 2
Samka **73** G 3
Sam Neua **73** H 3
Samoa Islands **82** D 3
Samokov **58** B 2
Sámos **58** C 3
Samothraki **58** C 2
Sampit **74** D 4
Samsang **72** D 1
Samsun **59** E 2
Samthar **72** C 2
Samusʾ **63** QR 4
Samut Prakan **73** H 5
Samut Songkhram **73** H 5
Sanʾaʾ **89** GH 5
Sanae **115**
Sanaga **91** G 5

Sanandaj **61** E 2
San Andrés **105** F 5
San Andrés Tuxtla **104** CD 4
San Angelo **102** F 5
San Antonia de Cortés
  104 E 4–5
San Antonio (Chile) **112** B 5
San Antonio (TX., U.S.A.)
  102 G 6
San Antonio, Cabo
  (Argentina) **113** E 6
San Antonio, Cabo (Cuba)
  104 EF 3
San Antonio Oeste **113** D 7
Sanâw **89** J 5
San Bernardino **102** C 5
San Bernardo **112** BC 5
San Borja **110** C 3
San Carlos (Nicaragua) **104** F 5
San Carlos (Philippines)
  75 F 1
San Carlos de Bariloche
  113 BC 7
San Carlos del Zulia **108** D 2
San Casme **112** E 4
San Cristóbal (Argentina)
  112 D 5
San Cristóbal (Dominican
  Rep.) **105** HJ 4
San Cristobal (Solomon Is.)
  81 H 4
San Cristóbal (Venezuela)
  108 D 2
San Cristóbal, Isla **108** B 6
San Cristóbal de las Casas
  104 D 4
Sancti Spíritus **105** G 3
Sandakan **74** E 2
Sandaré **90** B 3
Sand Hills **102** F 3
San Diego **102** C 5
San Diego, Cabo **113** C 9
San Dimitri Point **57** F 4
Sandnes **55** DE 4
Sandnesssjöen **54** F 2
Sandoa **92** C 6
Sandon **59** F 2
San Dona di Piave **57** F 2
Sandoy **52** A 1
Sandviken **55** G 3
Sandykachi **67** G 3
Sandy Lake **100** J 5
San Felípe (Chile) **112** B 5
San Felípe (Colombia) **108** E 3
San Felipe (Venezuela)
  108 E 1
San Fernando (Chile) **113** B 5
San Fernando (Mexico)
  104 C 3
San Fernando (Spain) **56** B 4
San Fernando (Trinidad and
  Tobago) **109** F 1
San Fernando de Apure
  108 E 2
San Fernando de Atabapo
  108 E 3
San Francisco (Argentina)
  112 D 5

San Francisco (CA., U.S.A.) **102** B 4
San Francisco, Paso de **112** C 4
San Francisco del Rincón **104** B 3
San Francisco de Macorís **105** HJ 4
Sangar **69** N 3
Sangatolon **69** R 3
Sangha **91** GH 5
Sangihe, Kepulauan **75** G 3
Sangli **72** BC 4
San Gregorio **113** B 9
Sanhe **68** M 5
San Ignacio (Bolivia) **110** C 3
San Ignacio (Paraguay) **112** E 4
Sanikiluaq **101** M 4
San Isidro **112** DE 5
San Jacinto **108** C 2
San Javier **110** D 4
Sanjawi **67** H 4
San Joaquín **110** D 3
San Joaquin River **102** BC 4
San Jorge, Golfo **113** C 8
San Jose (CA, U.S.A.) **102** B 4
San José (Costa Rica) **104** F 6
San José de Chiquitos **110** DE 4
San José de Jáchal **112** C 5
San José del Cabo **102** E 7
San José del Guaviare **108** D 3
San José de Mayo **112** E 5
San Juan (Argentina) **112** C 5
San Juan (Dominican Rep.) **105** H 4
San Juan (Peru) **110** A 4
San Juan (Puerto Rico) **105** J 4
San Juan Bautista Tuxtepec **104** C 4
San Juan del Norte **104** F 5
San Julián **113** C 8
San Justo **112** D 5
Sankt Gotthard-Pass **57** E 2
Sankt Pölten **57** G 2
Sankt Veit an der Glan **57** F 2
Sankuru **92** C 5
San Lorenzo **108** C 3
Sanlúcar de Barrameda **56** B 4
San Lucas, Cabo **102** E 7
San Luis (Argentina) **112** C 5
San Luís (Venezuela) **108** E 1
San Luis Obispo **102** B 4
San Luis Potosi **104** BC 3
San Luis Rio Colorado **102** D 5
San Marino **57** F 3
San Martín (Colombia) **108** D 3
San Martín de los Andes **113** BC 7
San Mateo **102** B 4
San Matías **110** E 4
San Matías, Golfo **113** D 7

San Miguel (Bolivia) **110** D 3
San Miguel (El Salvador) **104** E 5
San Miguel de Allende **104** BC 3
San Miguel de Huachi **110** C 4
San Miguel del Padrón **105** FG 3
San Miguel de Tucumán **112** C 4
Sannär **88** E 6
San Nicolás (Argentina) **112** DE 5
San Nicolás (Mexico) **104** B 2
Sannikova **114**
Sanok **53** H 5
San Onofre **108** C 2
San Pablo **113** C 9
San Pedro (Argentina) **110** D 5
San Pedro (Mexico) **104** B 2
San Pedro (Paraguay) **110** E 5
San Pedro de Arimena **108** D 3
San Pedro Sula **104** E 4
San Quintin **102** C 5
San Rafael **112** C 5
San Remo **57** E 3
San Salvador (El Salvador) **104** E 5
San Salvador (Watling Is.) **105** GH 3
San Salvador de Jujuy **110** C 5
Sansanding **90** C 3
San Sebastian (Argentina) **113** C 9
San Sebastián (Spain) **56** C 3
San Severo **57** G 3
Santa Ana (CA, U.S.A.) **102** C 5
Santa Ana (El Salvador) **104** DE 5
Santa Ana (Mexico) **102** D 5
Santa Ana (Solomon Is.) **81** H 4
Santa Barbara (CA, U.S.A.) **102** B 5
Santa Bárbara do Sul **112** F 4
Santa Catalina **112** C 4
Santa Catarina **112** FG 4
Santa Clara (CA, U.S.A.) **102** B 4
Santa Clara (Cuba) **105** F 3
Santa Clara (Mexico) **102** E 6
Santa Clotilde **108** D 4
Santa Cruz (Argentina) **113** C 9
Santa Cruz (Bolivia) **110** D 4
Santa Cruz (CA, U.S.A.) **102** B 4
Santa Cruz, Isla (Ecuador) **108** B 6
Santa Cruz de Mudela **56** C 4
Santa Cruz de Tenerife **86** BC 3
Santa Cruz do Sul **112** F 4

Santa Cruz Islands **81** J 4
Santa Elena **108** B 4
Santa Fé (Argentina) **112** DE 5
Santa Fe (N.M., U.S.A.) **102** EF 4
Santa Filomena **109** J 5
Santa Helena **109** JK 4
Santa Inés, Isla **113** B 9
Santa Isabel **82** B 3
Santa Isabel (Argentina) **113** C 6
Santa Isabel (Solomon Is.) **81** G 3
Santa Maria (CA., U.S.A.) **102** B 4
Santa Maria (Portugal) **86** A 1
Santa María (Rio Grande do Sul, Brazil) **112** F 4
Santa Maria, Cabo de **56** B 4
Santa Maria di Leuca, Capo **57** G 4
Santa Maria dos Marmelos **109** F 5
Santa Marta **108** D 1
Santana do Livramento **112** EF 5
Santander (Colombia) **108** C 3
Santander (Spain) **56** C 3
Sant' Antioco **57** E 4
Santarém **109** H 4
Santa Rita (Colombia) **108** D 3
Santa Rita (Venezuela) **108** E 2
Santa Rosa (Argentina) **113** CD 6
Santa Rosa (CA, U.S.A.) **102** B 4
Santa Rosa (N.M., U.S.A.) **102** F 5
Santa Rosa (Rio Grande do Sul, Brazil) **112** F 4
Santa Rosalia **102** D 6
Santa Sylvina **112** DE 4
Santa Teresa **111** G 3
Santiago (Chile) **112** BC 5
Santiago (Haiti) **105** HJ 4
Santiago (Panamá) **108** B 2
Santiago, Cerro **105** F 6
Santiago do Cacém **56** B 4
Santiago de Compostela **56** B 3
Santiago de Cuba **105** G 4
Santiago del Estero **112** CD 4
Santo André **111** G 5
Santo Ângelo **112** F 4
Santo Antão **90** A 6
Santo António de Jesus **111** HJ 3
Santo António do Icá **108** E 4
Santo Domingo (Dominican Rep.) **105** J 4
Santo Domingo (Mexico) **102** D 6
Santos **111** G 5
Santo Tomás **104** F 5

Santo Tomé de Guayana **109** F 2
San Valentin, Cerro **113** B 8
São Borja **112** E 4
São Carlos **111** G 5
São Domingos **111** G 3
São Felix **111** F 3
São Felix do Xingu **109** H 5
São Francisco **111** HJ 2
São Francisco do Sul **112** G 4
São João **111** G 5
São João del Rei **111** GH 5
São João do Piauí **111** H 2
São José do Río Prêto **111** FG 5
São José dos Campos **111** FG 5
São Leopoldo **112** FG 4
São Luís **111** H 1
São Mateus **111** J 4
São Miguel **86** A 1
São Miguel do Araguaia **111** FG 3
Saône **57** D 2
São Nicolau **90** B 6
São Paulo (Brazil) **111** FG 5
São Paulo (Brazil) **111** G 5
São Paulo de Olivença **108** E 4
São Raimundo Nonato **111** H 2
São Romão **111** G 4
São Roque, Cabo de **111** HJ 2
São Sebastião **111** GH 5
São Tiago **90** B 6
São Tomé **91** F 5
São Tomé and Principe **91** F 5
São Vicente (Cape Verde) **90** A 6
São Vicente (São Paulo, Brazil) **111** G 5
São Vicente, Cabo de **56** B 4
Sape **75** E 5
Sapele **91** F 4
Sapporo **71** LM 2
Sapulut **74** E 3
Säqand **61** G 2
Saqqez **61** E 1
Sara Buri **73** H 5
Sarafjagär **61** F 2
Sarajevo **57** G 3
Saraktash **62** L 5
Saralzhin **66** E 1
Saran' **63** O 6
Saran, Gunung **74** D 4
Saranpaul' **63** M 3
Saransk **62** J 5
Sarapul **62** KL 4
Sarasota **103** K 6
Saratok **74** D 3
Saratov **62** HJ 5
Sarawak **74** D 3
Saraya **59** E 3
Sarco **112** B 4
Sar Dasht **61** D 1
Sardegna **57** E 3
Sardinia **57** E 3

Sarek National Park **54** G 2
Sarektjåkkå **54** G 2
Sargasso Sea **105** JK 2
Sargodha **67** J 4
Sarh **91** H 4
Sâri **66** E 3
Sarigan **82** A 1
Sarıoğlan **59** E 3
Sarir Tibisti **87** J 4
Sariwon **71** HJ 3
Sarkand **63** P 6
Sarmi **75** J 4
Sarmiento **113** C 8
Sarnia **100–101** L 7
Saroako **75** F 4
Saronikos Kólpos **58** B 3
Saros Kôrfezi **58** C 2
Saroto **63** NO 2
Sarpinskaya Nizmennost'
59 G 1
Sartyn'ya **63** M 3
Sarva **58** A 2
Sarvestän **61** F 3
Saryassiya **67** H 3
Saryg-Sep **68** G 5
Sary-Ozek **67** K 2
Sary-Tash **67** J 3
Sasaram **72** D 3
Sasebo **71** J 4
Saskatchewan **99** Q 5
Saskatoon **99** Q 5
Saskylakh **68** KL 1
Sason Dağları **59** F 3
Sasovo **62** H 5
Sassari **57** E 3
Sassuolo **57** F 3
Sastre **112** D 5
Sasykkol', Ozero **63** Q 6
Satara (U.S.S.R.) **69** NO 2
Satawal **82** A 2
Satawan **82** B 2
Satipo **110** B 3
Satka **63** L 4
Satna **72** D 3
Satpura Range **72** BC 3
Sattahip **74** B 1
Satu Mare **58** B 1
Sauce **112** E 5
Sauda **55** E 4
Sauda Nathil **61** F 4
Saudi Arabia **89** GH 4
Sault Sainte Marie **100** L 6
Saumarez Reef **79** J 3
Saurimo **94** BC 1
Sava **58** AB 2
Savai'i **82** D 3
Savannah **103** K 5
Savannakhet **73** HJ 4
Savant Lake **100** JK 5
Save **95** E 4
Säveh **61** F 2
Savo **54** J 3
Savoie **57** E 2
Savonselkä **54** J 3
Sawäkin **88** F 5
Sawbä **92** E 3
Sawdiri **88** D 6
Sawhäj **88** E 3

Sawu Laut **75** F 5
Saydä **60** B 2
Sayhüt **89** J 5
Saynshand **70** F 2
Saywün **89** H 5
Sazin **67** J 3
Sbaa **86** E 3
Scafell Pike **52** C 4
Scaife Mountains **115**
Scammon Bay **98** DE 3
Scarborough **52** C 4
Schefferville **101** O 5
Schenectady **103** M 3
Schleswig **53** EF 4
Schleswig-Holstein **53** E 4
Schouten Islands **80** DE 2
Schwaner, Pegunungan
74 D 4
Schwarzwald **53** E 5
Schwatka Mountains **98** F 2
Schwedt **53** F 4
Schweinfurt **53** F 4
Schwenningen **53** E 5
Schwerin **53** F 4
Sciacca **57** F 4
Scicli **57** F 4
Scilly, Isles of **52** B 5
Scoresby Sound **114**
Scoresbysund **114**
Scotia Sea **115**
Scotland **52** C 3
Scott (Antarctica) **115**
Scott, Cape(Canada) **98** LM 5
Scott, Cape (N.T., Austr.)
78 D 1
Scott Island **115**
Scottsdale (AZ., U.S.A.)
102 D 5
Scottsdale (Tasmania, Austr.)
80 L 9
Seabra **111** H 3
Sea of Azov **59** E 1
Sea of Crete **58** BC 3
Sea of Japan **71** KL 3
Sea of Marmara **58** C 2
Sea of Okhotsk **69** R 4
Seattle **102** B 2
Sebastián Vizcaino, Bahía
102 D 6
Sebkha Azzel Matti **86** EF 3
Sebkha Mekerrhane **87** F 3
Sebkha Oumm ed Droûs Telli
86 CD 4
Sebkha Tah **86** C 3
Sebkhet Oumm ed Droûs
Guebli **86** C 4
Sechura **108** B 5
Sechura, Desierto de **108** B 5
Sedan **57** D 2
Seddenga **88** DE 4
Seeheim **94** B 5
Sefadu **90** B 4
Sefrou **86** E 2
Segesta **57** F 4
Segezha **54** K 3
Ségou **90** C 3
Segovia **56** C 3
Segozero, Ozero **54** K 3

Segre **56** D 3
Seguam **98** C 5
Seguin **102** G 6
Segura **56** C 4
Seiland **54** H 1
Seine **56** D 2
Seke **92** E 5
Sekoma **94** C 4
Sekondi-Takoradi **90** D 5
Selaru, Pulau **75** H 5
Selassi **75** H 4
Selatan, Tanjung **74** D 4
Selat Karimata **74** C 4
Selat Mentawai **74** A 4
Selat Salue Timpaus **75** F 4
Selawik **98** F 2
Selayar, Pulau **75** F 5
Seldovia **98** G 4
Selemdzhinsk **69** O 5
Selenge (Mongolia) **68** HJ 6
Selenge (Zaire) **92** B 5
Selgon **69** P 6
Selinunte **57** F 4
Selizharovo **62** F 4
Seljord **55** E 4
Selkirk Mountains **99** O 5–6
Selma **103** J 5
Selous Game Reserve **93** F 6
Selvagens, Ilhas **86** B 2
Selvänä **59** F 3
Selvas **108–109** EF 5
Selwyn Lake **99** R 3–4
Selwyn Mountains **98** LM 3
Semarang **74** D 5
Sembé **91** G 5
Semiozernoye **63** M 5
Semipalatinsk **63** Q 5
Semisopochnoi **98** AB 5
Semitau **74** D 3
Semmering **58** A 1
Semnän **61** F 2
Semporna **75** E 3
Senador Pompeu **111** HJ 2
Sena Madureira **108** E 5
Sendai **71** M 3
Sêndo **70** C 4
Sénégal **90** B 2
Senegal **90** AB 3
Senftenberg **53** F 4
Senhor do Bonfim **111** H 3
Senja **54** G 2
Senjavin Grop **82** B 2
Senneterre **101** M 6
Sens **56** D 2
Senta **58** A 1
Sentinel Peak **99** N 5
Seoni **72** C 3
Seoul **71** J 3
Sepik **82** A 3
Sepik River **80** D 2
Sept-Îles **101** O 5
Şerafettin Dağları **59** F 3
Serakhs **67** G 3
Seram **75** G 4
Seram, Laut **75** GH 4
Serang **74** C 5
Serdobsk **62** HJ 5
Seremban **74** B 3

Serengeti National Park
92 EF 5
Sergino **63** N 3
Sergipe **111** J 3
Seroglazovka **59** G 1
Serov **63** M 4
Serowe **94** D 4
Serpa **56** B 4
Serpukhov **62** G 5
Serra Acarai **109** G 3
Serra Bonita **111** G 4
Serra da Estrêla **56** B 3
Serra do Cachimbo **109** G 5
Serra do Estrondo **109** J 5
Serra do Marao **56** B 3
Serra do Mogadouro **56** B 3
Serra do Navio **109** H 3
Serra do Roncador **111** F 3
Serra dos Carajás **109** H 4–5
Serra dos Gradaús **109** H 5
Serra dos Parecis **110** D 3
Serra do Tombador **110** E 3
Serra Formosa **111** EF 3
Serrai **58** B 2
Serra Talhada **111** J 2
Serrezuela **112** C 5
Serrinha **111** J 3
Serrota **56** BC 3
Seruai **75** J 4
Serule **94** D 4
Sesfontein **94** A 3
Sesheke **94** CD 3
Sesibi **88** DE 4
Seskarö **54** H 2
Sestroretsk **55** JK 3
Séte **56** D 3
Sete Lagoas **111** H 4
Sétif **87** G 1
Settat **86** D 2
Sette Daban, Khrebet **69** P 3
Setúbal **56** B 4
Setúbal, Baía de **56** B 4
Seumanyam **74** A 3
Sevarujo **110** C 4
Sevastopol' **59** D 2
Sever **69** V 3
Severnaya Dvina **62** H 3
Severnaya Zemlya **114**
Severnoye **63** P 4
Severn River **100** K 4
Severnyy Anyuyskiy Khrebet
69 UW 2
Severodvinsk **62** G 3
Severomorsk **54** KL 2
Severo Sibirskaya
Nizmennost' **68** FK 1
Sevier Desert **102** D 4
Sevilla **56** B 4
Sevrey **70** D 2
Seward (AK, U.S.A.) **98** H 3
Seward (NE, U.S.A.) **102** G 3
Seward Peninsula **98** E 2
Sewell **112** BC 5
Seychelles **93** J 6
Seyhan **59** E 3
Seymchan **69** S 3
Sfax **87** GH 2
S. Félix Island **107** B 5

Shaanxi **70** EF 4
Shaba **92** CD 6
Shache **67** K 3
Shackleton Ice Shelf **115**
Shackleton Range **115**
Shaddādī **59** F 3
Shadrinsk **63** MN 4
Shaffhausen **57** E 2
Shahdol **72** D 3
Shahḥāt **87** K 2
Shahjahanpur **72** CD 2
Shahmīrzad **61** F 2
Shahr Kord **61** F 2
Shahtinsk **63** O 6
Shāʾib al Banāt, Jabal **60** A 4
Shaʾib Hasb **60** D 3
Shakhrisyabz **67** H 3
Shakhterskiy **69** XY 3
Shakhty **59** F 1
Shaki **90** E 4
Shalgiya **63** O 6
Shalkar **62** K 5
Shām, Jabal ash **89** K 4
Shamattawa **99** T 4
Shambe **92** E 3
Shāmīyah **60** C 2
Shammar, Jabal **60** CD 4
Shamrock **102** F 4
Shams **61** G 3
Shan **73** G 3
Shandan **70** D 3
Shandī **88** E 5
Shəndong **71** GH 3
Shandong Bandao **71** H 3
Shangcheng **70** FG 4
Shangdu **70** F 2
Shanghai **71** H 4
Shanghang **70** G 5–6
Shangqiu **70** G 4
Shangrao **71** G 5
Shangzhi **71** J 1–2
Shanh **68** H 6
Shankou **70** B 2
Shannon **52** B 4
Shannon, Mouth of the **52** A 4
Shanshan **70** B 2
Shantarskiye Ostrova **69** P 4
Shantou **70** G 6
Shanxi **70** F 3
Shaoguan **70** F 6
Shaowu **71** G 5
Shaoxing **71** GH 5
Shaoyang **70** F 5
Shaqrāʾ **89** H 6
Sharāf **66** C 4
Shark Bay **78** A 4
Shary **66** C 5
Shashamanna **93** F 3
Shashi **70** F 4
Shasta, Mount **102** B 3
Shatt al Arab **61** E 3
Shatt al Jarīd **87** G 2
Shaviklde **59** G 2
Shawinigan **101** N 6
Shaybārā **60** B 4
Shaykh, Raʾs ash **60** B 3

Shaykh Ṣaʿd **61** E 2
Shaykhʾ Uthmān **89** H 6
Shchara **55** J 5
Shchelʾyayur **62** KL 2
Shchuchinsk **63** N 5
Sheboygan **103** J 3
Shedin Peak **99** M 4
Sheffield **52** C 4
Shekhawati **72** C 2
Sheki **66** D 2
Shelburne **101** OP 7
Shelby **102** D 2
Sheldon Point **98** D 3
Shelikof Strait **98** G 4
Shellharbour **79** J 5
Shenandoah National Park **103** L 4
Shendam **91** F 4
Shenmu **70** F 3
Shenton, Mount **78** C 4
Shenyang **71** HJ 2
Shepetovka **55** J 5
Sherbro Island **90** B 4
Sherbrooke **101** N 6
Sheridan **102** E 3
Sherridon **99** RS 4
Shetland Islands **52** CD 2
Shevchenko **66** E 2
Shevli **69** O 5
Sheya **68** L 3
Sheyang **71** H 4
Sheyenne River **102** G 2
Shibarghan **67** GH 3
Shibazhan **69** MN 5
Shib Kūh **61** F 3–4
Shijiazhuang **70** FG 3
Shikarpur **67** H 5
Shikoku **71** K 4
Shilka **68** L 5
Shilkan **69** R 4
Shilla **72** C 1
Shillong **73** F 2
Shimanovsk **69** N 5
Shimizu **71** L 4
Shimoga **72** BC 5
Shingshal **67** JK 3
Shiping **70** D 6
Shipunovo **63** Q 5
Shiquanhe **72** C 1
Shirabad **67** H 3
Shirase Glacier **115**
Shīrāz **61** F 3
Shire **95** E 3
Shirikrabat **67** G 2
Shir Kūh **61** FG 3
Shishaldin Volcano **98** DE 5
Shishou **70** F 5
Shiveluch, Sopka **69** U 4
Shivpuri **72** C 2
Shizuoka **71** L 4
Shkodra **58** AB 2
Sholapur **72** C 4
Shoptykulʾ **63** P 5
Shorawak **67** H 4–5
Shoshone **102** D 3
Shoshoni **102** E 3
Shouguang **71** G 3
Showa **115**

Show Low **102** DE 5
Shqiperia **58** AB 2
Shreveport **103** H 5
Shrewsbury **52** CD 4
Shuangliao **71** H 2
Shuangyashan **71** K 1
Shucheng **71** G 4
Shuicheng **70** DE 5
Shule **67** K 3
Shumagin Islands **98** F 4–5
Shumerlya **62** J 4
Shuo Xian **70** F 3
Shurinda **68** K 4
Shūshtar **66** D 4
Shuwak **88** F 6
Siahan Range **67** GH 5
Siah-Chashmeh **59** F 3
Siargao **75** G 2
Šiauliai **55** H 4
Sibay **63** L 5
Šibenik **57** G 3
Siberut, Pulau **74** A 4
Sibirskoye Nizmennostʾ **63** NQ 3
Sibiti **91** G 6
Sibiu **58** B 1
Sibolga **74** A 3
Sibsagar **73** FG 2
Sibu **74** D 3
Sibuyan Sea **75** F 1
Sicasica **110** C 4
Sichote-Alin **69** P 6
Sichuan **70** CE 4
Sicilia **57** F 4
Sicilia, Canale de **57** F 4
Sicily **57** F 4
Sicuani **110** B 3
Siderno **57** G 4
Sidi-bel-Abbès **86** EF 1–2
Sidon **60** B 2
Siedlce **53** H 4
Siegen **53** E 4
Siena **57** F 3
Sierra Colorada **113** C 7
Sierra de Alcaraz **56** C 4
Sierra de Aracena **56** B 4
Sierra de Gata **56** B 3
Sierra de Gredos **56** B 3
Sierra de Guadarrama **56** C 3
Sierra de Gúdar **56** C 3
Sierra de la Cabrera **56** B 3
Sierra del Cadí **56** D 3
Sierra Leone **90** B 4
Sierra Madre **104** D 4
Sierra Madre del Sur **104** BC 4
Sierra Madre Oriental **104** BC 2–3
Sierra Madrona **56** C 4
Sierra Mojada **104** B 2
Sierra Morena **56** BC 4
Sierra Nayarit **104** B 3
Sierra Nevada (CA., U.S.A.) **102** BC 3–4
Sierra Nevada (Spain) **56** C 4
Sierra Pacaraima **109** F 3
Sierra Parima **109** F 3
Sierra Vizcaíno **102** D 6

Sífnos **58** B 3
Sighetu Marmaţiei **58** B 1
Signy Island **115**
Siguiri **90** C 3
Siirt **59** F 3
Sikar **72** C 2
Sikasso **90** C 3
Sikerin **69** Q 2
Sikkim **72** E 2
Siktyakh **69** N 2
Silchar **73** F 3
Silesia **53** G 4
Silet **87** F 4
Silifke **59** D 3
Siliguri **72** E 2
Silistra **58** C 2
Siljan **55** FG 3
Silkleborg **55** E 4
Siltou **91** H 2
Silver City **102** E 5
Silʾyeyaki **69** Q 1
Simanggang **74** D 3
Simav **58** C 2–3
Simenga **68** J 3
Simeulue, Pulau **74** A 3
Simferopolʾ **59** D 2
Simla **72** C 1
Simojärvi **54** J 2
Simplicio Mendes **111** H 2
Simpson Desert **79** F 3
Simpson Desert National Park **79** F 4
Simrishamn **55** FG 4
Sinaʾ **60** A 3
Sinai (Egypt) **60** A 3
Sināwan **87** H 2
Sincelejo **108** C 2
Sind **67** H 5
Sinda **69** P 6
Singapore **74** B 3
Singaraja **74** E 5
Singida **92** E 5
Singleton **79** J 5
Sinjaja **55** J 4
Sinjär **59** F 3
Sinkiang Uighur **67** L 3
Sinnamary **109** H 2
Sinop **59** E 2
Sinskoye **69** N 3
Sintang **74** D 3
Sinüiju **71** HJ 3
Sioux City **103** G 3
Sioux Falls **103** G 3
Siping **71** H 2
Sipiwesk **99** S 4
Siple Station **115**
Siracusa **57** G 4
Sir Edward Pellew Group **79** F 2
Sireniki **98** BC 3
Siret **58** C 1
Sirgän **67** G 5
Sirino **57** G 3
Sir James MacBrian, Mount **98** M 3
Sirsa **72** C 2
Sirt **87** J 2
Sisak **57** G 2

Sisophon **73** H 5
Sisseton **102** G 2
Sistema Iberico **56** C 3
Sistemas Béticos **56** C 4
Sistig-Khem **68** G 5
Sitapur **72** D 2
Sittwe **73** F 3
Sivaki **69** N 5
Sivas **59** E 3
Sivash **59** DE 1
Siverek **59** E 3
Siwah **88** D 3
Siwalik Range **72** CD 1–2
Siwan **72** D 2
Si Xian **71** G 4
Sjælland **55** F 4
Sjövegan **54** G 2
Skagen **55** F 4
Skagern **55** F 4
Skagerrak **55** EF 4
Skagway **98** K 4
Skåne **55** F 4
Skarsöy **54** E 3
Skarstind **54** E 3
Skarżysko-Kamienna **53** H 4
Skeldon **109** G 2
Skeleton Coast Park **94** A 3
Skellefteå **54** H 3
Skellefteälven **54** G 2
Skien **55** E 4
Skierniewice **53** H 4
Skiftet **55** H 3
Skikda **87** G 1
Skikotsu **71** N 2
Skíros **58** B 3
Skjoldungen **101** T 3
Sklad **68** M 1
Skópelos **58** B 3
Skopi **58** C 3
Skopje **58** B 2
Skövde **55** F 4
Skye **52** B 3
Slantsy **55** J 4
Śląsk **53** G 4
Slatina **58** B 2
Slave Coast **90** E 4
Slave River **99** P 3–4
Slavgorod **63** P 5
Slavonski Brod **57** G 2
Slavuta **55** J 5
Slavyansk **62** G 6
Sligo **52** B 4
Sliven **58** C 2
Slobodka **58** C 1
Slobodskoy **62** K 4
Slonim **55** J 5
Slovakia **53** H 5
Slovechno **55** J 5
Slovensko **53** H 5
Sluch' **55** J 5
Słupsk **53** G 4
Slutsk **55** J 5
Småland **55** G 4
Smallwood Réservoir **101** P 5
Smidovich **114**
Smirnykh **69** Q 6
Smith **99** P 4
Smokey Dome **102** CD 3

Smoky Cape **79** J 5
Smoky Hill River **102** FG 4
Smöla **54** E 3
Smolensk **62** F 5
Smooth Rock Falls **101** L 6
Snake River **102** C 2
Snezhnoye **69** W 2
Snoul **74** C 1
Snowdon **52** C 4
Snowdrift **99** PQ 3
Sobolevo **69** T 5
Sobral **111** HJ 1
Sochi **59** E 2
Society Islands **83** EF 4
Socorro **102** E 5
Sodankylä **54** J 2
Soddu **93** F 3
Söderhamn **54** G 3
Södermanland **55** G 4
Södertälje **55** G 4
Sofia **58** B 2
Sofiya **58** B 2
Sofiysk **69** O 5
Sofiysk **69** PQ 5
Sofporog **54** K 2
Sogamoso **108** D 2
Sogndalsfjöra **54** E 3
Sogn og Fjordane **54** E 3
Sog Xian **70** B 4
Söke **58** C 3
Sokhor, Gora **68** J 5
Sokodé **90** E 4
Sokółka **53** H 4
Sokolov **53** F 4
Sokosti **54** J 2
Sokoto **91** EF 3
Solberg **54** G 3
Soldatovo **69** V 3
Soledad **108** D 1
Soligorsk **55** J 5
Solikamsk **62** KL 4
Sol'-Iletsk **62** L 5
Solimões **108** E 4
Solitaire **94** B 4
Solomon Islands **81** G 3
Solomon Islands **82** B 3
Solomon Sea **81** F 3
Solomon Sea **82** B 3
Solov'yevsk **68** L 5
Solyanka **68** M 3
Somalia **93** GH 3–4
Somerset **79** G 1
Somme **56** D 1
Sonakh **69** P 5
Songea **95** F 2
Song Hong **73** H 3
Songhua Jiang **71** J 1
Songkhla **73** H 6
Songnim **71** J 3
Songo **95** E 3
Sonid Youqi **70** F 2
Sonid Zuoqi **70** F 2
Sonmiani Bay **67** H 5
Sonneberg **53** F 4
Sonoita **102** D 5
Sonoma Peak **102** C 3
Sonora **102** D 6
Sonoran Desert **102** D 5

Sonqor **66** D 4
Sonsonate **104** DE 5
Sopka Shiveluch **69** U 4
Sopochnaya Karga **68** DE 1
Sopron **58** A 1
Sopur **67** J 4
Sora **57** F 3
Soria **56** C 3
Sorikmerapi, Gunung **74** A 3
Sorkh, Küh-e **61** G 2
Sorkheh **61** F 2
Sor Mertvyy Kultuk **66** E 1
Sorong **75** H 4
Soroti **92** E 4
Söröya **54** H 1
Sör Rondane Mountains **115**
Sorsatunturi **54** J 2
Sorsele **54** G 2
Sorsogon **75** F 1
Sortavala **54** K 3
Sör-Tröndelag **54** F 3
Sosnogorsk **62** KL 3
Sosnovyy Bor **63** Q 3
Sosyka **59** EF 1
Sotra **55** D 3
Sotsial **63** P 6
Souanké **91** GH 5
Soudan **79** F 3
Soumenselkä **54** H 3
Soure **109** J 4
Souris River **99** R 6
Sousa **111** J 2
Sousse **87** H 1
Southampton **52** C D 4
Southampton Island **99** UV 3
South Andaman **73** F 5
South Australia **78–79** E 4
South Bend (IN, U.S.A.)
   103 JK 3
South Bend (WA, U.S.A.)
   102 B 2
South Carolina **103** K 5
South China Sea **74** CD 2
South Dakota **102** FG 3
South East Cape **80** L 9
Southend **99** R 4
Southend-on-Sea **52** D 4
Southern Alps **82** C 5
Southern Cook Islands **83** E 4
Southern Cross **78** B 5
Southern Uplands **52** C 3
Southern Yemen **89** HJ 5–6
South Geomagnetic Pole **115**
South Georgia **115**
South Island **80** P 9
South Korea **71** JK 3
South Magnetic Pole **115**
South Orkney Islands **115**
South Platte River **102** F 3
South Pole **115**
South Sandwich Islands **115**
South Saskatchewan **99** PQ 5
South Shetland Islands **115**
South Shields **52** C 3
South Uist **52** B 3
South Wellesley Islands
   79 FG 2

Southwest Cape **80** P 10
Soven **112** C 5
Sovetsk **62** J 4
Sovetskaya Gavan' **69** PQ 6
Sovetskaya Rechka **63** QR 2
Soya Strait **65** R 5
Sozimskiy **62** K 4
Spain **56** BC 4
Spanish Town **105** G 4
Spartanburg **103** K 5
Spartí **58** B 3
Spassk Dal'niy **71** K 2
Spearfish **102** F 3
Spence Bay **99** T 2
Spencer Gulf **79** F 5
Spicer Islands **101** M 2
Spitsbergen **114**
Split **57** G 3
Spokane **102** C 2
Spooner **103** H 2
Springbok **94** B 5
Springdale **103** H 4
Springfield (CO, U.S.A.)
   102 F 4
Springfield (IL, U.S.A.)
   103 HJ 4
Springfield (MA, U.S.A.)
   103 M 3
Springfield (MO, U.S.A.)
   103 H 4
Springfield (OR, U.S.A.)
   102 B 3
Springs **94** D 5
Squillace, Golfo di **57** G 4
Srbija **58** B 2
Sredinnyy Khrebet **69** TU 4–5
Sredna Gora **58** BC 2
Srednekolymsk **69** S 2
Sredne Sibirskoye
   Ploskogor'ye **68** FK 2–3
Sredniy **69** S 4
Srednyaya Itkana **69** U 3
Sremska Mitrovica **58** A 1–2
Srikakulam **72** DE 4
Sri Lanka **72** D 6
Srinagar **67** K 4
Staaten River National Park
   79 G 2
Stadlandet **54** D 3
Stafford **52** C 4
Stalowa Wola **53** H 4
Stamford **103** M 3
Standerton **94** D 5
Stanke Dimitrov **58** B 2
Stanley **113** E 9
Stanley Falls **92** D 4
Stanley Mission **99** R 4
Stanovka **63** O 4
Stanovoy Khrebet **68** LN 4
Stanovoy Nagor'ye **68** KL 4
Stara Planina **58** B 2
Staraya Russa **55** K 4
Staraya Vorpavla **63** N 3
Stara Zagora **58** C 2
Starbuck **83** E 3
Stargard Szczecinski **53** G 4
Starodub **62** F 5
Starogard Gdanski **53** G 4

Staryy Oskol 62 G 5
Staten Island 113 D 9–10
Stavanger 55 DE 4
Stavropol' 59 F 1
Stavropolka 63 N 5
Stavropol'skaya
    Vozvyshennost' 59 F 1
Steen River 99 O 4
Stefansson Island 99 Q 1
Steinkjer 54 F 3
Steinkopf 94 B 5
Stellenbosch 94 BC 6
Stenon 58 C 3
Stepanakert 66 D 3
Sterlitamak 62 KL 5
Steubenville 103 K 3
Stevenson Entrance 98 G 4
Stewart (AK, U.S.A.) 98 M 4
Stewart (Canada) 98 KL 3
Stewart (New Zealand)
    80 P 10
Stewart Crossing 98 K 3
Stewart Island (New Zeeland)
    80 P 10
Stewart Island (Solomon
    Islands) 82 B 3
Steyr 57 F 2
Stillwater 103 G 4
Stip 58 B 2
Stirling Range National Park
    78 B 5
Stjördal 54 F 3
Stockholm 55 G 4
Stockton 102 BC 4
Stockton Plateau 102 F 5
Stöde 54 G 3
Stoke-on-Trent 52 C 4
Stokksnes 54 BC 3
Stony Rapids 99 Q 4
Stony River 98 FG 3
Storån 54 G 3
Storavan 54 G 2
Stord 55 E 4
Storkerson Peninsula 99 Q 1
Stornoway 52 B 3
Storsjön 54 F 3
Storuman 54 G 2
Storvigelen 54 F 3
Stöttingfjället 54 G 3
Strait of Belle Isle 101 Q 5
Strait of Bonifacio 57 E 3
Strait of Dover 52 D 4
Strait of Gibraltar 56 B 4
Strait of Hormuz 89 K 3
Strait of Magellan 113 BC 9
Strait of Makassar 74 E 4
Strait of Malacca 74 B 3
Straits of Florida 103 KL 6–7
Stralsund 53 F 4
Strand 94 B 6
Stranraer 52 B 4
Strasbourg 57 E 2
Stratford 102 F 4
Straubing 53 F 5
Streaky Bay 78 E 5
Strelka-Chunya 68 H 3
Stretto de Messina 57 G 4
Streymoy 52 A 1

Strömsund 54 G 3
Stryy 53 H 5
Stung Treng 73 J 5
Sturt Desert 79 G 4
Sturt National Park 79 G 4
Stuttgart 53 E 5
Styr' 55 J 5
Subayhah 66 B 5
Suceava 58 C 1
Sucre 110 D 4
Sudan 88 DE 6
Sudbury 101 L 6
Suddie 109 G 2
Sudety 53 G 4
Suðuroy 52 A 1
Suez 60 A 3
Suez Canal 60 A 3
Şuhār 89 K 4
Sühbaatar 70 F 1
Suhl 53 F 4
Suide 70 EF 3
Suining 71 G 4
Suir 62 F 3
Suizhong 71 H 2
Sukaraja 74 D 4
Sukhana 68 L 2
Sukhona 62 H 4
Sukhumi 59 F 2
Sukkertoppen 101 R 2
Sukkur 67 H 5
Suksukan 69 S 3
Sula, Kepulauan 75 FG 4
Sulaimäniya 61 D 2
Sulaiman Range 67 H 4–5
Sulanheer 70 E 2
Sulawesi 75 EF 4
Sulawesi, Laut 75 F 3
Sulb 88 DE 4
Sulima 90 B 4
Suliskongen 54 G 2
Sullana 108 BC 4
Sultan Dağları 58–59 D 3
Sulu Archipelago 75 EF 2–3
Sulu Sea 75 EF 2
Sumarokovo 63 R 3
Sumatera 74 AB 3–4
Sumaúma 109 G 5
Šumava 53 F 5
Sumba 75 EF 5
Sumbawa 74 E 5
Sumbawanga 92 E 6
Sumbe 94 A 2
Sümber 70 E 1
Sumburgh Head 52 C 3
Sumgait 66 DE 2
Summel 59 F 3
Summit Lake 99 N 4
Sumperk 53 G 5
Sumter 103 L 5
Sumy 62 G 5
Suna 92 EF 6
Sunderland 52 C 4
Sündiren Dağları 58 D 3
Sundsvall 54 G 3
Sunflower, Mount 102 F 4
Sungai Barito 74 D 4
Sungai Kampar 74 B 3
Sungai Kutai 74 E 4

Sungai Mamberamo 75 J 4
Sunndalsfjorden 54 E 3
Suntar Khayata, Khrebet
    69 PQ 3
Suokonmäki 54 H 3
Suolahti 54 J 3
Suomenselkä 54 J 3
Suomi 54 J 3
Suoyarvi 62 F 3
Superior 103 H 2
Süphan Dağı 59 F 3
Suquṭrá 93 J 2
Şūr 60 B 2
Surabaya 74 D 5
Surakarta 74 CD 5
Surat (India) 72 B 3
Surat (Queensland, Austr.)
    79 H 4
Suratgarh 72 B 2
Surat Thani 73 GH 6
Surendranagar 72 AB 3
Surgut 63 O 3
Surgutikha 63 R 3
Surin 73 H 5
Surinam 109 G 3
Süriyah 60 BC 2
Surud Ad 93 H 2
Survey Pass 98 FG 2
Susa 61 E 2
Susah 87 H 1
Susques 110 C 5
Susuman 69 R 3
Sutlej 67 J 4–5
Sutton 98 H 3
Sutun'ya 69 NO 2
Suva 82 C 4
Suva Gora 58 B 2
Suva Planina 58 B 2
Suvorov 82 E 3
Suwałki 53 H 4
Suways, Qanat as 60 A 3
Suwon 71 J 3
Suzhou 71 GH 4
Suzun 63 Q 5
Svalbard 114
Svartisen 54 F 2
Svealand 55 FG 4
Sveg 54 F 3
Svendborg 55 F 4–5
Sverdlovsk 63 M 4
Sverige 54 G 3
Svetlogorsk (Belorussiya,
    U.S.S.R.) 55 J 5
Svetlograd 59 F 1
Svetlyy 69 N 4
Svetozarevo 58 B 2
Svobodnyy 69 N 5
Svolvœr 54 F 2
Swain Reefs 79 J 3
Swains 82 D 3
Swakopmund 94 A 4
Swan River 99 R 5
Swansea 52 C 4
Swaziland 95 E 5
Sweden 54 G 3
Swellendam 94 C 6
Świdnik 53 H 4
Swift Current 99 Q 5

Swinoujście 53 FG 4
Switzerland 57 E 2
Syadaykharvuta 63 OP 2
Syalakh 69 MN 2
Syangannakh 69 R 2
Syðri-Hagangur 54 B 2
Sydney (Canada) 101 Q 6
Sydney (N.S.W., Austr.)
    79 J 5
Syktyvkar 62 JK 3
Sylhet 73 F 3
Syracuse (N.Y., U.S.A.)
    103 L 3
Syr-Dar'ya 67 H 2
Syria 60 BC 2
Syria 88 F 2
Syrian Desert 60 C 2
Syuge-Khaya, Gora 69 P 2
Syurkum 69 Q 5
Syzran 62 J 5
Szczecin 53 F 4
Szczecinek 53 G 4
Szeged 58 A 1
Székesféhérvár 58 A 1
Szekszárd 58 A 1
Szentes 58 AB 1
Szolnok 58 B 1
Szombathely 58 A 1

T

Taarom 79 HJ 4
Tabacal 110 D 5
Tabaqah 60 C 2
Tabarqah 59 E 3
Tabas 61 G 2
Tabasco 104 D 4
Tabatinga 108 E 4
Tabelbala 86 E 3
Tabelbalet 87 G 3
Tabeng 73 HJ 5
Tabiteuea 82 C 3
Tabla 90 E 3
Table Mountain 94 B 6
Tábor 53 F 5
Tabor (U.S.S.R.) 69 R 1
Tabora 92 E 6
Tabou 90 C 5
Tabriz 66 D 3
Tabuaeran 83 E 2
Tabūk 60 B 3
Tacheng 67 L 1
Tacloban 75 F 1
Tacna 110 B 4
Tacoma 102 B 2
Tacuarembó 112 EF 5
Tademaït, Plateau du 87 F 3
Tadoule Lake 99 S 4
Tadzhikistan 67 HJ 3
Taegu 71 J 3
Taejŏn 71 J 3
Tagama 91 F 2
Taganrog 59 E 1
Taganrogskiy Zaliv 59 E 1
Tagounite 86 D 3
Taguatinga 111 G 3
Taguenout Haggueret 90 D 1
Tagula Island 79 J 1
Tahan, Gunung 74 B 3

Tahat, Mont **87** G 4
Tahiti **83** EF 4
Tahoe, Lake **102** C 4
Tahoua **91** EF 3
Tahrüd **66** F 5
Tahtali Daǧlari **59** E 3
Tahuata **83** F 3
Taibus Qi **70** FG 2
Taichung **71** H 6
Tailai **71** H 1
Taimba **68** G 3
Tainan **71** GH 6
Taipei **71** H 6
Taiping **74** B 3
Taipu **111** J 2
Taitao, Península de **113** AB 8
Taitung **71** H 6
Taivalkoski **54** J 2
Taiwan **71** H 6
Taiyuan **70** F 3
Ta'izz **89** G 6
Tajito **102** D 5
Tájo **56** B 4
Tajrīsh **61** F 2
Tajumulco, Volcán **104** D 4
Tak **73** G 4
Takáb **61** E 1
Takamatsu **71** KL 4
Takatshwane **94** C 4
Takeo **74** B 1
Takestan **61** E 1
Takhta-Bazar **67** G 3
Takht-e Soleiman **61** F 1
Takijuq Lake **99** P 2
Takla Landing **99** M 4
Takla Makan **67** L 3
Taklaun, Gora **69** Q 3
Taklimakan Shamo **67** LM 3
Takua Pa **74** A 2
Talak **91** EF 2
Talakan **69** O 6
Talandzha **69** O 6
Talara **108** B 4
Talaud, Kepulauan **75** G 3
Talavera de la Reina **56** C 3–4
Talawdi **88** E 6
Talaya (U.S.S.R.) **68** G 4
Talaya (U.S.S.R.) **69** S 3
Talca **113** B 6
Talcahuano **113** B 6
Taldy-Kurgan **63** PQ 6
Talence **56** C 3
Tálesh **66** D 3
Taliabu, Pulau **75** FG 4
Talimardzhan **67** H 3
Taliqan **67** HJ 3
Taliwang **74** E 5
Talkalakh **60** B 2
Talkeetna Mountains **98** H 3
Tall Afar **60** D 1
Tallahassee **103** K 5
Tall aş Şuwār **60** C 2
Tallinn **55** J 4
Tall Kayf **60** D 1
Tall Kūshik **60** C 1
Talo **53** F 2
Taltal **112** B 4
Tamale **90** D 4

Tamanrasset **87** G 4
Tamaulipas **104** C 3
Tambacounda **90** B 3
Tambalan **74** E 3
Tambisan **75** E 2
Tambo **79** H 3
Tambov **62** H 5
Tamch **68** F 6
Tamchaket **86** C 5
Tame **108** D 2
Tamel Aike **113** BC 8
Tamgak, Monts **91** F 2
Tamil Nadu **72** C 5
Tampa **103** K 6
Tampere **54** H 3
Tampico **104** C 3
Tamu **73** F 3
Tamworth **79** J 5
Tana (Kenya) **93** F 5
Tana (Norway) **54** J 1
Tana (Vanuatu) **82** C 4
Tanaga **98** A 5
Tanami **78** DE 2
Tanami Desert **78** E 2
Tanami Desert Wildlife
  Sanctuary **78** E 3
Tanana **98** G 2
Tanana River **98** H 3
Tanch'ŏn **71** JK 2
Tandaho **93** G 2
Tandil **113** E 6
Tane-ga-shima **71** K 4
Tanga **93** F 5–6
Tang-e Karam **61** F 3
Tanger **86** D 1
Tanggula Shan **70** AB 4
Tanggula Shankou **70** B 4
Tanghe **70** F 4
Tangmai **70** C 4
Tangshan **71** G 3
Tangyuan **71** J 1
Tanimbar, Kepulauan **75** H 5
Tanjung, Jabung **74** C 4
Tanjung Api **74** C 3
Tanjungbalai **74** AB 3
Tanjung Samak **74** C 4
Tanjung Selatan **74** D 4
Tanjungselor **74** E 3
Tanjung Vals **75** J 5
Tannu Ola **68** F 5
Tanță **88** E 2
Tan Tan **86** C 3
Tanzania **92** EF 6
Tao'an **71** H 1–2
Taolanaro **95** H 5
Taoudenni **90** D 1
Taoyuan **71** H 5
Tapachula **104** D 5
Tapajós **109** GH 4
Tapurucuara **108** E 4
Taquari (Brazil) **110** E 4
Taquari (Brazil) **111** F 4
Tara (U.S.S.R.) **63** OP 4
Tarābulus (Lebanon) **60** B 2
Tarābulus (Libya) **87** HJ 2
Taracua **108** E 3
Tarakan **74** E 3
Tarakki **67** H 4

Taranto **57** G 3
Taranto, Golfo di **57** G 3–4
Tarapoto **108** C 5
Tarasovo **62** J 2
Tarata **110** C 4
Tarauacá **108** D 5
Tarawa **82** C 2
Tarbes **56** D 3
Taree **79** J 5
Tareya **68** F 1
Tarīf **61** F 4
Tarija **110** D 5
Tarim Liuchang **70** A 2
Tarin Kowt **67** GH 4
Tarko-Zale **63** PQ 3
Tarkwa **90** D 4
Tarlac **75** J 1
Tarma **110** A 3
Tarn **56** D 3
Tarnobrzeg **53** H 4
Tarnów **53** H 4
Taroudant **86** D 2
Tarragona **56** D 3
Tarrasa **56** D 3
Tarsū Mūsā **87** J 4
Tarsus **60** B 1
Tart **70** B 3
Tartagal **110** D 5
Tartu **55** J 4
Tartus **60** B 2
Tarutung **74** A 3
Tashakta **63** R 6
Tashauz **66** F 2
Tashk, Daryācheh-ye **61** FG 3
Tashkent **67** H 2
Tashtagol **63** R 5
Tasman Bay **81** Q 9
Tasmania **80** KL 9
Tasman Sea **82** B 5
Tassili N-Ajjer **87** G 3
Tas-Tumus **69** O 1
Tasüj **59** G 3
Tatábánya **58** A 1
Tatakoto **83** F 4
Tatarbunary **58** C 1
Tatarsk **63** P 4
Tatarskiy Proliv **69** Q 6
Tatry **53** H 5
Taubaté **111** GH 5
Taunggon **73** G 3
Taungup **73** F 4
Taunton **52** C 4
Tauranga **81** R 8
Taurus Mountains **59** DE 3
Tavatuma **69** T 3
Tavda **63** N 4
Taverner Bay **101** N 2
Tavolara **57** E 3
Tavoy **73** G 5
Tawau **74** E 3
Tawitawi Group **75** F 2
Tawüq **60** D 1
Tawzar **87** G 2
Taxco de Alarcón **104** BC 4
Taxkorgan **67** K 3
Tayga **63** QR 4
Taylor **98** DE 2

Taymá' **60** C 4
Taymyr **68** F 2
Taymyr, Ozero **68** H 1
Tayshet **68** G 4
Taytay **75** E 1
Taz **63** P 2
Taza **86** E 2
Tāzah Khurmātū **60** D 2
Tazovskoye **63** P 2
Tbilisi **59** FG 2
Tcholliré **91** G 4
Teba **75** J 4
Tébessa **87** G 1
Tebingtinggi **74** A 3
Tebulos Mta **59** G 2
Tecer Daǧlari **59** E 3
Tecka **113** B 7
Tecomán **104** B 4
Tecuci **58** C 1
Tedzhen **66** FG 3
Teeside **52** C 4
Tefé **109** F 4
Tegal **74** C 5
Tegre **93** FG 2
Tegucigalpa **104** E 5
Tegyul'te-Tërde **69** O 3
Teheran → Tehrän **66** DE 3
Tehran **61** F 2
Tehuacán **104** C 4
Teiga Plateau **88** D 5
Tejo **56** B 4
Tekeli **67** K 2
Tekes **67** L 2
Tekirdaǧ **58** C 2
Telanaipura **74** B 4
Tel Aviv-Yafo **60** B 2–3
Telegraph Creek **98** LM 4
Telemaco Borba **111** FG 5
Telemark **55** E 4
Telén **113** C 6
Teles Pires **109** G 5
Teli **68** F 5
Tell al 'Amärna **88** E 3
Tello **112** C 5
Telok Anson **74** B 3
Tel'pos-Iz, Gora **63** L 3
Telukbatang **74** CD 4
Teluk Berau **75** H 4
Teluk Bone **75** F 4
Teluk Cendrawasih **75** HJ 4
Teluk Kumai **74** D 4
Teluk Tomini **75** F 4
Témacine **87** G 2
Tematangi **83** F 4
Tembenchi **68** G 3
Tembo **92** B 6
Tembo, Mont **91** G 3
Temirtau **63** O 5
Temiscaming **101** M 6
Temoe **83** G 4
Tempa **114**
Temple **103** G 5
Temuco **113** B 6
Tena **108** C 4
Tenali **72** D 4
Tenasserim **73** G 4–5
Tenere **91** FG 1–2
Ténéré, Erg de **91** G 2

Tenerife **86** B 3
Ténès **87** F 1
Tengchong **70** C 5
Tenggara, Kepulauan **75** G 5
Tengiz, Ozero **63** N 5
Teniente Marsh **115**
Teniente Matienzo **115**
Tenke (U.S.S.R.) **68** L 3
Tennant Creek **78** EF 2
Tennessee **103** J 4
Tenojoki **54** J 2
Teófilo Otoni **111** H 4
Tepatitlán **104** B 3
Tepic **104** AB 3
Teraina **83** E 2
Teramo **57** F 3
Tercan **59** F 3
Terceira **86** A 1
Terek **59** G 2
Teresina **111** H 2
Teressa **73** F 6
Terhazza **86** D 4
Termez **67** H 3
Terni **57** F 3
Ternopol' **62** E 6
Terpugovo **63** N 4
Terrace **98** M 5
Terracina **57** F 3
Terracy Bay **100** K 6
Tessalit **90** E 1
Tessenei **93** F 2
Testa, Capo **57** E 3
Tete **95** E 3
Tétouan **86** D 1
Tetovo **58** B 2
Tevere **57** F 3
Teverya **60** B 2
Tĕwo **70** D 4
Texarkana **103** H 5
Texas **102** FG 5
Texas City **103** G 6
Teya **68** F 3
Teykovo **62** GH 4
Teyuareh **67** G 4
Tezpur **73** F 2
Thailand **73** GH 4
Thakhek **73** HJ 4
Thames **52** C 4
Thana **72** B 4
Thangoo **78** C 2
Thanh Hoa **73** HJ 4
Thanjavur **72** CD 5
Thap Sakae **73** GH 5
Thar Desert **72** B 2
Thargomindah **79** G 4
Tharthār, Wādī ath **60** D 2
Thásos **58** BC 2
Thaton **73** G 4
The Alps **57** EF 2
The Bahamas **105** GH 2–3
Thebes **60** A 4
The Everglades **103** K 6
The Gambia **90** A 3
The Granites **78** DE 3
The Hague **52** D 4
The Johnston Lakes **78** BC 5
The Pas **99** R 5
Thermaïkós Kólpos **58** B 2–3

Thessalía **58** B 3
Thessaloníki **58** B 2
The Wash **52** D 4
Thiès **90** A 3
Thimphu **72** E 2
Thio (Ethiopia) **93** G 2
Thio (New Caledonia) **81** J 6
Thíra **58** C 3
Thompson **99** S 4
Thompson Falls **102** CD 2
Thon Buri **73** GH 5
Thonon **57** E 2
Thraki **58** BC 2
Thrakion Pélagos **58** BC 2
Three Forks **102** D 2
Three Kings Islands **81** PQ 7
Three Pagodas Pass **73** G 4
Thule **114**
Thunder Bay **100** K 6
Thung Song **73** GH 6
Thurston Island **115**
Thy **55** E 4
Tiandong **70** E 6
Tiangua **111** H 1
Tianjin **71** G 3
Tianjun **70** CD 3
Tianmen **70** F 4
Tiantai **71** H 5
Tiaret **87** F 1
Tiber **57** F 3
Tibesti **91** H 1
Tibet **72** E 1
Tichla **86** B 4
Tidjkdja **86** C 5
Tidra, Ile **86** B 5
Tieli **71** J 1
Tielongtan **67** K 4
Tientsin **71** G 3
Tierra de Campos **56** BC 3
Tierra del Pan **56** B 3
Tigil **69** T 4
Tigris **60** D 2
Tiguent **86** B 5
Tihāmat **89** G 5
Tijuana **102** C 5
Tikal **104** E 4
Tikhoretsk **59** F 1
Tikhvin **62** FG 4
Tilburg **52** DE 4
Tillabéri **90** E 3
Tillamook **102** B 2
Timanskiy Kryazh **62** J 2–K 3
Timaru **81** Q 9
Timashevskaya **59** EF 1
Timbauba **111** J 2
Timétrine **90** D 2
Timétrine, Monts **90** D 2
Timia **91** F 2
Timir-Atakh-Tas **69** S 2
Timişoara **58** B 1
Timkapaul' **63** M 3
Timmins **101** L 6
Timmoudi **86** E 3
Timor **75** G 5
Timor, Laut **75** G 6
Timor Sea **75** GH 5
Timote **113** D 6

Tinaca Point **75** G 2
Tindouf **86** D 3
Tinfouchy **86** DE 3
Tingmiarmiut **101** T 3
Tingri **72** E 2
Tinian **82** A 2
Tini Wells **88** C 6
Tinogasta **112** C 4
Tínos **58** C 3
Tinsukia **73** G 2
Ti-n Zaouâtene **87** F 4
Tirán **60** B 4
Tirana **58** AB 2
Tiraspol' **58** CD 1
Tire **58** C 3
Tirgovişte **58** C 1–2
Tîrgu Jiu **58** B 1
Tîrgu Mureş **58** BC 1
Tirnãveni **58** B 1
Tirol **57** F 2
Tirso **57** E 3
Tiruchchirappalli **72** CD 5
Tirunelveli **72** C 6
Tirupati **72** CD 5
Tiruvannamalai **72** C 5
Tisdale **99** R 5
Tisza **58** B 1
Tiszántúl **58** B 1
Titicaca, Lago **110** C 4
Titograd **58** A 2
Titovo Užice **58** AB 2
Titov Veles **58** B 2
Titusville **103** K 6
Tiveden **55** F 4
Tizatlan **104** C 4
Tizimín **104** E 3
Tiznit **86** CD 3
Tjåhumas **54** G 2
Tkhach **59** F 2
Tkvarcheli **59** F 2
Tlemcen **86** E 2
Toamasina **95** HJ 3
Tobago, Isla **109** F 1
Toba & Kakar Ranges **67** H 4
Tobermorey **79** F 3
Tobol **63** N 4
Tobol **63** M 5
Tobol'sk **63** NO 4
Tobseda **62** K 2
Tocantinia **109** J 5
Tocantins **109** J 4
Tocapilla **110** B 5
Tocorpuri, Cerro de **110** C 5
Togiak **98** E 4
Togian, Kepulauan **75** F 4
Togni **88** F 5
Togo **90** E 4
Togtoh **70** F 2
Togyz **67** G 1
Tohma **59** E 3
Toijala **54** H 3
Tok **98** J 3
Tokara-rettō **71** J 4–5
Tokat **59** E 2
Tokelau Islands **82** D 3
Tokko **68** L 4
Tokmak (U.S.S.R.) **59** E 1
Tokmak (U.S.S.R.) **67** K 2

Toksun **67** M 2
Toktogul **67** J 2
Toku-no-shima **71** J 5
Tokur **69** O 5
Tokushima **71** KL 4
Tōkyō **71** L 3
Tolbukhin **58** C 2
Toledo(OH, U.S.A.) **103** K 3
Toledo (Spain) **56** C 4
Toledo, Montes de **56** C 4
Toli **67** L 1
Toliara **95** G 4
Tolima **100** D 3
Toltén **113** B 6
Toluca **104** BC 4
Tol'yatti **62** J 5
Tomakomai **71** M 2
Tomaszów Mazowiecki **53** H 4
Tomatlán **104** AB 4
Tombador, Serra do **110** E 3
Tombigbee River **103** J 5
Tombouctou **90** D 2
Tomé **113** B 6
Tomelloso **56** C 4
Tomini, Teluk **75** F 4
Tomkinson Ranges **78** D 4
Tomma **54** F 2
Tommot **69** N 4
Tompa **68** JK 4
Tomsk **63** R 4
Tonantins **108** E 4
Tondano **75** G 3
Tonekābon **61** F 1
Tonga **82** D 4
Tonga (Sudan) **92** E 3
Tonga Islands **82** D 4
Tongariro National Park **81** QR 8
Tongatapu Group **82** D 4
Tongchuan **70** E 3
Tonghai **70** D 6
Tonghe **71** J 1
Tonghua **71** J 2
Tongliao **71** H 2
Tongoy **112** B 5
Tongren (Guizhou, China) **70** E 5
Tongren (Qinghai, China) **70** D 3
Tongtian He **70** C 4
Tongyu **71** H 2
Tonj **92** D 3
Tonk **72** C 2
Tonle Sap **73** H 5
Tonopah **102** C 4
Tönsberg **55** F 4
Toompine **79** G 4
Toowoomba **79** J 4
Topeka **103** G 4
Topolinyy **69** P 3
Topozero, Ozero **54** K 2
Toraya **110** B 3
Torbat-e Heydariyeh **66** FG 2–3
Torbay **52** C 4
Torbino **62** F 4
Torey **68** H J 5

Tori 92 E 3
Torino 57 E 2
Torneälven 54 H 2
Torneträsk 54 GH 2
Toro, Cerro del 112 C 4
Torom 69 P 5
Toronto 101 M 7
Toropets 62 F 4
Tororo 92 E 4
Toros Dağlari 59 D 3
Torquato Severo 112 F 5
Torrelavega 56 C 3
Torrens, Lake 79 F 5
Torrens Creek 79 H 3
Torrente 56 C 4
Torreón 104 B 2–3
Torres Strait 79 G 1
Torrington 102 F 3
Tortkuduk 63 O 5
Tortosa 56 D 3
Torud 61 G 2
Toruń 53 G 4
Toscana 57 F 3
Tosontsengel 68 G 6
Tostuya 68 K 1
Totma 62 H 4
Totness 109 G 2
Totoras 112 D 5
Totten Glacier 115
Tottori 71 K 3
Touggourt 87 G 2
Toulon 57 E 3
Toulouse 56 D 3
Toungoo 73 G 4
Touraine 56 D 2
Tourcoing 56 D 1
Tourine 86 C 4
Tours 56 D 2
Towakaima 109 G 2
Townsend 102 D 2
Townsville 79 H 2
Toyama 71 L 3
Toygunen 98 C 2
Toyohashi 71 L 4
Toyota 71 L 3
Trabzon 59 E 2
Trafalgar, Cabo 56 B 4
Trâghan 87 HJ 3
Trang 73 G 6
Trangan, Pulau 75 H 5
Transantarctic Mountains 115
Transilvania 58 B 1
Transkei 94 D 6
Transtrandsfjällen 54 F 3
Transvaal 94 D 5
Trapani 57 F 4
Traun 57 F 2
Treinta y Tres 112 EF 5
Trelew 113 CD 7
Trelleborg 55 F 4
Tremonton 102 D 3
Trenčín 53 G 5
Trenel 113 D 6
Trenque Lauquen 113 D 6
Trento 57 F 2
Trenton 103 M 3
Trepassey 101 R 6
Tres Arroyos 113 D 6

Tres Cerros 113 C 8
Tres Esquinas 108 CD 3
Três Lagoas 111 F 5
Tres Puentes 112 BC 4
Treviso 57 F 2
Triabunna 80 L 9
Trialetskiy Khrebet 59 F 2
Trichur 72 C 5
Trier 52 E 5
Trieste 57 F 2
Trikala 58 B 3
Trincomalee 72 D 6
Trindade Island 107 G 5
Trinidad (Bolivia) 110 D 3
Trinidad (CA, U.S.A.) 102 B 3
Trinidad (Colombia) 108 D 2
Trinidad (Cuba) 105 G 3
Trinidad (Uruguay) 112 E 5
Trinidad, Isla 109 F 1
Trinidad and Tobago
109 FG 1
Trinity Islands 98 G 4
Trinkitat 88 F 5
Tripoli 60 B 2
Tripoli (Libya) 87 H 2
Tripolitania 87 HJ 2
Tripura 73 F 3
Trivandrum 72 C 6
Trnava 53 G 5
Trobriand or Kiriwina Islands
81 F 3
Trois-Pistoles 101 O 6
Trois Rivières 101 N 6
Troitsk (U.S.S.R.) 63 M 5
Troitsk (U.S.S.R.) 68 F 4
Troitsko-Pechorsk 62 KL 3
Trollhättan 55 F 4
Trollhetta 54 E 3
Tromelin 85 H 6
Troms 54 G 2
Tromsö 54 G 2
Trondheim 54 F 3
Troodos 59 D 4
Trout Peak 102 E 3
Trout River 101 Q 6
Troy 103 J 5
Troy (Turkey) 58 C 3
Troyan 58 BC 2
Troyez 56 D 2
Troy Peak 102 C 4
Trucial Coast (United Arab
Emirates) 61 FG 4
Trujillo (Peru) 108 C 3
Trujillo (Venezuela) 108 D 2
Truk Islands 82 B 2
Truro 101 P 6
Trust Territory of the Pacific
Islands 82 AB 2
Truth or Consequences
102 E 5
Truva 58 C 3
Trysilfjellet 54 F 3
Tsavo National Park 93 F 5
Tselinograd 63 NO 5
Tsenhermandal 68 JK 6
Tsenogora 62 J 3
Tsentralno Tungusskoye
Plato 68 H 3–4

Tsetseg 68 F 6
Tsetserleg 68 G 6
Tshane 94 C 4
Tshesebe 94 D 4
Tshikapa 92 C 6
Tsiafajavona 95 H 3
Tsimlyanskoye
Vodokhranilishche 59 F 1
Tsingtao 71 H 3
Tsipanda 69 OP 4
Tsjokkarassa 54 HJ 2
Tskhinvali 59 F 2
Tsodilo Hills 94 C 3
Tsuchiura 71 M 3
Tsumeb 94 B 3
Tsumkwe 94 C 3
Tsuruoka 71 L 3
Tuamotu Archipelago
83 FG 4
Tuan 73 H 3
Tuapse 59 E 2
Tuba 68 H 4
Tubal, Wādī aṭ 60 C 2
Tubarão 112 G 4
Tubayq, Jabal aṭ 60 B 3
Tubruq 87 K 2
Tubuai 83 F 4
Tubuai Islands 83 EF 4
Tucano 111 J 3
Tucavaca 110 E 4
Tucson 102 D 5
Tucumcari 102 F 4
Tucuruí 109 HJ 4
Tufi 82 A 3
Tuguegarao 75 J 1
Tugur 69 P 5
Tukangbesi, Kepulauan
75 F 5
Tuktoyaktuk 98 L 2
Tukzar 67 H 3
Tula 104 C 3
Tula (U.S.S.R.) 62 G 5
Tulancingo 104 C 3–4
Tulbagh 94 B 6
Tulcán 108 C 3
Tulcea 58 C 1
Tulchin 58 C 1
Tuloma 54 K 2
Tulsa 103 GH 4
Tuluá 108 C 3
Tulun 68 H 5
Tumaco 108 C 3
Tumany 69 T 3
Tumat 69 PQ 1
Tumbes 108 B 4
Tumd Youqi 70 F 2
Tumeremo 109 F 2
Tümü 87 H 4
Tunas 111 H 5
Tunduru 95 F 2
Tunga 91 F 4
Tungsten 98 M 3
Tunguska, Nizhnyaya 68 F 2
Tungus-Khaya 69 N 3
Tûnis 87 G 1
Tunisia 87 GH 1
Tunja 108 D 2
Tununak 98 D 3

Tunxi 71 G 5
Tuöroyri 52 A 1
Tuostakh 69 P 2
Tuotuo Heyan 70 B 4
Tupã 111 F 5
Tupelo 103 J 5
Tupiza 110 C 5
Tuquan 71 H 1
Tura (U.S.S.R.) 68 H 3
Turakh 68 MN 1
Turana, Khrebet 69 O 5
Turanskaya 66 F 2
Turanskaya Nizmennost
66–67 FG 2
Turbo 108 C 2
Türeh 61 E 2
Tureia 83 F 4
Turgay 67 G 1
Turgayskaya Dolina
63 M 5–6
Turgayskaya Stolovaya
Strana 63 M 5
Türgen Uul 68 F 6
Türgovîshte 58 C 2
Turgutlu 58 C 3
Turhal 59 E 2
Turin 57 E 2–3
Turkestan 67 H 2
Turkey 59 DE 3
Turkey 60 AB 1
Türkiiye 59 DE 3
Turkmeniya 66 F 3
Turks and Caicos Islands
105 HJ 3
Turks Islands 105 H 3
Turku 55 H 3
Turnu Măgurele 58 BC 2
Turpan 70 A 2
Tursha 62 J 4
Turukhansk 63 RS 2
Turukta 68 L 3
Tuscaloosa 103 J 5
Tuticorin 72 C 6
Tutonchany 68 FG 3
Tutubu 92 E 6
Tutuila 82 D 3
Tuvalu 82 D 3
Tuwayq, Jabal 61 D 4
Tuxpan de Rodríguez Cano
104 C 3
Tuxtla Gutiérrez 104 D 4
Tuz Gölü 59 D 3
Tûz Khurmātū 61 D 2
Tuzla 57 G 3
Tyan'-Shan' 67 JK 2
Tychy 53 G 4
Tygda 69 N 5
Tyler 103 G 5
Tynda 69 M 4
Tynset 54 F 3
Tyre 60 B 2
Tyrma 69 O 5
Tyrrhenian Sea 57 F 3–4
Tyubelyakh 69 Q 2
Tyukalinsk 63 O 4
Tyumen' 63 MN 4
Tyungulyu 69 O 3
Tzaneen 94 DE 4

U

Uad el Jat **86** C 3
Ua Huka **83** F 3
Uatumá **109** G 4
Uauá **111** J 2
Uaupés **108** E 4
Ubá **111** H 5
Ubangi **92** B 4
'Ubayyid, Wādī al **60** CD 2
Ubeda **56** C 4
Uberaba **111** G 4
Uberlândia **111** G 4
Ubolratna Dam **73** H 4
Ubombo **95** E 5
Ubort' **55** J 5
Ucayali **108** D 5
Uch-Aral **63** Q 6
Uch Kuduk **67** GH 2
Udachnaya **68** K 2
Udaipur **72** B 3
Udanna **69** Q 2
Uddevalla **55** F 4
Uddjaure **54** G 2
Udgir **72** C 4
Udine **57** F 2
Udipi **72** B 5
Udon Thani **73** H 4
Udskoye **69** O 5
Udzha **68** L 1
Uele **92** C 4
Uelen **98** C 2
Uel'Kal' **98** AB 2
Uelzen **53** F 4
Ufa **62** L 4–5
Ugalla **92** E 6
Ugalla River Game Reserve
   92 E 6
Uganda **92** E 4
Uglegorsk **69** Q 6
Ugoyan **69** N 4
Ugulan **69** T 3
Ugumun **68** L 2
Ugun **69** N 4
Uherské Hradiště **53** G 5
Uil **66** E 1
Uis Mine **94** AB 4
Uitenhage **94** DE 6
Ujae **82** C 2
Ujelang **82** B 2
Ujiji **92** D 6
Ujjain **72** C 3
Ujung **75** E 5
Ujung Pandang **75** E 4–5
Uka **69** U 4
Ukelayat **69** WX 3
Ukhta **62** K 3
Ukmergė **55** HJ 4
Ukraina **62** FG 6
Ukrainka **54** K 5–6
Uktym **62** J 3
Ukwaa **92** E 3
Ulaanbaatar **68** J 6
Ulaga **69** O 2
Ulan Bator **68** J 6
Ulan-Ude **68** J 5
Ularunda **79** H 4
Uleåborg **54** J 3

Ulety **68** K 5
Ulhasnagar **72** B 4
Uliastay **68** G 6
Uliga **82** C 2
Ullapool **52** B 3
Ulovo **69** S 1
Ulsan **71** JK 3
Ulster **52** B 4
Ulu **88** E 6
Uludağ **58** C 3
Ulutau, Gory **67** H 1
Ul'yanovsk **62** J 5
Uma **68** M 5
Uman' **58** D 1
Umanak **114**
Umari **75** J 4
Umba **54** K 2
Umboi **80** E 3
Umbria **57** F 3
Umeå **54** H 3
Umm al Qaywayn **61** G 4
Umm Durmān **88** E 5
Umm Lajj **60** B 4
Umm Ruwābah **88** E 6
Umm Urūmah **60** B 4
Umnak **98** D 5
Umtata **94** D 6
Umuarama **111** F 5
Umvuma **95** E 3
Unaí **111** G 4
Unalakleet **98** E 3
Unalaska **98** D 5
Unayzah (Jordan) **60** B 3
'Unayzah (Saudi Arabia)
   60 D 4
Ungava Bay **101** O 4
União do Vitória **112** F 4
Unimak **98** E 5
Union of Soviet Socialist
   Republics **65** HP 4
United Arab Emirates
   61 FG 5
United Kingdom **52** DC 3
United States **102–103**
Unity **99** Q 5
Universales, Montes **56** C 3
Unst **52** C 2
Uoyan **68** K 4
Upata **109** F 2
Upemba, Lac **92** D 6
Upemba National Park **92** D 6
Upernavik **114**
Upington **94** C 5
Upolu **82** D 3
Upper Red Lake **103** GH 2
Uppland **55** G 3
Uppsala **55** G 4
Urak **69** Q 4
Ural **66** E 1
Ural Mountains **63** LM 2–4
Ural'sk **62** K 5
Urandangie **79** F 3
Urandi **111** H 3
Uranium City **99** Q 4
Uraricoera **109** F 3
Ura Tyube **67** H 3
Urayq, Natud al **60** D 4
Urbano Santos **111** H 1

Uren **62** J 4
Urewera National Park **81** R 8
Urfa (Turkey) **59** E 3
Urfa Platosu **59** E 3
Urgench **66** FG 2
Uribia **108** D 1
Uromi **91** F 4
Ur Suq ash Shuyūkh **61** DE 3
Ursus **53** H 4
Uruaçu **111** G 3
Uruapan **104** B 4
Urucará **109** G 4
Uruçuí **111** H 2
Uruguaiana **112** E 4–5
Uruguay **112** EF 5
Uruguay **112** EF 5
Urumchi **67** M 2
Ürümqi **67** M 2
Uruqnay **112** E 5
Uryupinsk **62** H 5
Uşak **58** C 3
'Ushayrah **61** DE 4
Ushuaia **113** C 9
Üsküdar **58** C 2
Ussuriysk **71** K 2
Ust'-Bol'sheretsk **69** ST 5
Ust'-Chayka **68** J 3
Ust'-Ilimsk **68** H 4
Ustinov **62** K 4
Ust-Kada **68** H 5
Ust'-Kamchatsk **69** U 4
Ust'-Kamenogorsk **63** QR 5–6
Ust'-Karenga **68** L 5
Ust'-Karsk **68** L 5
Ust'-Khayryuzovo **69** ST 4
Ust'-Kulom **62** K 3
Ust'-Kut **68** J 4
Ust-Labinsk **59** EF 1
Ust'-Nera **69** Q 3
Ust'-Olenëk **68** LM 1
Ust'-Ozernoye **63** RS 4
Ust'-Pit **68** F 4
Ust'-Port **63** Q 2
Ust'-Sugoy **69** S 3
Ust'-Tatta **69** O 3
Ust'-Tym **63** Q 4
Ust'-Ura **62** H 3
Ust'-Urgal **69** O 5
Ust'-Us **68** F 5
Ust'-Usa **62** L 2
Ust'-Uyskoye **63** M 5
Ustuyurt, Plato **66** F 2
Ust'-Vyyskaya **62** J 3
Ust'Yuribey **63** NO 2
Usu **67** L 2
Usulután **104** E 5
Usumacinta, Rio **104** D 4
Utah **102** D 4
Utah Lake **102** D 4
Utata **68** H 5
Utės **63** P 5
Utesiki **69** W 2
Utiariti **110** E 3
Utica **103** M 3
Utirik **82** C 2
Utrecht **52** DE E 4
Utrera **56** B 4
Uttyakh **69** O 2

Uuldza **68** K 6
Uusimaa **55** J 3
Uvarovo **62** H 5
Uvinza **92** DE 6
Uvs Nuur **68** F 5
Uwayrid, Harrat al **60** B 4
Uxituba **109** G 4
Uyaly **67** G 2
Uyandi **69** Q 2
Uyega **69** Q 3
Uyuni **110** C 5
Uyuni, Salar de **110** C 5
Uzbekistan **67** GH 2
Uzbel Shankou **67** J 3
Uzhgorod **58** B 1
Uzhur **63** R 4
Uzunköprü **58** C 2

V

Vaal **94** C 5
Vaasa **54** H 3
Vác **58** A 1
Vacaria **112** FG 4
Vadodara **72** B 3
Vadsö **54** J 1
Vaduz **57** E 2
Vágar **52** A 1
Vaghena **81** G 3
Vairaatea **83** F 4
Vaitupu **82** C 3
Vakarevo **69** W 3
Valachia **58** BC 2
Valcheta **113** C 7
Valday **62** F 4
Val de Loire **56** D 2
Valdepeñas **56** C 4
Valdés, Península **113** D 7
Valdez **98** H 3
Valdivia **113** B 6
Val-d'Or **101** M 6
Valdosta **103** K 5
Valença **111** J 3
Valenca do Piauí **111** H 2
Valence **57** DE 2–3
Valencia (Spain) **56** CD 4
Valencia (Venezuela) **108** E 2
Valentine **102** F 3
Valera **108** D 2
Valga **55** J 4
Valjevo **58** AB 2
Valladolid (Mexico) **104** E 3
Valladolid (Spain) **56** C 3
Vall de Uxó **56** C 4
Valle de la Pascua **108** E 2
Valledupar **108** D 1
Valle Grande **110** D 4
Vallenar **112** BC 4
Valletta **57** F 4
Valleyview **99** O 4
Valparaíso **112** B 5
Vals, Tanjung **75** J 5
Vammala **54** H 3
Van **59** F 3
Vanavara **68** H 3
Vancouver **99** N 6
Vancouver Island **99** M 6
Vanda **115**
Vanderbijlpark **94** D 5

Vanderhoof **99** N 5
Van Diemen, Cape **78** D 1
Van Diemen Gulf **78** E 1
Vanduzi **95** E 3
Vänern **55** F 4
Van Gölü **59** F 3
Vangunu **81** G 3
Vanikolo Islands **81** J 4
Vanikoro Island **82** C 3
Vankarem **98** B 2
Vannes **56** C 2
Vanoua Lava **81** J 4
Vanrhynsdorp **94** B 6
Vanua Levu **82** C 4
Vanuatu **81** J 5
Vanuatu **82** B 3
Vanzhil'kynak **63** QR 3
Varanasi **72** D 2
Varangerfjorden **54** K 1–2
Varangerhalvöya **54** JK 1
Varaždin **57** G 2
Varberg **55** F 4
Vardö **54** K 1
Vardofjällen **54** FG 2
Varginha **111** GH 5
Varkaus **54** J 3
Värmland **55** F 4
Varna (Bulgaria) **58** C 2
Värnamo **55** F 4
Varsinais Suomi **55** H 3
Var'yegan **63** P 3
Vashnel **63** N 3
Vasiss **63** O 4
Vassdalsegga **55** E 4
Västerås **55** G 4
Västerbotten **54** G 3
Västergötland **55** F 4
Västervik **55** G 4
Vasto **57** F 3
Västra Granberget **54** H 2
Vasyugan **63** P 4
Vaticano, Citta Del **57** F 3
Vatnajökull **54** B 3
Vatoa **82** D 4
Vättern **55** F 4
Vatyna **69** W 3
Vaughn **102** E 5
Vaupés **108** D 3
Vava'u Group **82** D 4
Växjö **55** FG 4
Vayvida **68** FG 3
Vazhgort **62** J 3
Veadeiros **111** G 3
Vefsna **54** F 2
Vega **54** F 2
Vegreville **99** P 5
Vejle **55** E 4
Velež **57** G 3
Vélez-Málaga **56** C 4
Velikiye Luki **55** K 4
Velikiy Ustyug **62** HJ 3
Veliko Türnovo **58** C 2
Vella Lavella **81** G 3
Vellore **72** CD 5
Velsk **62** H 3
Vel't **62** K 2
Vemor'ye **69** Q 6
Venado Tuerto **112** D 5

Venda **95** E 4
Venezia **57** F 2
Venezuela **108–109** EF 2
Venezuela, Golfo de **108** D 1
Vengerovo **63** P 4
Venice **57** F 2
Venta **55** H 4
Ventoux, Mont **57** E 3
Ventspils **55** H 4
Ventura **102** C 5
Venustiano Carranza **104** D 4
Vera **112** DE 4
Veracruz **104** CD 4
Veraval **72** AB 3
Verbania **57** E 2
Verdalsöra **54** F 3
Verdun **57** E 2
Vereeniging **94** D 5
Verkhn'aya Salda **63** M 4
Verkhneimbatskoye **63** RS 3
Verkhneural'sk **63** LM 5
Verkhnevilyuysk **68** LM 3
Verkhneye Kuyto,Ozero
    54 K 3
Verkhnyaya Amga **69** NO 4
Verkhnyaya Vol'dzha **63** PQ 4
Verkhoyansk **69** O 2
Verkhoyanskiy Khrebet
    69 N 2–P 3
Verkhoyansk Range **69** N 2
Vermilion Bay **100** J 5
Vermont **103** M 3
Verona **57** F 2
Vérroia **58** B 2
Versailles **56** D 2
Vershina **63** M 3
Vershino-Shakhtaminskiye
    68 L 5
Vest-Agder **55** E 4
Vesterålen **54** FG 2
Vestfirðir **54** A 2
Vestfjorden **54** F 2
Vestvågöy **54** F 2
Vesuvio **57** F 3
Vetlanda **55** G 4
Vetrenyy **69** R 3
Viacha **110** C 4
Viborg **55** E 4
Vibo Valentia **57** G 4
Vicecommodoro Marambio
    115
Vicenza **57** F 2
Vichada **108** E 3
Vichy **56** D 2
Vicksburg **103** HJ 5
Victoria (Australia) **79** G 6
Victoria (Canada) **99** N 6
Victoria (Chile) **113** B 6
Victoria (Hong Kong) **70** F 6
Victoria (Seychelles) **93** JK 5
Victoria (TX, U.S.A.) **103** G 6
Victoria, Mount (Burma)
    73 F 3
Victoria, Mount (Papua New
    Guinea) **82** A 3
Victoria de Durango **104** B 3
Victoria de las Tunas **105** G 3
Victoria Falls **94** D 3

Victoria Island **99** PQ 1
Victoria Land **115**
Victoria River **78** E 2
Victoria Strait **99** R 2
Victoria West **94** C 6
Vicuña Mackenna **112** D 5
Vidin **58** B 2
Vidisha **72** C 3
Vidsel **54** H 2
Viduša **57** G 3
Vidzemes Augstiene **55** J 4
Viedma **113** D 7
Viedma, Lago **113** B 8
Vieng Pou Kha **73** H 3
Vienna **57** G 2
Vienne **57** DE 2
Vientiane **73** H 4
Vientos, Paso de los
    105 H 3–4
Vierzon **56** D 2
Vietnam **73** JK 5
Vifosa **58** B 2
Vigan **75** J 1
Vigevano **57** E 2
Vigo **56** B 3
Viiala **54** H 3
Vijayawada **72** D 4
Vikna **54** F 3
Vila **81** J 5
Vila Conceição **109** F 3
Vilanculo **95** F 4
Vila Nova de Gaia **56** B 3
Vila Velha (Amapá, Brazil)
    109 H 3
Vila Velha (Espírito Santo,
    Brazil) **111** HJ 5
Vıldız Dağları **58** C 2
Vilhena **110** D 3
Villa Abecia **110** CD 5
Villa Bella **110** C 3
Villach **57** F 2
Villa Constitución **112** D 5
Villa Coronado **104** B 2
Villa Dolores **112** C 5
Villa Frontera **104** B 2
Villagarcia de Arosa **56** B 3
Villaguay **112** E 5
Villahermosa **104** D 4
Villa Huidobro **112** D 5
Villa Ingavi **110** D 5
Villalonga **113** D 6
Villa María **112** D 5
Villa Mazán **112** C 4
Villa Montes **110** D 5
Villanova y Geltrú **56** D 3
Villa Ocampo **104** AB 2
Villareal de las Enfants
    56 CD 4
Villa Regina **113** C 6
Villarreal de los Infantes
    56 CD 4
Villarrica (Chile) **113** B 6
Villarrica (Paraguay) **112** E 4
Villatoro, Puerto de **56** B 3
Villa Unión **112** C 4
Villavicencio **108** D 3
Villazón **110** C 5
Villefranche **57** DE 2

Villena **56** C 4
Vilnius **55** J 5
Vilyuy **69** MN 3
Vilyuyskoye Plato **68** J 2
Vilyuyskt **68** M 3
Viña del Mar **112** B 5
Vindhya Range **72** BC 3
Vinh **73** J 4
Vinh Giat **73** JK 5
Vinh Linh **73** J 4
Vinh Loi **73** J 6
Vinkovci **57** G 2
Vinnitsa **62** E 6
Vinson Massif **115**
Virac **75** F 1
Virandozero **62** FG 3
Viranşehir **59** F 3
Virden **99** R 6
Virgem da Lapa **111** H 4
Virginia (South Africa) **94** D 5
Virginia (U.S.A.) **103** L 4
Virginia Beach **103** LM 4
Virginia Falls **99** N 3
Virgin Islands **105** JK 4
Virrat **54** H 3
Virtsu **55** H 4
Virtul Gutii **58** B 1
Visayan Sea **75** F 1
Visby **55** G 4
Viscount Melville Sound
    99 P 1
Vishakhapatnam **72** DE 4
Vista Alegre **109** F 3
Vistula **53** G 5
Vitebsk **55** K 4
Vitiaz Strait **80** E 3
Viti Levu **82** C 4
Vitim **68** K 4–5
Vitimskoye Ploskogor'ye
    68 K 5
Vitória (Espírito Santo, Brazil)
    111 HJ 5
Vitória (Pará, Brazil) **109** H 4
Vitoria (Spain) **56** C 3
Vitória da Conquista **111** H 3
Vittorio Veneto **57** F 2
Vivorata **113** E 6
Vizianagaram **72** D 4
Vladimir **62** H 4
Vladimir **71** L 2
Vladimirovka **62** K 5
Vladimir-Volynskiy **55** H 5
Vladivostok **71** K 2
Vlissingen **52** D 4
Vlorë **58** A 2
Vltava **57** F 2
Vogan **90** E 4
Voghera **57** E 2
Voi **93** F 5
Voinjama **90** C 4
Volcán Citlaltépetl **104** C 4
Volcán Llullaillaco **110** C 5
Volcán Miravalles **104** EF 5
Volcán Misti **110** B 4
Volcán Ollagüe **110** C 5
Volcán Popocatéptl **104** C 4
Volcán Tajumulco **104** D 4
Volga **62** J 5

Vol – Win

Volgo-Balt (I.V. Lenin) Kanal 62 FG 3
Volgodonsk 59 F 1
Volgograd 62 H 6
Volkhau 54 K 4
Volkhov 55 K 4
Volochayevka 69 O 6
Vologda 62 GH 4
Volokon 68 J 4
Volos 58 B 3
Vol'sk 62 J 5
Volta 90 E 4
Volta Redonda 111 GH 5
Volynskoye Polesye 55 J 5
Volzhsk 62 J 4
Volzhskiy 62 J 6
Vopnafjörður 54 C 2
Vórioi Sporádhes 58 B 3
Vorkuta 63 MN 2
Vormsi 55 H 4
Voronezh 62 GH 5
Voroshilovgrad 59 EF 1
Võrts Järv 55 J 4
Võru 55 J 4
Vosges 57 E 2
Voss 55 E 3
Vostochnaya Litsa 62 G 2
Vostochnyy Sayan 68 G 5
Vostok (Antarctica) 115
Vostok (Kiribati) 83 E 3
Votkinsk 62 K 4
Voyampolka 69 T 4
Vozhega 62 H 3
Voznesensk 58 D 1
Vozvyshennost' Karabil' 67 G 3
Vran 57 G 3
Vranje 58 B 2
Vratsa 58 B 2
Vršac 58 B 1
Vryburg 94 C 5
Vryheid 95 E 5
Vsetin 53 G 5
Vsevidof, Mount 98 D 5
Vsevolozhsk 55 K 3
Vukovar 57 G 2
Vung Tau 73 J 5
Vuoksa 54 J 3
Vyaltsevo 62 H 4
Vyatskiye Polyany 62 K 4
Vyazemskiy 69 OP 6
Vyaz'ma 62 F 4
Vyborg 54 J 3
Vychegda 62 J 3
Vyksa 62 H 4
Vyngapur 63 P 3
Vysotsk 55 J 3
V'yuny 63 Q 4

W

Wabowden 99 S 5
Wabrah 66 D 5
Waco 103 G 5
Wad 67 H 5
Waddän 87 J 3
Waddington, Mount 99 M 5
Wādi al 'Arabah 60 B 3

Wādi al Bātin 61 DE 3
Wādi al Ghudāf 60 D 2
Wādi al Khurr 60 C 3
Wādi al 'Ubayyid 60 CD 2
Wādi ath Tharthār 60 D 2
Wādi at Tubal 60 C 2
Wādi Halfa' 88 E 4
Wādi Hawrān 60 C 2
Wādi Jimāl 60 B 4
Wādi Qina 60 A 4
Wadley 103 K 5
Wad Madani 88 EF 6
Wafrah 66 D 5
Wagga Wagga 79 H 6
Wagin 78 B 5
Wah 67 J 4
Wahai 75 G 4
Wāhāt al Khārijah 88 E 3–4
Waigeo, Pulau 75 H 4
Waingapu 75 F 5
Wajir 93 G 4
Wakayama 71 L 4
Wake 82 C 1
Wakkanai 71 M 1
Wałbrzych 53 G 4
Waldia 93 F 2
Wales 52 C 4
Walewale 90 D 3
Walgett 79 H 4–5
Wallaroo 79 F 5
Wallis 82 D 3
Wallis and Futuna 82 CD 3
Walnut Ridge 103 H 4
Walvis Bay 94 A 4
Wanaaring 79 G 4
Wanaka 82 C 5
Wandel Sea 114
Wanganui 81 R 8
Wangka 73 G 5
Wangqing 71 J 2
Wan Hsa-la 73 G 3
Wankie 94 D 3
Wankie National Park 94 D 3
Wanxian 70 E 4
Warangal 72 CD 4
Warbumi 75 H 4
Warburton Mission 78 D 4
Waren 75 J 4
Warner Peak 102 C 3
Warner Robins 103 K 5
Warragul 79 H 6
Warren 103 K 3
Warrenton 94 C 5
Warri 91 F 4
Warrnambool 79 G 6
Warrumbungle Range 79 H 5
Warsaw 53 H 4
Warszawa 53 H 4
Warta 53 G 4
Warwick 79 J 4
Wasatch Range 102 D 3–4
Washington (D.C., U.S.A.) 103 L 4
Washington (U.S.A.) 102 BC 2
Wasua 80 D 3
Wasum 81 E 3
Watampone 75 F 4
Waterberg 94 B 4

Waterford 52 B 4
Waterloo 103 H 3
Waterton Lakes National Park 99 OP 6
Watertown 103 LM 3
Watheroo 78 B 5
Watrous (Canada) 99 QR 5
Watrous (N.M., U.S.A.) 102 F 4
Watsa 92 D 4
Watson Lake 98 LM 3
Wauchope 79 J 5
Wausau 103 J 3
Wave Hill 78 E 2
Wāw 92 D 3
Wawotobi 75 F 4
Waycross 103 K 5
Wayland 103 K 4
Weagamow Lake 100 J 5
Webbe Shibeli 93 G 3
Weddel Sea 115
Weichang 71 G 2
Weiden 53 F 5
Weifang 71 GH 3
Weimar 53 F 4
Weining 70 D 5
Weipa 79 G 1
Wejherowo 53 G 4
Welkom 94 D 5
Wellesley Islands 79 F 2
Wellington (New Zealand) 81 R 9
Wellington, Isla (Chile) 113 AB 8
Wells (NV, U.S.A.) 102 C 3
Wels 57 F 2
Wendeng 71 H 3
Wenshan 70 DE 6
Wentworth 79 G 5
Wenzhou 71 H 5
Wepener 94 D 5
Weser 53 E 4
Wesleyville 101 R 6
Wessel, Cape 79 F 1
West Antarctica 115
Westbank 60 B 2
West Berlin 55 F 5
West Berlin 55 F 5
West Cape 82 C 6
Western Australia 78 C 3–4
Western Ghats Kerala 72 BC 4–5
Western Sahara 86 C 4
Western Samoa 82 D 3
West Falkland 113 D 9
West Ice Shelf 115
West Indies 104 HJ 3
West Indies 105 HJ 3
Westlock 99 P 5
West Memphis 103 H 4–5
West Palm Beach 103 L 6
West Plains 103 H 4
Westport 81 Q 9
Westree 101 L 6
West Siberian Plain 63 OQ 3
West Virginia 103 K 4
West Wyalong 79 H 5
West Yellowstone 102 D 3

Wetar, Pulau 75 G 5
Wetaskiwin 99 P 5
Wete 93 FG 5
Wewak 80 D 2
Weyburn 99 R 6
Whale Cove 99 T 3
Whangarei 81 Q 8
Wheatland 102 F 3
Wheeler Peak 102 E 4
Wheeling 103 KL 4
Whitecourt 99 O 5
Whitehaven 52 C 4
Whitehorse 98 KL 3
White Mountain Peak 102 C 4
White Nile 88 E 6
White Pass 98 L 4
White River 100 L 6
White Russia 55 J 5
White Sea 62 G 2
Whitewood 79 G 3
Whitmore Mountains 115
Wholdaia Lake 99 QR 3
Wichita 102 G 4
Wichita Falls 102 G 5
Wick 52 C 3
Wickenburg 102 D 5
Wien 57 G 2
Wiener Neustadt 57 G 2
Wieprz 53 H 4
Wiesbaden 53 E 4
Wilhelm, Mount 80 D 3
Wilhelmshaven 53 E 4
Wilkes-Barre 103 L 3
Wilkes Land 115
Willcox 102 E 5
Willemstad 108 E 1
Willeroo 78 E 2
Williams 102 D 4
Williams Lake 99 N 5
Williamsport 103 L 3
Williston (South Africa) 94 C 6
Williston (U.S.A.) 102 F 2
Williston Lake 99 N 4
Wilmington (DE, U.S.A.) 103 L 4
Wilmington (N.C., U.S.A.) 103 L 5
Wilowmore 94 C 6
Wilson 103 L 4
Wilson Bluff 78 D 5
Wilsons Promontory 79 H 6
Windhoek 94 B 4
Windsor 103 K 3
Windward Islands (French Polynesia) 83 F 4
Windward Islands (Lesser Antilles) 105 L 4–5
Winisk 100 K 4
Winisk River 100 K 5
Winneba 90 D 4
Winnemucca 102 C 3
Winnipeg 99 S 6
Winnipeg, Lake 99 S 5
Winnipegosis, Lake 99 RS 5
Winona 103 H 3
Winslow (AZ., U.S.A.) 102 DE 4
Winslow (Kiribati) 82 D 3

182

Winston-Salem **103** K 4
Winterthur **57** E 2
Wisconsin **103** HJ 2
Wiseman **98** G 2
Wista **53** G 4
Wismar **53** F 4
Wittenberg **53** F 4
Wittenberge **53** F 4
Włocławek **53** G 4
Wokam, Pulau **75** H 5
Woleai **82** A 2
Wollastone Lake **99** R 4
Wollaston Lake **99** R 4
Wollaston Peninsula **99** OP 2
Wollongong **79** J 5
Wolverhamton **52** C 4
Wonju **71** J 3
Wŏnsan **71** J 3
Wonthaggi **79** GH 6
Wood Buffalo National Park
   99 OP 4
Woodlark **81** F 3
Wood River Lakes **98** F 4
Woodstock (Queensland,
   Austr.) **79** G 2
Woodward **102** FG 4
Woomera **79** F 5
Wooramel **78** A 4
Worcester (South Africa)
   94 BC 6
Worcester (U.K.) **52** C 4
Worchester (MA, U.S.A.)
   103 M 3
Worland **102** E 3
Wosi **75** G 4
Wotho **82** BC 2
Wotje **82** C 2
Wrangel Island **114**
Wrangell **98** L 4
Wrangell Saint Elias National
   Park and Preserve **98** J 3
Wrigley **99** N 3
Wrocław **53** G 4
Wuchuan **70** E 5
Wudaoliang **70** B 3
Wudu **70** D 4
Wugang **70** F 5
Wugong **70** E 4
Wuhai **70** E 3
Wuhan **70** FG 4
Wuhu **71** G 4
Wüjang **72** D 1
Wukari **91** F 4
Wuliang Shan **70** D 6
Wun Rog **92** D 3
Wuppertal **53** E 4
Wurung **79** G 2
Würzburg **53** F 5
Wutunghliao **70** D 5
Wuvulu **82** A 3
Wuwei **70** D 3
Wuxi **71** H 4
Wuxing **71** H 4
Wuyiling **69** N 6
Wuyuan **70** E 2
Wuzhi Shan **70** E 7
Wuzhong **70** E 3
Wuzhou **70** F 6

Wynbring **78** E 5
Wyndham **78** D 2
Wyoming **102** E 3
Wyoming Peak **102** DE 3
Wyperfeld National Park
   79 G 6
Wysoczyzna Ciechanowska
   53 GH 4

X

Xainza **72** E 1
Xai-Xai **95** E 5
Xambioá **109** J 5
Xangongo **94** AB 3
Xánthi **58** B 2
Xanthos **58** C 3
Xapecó **112** F 4
Xapuri **110** C 3
Xayar **67** L 2
Xenia **103** K 4
Xiaguan **70** D 5
Xiamen **71** G 6
Xi'an **70** EF 4
Xiangfan **70** F 4
Xiangshan **71** H 5
Xiangtan **70** F 5
Xiangyin **70** F 5
Xianju **71** H 5
Xianyang **70** E 4
Xiao'ergou **69** M 6
Xiao Hinggan Ling **69** N 5–6
Xiapu **71** H 5
Xichang **70** D 5
Xigazê **72** E 2
Xiliao He **71** H 2
Ximiao **70** D 2
Xin Barag Zuoqi **68** L 6
Xingcheng **71** GH 2
Xingdi **70** A 2
Xingren **70** E 5
Xingtai **70** F 3
Xingu **109** H 4
Xing Xian **70** EF 3
Xingxingxia **70** C 2
Xingyi **70** D 5–6
Xining **70** D 3
Xinjiang Uygur Zizhiqu
   67 KM 2
Xinjin (Liaoning, China)
   71 H 3
Xinjin (Sichuan, China) **70** D 4
Xinlitun **69** N 5
Xin Xian **70** F 3
Xinxiang **70** FG 3
Xinyang **70** F 4
Xinyi **71** G 4
Xinyuan **67** L 2
Xique-Xique **111** H 3
Xiushui **70** F 5
Xiuyan **71** H 2
Xiwu **70** C 4
Xixiang **70** E 4
Xizang Zizhiqu **72** DE 1
Xpuhil **104** E 4
Xuanhan **70** E 4
Xuanhua **70** F 2
Xuanwei **70** D 5
Xuchang **70** FG 4

Xuguit Qi **68** LM 6
Xümatang **70** C 4
Xuwen **70** F 6
Xuyong **70** DE 5
Xuzhou **71** G 4

Y

Yablonovyy Khrebet **68** JL 5
Yabrūd **60** B 2
Yacuiba **110** D 5
Yadgir **72** C 4
Yagoua **91** GH 3
Yagradagze Shan **70** C 3
Yakima **102** BC 2
Yakmach **67** G 5
Yakoma **92** C 4
Yakrik **67** L 2
Yakumo **71** LM 2
Yakutat **98** K 4
Yakutsk **69** N 3
Yala (Sri Lanka) **72** D 6
Yala (Thailand) **73** H 6
Yalgoo **78** B 4
Yalnızçam Dağları **59** F 2
Yalong Jiang **70** D 4–5
Yalta **59** D 2
Yalutorovsk **63** MN 4
Yamagata **71** LM 3
Yamal Peninsula **63** NO 1
Yambio **92** D 4
Yambol **58** C 2
Yamburg **63** OP 2
Yamdena, Pulau **75** H 5
Yamoussoukro **90** C 4
Yamuna **72** D 2
Yana **69** P 1
Yan'an **70** E 3
Yanartaş Dağları **58** CD 3
Yanbu' **60** C 4
Yanchang **70** EF 3
Yandrakinot **98** C 2
Yangambi **92** CD 4
Yangjiang **70** F 6
Yangquan **70** F 3
Yangtze Kiang **70** C 4
Yangtze Leiang **71** G 4
Yang Xian **70** E 4
Yanhe **70** E 5
Yanhuqu **72** D 1
Yankton **102** G 3
Yano-Indigirskaya
   Nizmennost **69** PR 1
Yanov Stan **63** Q 2
Yanqi Huizu Zizhixian
   67 LM 2
Yanshou **71** J 1
Yanskiy Zaliv **69** OP 1
Yantai **71** H 3
Yaoundé **91** G 5
Yapen, Pulau **75** J 4
Yapura **108** D 4
Yaraka **79** G 3
Yaranga **69** X 3
Yaransk **62** J 4
Yari **108** D 3
Yarlung Zangbo Jiang **70** B 5
Yarmouth **101** O 7
Yaroslavl' **62** G 4

Yarram **79** H 6
Yarroto **63** O 2
Yartsevo **63** RS 3
Yarumal **108** CD 2
Yashkino **69** P 5
Yasnyy **69** N 5
Yaté-Village **81** J 6
Yathkyed Lake **99** S 3
Yatsushiro **71** JK 4
Yavi, Cerro **108** E 2
Yawng-hwe **73** G 3
Ya Xian **70** E 7
Yazd **61** G 3
Yazdān **67** G 4
Yaz-ed Khvāst **61** F 3
Yecheng **67** K 3
Yedoma **62** H 3
Yeeda River **78** C 2
Yefremov **62** G 5
Yegorlykskaya **59** F 1
Yei **92** E 4
Yelabuga **62** K 4
Yelets **62** G 5
Yelizarovo **63** N 3
Yelizovo **69** T 5
Yellowhead Pass **99** O 5
Yellowknife **99** P 3
Yellow Sea **71** H 4
Yellowstone National Park
   102 D 3
Yellowstone river **102** EF 2
Yelovka **69** U 4
Yelvertoft **79** F 3
Yemanzhelinsk **63** M 5
Yematan **70** C 3
Yemen **89** GH 5
Yengisar **67** K 3
Yengo **91** H 5
Yengue **91** F 5
Yenice **59** E 3
Yenisey **63** R 2
Yenisey, Malyy **68** FG 5
Yeniseyskiy Kryazh **68** F 3–4
Yepoko **63** OP 2
Yercha **69** R 2
Yerema **68** J 3
Yerevan **59** FG 2
Yergeni **59** F 1
Yermak **63** P 5
Yerofey-Pavlovich **69** M 5
Yeropol **69** V 2
Yertom **62** J 3
Yerupajá, Nevado **110** A 3
Yerushalayim **60** B 3
Yesil **63** N 5
Yeşilırmak **59** E 2
Yessentuki **59** F 2
Yetman **79** J 4
Yeu, Ile d' **56** C 2
Yevpatoriya **59** D 1
Yeya **59** E 1
Yeysk **59** E 1
Yi'an **69** N 6
Yibin **70** D 5
Yichang **70** F 4
Yichun **69** N 6
Yidu **70** F 4
Yıldız Dağı **59** E 2

Yilehuli Shan **69** MN 5
Yiliang **70** D 6
Yinchuan **70** E 3
Yingde **70** F 6
Yingkou **71** H 2
Yining **67** L 2
Yirga Alem **93** F 3
Yitulihe **69** M 5
Yiyang **70** F 5
Ylikitka **54** J 2
Yllastuntun **54** H 2
Yoboki **93** G 2
Yogyakarta **74** CD 5
Yokohama **71** LM 3–4
Yokosuka **71** LM 3–4
Yokote **71** LM 3
Yola **91** G 4a
Yolombo **92** C 5
Yonago **71** K 3
Yŏngan **71** JK 2
Yongchang **70** D 3
Yong deng **70** D 3
Yongren **70** D 5
Yonkers **103** M 3
Yonne **56** D 2
York (PA, U.S.A.) **103** L 4
York (U.K.) **52** C 4
York (Western Australia) **78** B 5
Yorke Peninsula **79** F 5
Yorkton **99** R 5
Yosemite National Park **102** BC 4
Yoshkar Ola **62** J 4
Yōsu **71** J 4
Young **79** H 5
Youngstown **103** KL 3
Yozgat **59** D 3
Ytyk-Kel' **69** O 3
Yuanping **70** F 3
Yucatán Peninsula **104** E 3–4
Yucheng **71** G 3
Yuci **70** F 3
Yudoma **69** P 4
Yuexi **70** D 5
Yueyang **70** F 5
Yugorskiy Poluostrov **63** M 2
Yugoslavia **57** G 3
Yukagirskoye Ploskogor'ye **69** ST 2
Yukon **98** EF 3
Yukon-Charley Rivers National Preserve **98** J 2–3
Yukon Flats **98** H 2
Yukon Flats National Monument **98** H 2
Yukon Plateau **98** K 3
Yukon River **98** J 2
Yukon Territory **98** KL 3
Yulin (China) **70** EF 6
Yulin (Shaanxi, China) **70** E 3
Yuma **102** F 3
Yumari, Cerro **108** E 3
Yumen **70** C 3
Yumenzhen **70** C 2
Yunaska **98** C 5

Yunling Shan **70** C 5
Yunnan **70** D 6
Yunxiao **71** G 6
Yuriby **63** P 1
Yurimaguas **108** C 5
Yurty **69** U 4
Yushan (China) **71** G 5
Yushan (Taiwan) **71** H 6
Yushnoye **69** Q 6
Yuxi **70** D 6
Yu Xian **70** FG 2–3
Yuzhno-Sakhalinsk **69** Q 6
Yuzhnyy Bug **58** CD 1

Z

Zabarjad **60** B 5
Zabol **67** G 4
Zabrze **53** G 4
Zacapu **104** B 4
Zacatecas **104** B 3
Zadar **57** G 3
Zadetkale Kyun **73** G 5
Zadran **67** H 4
Za'faranah **60** A 3
Zag **86** D 3
Zägheh-ye Bálá **61** E 2
Zagorsk **62** G 4
Zagreb **57** G 2
Zagros, Kühha ye **61** EF 2
Zagros Mountains (Iran) **61** F 3
Záhedán **67** G 5
Záhirah **61** G 5
Zahlah **60** B 2
Zaire **92** BD 5
Zaire (Angola) **94** A 1
Zakamensk **68** H J 5
Zakharov **69** O 3
Zákhú **66** C 3
Zákinthos **58** B 3
Zalábiyah (Syria) **60** C 2
Zalaegerszeg **58** A 1
Zalim **89** G 4
Zaliv Akademii **69** P 5
Zaliv Kara-Bogaz Gol **66** E 2
Zaliv Shelikhova **69** T 3–4
Zaliv Terpeniya **69** Q 6
Zallah **87** J 3
Zamakh **89** H 5
Zambeze **95** E 3
Zambezi **94** C 2
Zambia **94** D 2
Zamboanga **75** F 2
Zamora (Ecuador) **108** C 4
Zamora (Spain) **56** B 3
Zamość **53** H 4
Zanesville **103** K 4
Zanján **66** D 3
Zanthus **78** C 5
Zanul'e **62** K 3
Zanzibar **93** FG 6
Zanzibar Island **93** FG 6
Zaouatallaz **87** G 4
Zaoyang **70** F 4
Zaozernyy **68** FG 4
Zaozhuang **71** G 4

Zaragoza **56** C 3
Zarand (Iran) **61** F 2
Zarand (Iran) **66** F 4
Zárate **112** E 5
Zaraza **108** E 2
Zard Küh **61** F 2
Zarechensk **54** K 2
Zarghun **67** H 4
Zaria **91** F 3
Zaruma **108** C 4
Zaskar Mountains **67** K 4
Zastron **94** D 6
Zatish'ye **69** T 2
Zatoka Gdańska **53** G 4
Zav'yalova, Ostrov **69** RS 4
Záwiyat Masüs **87** K 2
Zawr, Ra's az **61** E 4
Zayü **70** C 5
Zduńska Wola **53** G 4
Zeehan **82** A 5
Zêkog **70** D 4
Zelenoborskiy **54** K 2
Zelenodol'sk **62** JK 4
Zelenokumsk **59** F 2
Zell am See **57** F 2
Žemaičiu Aukštuma **55** H 4
Žemaitija **55** H 4
Zemgale **55** H J 4
Zemio **92** D 3
Zenica **57** G 3
Zeya **69** N 5
Zêzere **56** B 4
Zhag'yab **70** C 4
Zhailma **63** M 5
Zhaksylyk **63** O 6
Zhanabas **67** H 1
Zhanabek **63** P 6
Zhangjiakou **70** FG 2
Zhangping **71** G 5
Zhangwu **71** H 2
Zhangye **70** CD 3
Zhangzhou **71** G 5–6
Zhangzi **70** F 3
Zhanjiang **70** F 6
Zhantekets **63** Q 6
Zhao'an **70** G 6
Zhaodong **71** HJ 1
Zhaojue **70** D 5
Zhaotong **70** D 5
Zhaoyuan **71** J 1
Zhaozhou **71** HJ 1
Zharkamys **66** F 1
Zharkova **63** R 4
Zharlykamys **63** P 6
Zharma **63** Q 6
Zharyk **63** O 6
Zhdanov **59** E 1
Zhejiang **71** H 5
Zhel'dyadyr **67** H 1
Zhelezinka **63** P 5
Zheleznodorozhnyy **62** K 3
Zheleznogorsk **62** FG 5
Zhenghe **71** G 5
Zhengzhou **70** F 4
Zhenjiang **71** GH 4
Zhenlai **71** H 1

Zhenning **70** DE 5
Zhenxiong **70** D 5
Zapadnaya Dvina **55** J 4
Zapadno **63** OP 3
Zapala **113** B 6
Zaporosh'ye **59** E 1
Zhenyuan **70** E 5
Zhigalovo **68** J 5
Zhijiang **70** E 5
Zhitomir **55** J 5
Zhlatyr **63** P 5
Zhmerinka **58** C 1
Zhongba **72** D 2
Zhongning **70** E 3
Zhongwei **70** DE 3
Zhong Xian **70** E 4
Zhongxiang **70** F 4
Zhoukouzhen **70** FG 4
Zhovtnevoye **59** D 1
Zhuanghe **71** H 3
Zhuo Xian **70** G 2
Zhupanovo **69** TU 5
Zhurban **69** N 5
Zhushan **70** EF 4
Zhuzhou **70** F 5
Zibà **60** B 4
Zielona Góra **53** G 4
Zigong **70** DE 5
Ziguinchor **90** A 3
Zihuatanejo **104** B 4
Zilair **63** L 5
Zile **62** E 2
Žilina **53** G 5
Zima **68** H 5
Zimba **94** D 3
Zimbabwe **94–95** DE 3
Zimbabwe **95** E 4
Zimi **90** B 4
Zimovniki **59** F 1
Zincirli **59** E 3
Zinder **91** F 3
Zlatoust **63** L 4
Zlatoustovsk **69** OP 5
Znamenka **59** D 1
Znojmo **53** G 5
Zoigê **70** D 4
Zolotaya Gora **69** N 5
Zomba **95** F 3
Zonga **92** B 4
Zonguldak **59** D 2
Zorritos **108** B 4
Zrenjanin **58** B 1
Zufär **89** J 5
Zugdidi **59** F 2
Zugspitze **57** F 2
Zújar **56** B 4
Zunyi **70** E 5
Zurbätiyah **61** D 2
Zurich **57** E 2
Zurmat **67** H 4
Zuwärah **87** H 2
Zvolen **53** G 5
Zwickau **53** F 4
Žyrardów **53** H 4
Zyryanka **69** S 2
Zyryanovsk **63** Q 6

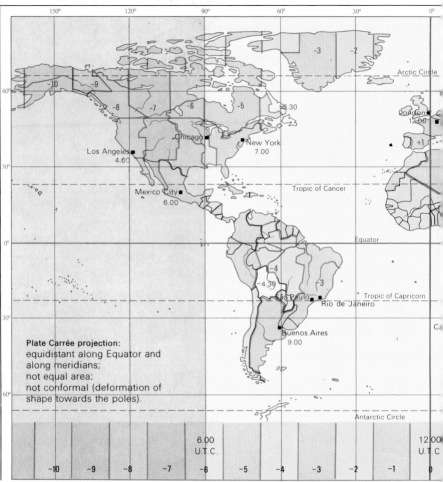

Plate Carrée projection:
equidistant along Equator and
along meridians;
not equal area;
not conformal (deformation of
shape towards the poles).

INTERNATIONAL DIALING CODES

To make an international call it is necessary to dial first the dialing-out code (011 in USA), then the dialing-in code followed by the subscriber number, including the city code.

Country	Code	Country	Code	Country	Code	Country	Code
Algeria	213	Greece	30	Mexico	52	Spain	
Argentina	54	Hong Kong	852	Netherlands	31	Sweden	
Australia	61	India	91	New Zealand	64	Switzerland	
Belgium	32	Iraq	964	Nigeria	234	Taiwan	88
Brazil	55	Ireland	353	Norway	47	Trinidad/Tobago	3
Canada	1	Israel	972	Pakistan	92	Turkey	
Chile	56	Italy	39	Panama	507	United Arab Emirates	9
Denmark	45	Jamaica	809	Philippines	63	United Kingdom	
Dominican Republic	809	Japan	81	Portugal	351	USA	
Finland	358	Kuwait	965	Saudi Arabia	966	USSR	
France	33	Libya	218	Singapore	35	Venezuela	
Germany	49	Malaysia	60	South Africa	27	Yugoslavia	